SYLVIA ARDYN BOONE has made seven trips to Africa and has lived there for extended periods of time, visiting most of northern, western, central and eastern Africa. Fluent in French, she has traveled in a variety of roles — work-camper, student, teacher, lecturer, researcher, translator, writer, radio announcer, escort-interpreter, guide and journalist.

At present, Miss Boone is a Fellow of the Yale University Graduate School, where she is a candidate for the Doctorate in the History of Art, specializing in the Arts of Africa.

West African Travels

A Guide to People and Places

West African Travels

Travels

A Guide to People and Places

by Sylvia Ardyn Boone

Random House   New York

Grateful acknowledgment is made to Eve de Negri and Nigeria Magazine for permission to reproduce drawings and captions which appeared in Nigeria Magazine, Nos. 72 and 73, and to the United Nations for permission to use all photographs throughout the book except the one noted.

Endpaper photograph: Painted-Resist-Dyed Cloth. Yoruba, Nigeria. 78 x 66 inches. Collection Mr. and Mrs. Jo Dendel, Costa Mesa, California. Collected in 1941. One of the traditional cassava-paste-painted-resist cloths. This design is called olokun. It is from African Textiles and Decorative Arts. Copyright © 1972 The Museum of Modern Art. Photograph courtesy of Frank J. Thomas—Los Angeles, California.

Library of Congress Cataloging in Publication Data

Boone, Sylvia Ardyn.
West African travels.

1. Africa, West—Description and travel—
1951– —Guide-books. I. Title.
DT472.B65   916.6'04   73-19521
ISBN 0-394-46154-1

Manufactured in the United States of America
2 4 6 8 9 7 5 3
First Edition

Dedicated to my niece
Tracey Ardyn Boone

. . . Ezekiel saw the wheel
Way in the middle of the air.
Big wheel run by faith,
Little wheel run by the grace of God.
A wheel in a wheel—
   Way in the middle of the air.

—Traditional

Acknowledgments

It is a pleasure to publicly express my appreciation to a number of people whose assistance and influence have encouraged me in my work:

To Deborah Szekeley for offering me world enough and time when I needed it most.

To Margaret and Paul Thorsen for their friendship and support.

To Maya Angelou, Rosa Guy and Janet Morales for their example, experience and instruction.

To John W. Blassingame and Roy S. Bryce-Laporte for their interest and understanding.

To Charles H. Cutter and Robert P. Thompson for reading the manuscript in draft and correcting many embarrassing errors.

To Air Afrique for extending many courtesies.

To Anne Granger for preparing the manuscript and abiding with me.

To Barbara Greene, Arlene Mancuso, Julius Rosenthal and Vera Wells for helping steady this trembling hand. And to Dr. Jim; he knows why.

*   *   *

Successful completion of this book was made possible through direct intervention in the eleventh hour by a Hawaiian angel. For this timely visitation I owe him deep gratitude and tender regards.

I hope this book pleases three special people and justifies their faith in me: my heroine—Josephine Baker; my editor—Robert D. Loomis; and my mentor—Robert Farris Thompson.

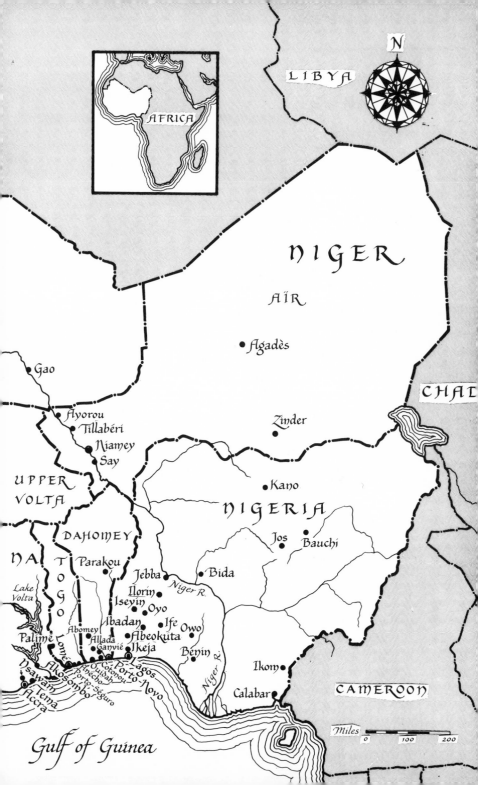

N

LIBYA

AFRICA

NIGER

AÏR

• Agadès

Gao •

CHAD

Ayorou •
Tillabéri
Niamey •
Say •

Zinder •

UPPER
VOLTA

• Kano

NIGERIA

DAHOMEY

Jos • Bauchi •

Parakou •

Lake
Volta

Jebba • • Bida

• Niger R.

Ilorin
Iseyin
Oyo •
Ibadan
Ife • Owo •
Abomey Abeokuta
Palimé Allada
Ganvié Ikeja
Lomé Porto-Lagos
Akosombo Cotonou Benin •
Nsawam Ouidah
Accra Porto-Séguro
Tema Abecho Porto-Novo

Ikom •

Niger R.

Calabar •

CAMEROON

Gulf of Guinea

Miles
0   100   200

Contents

Perspectives

OMEGA

There is one single key to seeing Africa as it is, not as a reflection of bogus stories you have been told. It is an easy and simple rule, but very hard for Europeans and Americans to follow.

Try to think of every African you meet as a person just like yourself, with the same needs and desires, hopes and dreams. The African, at *his* best, is like *you* at *your* best. When you *both* are striving for the finest of creativity and spirituality, you are alike on a high humanist plane.

Everyone in the world wants great things. Everyone wishes to be beautiful and to live in beautiful surroundings. Everyone wants to build something or to make something grow. Everyone wants to see some idea of his take on material form and life. Everyone loves to feel his intellect stimulated and clicking, whether through a conversation or a poker game. Everyone longs to express his thoughts and feelings and to communicate his conceptions to others. We all yearn for transcendence, for immortal life, to be part of the future.

An African is no different—an obvious fact that must nonetheless be emphasized. Connecting on these wavelengths, being open to these touches, being aware of these aspirations and desires—all these put us in rapport with the Africans we meet.

SPECIAL BENEFITS OF TRAVEL IN AFRICA: AN ATTEMPT TO EXPLAIN

The preacher says it's no secret when you start living a good life. Everyone can see, because you begin to walk better, talk better, look better and act right. The promise is that after your trip to Africa you will be "better."

Travel to Africa has all the benefits of travel to other places, but it also has something *special*. For one friend it is the end of the big-city paranoia that grips us every day. You can walk down the street without terror, get in an elevator without feeling trapped, and there aren't any more of those funny clicks on your phone. The stores don't have convex, reflecting mirrors, and the closed-circuit protection-agency cameras aren't whirring. The bomb isn't going to fall on your head, the world isn't going to end, your life is not in imminent danger—so you can let down your defenses. Because your being is not threatened, you don't have to be tensed for flight or battle.

Your personality is not being shredded by a cascade of words and images on television that corrodes your integrity and self-esteem. No beautiful people, no jet setters, no odious comparisons between yourself and your possessions and the vastly superior minds, bodies and possessions of mannequins and movie stars and public figures constantly splashed on the TV screen. It will occur to you one day on your trip that the voices are not snarling and that the fire-drill bell of alarm and danger isn't ringing, as so often happens in the urban setting. With the pressure cooker off, your better self emerges.

It may be the vividness of colors and shapes. Perhaps it is the endless variety of images, the kaleidoscope of movement and shading. Or the sensation of warmth and leisure, or the feeling of space and ease. Some people say it is the quality of the air—its clarity and cleanliness. Another explains that the primary source of energy is the sun, and in Africa the sun's rays are most direct and most healthful. Whatever it is, it is good for making flowers and people bloom.

VOCABULARY

Most of the words used to refer to Africa and Africans are insulting and pejorative. Common parlance learned from Tarzan movies and television serials is full of words and phrases that demean Africans and hold them in condescension and contempt.

The old vocabulary reveals the values and opinions of the colonialist/imperialist mentality. It says, in effect, Africans are inferior and thus incapable of ruling themselves; it says Africans are children to be managed, brutes to be tamed, wanderers in darkness to be brought to the light. Europeans have the real thing, Africans only the short, underdeveloped version. It is now time to learn a new vocabulary based on modern realities and sensibilities —and facts.

1. *People of African origin are to be called "African," "black" or by nationality.* They are *not* "natives" and they are not "Negroes." The word "native" should never be used. It implies an anonymous person who is inferior and primitive. She is not a "native woman"—rather, she is an African woman; he is not a native of Nigeria, he is a Nigerian.

2. *The word "native" is not used as an adjective either.* You may be tempted to describe something as native—say, his "native" food. Use instead his "local," "traditional" or "customary" food.

3. *"Primitive" and "savage" should be completely eliminated.* No two words are more disparaging and offensive; they should be stricken from your vocabulary. There is no polite substitution for these two words as nouns. As adjectives, for "primitive" one may substitute traditional, rustic, rudimentary, simple, old-fashioned; for "savage," exotic, original, surprising.

4. *The word "tribe" is no longer used*; instead one says "ethnic group" or "people." "Tribe" is another one of those colonial words based on European arrogance and ignorance that fit people into slots and froze them onto little parcels of land. It is ridiculous to refer to ten million Yoruba or five million Akan as a tribe. (Are the eight million Swedes a tribe, or the four million Finns?)

5. *African people are men and women, youths, adolescents, children, boys and girls, as the name fits the age range. No other words are acceptable.* A lovely young African girl is not a maiden . . . how can you tell? Her eighteen-year-old brother is not a young buck or a warrior or a brave; he is, rather, a young man or a youth. If they are both graceful of manner and richly dressed, don't suppose that they are "princess" and "prince." (Ó, the number of African princes there are!) Their fifty-year-old father is not a

"boy," although he does servant's work, and their mother is not a "mammy."

6. *African people wear clothes*, not "costume" or "garb" or "native dress." Learn the names of African clothes, or call them suits, outfits, ensembles or national dress.

7. *Africans speak languages, not "dialects."* They speak in their African languages, or in the "vernacular." At home, as a child, an African learned his mother tongue, not a "native dialect." Aren't there such things as dialects? Yes, and if you are a linguist or an anthropologist discussing classifications of languages, you will be understood by your profes ᵓnal colleagues. But for general purposes such a category applied to African languages is belittling.

8. *African people live in cottages or houses, not in "huts" or "shacks."* Yes, many habitations are small and made of earthen bricks and have thatched roofs. In rural England it would be considered a cottage; call it a cottage when Africans live there too. Houses vary in design and quality, but they are still houses. If you see slums or crumbling buildings, call them that.

9. *Africa is not the "jungle."* Places with thick vegetation are called country, bush or forest. The old jungle image comes from Tarzan movies, with their white man swinging apelike through the trees. The forest belt of Africa is not large compared to the savannah, scrub and desert areas.

10. *African people have medicine*, not "witchcraft" or "juju" administered by witch doctors and medicine men. African folk medicine is a treasure house of knowledge rivaling that of the Chinese; one day it will be appreciated and developed. If AMA scruples prevent you from calling an African medical practitioner a "doctor," refer to him as a "healer" or an "herbalist" or a "traditional doctor." What he practices, then, is traditional healing or herbalism. If he specializes in emotional disorders, he is doing psychic healing.

11. *African people have their own systems of religion and philosophy.* To call their beliefs juju or witchcraft is again disrespectful and mocking. Their religious leaders are priests and priestesses, prophets or holy men, not fetishers. The place of worship is a shrine or temple, not a fetish house, and the objects used in ceremonies are not fetishes or juju.

PEJORATIVE	PREFERRED
1. a) native (noun) Negro b) native (adjective)	African black man country of origin (Nigerian, Togolese, etc.) local, customary, traditional
2. a) primitive (noun) b) primitive (adjective)	none traditional, rustic, rudimentary, simple, old-fashioned
3. a) savage (noun) b) savage (adjective)	none unusual, exotic, surprising, original
4. tribe	ethnic group, people
5. native, boy, maiden, warrior young buck, prince princess, pickaninny mammy	man, youth, woman, adolescent young man young woman, child, boy, girl none
6. costume, garb, native dress	clothes, outfit, ensemble, national dress
7. dialect	language, tongue, vernacular
8. hut	cottage, house, dwelling
9. jungle	country, bush, forest
10. a) juju, witchcraft (referring to healing practices) b) witch doctor, medicine man (referring to healing practices)	a) folk medicine, herbalism, traditional medicine, psychic healing b) doctor, traditional healer, herbalist, psychic healer
11. a) juju, cult, fetish, witchcraft (referring to belief in the Divine) b) witch doctor, fetish priest (referring to things spiritual)	a) religion, beliefs, customary or traditional religion b) priest, priestess, prophet
12. a) fetish house (referring to place of worship) b) fetish, grigri, juju (referring to objects used in worship)	a) shrine, temple b) talisman, amulet, holy medal, sacred object

7

LANGUAGES

West Africans speak dozens of languages, but the visitor must deal with only three: English, French and the vernacular. English and French are convenient lingua francas, borrowed from metropolitan powers, used in public and commercial affairs. The vernacular is any one of the local African languages (recall that English, French, Italian, German, and other major European languages, were imposed on certain geographical territories, the people of which still continue to speak local tongues, Provençal and Basque and Sicilian, for example). An educated West African wants to speak both English and French so that he may communicate across false barriers erected by colonial powers, and in general, most Africans speak or at least understand three local languages.

English is spoken in five of the countries discussed in this book (The Gambia, Sierra Leone, Liberia, Ghana and Nigeria); the other nine are French-speaking. All business is conducted in the official language, and while most people you meet in towns can converse in the official language, in the countryside the vernacular is used almost exclusively. Even though you don't speak French, you will be able to manage with good humor and a phrase book; hospitable Africans will round up people to speak English to you, and someone will always turn up to translate and help you through.

In almost every country there is an indigenous language holding sway over the others: Bambara is the increasingly dominant language in Mali, and in the Ivory Coast it is Baulé. The thrust of a particular vernacular language depends on several factors: mother tongue of the President and ruling elites; location of popular secondary schools; fashion in the colleges; or vigor of the group's traders and merchants.

One great gift of your trip is the surprise of hearing English; your own grasp of English returns as you stop speaking TV brand-name shorthand and begin to converse using a vocabulary of generic terms! Sparkling and amusing turns of phrase and the musical tones used by Africans will give your listening a pleasant jolt. Upper classes use a sonorous, formal, often archaic handling of English, a reminder of how burnished the language can be. West

Africans have also developed an original idiom of expression for the streets, and a thriving popular literature written for the masses.

West Africans haven't just learned English, they have gobbled it up whole with enthusiasm and relish. Their mother tongues are much richer in nuances than English: the average African uses a vocabulary of 50,000 words when speaking in a vernacular, while most of us use only 20,000 words in English. As a consequence, ordinary spoken English seems sparse and bare to West Africans, not fully packed, not rich enough. The Briton or American likes to speak economically, efficiently; the West African prefers to allude, alliterate and speak in metaphors. He will never use five words where fifteen will do!

Another note on language: it is clean. West Africans rarely swear or use the careless profanity we all utter mindlessly. Restrain yourself, because a dirty mouth labels you as a boor. Also, don't call people names in anger. It can be a *legal offense* to call a man a fool, or an idiot; in Ghana you can be prosecuted for "assault with the tongue" for calling someone a bad name. It is terrible to say that a person is "not human," or to call him "rat," "monkey," "skunk," "snake." Anything implying that a person is less than human is devastating and *criminal*! Try, too, to speak in a softer voice, a couple of decibels below your usual pitch.

Say What You Mean

The young music professor visiting in Freetown went to the counter at the airlines office to inquire about a plane.

"Do you fly to Lagos?" he asked.

"Yes."

"Is there a plane today?"

"Yes, there is."

"When is it leaving?"

"This evening at six P.M."

"Perfect, when does it arrive at Lagos?"

"At seven forty-two P.M."

"How much is the fare?"

"One way or round trip?"

"One way."

"Thirteen pounds."

"Great, I'd like to reserve a place on the plane; I'll buy my ticket now."

"Oh, no, that plane is fully booked."

It's one of those "little things" that happens all the time. The moral is: Ask your question directly and never take the obvious for granted.

MYTHS AND LIES

Dwelling in our imagination is "the Africa That Never Was," the Africa painted for us by centuries of literary fiction and propaganda. African life was pictured as barbaric and savage, backward and primitive, its kings as bloody and despotic, its people cowardly, diseased and ignorant. The continent of Africa vast and uncontrollable, the sun scorching hot, bananas, monkeys and Tarzan dangling from the trees have been dominant themes describing the "dark continent," so-called. We know now that these crude images were reflections of the English writer's need to invent a place in which he could be a lordly superman in a primeval forest, where he was unfettered and untamed by the inhibitions and restrictions of modern industrial life. That fiction of Africa fed the psyche of the white man, and by making believe that there was a wild terrain out there waiting for his dominion, induced the adventurous misfits to go out to the colonies, and the well-adjusted stay-at-homes to accept the limitations of the *here*, while dreaming of the freedom of *there*.

Colonizers and explorers came back from Africa claiming that there was no beauty, no culture, no learning. The myth of a heathen, savage Africa gained great currency in the late 1800s, and was used to justify European slaving and colonizing. Today, with our new view, we must ask how those earlier travelers could have passed by African arts and music, but had no trouble finding the copper, gold and oil. How come they overlooked the literature and science above ground, and yet managed to discover the diamonds, tin and uranium far below the surface? They easily located the bauxite and iron, but said they could find no history or religious faith.

They were lying, of course, lying to protect their concerns and increase their profits. They were not interested in African harmony and symmetry, only in extracting its wealth with no troublesome interference. European colonial powers built a wall of cartels, monopolies and military force around Africa, using the myth of African backwardness to buttress their claims to a right to rule, cutting weak Africa off from normal, reciprocal arrangements of exchange and trade with the rest of the world, successfully "underdeveloping" Africa.

Movies and television are probably the biggest continuous sources of vicious misinformation about Africa. From Mexico to Japan, from the United States to Greece, everywhere they have spread falsehoods and insults. The anthropologist Edmund Carpenter (in his book *Oh, What a Blow That Phantom Gave Me*) tells the story. In the fifties, when films with an African locale were made in number, the big studios "to avoid offending African governments insisted that no film on Africa resemble Africa." They hired consultants whose task it was to create this phony Africa— "buildings, songs, shields, dances, masks, even 'languages,' all of which Americans would accept as authentically African but which no African would recognize as his." Some Africans were convinced, though, thinking that other Africans in a faraway corner of the continent were the ones depicted on the screen. So when they were asked for a display of African culture they often repeated the falsehoods in order to please the audience!

Thus the myth evolved that Africans had nothing, had accomplished nothing, had made no contribution to human enlightenment and culture. Gradually the myths are being dissolved by information and truth, but lies die hard.

FANTASIES

Since we all have been deeply conditioned and influenced by the falsehoods about Africa, we carry with us many distorted notions of what our experiences will be. While traveling in Africa there are several fantasies that invariably bubble to the surface. These fantasies show up in behavior responsive to a situation that rings a bell of recognition in our psyches. A steady line of cartoons amuse us because they, too, strike a responsive chord.

The First-White-Man Fantasy. In this one the visitor from Europe or America imagines he is "the first white man ever to visit this village." Or, sometimes, "the villagers have probably never seen a white man before." When the traveler ventures off the beaten track he feels like an explorer, a "discoverer" of people who "have no contact with the outside world," "people who have lived this same way for centuries." Perhaps he stumbles upon a practically inaccessible but glorious waterfall or brook. He will wonder whether he is the "first white man" to see this waterfall. The problem is, "first *white* man" is easily transformed into "first man."

This concept is deeply imbedded in the psyche of Europeans and Americans. The sophisticated laugh at the notion of Columbus "discovering" America or Hudson being the "first person" to navigate New York's waters. Nonetheless, these stories are taught the same way today and form the basis of the imaginings of young Americans. Every boy dreams of being "first" on Mars, or to "discover a cure," or find the "oldest man alive." In Africa these firsts are familiar feats: the explorer who "first" sees the headwaters of the Nile, or Stanley pushing forward to be "first" to gaze on Livingstone Falls, a scene literally concretized by the colonial regime by a statue in Kinshasa of Stanley on the rock from which he looked at the Congo River rapids.

The philosophical stance is the same—things only exist *once they are linked to European experience;* they exist as a consequence of European observation. It is the concept of a Garden of Eden whose creatures are to be named not by its inhabitants, but by a "first man," living a world apart, who comes and whose mere presence gives life, name and existence to all things seen.

Female Fantasies and Fears. Though they share in the first-white-man concept, there are attitudes peculiar to women. A woman learns them on her first trip if she is in a group; they come from stories she hears and the instructions she receives. They are of three types. *The "Harem" Fantasy*: Here a white woman fears that she will be surrounded by a mass of dark-skinned people and carried off. She is violated by a wild crowd, or kidnapped to become a member of a harem. *The "Going Native" Fantasy*: This is

"They are *nice falls, aren't they? I've always
hoped someone would discover them."*

13

a variant of the Harem Fantasy. She fears being swallowed up by a crowd of Africans. She is told not to go too deep into the market because she might "never come back" or "get lost." Stories are exchanged of at least one English (American, French) girl whom someone "found by chance" deep in the bush, "living just like a native woman." Africa is so strong that resistance is impossible. The woman separated from her group is easily seduced and captured by the call of the "primitive." *The "White-Queen" Fantasy*: A more engaging variant is that the woman will end up as a "white queen" ruling over fawning dark subjects. Any white woman is intrinsically so special that she is chosen ruler among darker people. Sexually, the illusion is to her power to command the services of her subjects. The black man is reduced to the image of stud.

Sex: The Biggest Fantasy

In the United States, sex between blacks and whites is an ever-present theme with four fascinating variations. When you get to Africa, the whole subject becomes enormously more complex and intricate. There are *new* kinds of white and black there now—exotic white and soft black.

Granted, there are standard titillations of all voyages, stemming from a heightened awareness, a feeling of well-being, and a desire to take a fling. The fantasies begin here. You become more daring in your anonymity far away from usual surroundings; you ventured away from home, did you not, because you *are* attracted by the strange and unknown, willing to learn and experiment? Freed from the world of work and reason, you seek distraction and play. For all these good reasons and more, you may find that romance in its intricacies and involvements may occupy a goodly portion of your imagination when you are in West Africa.

This is the land of fantasies, dreams and imaginings: the dark continent, the heart of darkness, the dark eye in Africa. The taboo land is lush and green, the air is soft and moist. All that heat from the sun—it stirs up passions at the same time that it invites languid, lazy dalliance.

Your head may be full of Museum of Natural History fantasy images (people on display like bees, dinosaurs and deer) of

"Miss Marchand, you know very well that this is
contrary to Peace Corps policy."

"natural" people: bare-bosomed women, men clad only in loin-cloths, living next to nature. They are naked and frank; their sexuality is no secret. Africans would seem to have a relaxed, open attitude toward sex, so different from the uptight, inhibited and socially restrained behavior of the middle-aged American. They are people whose energies are not sapped by the demands of Western city life and by the grind of competitive moneymaking. Their powers are intact. They are secure, guilt-free children of nature, says the fantasy.

Nubile teen-age girls and stalwart young men with glistening skin drawn over rippling muscles—picture the tropical nights when maidens dance in the moonlight to attract eager swains, while insistent, throbbing drums drive them to orgiastic abandon. And they have those "customs." One man can have several wives, each vying for his attention and waiting on his needs. Surely the girls are willing. Everyone knows of "the tribe where" to be eligible for marriage a girl must first give birth to prove her fertility. Then too, "there is the village where" the fortunate stranger is presented one of the chief's wives as companion for the night. All of it is pure fantasy.

15

Africa is the terrain of Western man's libido, the dark land of slithering snakes (remember Freud) in person and sweet forbidden fruits. The lid on the id may crack from the pressure of sublimated sexual desires, warmed by the sun, boiling now, threatening to bubble over. It is a wild place of graceful gazelles prancing on the edge of sight, and lurking animals coiled to spring. Electra and Oedipus relive their childhood sexual impressions of father and mother made "black" by night—the woman is voluptuous, the man huge and indefatigable, their coupling heroic and bestial. It is from this untamed part of consciousness, from this receptacle of unsatisfied desires and painful disappointments, from this wild place where the violence of human sexuality never fades, it is from *here* that the words are screamed: Primitive! Savage!

On and on go the forbidden dreams and infantile fantasies. They are part of us all, part of our image of Africa. They are thoughts embodied in dirty jokes, filthy pictures and smutty souvenirs. It all may be amusing to some, but it is totally unreal. It is not heightened reality or enhanced life, but just plain distorted, ignorant unreality. It is quite a load. And certainly for a long journey, it is definitely excess baggage. Forget it.

Realities   Our heads are filled with a kind of lord-of-the-universe mythology that obscures our vision of the seriousness and reality of other peoples' feelings and experiences. This whole book is an attempt at an honest representation of West African life, an attempt to describe it, in some beginning way, as it is.

ETIQUETTE: RIGHT-HANDEDNESS

In West Africa, where the ways of courtesy are elaborate, rococo, the deportment that marks a true lady and gentleman is complicated to explain. If you learn the Rules for the Right Hand you are well on your way to being considered well-mannered; violate these strictures and you will be considered coarse and gauche.

First of all, *use only your right hand for greeting another person.* Waving good-bye, shaking hands, friendly touching, all are performed *only* with the right hand. (After a coup d'état toppled a prominent African head of state, one of his ambassadorial appointees testified that he knew the President was becoming an "evil man" because, at a state dinner party, he had reached out to him with his left hand. The statement brought nods of understanding from the court, and was entered as damaging evidence.)

Next, give *things to people only with the right hand, never with the left*. There are no exceptions to this. If you have something in your left hand, transfer it to your right hand before you pass it. If your right hand happens to be wet or dirty at the moment you are asked to accept or pass something, what you do is crisscross your arms with the right over the left so that the left hand you reach with is at least coming from the right side of your body. You thus indicate that you know the rules but are asking forgiveness for the breech of etiquette.

Third, and most important, *use your right hand for eating and never touch or pass food with the left hand.* If you are cutting a piece of meat and holding the fork in your left hand, take the time to transfer it to the right, then bring it to your mouth. If you are eating with your fingers, keep your left hand in your lap; again, only your right hand touches the food.

The symbolism of right and left is strong in most African societies. The left side is considered strongly negative—the meaning retained in the English word "sinister" (from the Latin meaning both "on the left" and "disastrous"). The right side is of good spirits; the left of prankster troublemakers. The right hand brings good, the left evil. On traditional state occasions, the visiting dignitary will even shake hands with his left hand clasping his right wrist as added proof that he holds no weapon hidden in his left hand, and thus comes only in friendship. Touching food with the left hand is forbidden because in traditional life the left hand is used for matters of personal hygiene, and so is thought of as unclean.

Though the rules seem simple to remember and follow, there are times when African courtesy conflicts with Western theories. This situation happened to one visitor. She was invited to a feast at the home of a high-ranking chief of the Akan. For several hours she met guests who came to pay respects to the household. By the end of the afternoon she must have shaken hands with sixty people. At a quiet moment the chief gestured to her, and handed her a piece of cake to eat. She hesitated for a second, debating between the germs she imagined on her right hand from all the handshaking, and the rules of courtesy, decided against germs and reached out with her left hand! Recall the movie scene in which a great insult is made to the king and everyone in court gasps and shrinks back in horror. Well, it happens in real life. Hers was a triple faux pas, violating everything at once: using the left hand to return a friendly gesture, accept a gift and touching food. And, moreover, all this wickedness done against the chief in front of a large public in answer to his respectful courtesy. It was just terrible, never really forgiven or forgotten.

A Lesson in Politeness

Two tourists stop the car outside a bakery in Bamako. The woman runs in and hurriedly asks for a loaf of bread. She is ignored by the baker chatting with some friends at the back of the shop. She asks again, louder this time. Still no response from the others. Impatiently she insists. The baker turns and walks slowly over to the counter.

"Good evening," he says, squarely and deliberately.

"Good evening," she must answer.

"How are you this lovely evening?"

"Very well, thank you."

"Are you in good health?"

"Yes, thank you, I feel fine."

"And how is your family?"

"They are all well, thank you."

"Is there something you would like?"

"Yes," she replies, humbled, tears in her eyes, "a loaf of bread."

"Happy to serve you," he says, finishing the lesson.

CUISINE

Tasting and savoring foreign dishes is part of the excitement of any trip. Your mouth can water when thinking of the treats awaiting you in France or Italy. Travelers to China write of groaning banquet boards, and visitors to Holland dote on the hearty meals. It's caviar and vodka in Russia, smörgåsbord in Sweden, paella in Spain, pastries in Austria.

But when you get to Africa, what do you do? All the reports about African food may be negative—burning hot on the palate, sticky, low in nutritional value, and perhaps none too clean. If Americans are apprehensive about Mexican food, imagine what they think about tropical African.

Of course we all prefer "our own" familiar, customary foods, but often fear of microbes and upset stomachs masks fear of close relationships with other human beings. If you respect what nourishes a man, you are respecting the very fiber of his being. If you are reluctant to break bread with him you are saying that he will contaminate you. Contempt for African food indicates a contempt for African people.

Attitudes toward food can become a serious point of division between people, putting an African person into a subhuman position—that is, *you* wouldn't eat something dirty, but he doesn't mind, or know better; germs and microbes make *you* sick, but *him*—well, *he* is somehow "used to it." The whole sorry litany of insults as a cover for prejudice and discrimination is to be heard in any discussion of African food.

Ironically Africans, especially African men, are very fussy about their food: they expect their meals to be carefully and lovingly prepared to suit their particular taste. Fish has to be fresh from the sea that day, tomatoes just from the vine. It is essential that a girl have a reputation as a good cook—not only must her dishes be delicious, she must also be frugal and imaginative, industrious and painstaking. One pretty young lady was called "lazy" because she did not trouble to grind the eggplant seeds in her stew; another was called extravagant because she liked the taste of butter. A polygamist won't tell which of his wives he "likes best" but will give away his preference by telling which one is "the best cook."

European-style cooking is featured in all hotels and in most restaurants in Africa. Unfortunately, like the cuisine of Andalusia or Lebanon, African food is "home food," not well reproduced in a restaurant. To taste good African food you must be fortunate enough to get invited to an African home. At its best, in an affluent home prepared by a skilled cook, African food soars to great peaks. If you are lucky, you may come upon a wedding with a sumptuous spread, or you may be invited to a large party at the home of a dignitary, or be the frequent guest at the home of a good cook. The soul of courtesy, African families may prepare Western-style food when you come to dine—if they are not sure you like local cooking.

Basic African food is of two types: "dry"—roasted, grilled and barbecued dishes; and "wet"—soups and stews. Chicken, squab, fish, shrimp and chops are brushed with shortening, grilled, then laced with herbs and spices in a pepper sauce. Simple kebabs are popular as snack food. The most dramatic and festive of grilled foods is the *méchoui*—a whole stuffed spring lamb spit-roasted over open coals, served at feasts and parties. The African cook, however, is judged by the quality of her soups, stews and sauces. For her sauces and gravies, she usually uses eggplant, onion, tomato, light oil and seasoning. A stew has all these ingredients, plus beans, okra or green vegetables and stock fish in combination. It is then filled with meat, fish or hard-boiled eggs. Vitamin-rich palm oil gives stew a red color; otherwise peanut oil and corn oil are used.

Grains and tubers are a staple of home meals. Rice and millet or other grains are served boiled; root yam, cassava or plantain are boiled first, then served sliced, mashed or pounded with a mortar and pestle into a dumpling called *fufu*. The outlines of a meal: staple base of cereal or tuber, a sauce or stew of meat, vegetables and seasonings, a side dish of another vegetable. All very "balanced." West Africans rarely serve appetizers, but savory side dishes such as fritters and stuffed dumplings are popular; dessert is fresh fruit.

Every region has its special dishes: fish-and-rice in Senegal, palm-butter stew in Liberia, couscous in Mauritania, and pepper chicken in Nigeria. Two dishes are prepared everywhere in West Africa and enthusiastically received by even the most timid visitor—peanut-butter stew and Joloff rice. Peanut-butter stew, known also as *mafé* or groundnut stew, is a gravy made of ground peanuts, tomato, onion and spices mixed with meat, chicken and fish. Joloff rice is a casserole of rice cooked with tomato sauce and spices, with morsels of lamb or beef added.

You are invited to taste and to try. You won't like everything; it's not expected that you will. But part of your African experience is experimenting with new dishes, and sharing the food offered in hospitality by the gracious people you meet.

THE SERVANT PROBLEM

An eminent Ghanaian scholar has written that West African city life could not exist without its army of domestic workers. Woven throughout a classless culture or a communitarian society, lands of African personality and Negritude, are the cooks, stewards, baby-sitters, chauffeurs, waiters, watchmen and laundresses who hold the fabric of modern life together. After a while the visitor gets the impression that everyone in town has a servant—the young lieutenant has a steward, the political exile has a cook, the cabdriver has a nursemaid, the saleslady has a laundress, the schoolteacher has a maid. And if you stay for any length of time, you'll be told that you need a servant too.

Domestic workers occupy a variety of positions in the larger society. Some of them—for example, the men who are cleaners and waiters in the large hotels—are usually countrymen, controlled and protected by unions and associations. The older man who cleans hotel rooms by day leaves work in the evening elegant in a sharply cut djellabah and fez, fingering his beads. At the other end of the scale are young girls of fifteen and sixteen looking for housework at a "shape-up" corner or by going door-to-door in rich neighborhoods. Sometimes they are the poor relations from the country sent to town to wait on a more prosperous family member, or runaways hoping to earn enough money to study a trade.

The presence of so many servants makes most Americans uncomfortable. A sleep-in maid is a great luxury in the States; only the wealthiest households can afford to keep a whole retinue of servants. With the availability of labor-saving appliances and a desire for nuclear-family privacy, even affluent households have only part-time help with the cleaning. Now here are all these dark-skinned men and women, working long hours for little pay; they inspire guilt and uneasiness.

Black Americans especially find dealing with all the maids and chauffeurs very trying. Long relegated to performing menial jobs, they immediately identify and empathize with domestics, much to the embarrassment of their hosts. Afro-Americans are often shocked by callous treatment meted out to workers, and are dismayed at feeling a part of the exploitation, finding themselves for once "on the other side." The sight of one black man contemptuously ordering around a poorer black brother is galling and confusing. So the black freshman on her first trip will complain angrily that "Africans treat their servants like slaves." No, it is not slavery, but it is ill-paid, dead-end drudgery, work done by people with little choice.

In economies where jobs are scarce, the white and black Americans' dislike of "having servants around" is not considered estimable. Translated into practice, that attitude would mean even more people out of work. In Africa no one does anything for himself—one of the more disconcerting aspects of life there. A battlefield of class and privilege—a different kind of "servant problem."

HEALTH

One of the most common and oft-repeated images of Africa is the witch doctor; every schoolchild can do a menacing mock medicine-man dance. And the African witch doctor, with bone through his nose, feathers, rattles and boiling cauldrons of bogus cures, is a stock character in cartoons. By repetition and pervasiveness, from Disneyland to *Playboy*, it provides another part of the mental picture we have of Africa.

The witch-doctor image typifies the colonial idea of the African—ignorance trying to fight disease, magical masks and music as substitutes for knowledge. These ideas are combined with the charlatanism of a man who may know a little something, hoodwinking fellow Africans and, in modern times, endangering lives by keeping people from "real" medicine. It represents another perfect situation permitting the European conqueror-colonist to enter and put things right, bringing the "benefits of modern medicine."

Reality is quite different. Africans have lived in the world longer than anyone else has. The black man has been in demand as a laborer because of his vigor, energy and endurance. The basis of this force and dynamism is in good health, is it not? The spectacular growth of life expectancy in the West has come, as the ecologist and physician Dr. Dubos teaches us, not so much as a product of medical technology, but rather because of an improvement of general living standards and hygiene through economic development (for example, most African areas lack sophisticated sewage systems and well-built houses). Research shows that the incidence of infection and waterborne diseases in Africa is the same as it was in the United States when *it* had not yet developed a sophisticated disposal system.

Dr. Schweitzer aside, European contact with Africa has been as cruel and devastating in matters of health as in everything else. The glamorous sugar and white flour introduced by the West·has replaced more wholesome items in the traditional diet. (There are staunch, independent men in Mauritania who will not eat sugar, *on principle*.) Under colonialism, ancient knowledge was ridiculed as superstition, tested traditional methods of healing were jettisoned, and the African man labeled "diseased and ignorant."

This fear of "disease," and the idea that the African was dirty, a carrier of all sorts of infections, is, of course, part of the mystique of the colonial situation. It became a more polite reason for discrimination against blacks, and segregation into separate living areas. With the world wars, fought in malarial areas, the Western nations were interested in finding relief from tropical diseases, initially to protect their own populations living in those areas. So, since the 1940s, the West has had something of value to offer indigenous populations: anti-malaria drugs, some antibiotics, development of sterile techniques, and nursing care.

Solving African health problems is a monumental task to be accomplished through social organization that translates the population's desire for the fullness of vitality into concrete social action.

It will come from a general raising of living standards, from a refinement of traditional knowledge, and from research into the healing powers of local, traditional pharmacopoeia combined with information and techniques from the West. No "shipment of miracle medicines" from the United States is going to have much of a good effect on raising health standards in Africa. Good health is a political, social and scientific issue, and it will be solved as such.

THE AMERICAN'S LIVING ROOM

In every African city there is an American presence, a group of people staying in Africa for a while. Most are on a two-year contract of some sort, working for a government-connected agency—U.S. embassy, the U.S. Information Agency, the U.S. Agency for International Development, the Peace Corps or an English-language teaching program. The typical American is writing his thesis financed by a research grant, or he is working for a foundation, institute or any one of the American organizations and firms that have employees in Africa. Depending on status and disposable income he has a spacious house called a "villa" or a "bungalow" in a residential section of town. He has a car, or at least a motorbike. He employs a steward who does all the domestic chores in a relaxed and probably peculiar fashion, and cooks him plain, homey meals. Because it's no trouble, he loves having company for dinner.

As he gets to know Africa he begins to talk about it in a special way—a certain paternalistic tone of voice when describing how the founding of a new university or adoption of a new kind of corn "gives one hope for the future." He has a way of looking for "signs"—the popularity of a new song or the emergence of a new political group—as an indication of "the direction the country is taking." As a representative of the "free, developed" world he shows proprietary concern and wry amusement as he watches the clumsy steps of the baby nation.

So the young biology teacher who is cozily ignorant of goings-on in his American hometown speaks knowingly of the latest bits of local intrigue—the contract awarded through nepotism, the scandal of the minister's shapely mistress, the inside story on that ambassadorial appointment. And New Yorkers, these citizens of a corrupt city where crime commissions and investigative hearings go on nonstop and where official estimates of underworld activities stagger the imagination, relate juicy tales about bribes and influence with shocked amusement, as a menace for the future.

From your American host you learn the folklore of white life in Africa. "WAWA" is a popular term, the initials for "West Africa Wins Again"—a phrase expressing the intractability of the African situation and the futility of trying to set it right. Another is "The longer you stay here, the less you understand," meaning that Africa is hopelessly complicated and also that it doesn't fit Western themes. There's a lot of talk about how French colonialism developed "Black Frenchmen" and philosophers, and "that French mixed freely with their subjects"—all false. Or that Africans need to be taught to "work with their hands," as though there weren't millions of farmers tilling the soil, others building, mining, as well as thousands of fine artists carving and decorating. (This moral is told at the end of the story of the American teacher in the interior who in addition to giving English classes also grows a vegetable garden and shows his pupils the "dignity of work with one's hands.")

A young couple has stories of high adventure based on inefficiency and delays. The housewife loves to tell you of the little bug that lays its eggs on clothes out to dry whose larvae then burrow under the skin of the clothes wearer, or of having to wash the vegetables in antiseptic. Her children, meanwhile, far from feeling any hardship, are sprouting like Vikings. The husband will tell you about the danger of armed robbers and heart snatchers, as well as the price currently fetched by white prostitutes.

The fictions and misinformation continue and grow, repeated, carelessly, not as fact, but as *orientation* to the proper attitudes. At first you think it would be worthwhile to do a book of all the fibs and fantasies about Africa, contrasting them with the realities. But the expatriate *knows* better, he has the facts, and he is having the time of his life.

There is a tendency to dramatize, to accentuate dangers, to report on the difficult and the strange. It's a feeling of "Here I am in Africa braving the unknown, roughing it, struggling with forces of confusion and darkness." The expatriate is responding to his own national concerns, looking in Africa for solutions to his own problems. He is in great company, but when you go back to towns where the phones are bugged, the dockers are still out on strike and the pollution can't be washed off the tomato, reflect on his needs and your own.

MEETING PEOPLE

A vacation in Africa offers golden occasions for casual companionship and friendship. Perhaps you have come to summer school at the University of Ghana, to visit Mali's historical cities, or to a festival in Nigeria. You also want to meet some pleasant people who may become permanent friends; you want to be appealing to others and have a satisfying and enjoyable time.

With Non-Africans Africa's capital cities attract diplomats, businessmen, students, engineers and technical-assistance people from all over the world; with good fortune you may socialize with them. There may be a Danish construction company in town, a group of Italian film makers, Canadian voluntary workers or some Rumanian doctors. You can be assertive without being afraid, for they are also eager to meet you. The easiest way is simply to strike up a conversation with chance acquaintances, especially on visits to embassies and airlines.

For better or worse, West Africa gives you the opportunity to see the French and the English up close. Much of the administrative and political structure is modeled after metropolitan plans—so you get to learn about "A" levels and "O" levels, dual carriage ways, cold stores, leeks, walnut oil, kilometers, and other unfamiliar terms. And don't scorn the company of other Americans; the new people you meet abroad can become long-time friends back home.

With Africans   Before your trip, ask everyone you know for the names of people you can look up in the countries you are visiting. Friends of friends, relatives of students, colleagues, anyone who is recommended. It is good to write ahead to introduce yourself and let people know you are coming. It is also all right just to drop in on them without notice, once you arrive. People are amazingly cordial and hospitable, gracious with their time. If you are fortunate enough to be *adopted* by an African family or invited on a regular basis, you will have an invaluable entrée to African society available in no other way. It is best to keep close to your host family; it can become complicated if you try to mix too many people.

There are two things you can do on your own to enlarge your circle of African acquaintances and get a more intimate glimpse of African life. First, try having something made by a seamstress—not one who owns a shop but one who works at home. Get a name from the desk clerk, from a friend, from someone on the street. Seamstresses are all frazzled, rumpled, busy *and* friendly. You'll be invited to sit around and wait, usually in the jolly company of children, apprentices, friends, and other customers. Second, go to any religious gathering of any kind, according to your taste. Western-style Christian churches are a good place for meeting people; local African Christian churches, especially those with ministers known for powers of healing and blessing, are even better because the services are livelier, the participants more fervent, the atmosphere more stimulating.

Chances are the young African men you'll be meeting are smooth and sociable, with a bright, warm nature. Coming from the States, where men are supposed to be stolid and inscrutable, you will find it delightful to be in the company of a man who is a gentleman and at the same time exuberant. What's more, African men are marriers, so if they like you they will approach you with frank admiration never displayed by American altar-shy bachelors.

The crucial thing to remember in their company is that *African men chase the women*, not the other way around. Here in the States "the woman chases the man until he catches her." An African man will *choose* you and court you; the choice is *not* yours (this can be disconcerting). He will show you extravagant courtesies on short acquaintance. He is gallant as an escort, delightful as a companion, generous as a friend. He will make many displays of understanding concern and will try during your visit to make your wishes a reality, things that will make your heart melt.

An African woman is often a very private, self-contained kind of person, of enormous poise and self-confidence, but naturally harder to meet and get to know than the men. Men feel she has the quality of softness and modesty shared by so many women in the non-Western world. What doesn't show right away is her great independence, enterprise and sense of security in her family and power in her society.

With Humanity   There are two ways of looking at the problem of cultural differences. You may feel that deep communication is almost impossible, or else, that people are more alike than they are dissimilar. One of the most experienced and knowledgeable people in international work feels that problems in translation of conversation or situation are insurmountable, and that even simple concepts cannot be accurately imparted. He thinks that things are always a bit off, and points to the rigors of trying to draft bilingual diplomatic agreements that will mean the same to both parties. Personal concords are equally unachievable, he thinks, though not as obvious.

Some of us are more sentimental and optimistic about the possibility for meaningful interchange, and feel that for a temporary, sociable relationship it isn't worth the time to thrash out the nuances. I like to think that much appeal and mutual attraction is inexpressible, that it has to do with emotional touching and a sense of stimulation and satisfaction. Some of the most profound messages may be transmitted through stumbling phrases and gentle gestures. Perhaps it is not that necessary for two people to "understand" each other easily; it may be a pleasure to have mysteries and surprises.

Your attitudes will make all the difference. If you are *sympathique*, not condescending, patient, not irritated, eager to learn, flexible, accepting, ready to step out of your customary groove, then you will find it easy meeting people and beginning friendship and communication. As Leon Thomas sings: "There's a thing about nature—when your heart is good, people understand."

LIKING A COUNTRY

After you've been in Africa a short time you'll find that many travelers are fiercely opinionated and partisan about their favorite countries. At the moment I am enamored of Dahomey and countries bordering the desert; formerly it was Ghana and Guinea, next it may be Sierra Leone and Mauritania; with the slightest provocation I'll tell you why. Some people only like French-speaking Africans and have awful things to say about English-speaking ones. Or you'll meet a man who finds Liberians vastly superior to Gambians, or Nigeria so much better than the Ivory Coast.

Every place is every place. So much of the way you are going to feel about any particular country or any particular trip will depend on how well you "click" personally, whom you travel with, or whom you happen to meet; part luck, part chemistry. You are entitled to be enthusiastically biased too. But on your first trip, try to keep an open mind, and remember that if somehow you didn't hit it off in Senegal, Mali is bound to be better.

Countries and Cities

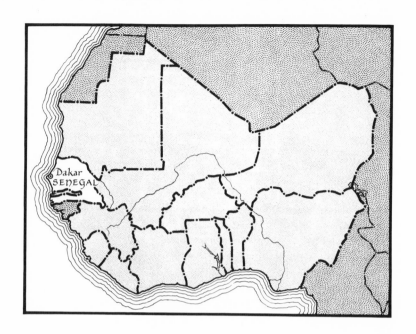

Senegal
DAKAR

The time is early morning. Your Air Afrique jet took off from New York City's Kennedy International Airport seven and a half hours ago. Now you are landing in Senegal, your first stop in West Africa. In one hop you have crossed 3,812 air miles; you have come from the New World to the Third World, a voyage of emotion, thought and new physical sensations. Your first stop is Senegal—the gateway to West Africa, the place where Black Africa begins.

Senegal is in a strategic position geographically. It is on the westernmost bulge of Africa, so it is the African nation closest to

North and South America. It has a long, smooth coastline along the Atlantic Ocean, and borders five other countries. Geographically, Senegal is a land of variation: dry savannah in the north, dense tropical forests in the south. Dakar, the capital, built on the Cap Vert peninsula, is a seaport and benefits from one of the world's finest natural harbors. Here begins your visit to West Africa.

Dakar gleams in the sun. The sun shines every day in a cloudless sky for eight months at a stretch. The air is crystal-clear, with a sharp, crisp sparkle, and the light—reflecting from the whitewashed buildings and the surrounding sea—makes Dakar glimmer with brightness. The breeze comes in from the ocean, giving the whole atmosphere a freshness that is exhilarating. For most of the year Dakar temperatures are a bit cool, in the low seventies. Then in late July they jump into the eighties; formerly dry, crisp air becomes softly tropical; it showers and the earth turns green again.

Dakar is an intense introduction to West Africa—everything about it is extreme. Dakar represents the range of the African/European experience; so, as you become familiar with the layout of its urban sections and the social structure of its 580,000 inhabitants, you begin to understand the pattern of other African cities. Dakar is "typical" and at the same time exaggerated.

Most of the capital cities of African nations are coastal towns originally set up by colonizing Europeans as administrative and commercial posts. (The great old African cities—Ibadan, Kumasi, Djenné, Kano, for example, are well inland but tightly linked to the grasslands, forests and deserts by traditional trade routes.) The colonial sites were generally chosen for their proximity to the ocean, the availability of natural harbors, and, where possible, control of a river into the interior. Starting from a small settlement of Europeans, these towns have grown and developed in a somewhat similar fashion.

The first Europeans who came to this area made trading posts on Gorée Island, and in the coastal towns of Rufisque and Saint-Louis. Gorée thrived from all aspects of the slave trade; Rufisque was an old African town, the traditional terminus of caravan routes from the interior, but is now adapted to more modern trends; and Saint-Louis was the capital of the French colonial administration.

By 1857 Dakar had a small nucleus of whites. It grew steadily over the next fifty years, but only came to real importance in 1907 when the governor general of all French West Africa moved into the governor's mansion and Dakar became the center and show-piece of colonial administration and military presence. Its prime resource was a remarkable natural harbor, but as the port was developed, as commerce, industry and transport became concentrated in Dakar, as the problems of public health and sanitation were solved, as a communications network grew, Dakar became the most important city in West Africa.

Right after World War II, Dakar experienced an enormous financial upsurge. With commerce and industry developing and expanding rapidly, lavish sums were invested in excellent new housing, spacious government and commercial offices. During this time too, the European population trebled. Rita Cruise O'Brien, an outstanding young sociologist who has studied the French in Senegal, discusses the reasons for this:

> The disruption of personal and family life during the war in France, together with the limited possibilities for employment in the immediate post-war period, made a "promised land" of her overseas colonies. In Dakar there was in particular a wide variety of opportunities for those with little educational background, or training: even a primary school certificate was sufficient to command quite a good salary. . . . Ex-servicemen were a prominent group among the recruits for overseas employment from 1946. Young men who had traveled to Africa and Asia during the war developed a taste for expatriate living and remained dissatisfied when they returned to the circle of their families and friends in France. . . . By the decade following the war, Dakar no longer looked like a small colonial town: it was the only really European-type city along the coast, providing shops, services and leisure activities demanded by the growing white resident population.

Dakar is a multiracial town, but each of the three component groups—Africans, Europeans and Lebanese—is involved in a distinct life style of its own governed by a separate set of economic, political and cultural aspirations and realities. The differences will be obvious to even the most casual visitor, for Dakar is generally divided into three separate areas. These major geographic divisions lie side by side and at points they overlap and interweave, but their characters remain distinct as residential bases for the three color groups. The *Plateau* is the modern, neat, prosperous section of the city, occupied by the French. The *Médina* is the name given to those much larger and more numerous areas where the black population lives. The third section, the *downtown commercial area,* is the home of the Levantine community.

The Plateau area is the Dakar you will come to know first. This is the tourist's Dakar, the Dakar of picture postcards. The buildings are white; so are their proprietors and residents. Europeans make their homes in the luxury apartment buildings and well-designed private houses. Businesses operate out of the large office buildings. The cafés, restaurants, the stores for fabrics, jewelry, foodstuffs and housewares, the beauty parlors, travel agents, butchers, bakers, cinemas, doctors, dentists, schools, drugstores, florists, nursery schools, churches, confectionary shops, bookstores, photographers—all of them are owned and run by Europeans to suit European taste and values. The whites who do not live here live in other well-appointed enclaves out near the university at Fann, and at Point E, then on the other side of the peninsula at Hann and Bel-Air.

This photogenic Dakar, this "Paris of Africa," is really a small nerve center of banking, commercial, educational, governmental and communications services, concentrated in one area alongside choice, expensive housing with well-developed leisure facilities and beautiful scenic views.

If this European town is made of white stone and cement buildings of different heights clustered together, the African town, the Médina, is the opposite—gray, flat, sprawling. Médinas exist as a result of colonial policy of racial separation and differential development. The first of them was laid out around 1914–1918 when both Frenchmen and Africans were moving to Dakar in numbers. Since urban agglomerations require certain levels of hygiene and sanitation to ensure healthful living, the colonial government knew it had to make improvements in living standards. Its answer to the expense such improvements would entail was to invest in only one portion of the city, that part which would be used for European residence, business and administration. It was decided that this white area would have facilities to rival those of any provincial town in France. The rest of Dakar, the large areas required for African use, was left in neglect. Thus the European community was separated from the African community, and the African was barred both by law and by expense from living in the modern, central area of the city.

The investment was made to make the European areas comfortable and safe, while substandard housing was deliberately built for Africans during the colonial period on the flippant assumption that it was "good enough for them" and "better than the bush." Having rudimentary facilities is not squalid in the countryside, however, because space and nature combine to cleanse the environment. Unsanitary conditions in a congested urban area are ugly and dangerous.

In Dakar the Médinas are named Grand Dakar, Pikine, Gambetta, Gueule Tapée, Médina East and Médina West. Though some of the houses are substantial, most of them are made of wood, hammered sheets of metal, homemade earthen brick ("swish" or *banco*), stucco and stone. Several seem to be just a few boards held together with string and a few nails. Roofs are of thatch or corrugated iron.

Slums without sanitation, with only two water spigots per block, and no urban services—this is the *other* Dakar. But it's not just Dakar. It is also Lagos, and Montevideo, Port-au-Prince, San Juan, Rio de Janeiro and Mexico City. It is what Americans refer to as "appalling poverty." It is that whole tangle of losses and defeats which are the backwash, the stench of economic, political and cultural exploitation. The Médina is a result of the policy of milking and mining the African continent, of draining off its brains, muscles and riches to build the capitals of Europe. Everything that Europe ever wanted or needed was to be found in Africa. I can only wonder, how will Africa develop without "an Africa," where will *Africa* turn?

If you happen to go through these areas you will quickly be told that the government intends to knock these shelters down and put up good housing. It is clear that the streets are meant to be streets: they have been paved and the areas are marked out in an orderly grid pattern, all in anticipation of the day when the old shelters will be removed and the whole place rebuilt. In the meantime, shantytowns continue to grow as folks pour in. There is a bit of good news, however. SICAP, a private development firm, has built long tracts of new, moderate-priced apartments and bungalows in solid materials; many Africans are living there now. In addition, there are some public-housing projects offering low-cost accommodations to a few lucky families.

Invariably between the Médina and the Plateau is the living area of the Levantine community. In each and every West African town you visit there is a group of merchants and traders, and their families, called usually "the Lebanese." True, most of them are from Lebanon or are of Lebanese parentage, but a good number are Syrians, Armenians, Turks and Greeks. They run most of the "middleman" trade and the smaller shops, restaurants, hotels and markets. They live right in the center of town, usually upstairs over their businesses. The Lebanese interact with the Africans, often exploiting them, and have little contact with Europeans, who treat them with contempt. They have endured many hardships over the years to accumulate the bit of wealth that they have. As a rule they speak the local language, and have come to stay.

The pattern, then, is typical—though exaggerated—of every town you will see in West Africa. A posh white residential area, Levantine people living over their stores, and large African sections. In the white Plateau areas there is a sprinkling of black faces—wealthy businessmen, high-ranking officials, foreign diplomats, and such. And often piled in the backyards or the courtyards, squeezed out of sight, there are African dwellings for single men, domestics, market families, retainers of the powerful.

Of course there are variations from town to town. Dakar and Abidjan display very striking differences from district to district, while Bamako is a more coherent whole without these brutal divisions. In the English-speaking countries the three-part pattern is still the norm, but with one difference. Geoffrey Gorer, a perceptive English anthropologist, reminds us that Anglo-Saxons don't like to live in town; instead they prefer housing "out of the town in a garden suburb of bungalows. The Frenchman abroad tries to reproduce the illusion of provincial urban conditions, the Englishman the illusion of the country."

Observation: The Poet, the Peanut, and George Washington Carver The delightful aroma often in the air of Dakar is the smell of roasting peanuts: several mills around town process the peanuts into oil and dry bean cakes. The scent wafts over the city in the early evening—a hearty, wholesome perfume evoking nostalgia for fall afternoons in clean, cheerful kitchens. The peanut breeze comes unexpectedly, then fans away as the wind turns.

Senegal is a "peanut republic"; its principal earnings in foreign exchange come from the sale of its peanuts on the international market. The building and trade you see in bustling Dakar are based on income drawn from the export of peanuts. In the town of Kaolack to the south of Dakar the peanut pyramids rise: stacks of bags of the raw pods, piled neatly in steps, arranged in a coherent, beautiful geometric form.

The peanut is a boon to West Africa because it thrives in the poor, sandy soils characteristic of the Sahel, the huge savannah area between the coastal forests and the Sahara desert. Not only does it grow profusely in dirt too feeble to support other crops, the peanut actually helps improve the soil by enriching it with nitrogen. Most important for the hot dusty lands of northern West Africa, the peanut is one of the few crops able to withstand the rigors of long dry spells; in times of drought the peanut plant just curls up and waits for rain, then leaps to maturity once moisture arrives.

The peanut is called "groundnut" in West Africa (*arachide* and *cacahouète* in French), the English name referring to the plant's stalk bending down, forcing the pods underground where they ripen. In some parts of the States, peanuts are called "goobers," a West African word. It is thought that peanuts were introduced to Africa from South America in the 1600s by Spanish explorers. The peanut then made its way to North America from West Africa as the sustaining food for African captives; slave ships brought the peanut plants along with the cargo of black bodies. Like the African, the goober survived the transplant and put down roots in the New Land.

Senegal is not the only West African country dependent on a peanut crop. The peanut is The Gambia's *sole* export, and it is the major cash crop of Niger. It is important produce in Mali and Upper Volta, and

Togo. Even in richly endowed Nigeria, peanuts are second only to petroleum as a cash-earning export.

Is it that we all eat so much peanut butter? In part, yes. The peanut is a rich foodstuff. Pound for pound it has more protein than steak, more complex carbohydrates than potatoes, more fat than creamery butter. Its delicious flavor and easy digestibility make it a favorite food all over the world. Peanuts are also in demand as feed for livestock, for peanuts contain a maximum of flesh-forming nutrients.

But the enormous importance of peanuts goes beyond its popularity as a tasty, nutritious food. Peanuts are so valuable because they can be processed into an extraordinary variety of secondary products. To do this the peanut is factored into its constituent proteins, resins, starches, sugars, fats and minerals. Then these components are put together in different combinations under varying pressures and temperatures. In this way are new products formed.

The list of things made from the peanut as raw material numbers over three hundred. There are at least a hundred food items ranging from flour, oil, milk, margarine, cheese, candy and ice cream to nondairy butter, vegetarian mock meat and Worcestershire sauce. No part of the peanut is wasted; hull, skin, nut—every bit of it has commercial possibilities. More than two hundred other items have been made, among them linoleum, synthetic rubber, bleach, printer's inks, dyes, paper, soap, axle grease, and most important, all manner of plastics used in modern industry.

This cornucopia of riches flowing out from the lowly peanut is due to the genius of one man, the Afro-American scientist George Washington Carver (1864–1943). Working in his laboratories at Tuskegee Institute in Alabama, Carver unlocked the secret of plants: he discovered the methods of separating the natural vegetable into its basic chemical elements. Then he developed ways of rearranging these elements and transforming them into new and different materials.

It is not just the peanut that has been dissected; since Carver outlined his methods of experimentation, work has gone on systematically with one crop after another. Cocoa, cotton, sweet potatoes, soybeans, sorghum, corn, bananas—many plants have been studied to reveal their hidden potential. And as each plant is analyzed, it has yielded galaxies of products on which our modern economies depend, all coming from the basic research done by Carver.

The magnificence of Carver's intellect, the socially responsible, life-enhancing orientation of his ingenuity, the prosperity and wealth that have been generated by his discoveries place him as one of the greatest scientific figures of our era. His only peers are men the height of Edison and Einstein who have made basic, inspirational contributions to human knowledge and progress.

Now, back to Dakar. The long-time President of Senegal is Léopold Sédar Senghor, a reknowned politician, poet and philosopher. As a politician he successfully led his country in the struggle for independence and has guided it in its young nationhood. Senghor is one of the greatest living poets in the French language. His African imagination brought a new idiom into French poetry and earned him world-wide acclaim for his artistry and creativity. Also, Senghor has long been in the forefront of African thinkers. He has developed ideas on the essence of black aesthetics and metaphysics. He is one of the originators of the cultural philosophy of Negritude, and he has promulgated the doctrine of African socialism.

So, we want to know why Senghor—President of a country whose economy is based on the peanut, poet celebrating black genius, philosopher interested in proceeding from African modes of thought— *why hasn't Senghor written a ballad, a poem, an ode, an epic to the glory of George Washington Carver?* Where are the grand boulevards and plazas named Carver, and where are the statues in his image? Carver labored all his life in an academic setting; why isn't there a college or agricultural institute in his honor? Carver was an accomplished painter and pianist, so why isn't an arts festival given in his praise? The harbor of Dakar berths freighters loaded with peanuts; why doesn't even one of the ships have the words George Washington Carver painted on her side? Oh, sharper than a serpent's tooth . . .

It is wrong to isolate Carver as a humble botanist, the "man with the peanut," and then remember him only during Black History Week. It is time now to appreciate his discoveries in their 360-degree relationships with world economics and politics. There is no way to overestimate his impact on the material prosperity of our everyday lives. Senghor, of all people, should understand this.

* * *

LEISURE AND PLEASURE

In the morning
—Make a visit to the university. You can arrange to see the museum, faculties and institutes.
—Go and buy flowers at Kermel Market.
In the afternoon
—Choose a sidewalk café along Avenue William Ponty, buy a beer or some Perrier, and then while away the afternoon people-watching.
—Take a taxi to the Grande Mosquée. For 100 CFA (West African francs) you can take an elevator to the top of the minaret and see the sun setting over Dakar.
In the evening
—Dine al fresco in one of the garden or seaside restaurants.
—Attend a performance of the Senegal National Dance Company or whatever theatrical troupe is in town.

GETTING AROUND

Dakar Plateau is built on the Parisian plan with straight, wide avenues and boulevards leading into spacious squares and plazas. Enjoying the advantages of its geography, the city is rimmed by oceanside roads, the West Corniche and East Corniche, which offer pleasant, refreshing drives. The longest and most important street is Avenue du Président Lamine Guèye, recently formed from Avenue Gambetta and Avenue Maginot. Many businesses still list the old familiar street names, but this guide prefers to use the popular designation of Avenue Lamine Guèye.

Taxis
There are lots of little taxis in Dakar. Their prices are fair by New York standards but expensive for Dakar; consequently, they are not hard to find. In fact, they are always tooting at a possible customer, so that even when you intend to walk, they can beat you down. The cost to the airport is outrageous ($10) and fixed. Therefore, try to be met on arrival by your hotel's bus for free.

Taxicab drivers are extremely dependable about appointments, especially early-morning pickups. The desk clerk at your hotel will make arrangements.

Buses

Dakar has an excellent bus system and a 10-cent fare. As you would expect, all the buses are jammed during rush hours, and those which service the Médina areas are always packed. There are several lines which go to places of interest to tourists. The buses have numbers preceded by the letter *P* and they stop at designated spots. If you ask someone, he will tell you where. From the Tourist Bureau at 28 avenue Roume, you can get a detailed map of the bus routes.

The *P-1* leaves the Palais de Justice and passes the Zoo and Botantical Gardens at Hann. The *P-5* goes from the Palais de Justice along the West Corniche, through Médina, to the university. The famous *P-7* starts at the Place Ballay at the port, passes the N'Gor Hotel and Beach, and ends up at the airport at Yoff. Yoff is also the destination of the *P-8*, but it starts at the Palais de Justice, touches the Médina market and goes through SICAP. Take the *P-14* starting at the Palais de Justice to get to M'Bao Beach, and the *P-17* from the same place to get to Camberène Beach. The *P-18*, which you can get right at the Place de l'Indépendance, will take you to N'Gor Beach. The *P-15* goes to Rufisque.

Trains

You can buy tickets and get information about trains at 38 boulevard de la République. There is train service to Saint-Louis, to the game park at Tambacounda, and to Bamako, Mali. Accommodations are acceptable. First class to Bamako costs around $28. It is recommended to get a sleeper for about $8 more. Second class rides wooden benches and is first come, first served.

Long-distance taxis

At the stations near the auto routes you can get station-wagon taxis carrying nine passengers that go to Saint-Louis, Kaolack, Rufisque, Thiès, Ziguinchor, M'Backé, Touba, M'Bour, and to Banjul, The Gambia.

Car rentals

Hertz is here (26–28 rue Jules Ferry), as is Sintra-Europcar (21 rue Blanchot), *S.A.M.A.* (31 avenue Gambetta) and Locauto (3 avenue Faidherbe). You must shop around for the best rates, but you can rent a Fiat 600 or a Volkswagen for around $10 a day, and an air-conditioned Peugeot 404 for $23. There is an additional cost of 5 cents per km. above 70 km.; oil and insurance are included; gas is 80 cents a gallon.

AREAS AND WALKS OF INTEREST

Old Dakar

When you are at the **Hotel des Postes** (Central Post Office) you are in the heart of Old Dakar. Instead of the wide avenues and boulevards of the Plateau, you have here small, crooked streets with low buildings crowded with people, shops, restaurants, cafés, schools and offices. Grouped in Old Dakar are the offices and warehouses of the giant old and powerful French trading companies—SCOA, CFAO, Chavanel, Peyrissac. Wander as you wish, then gradually make your way to **Kermel Market.** After all those colors and shapes, take Avenue Albert Sarraut, passing by the specialty and department stores, back to the Place de l'Indépendance.

The Port

The port is the whole reason for Dakar being here! The city began as a trading center, and its raison d'être continues to be its enterprise in exporting and importing. Start your walk from the **Place de l'Indépendance** down Rue Canard, near the Ministry of Commerce Building. Continue to the very end of this street; where it meets Boulevard de la Libération you will be facing the Port Authority. To your left, opening onto a huge plaza (**Place Maréchal Leclerc**), is the railroad station, and stretching to your right is the main port area.

You will be drawn to visiting the railroad station—it has its own special allure. The architecture is strong and simple; you can't help but feel its importance in the imagination of the Senegalese. On Tuesdays and Fridays at 7:30 P.M., the crowds gather to send the train off to Bamako. Whole families show up, people of all sizes, ages and stations in life. This is a good time and place for observing the people of black Dakar at their flamboyant best. The embroidered *bubus* of the women billow and swirl in a kaleidoscope of colors. The wrap of their head ties and the delicacy of their sandals punctuate the ensemble. They drip with gold filigree jewelry and necklaces of semiprecious stones. Their exquisite cleanliness, velvety skin and magnificent carriage are stunning to behold. The men's outfits are pale-blue or brown, more restrained but equally flattering.

To the right, down the boulevard, is the port itself. Because of the strategic location between Europe and South America (look at your world map again) and between southern Africa and Europe, the port of Dakar is active and thriving.

Cap Manuel

At the **Place Tascher,** near the National Assembly, you take Avenue Pasteur, walking straight for Cap Manuel, which was named by Portuguese explorers in honor of their King Manuel (1495–1521). You will pass a variety of public buildings (the African Maternity Hospital, the Hospital le Dantec, Pasteur Institute) and residences along the way, but your goal (tell the driver if you are going by taxi) is the **Palais de Justice.** Behind this building complex there is a walk that leads to the Cap Manuel Lighthouse. The lighthouse, painted red and white, can be visited during the day.

This whole area is open, fresh and flooded with dazzling light—truly an opening onto the ocean, a straining to the limitless. Now, from the lighthouse, you get back on Avenue Pasteur, pass the Palais de Justice, the residence of the American ambassador, and then at your left, take the road that crosses through the pretty park bordering Madeline Beach. There is a parking lot for cars, and a footpath that continues down the cliffs.

You are now approaching one of the most picturesque places in West Africa, *Les Orgues Balsatiques du Cap Manuel. (Note:*

Freely translated, this means a colonnade of basalt. Basalt is the name for the dark-gray to black marblelike igneous rock formed by the cooling of molten rock materials that oozed out of the earth.) These cliffs are dark and brooding, cut and shaped into singular figures that are constantly being pounded by the sea. Farther out, the waters enter an underwater grotto where they thunder and echo. Very exciting.

Almadies Point and Mamelle Lighthouse

Back in the 1500s, Portuguese sailors named Almadies Point with their word for "canoe" because they were so impressed by the dugout canoes of the local fishermen. The significance of the point lies in its being the westernmost extremity on the African continent. Its popularity seems due to the force and froth of the striking ocean waves, the weird configurations of its rocks, and a certain quality of primeval solitude. The solitude ends on the weekend when scores of people come to climb around the point and enjoy the refreshments served by three small restaurants. From this point you can get to the Mamelle Lighthouse; the lighthouse is large and its light extremely powerful.

SIGHTS TO SEE

Churches and Mosques

The Catholic cathedral on Avenue de la République, **Cathédral du Souvenir Africain,** is an impressive example of the "neo-Sudanese" architecture. The dome looks Byzantine, and its two towers resemble minarets on a Muslim mosque. It is a fine handling of light, space and mass. At the right of the entrance is a lovely little chapel, donated by the Portuguese community of Dakar and dedicated to Our Lady of Fatima. **Sacré-Coeur**, in Rue Malenfant, is another good-looking Catholic church. The big **Protestant church** is on Rue Carnot.

One of the most beautiful religious buildings in all of West Africa is to be found in Dakar: it is the **Grande Mosquée**, located at the Allées Coursin. Remove your shoes as you enter, and give a small offering. You may walk around the patio, courtyards and the large prayer hall, and also visit the small women's mosque at the side. For a small donation you may ride an elevator to the top of the minaret. From there you look down to the mosaic tiles of the courtyard and patio, watch the splashing of the fountains, and see the faithful in meditation and prayer. This spot also offers the best panoramic view of Dakar. The Grande Mosquée is a place of serenity and nobility, and an oasis of beauty and calm amidst the dusty hubbub outside.

Another mosque to visit is the one on Rue Blanchot. Again, non-Muslims are allowed to enter and look around. Part of the interest in visiting the mosques is the opportunity it offers to see the Senegalese patriarchs at their *own thing,* in the full dignity of their religion, learning and community; you can discreetly watch the comings and goings. Outside of both mosques there are men selling an intriguing spread of prayer beads, amulets, holy scriptures and paraphernalia.

Public Buildings

Dakar was built as a showcase of French imperialism, and the administrative center of all French West Africa. So a must for the traveler is a tour of the public buildings.

The **Presidential Palace** is a "White House" type mansion on Avenue Roume. It is sparkling and brilliant in the sunlight. It is locked and guarded, of course, but you can look in at the buildings and the gardens. The Administrative Building, across from the Palace, is the ten-story governmental building that houses the administrative services. There is a terrace upstairs from which you have a view of Dakar, the sea and the peninsula.

The **National Assembly Building**, on the Place Tascher, has a soaring, grand sweep of an entrance. There is a very attractive restaurant, and upstairs a simple café, both open to the public, but frequented mainly by the legislators.

Palais de Justice. The Senegalese Supreme Court occupies this impressive edifice. It has a huge public hall built in the style of North African architecture and is set in beautiful gardens.

Museums

Institut Fondamental d'Afrique Noire (Ethnographic Museum), Place Tascher   Open daily 9 A.M.–1 P.M., and 4–7 P.M. Closed Mondays and Tuesdays.   I.F.A.N. (pronounced ee-*fan*), as the Institute is called, carries on many research projects in the sciences and humanities. Part of the results of the work done on African ethnology is on display here at the museum. The guardian is a man of intellect, and the displays are rich and well arranged.

Musée Dynamique, West Corniche   Open daily 8:30 A.M.–12:30 P.M., and 2:30–6:30 P.M.   This museum was established in 1966 for the *Festival des Arts Nègres.* The exhibitions change frequently, and are mainly about African antiquity.

Institut Fondamental d'Afrique Noire, Campus of the University of Dakar   Open daily 9 A.M.–12 noon, and 3–7 P.M. Closed Mondays and Fridays.   There are eight large exposition rooms in this museum of natural science, history and art. You will find displays relating to anthropology, geography, history, Isläm, linguistics, ethnography, archaeology, zoology and botany. It functions as an educational resource for the students of the university, and as a center for research and documentation. Those with student identification are invited to visit the university's Botanical Gardens, were hundreds of examples of Senegal flora are on display.

Gardens and Parks

Dakar is blessed with several gardens and parks that are spacious and inviting. People go strolling in the evening, or any time of day.

Place de l'Indépendance   Right in the center, the heart of town, is this large park. It is planted with lawns, flowers and trees. There are stone benches for the weary, and a central fountain that works sometimes. You can't miss it.

Hann Park of Forestry and Zoology, Hann-Dakar   Open daily 11 A.M.–12 noon, and 3–7 P.M.   The Hann botanical and zoological gardens are sort of a mixed bag. The botanical gardens are pleasant, planted with shade trees and about two hundred different species of plants. This is a nice place to stroll in, to sit and chat. Unfortunately, the zoo is just grim; there are thirty or forty kinds of animals, caged and harassed by the visiting children.

Madeline Cove Park, at the foot of Avenue André Peytavin and Boulevard de la République   The easiest way to get here is by walking straight down the famous Avenue William Ponty. As you continue, William Ponty changes to André Peytavin. At the very end of the street there is a large traffic circle and beyond that, stretching to your left, is a magnificent park, built on the cliffs overlooking the cove. It is a magical spot: there are flowers, trees, benches and walks, arranged for variety and comfort. The attraction, though, is the sea. Down below the waves pound and break incessantly, drawing you to the hypnotic fascination of the waters.

Yoff Airport

Built to accommodate the crowds expected for the First World Festival of Negro Arts in 1965, Yoff Airport is a mellow place. In contrast to other airports, where security is strict and customs officers mean, the personnel at Yoff are courteous and welcoming. They are kept busy around the clock with jet arrivals and departures to and from North and South America and Europe. Many smaller local airlines use this airport also. There are a lot of people wandering around all the time, and they are all quite friendly. Among the amenities is a gift shop that has delightful items at outrageous prices. The airport restaurant will cook you a full meal at any hour of the day or night, and the bar is almost always open. Note that the post office at the airport is open twenty-four hours a day for stamps, telegrams and long-distance phone calls. The clerk may be curled up under the counter asleep, but he is *there,* and can be awakened.

MARKETS

If you are to fully enjoy the color, swirl, and smell of life in Africa, you must learn to know and appreciate its markets. The market offers the visitor a chance to meet and interact with a number of Africans from all walks of life.

Kermel Market, Place Kermel, behind the Central Post Office. Built in 1910, this market in old Dakar is a carousel of steel and stone. It functions from early in the morning, reaches fever pitch around noon and is hosed down and closed by 3 P.M.

Kermel Market is frequented mainly by Europeans; very few Senegalese come here to shop. So, as you expect, there is a great variety of foodstuffs, especially fruits and vegetables. The main flower market is here, too—gorgeous banks of zinnias, lilies, nasturtiums, carnations and sunflowers. Their colors are matched by the plumage of the birds for sale—dazzling in their iridescence.

Again, because this is a market for Europeans, the prices are a bit higher, but everything is displayed in an eye-catching manner. The merchants who sell there are a special type—they are men and women who make it their business to know the psychology of Europeans. So they smile at you a lot, cajole and flatter. They offer you gifts of flowers and compliment you on your good looks. You are *"Madame Jolie," "Ma chérie," "Mon client," "Mon ami."* You still have to bargain, but the playing adds charm to even as mundane an act as buying some lettuce and tomatoes for a salad.

Sandaga Market, corner Avenue William Ponty and Avenue Lamine Guèye   Sandaga Market is Dakar's main trading spot for foodstuffs, both wholesale and retail. There are sections for meat, fresh fish, dried fish, fruits, vegetables, starchy roots, cereals, grains and spices. But these are just the beginning. There are pots and pans, dishes, hardware and small furnishing. The place is busy, the trading is sharp. Everything and everybody moves at a fast pace, and good-natured bargaining turns into hard-nosed haggling. Kermel is a game; Sandaga is serious.

After staying in Dakar for a while, I started to buy my mangoes and pineapples from a particular fruit man who had the choicest selections at the best prices. Also, he stayed open very late in the evening. So it was already getting dark this particular night when I came in for some fruit. The market was resounding with the sound of drums, but nobody seemed to be interested. When I asked the grocer about it, he told me "his brother" would show me the way to the music. A limber young man appeared and led me up to a side entrance of the market stall. After two flights of stairs we were in pitch-black, climbing round upon round of spiraling stairs. I could see nothing—I clung to the walls and felt for each step. In the darkness my little New York paranoia sprouted into dirigible-sized mushrooms. I was *terrified!* What am I doing here? Who is this man? Where is he taking me? What happens if he decides to turn and attack? I don't know him from Adam. Why should I be following him? Nobody even knows where I am, nobody will miss me. If I manage to escape with my life, how shall I ever explain what I was doing in Dakar climbing the back stairs of Sandaga Market alone at night?

The young man bounded ahead with self-confident familiarity with the terrain. Struggling with my fears, I managed a halting, painful pace. Trapped as I was, I could only go forward, begging "Is it much further?" his replying "No, not much more." As despair and trembling were getting the better of me, we suddenly reached the top of the stairs. I was safe! We were out in the open again.

We were on the roof of the market, much higher than I had realized. And here on this roof we were in the midst of a community of activity. Families live on top of the market, in lean-tos and shanties, and in regular solid structures. At this time of night, women were preparing food. The stew pots were so huge, no doubt they were being prepared to be sold downstairs. There were a few sheep and chickens. All this time the drums were pounding out over this quiet, self-contained world, open to the skies, overlooking the roofs of Dakar.

There was still more climbing to do to reach the music. Steep ladder steps led up to a hastily opened and slammed-shut door. It was just a huge bare concrete room, transformed, as it were, into a rehearsal hall for one of the local troupes. The choreographer/director was as a man inspired. He moved with leopard strength and grace, seeming to compose new combinations as he proceeded.

The women dancers were good, the men were excellent, and one of the drummers was a genius.

I stayed a long time, my companion a discreet distance away. A while later we left—across the roof, down the gloomy stairs, out to the street. My head was filled with the rhythms and the movements, and I was weary and spent from the intensity of my feelings. I thanked my guide, gave him a tip for his troubles and made my way back to the hotel, through the busy streets, realizing that I had been touched by the spirit of Africa.

Tilene Market, Avenue Blaise Diagne Tilene Market is in the heart of the Médina, and it caters almost exclusively to the poor, slum-dwelling African community. The whole place is packed with a noisy, agitated crowd. The penny-pinched African housewife shops here for the fish head to put in her rice, and for a bit of okra to make her gumbo sauce. Your supermarket sensibilities may be shocked by the minute quantities of the exchange—a teaspoon of salt, a thimble of oregano, half a carrot, two bayleaves, a cup of beans or rice, an ounce of dried fish or shrimp. The housewife probably gets a small sum every day, never enough for her to buy by the kilo, and it is unlikely that she has a refrigerator.

The dust and stench rise as you continue walking. Rotting food and old clothes. You may find an alley of old magazines without covers, or a row of apothecaries selling magical substances. So when you eventually stumble onto the vast stores of enamelware you are relieved by their cleanliness, odorlessness, and their calming, smooth stillness.

When you leave the market, you'll be back on the main avenue. This time, cross to the other side to find a large school, and to the right, **La Résidence Médina.** This old-style building used to be the home of the French governors of Dakar. It is set in the middle of a garden blessed with unusual old trees, a good place for a stroll to collect your thoughts.

Le Village Artisanal de Soumbedioune (The Soumbedioune Artisan Village)

The Artisan Village was opened in 1961, on the anniversary of Senegal's first independence day. Students and voluntary workers helped in the construction, made to resemble the traditional domestic architecture of the region. It was hoped that it would serve as a display area for craftsmen, and a pleasant spot for tourist strolling. It has been a great success. After great ups and downs, the village remains as an institution and one of the few places in West Africa where a visitor may easily and casually see artists at work in their studios and workshops.

The village is in the Médina area, just off the Plateau. A ten-minute drive from the center of town brings you to its ornamented gates. Located near a cove, the Village is on sandy land right at the seaside. You will find at work weavers, jewelers, sculptors, ivory carvers, shoemakers, leatherworkers, potters, blacksmiths. It is enjoyable to watch their activities. The artisans vary in their prerogatives, of course. It is hardest to get close to the goldsmiths—their goods are laid out in splendor, but the artisans are deep in the dark of the interior. Their manipulation of powerful forces—fire, water and air—in combination with the most spiritually significant of earth's metals demands a gloom of mystery and reverence. Nevertheless, the leatherworkers are usually friendly and jocular.

YOUR VISIT TO THE VILLAGE

Morning: The Village comes alive around 10:30 or 11 A.M. If you arrive around then, you have time for a leisurely tour. You can take a quick look around, then come back slowly to particular stands and workshops. When you have seen enough, you can have lunch in the restaurant before going back to your hotel for a siesta.

Afternoon: During siesta time, the Village goes to sleep. By 4 P.M. it is in high gear again, so that is a good hour for you to visit the exhibits and workshops. As the evening approaches, go to the restaurant for refreshments. They serve juices and drinks at the oceanfront and in the café on the pier. Then, you complete the afternoon by strolling down to the beach to watch as the fishermen arrive with their catch.

The Crafts   The Village is there for the display and sale of works made by local artisans; latest reports on the quality of work is mixed. Some is excellent, other stuff very poor. Unfortunately, the general tone is below the standards of Senegalese guild craftsman-

53

ship. Highest marks go to the goldsmiths, followed by the cloth weavers, straw weavers and ceramic makers. The wood-carvers' crass, imitative work seems the most distressing.

You can take your pick from the items on display, or you can place an order to have an item made to your special requirements. The weavers make the traditional African fabrics. They work on handlooms, producing strips of material of mainly white with black abstract design. These are then sewn together to make bedspreads and blankets. The wood carvers only make glossy tourist souvenir pieces; deer, elephants, busts and copies of masks are the most popular. The models of long canoes containing lots of little fishermen have a great deal of charm. The goldsmiths are the very best. Styles change, and they keep up with them. They make the bracelets and brooches desired by the tourist, and also the weighty, intricate dowry jewelry for the local African women. Business is brisk at the stands that sell goods made of skins. There is some work in leather, but most of the items for sale are made of reptile skins—boa, crocodile and iguana—fashioned into shoes, handbags, briefcases, sandals, belts, wallets, and that sort of thing.

The photographer has some fine pictures on display. He makes the selection available in all sizes from postcard to poster. My favorite place is the bookbinders at the far end, down near the restaurant. They bind books in beautiful hand-dyed cloth, leather and skin. Also, they make up boxes, covered in fine cloth, designed to be used to hold keepsakes and jewelry. Nearby the basket makers really go into new dimensions. They work rope and reeds into everything: chains, baskets, lampshades, wall hangings, and best of all, great hammocks!

Women artisans make the ceramics and traditional pottery. They work on dressmaking and needlework, and make little souvenir dolls. Indigo tie-dyes and batik fabrics are the current choice of well-dressed women of Dakar.

Café and Restaurant   One of the amenities of the Village is its café and restaurant. It has three parts: a cocktail lounge, an outdoor café and a restaurant. The lounge is pleasant enough, the café is very good and the restaurant is poor. The café, out on a wharf, with a pier into the ocean, is a quiet, relaxing spot.

Environs   Long before the establishment of the Village, this area was special for Dakar residents as the location of the Muslim cemetery. There are entry gates near the Village. The cemetery spreads quietly out to the seaside as you walk through it, its large stone grave markers oriented east to Mecca.

Then comes the Village, and a few feet beyond is the Soumbedioune Fishing Port, located on the cove. For some fishermen this is an ideal spot—the fishing is good, the waters of the cove are well sheltered, making takeoff and docking easy, and it is near enough to a major road for restaurants, fishmongers and individual customers to come from all over the city. A whole market garden flourishes because of the brisk business in fish.

SHOPPING

Jewelry

The people of Dakar take their jewelry very seriously. Both the French and the Senegalese believe in investing sizable sums in women's gold baubles. The world's bankers and economists tremble at the mention of the vast quantities of gold held by private French citizens. Here in Dakar they are at it again, buying gold as frequently as they can manage it. For them it is the best buy because all manufactured goods are cheaper and of better quality back home where they're imported from, and other things, like cloth, simply don't absorb much capital. Gold is valuable, beautiful and portable (and concealable). The Senegalese have always been a part of the West African gold trade; earliest archive pictures show wealthy ladies splendorously bedecked. Jewelry is a woman's bank account, her separate wealth, her security.

As an object, in its thing-ness, a hunk of wrought gold jewelry—enhancing the beauty and prestige of the wearer and still remaining of constant negotiable value—presents one of those happy instances in life (too, too few) when one can have one's cake and eat it too.

Goldsmiths in Dakar specialize in making jewelry of filigree. Their world-wide reputation rests on their ability to spin an airy design of gold that is strong and durable. The patterns are graceful and fluid, and because they are open, allow a play of light and shadow that gives the jewelry a special alive quality.

My problems through the years as a jewelry nut would tug your heartstrings. Rather than go into all the sorry details, let me just say that there lives in Dakar the best goldsmith I have found anywhere. His name is **Mor Guèye** and he is in booth No. 1 (first one on the left as you enter through the gate), in the Artisans Village at Soumbedioune. Born into the goldsmith caste, married to the daughter of a goldsmith, in a cooperative company with other goldsmiths, Mor Guèye has lived all his young life in *le beau métier.* He is especially apt at making objects to order that match your dreams, or in copying in gold a costume piece of good design.

In town there are a number of jewelry shops along Rue Mohamed V. You can choose from samples; the artisans work very quickly and skillfully. If you wish to see a complete display of the whole gamut of the goldsmiths' craft, you are invited to visit the office of the **Coopérative de Bijoux Sénégalais** at 120 avenue Clemenceau (a tiny street which is a continuation of Avenue Jaureguiberry, leading into Avenue Blaise Diagne.) They show a sample of every single, traditional and national design known in the field. You will notice quite a few European jewelry shops also along the main shopping streets. Because diamonds are cheaper in Senegal than in most other countries, you will see some remarkable (and sometimes gaudy) items of diamond-studded jewelry. These shops also sell gold in both European and African styles.

Note: Gold jewelry in Dakar is fabricated from standardized gold of 18 carats, the lowest unit that is legal in Senegal or in France. The piece of jewelry itself is usually sold by its gram weight. The jeweler will weigh it before you on his little scale. By convention, the customer pays for the gold, not the workmanship, so that a solid circle of gold that required little crafting will cost the same as a piece of intricate filigree of the same weight. The price of gold is fixed by the government; it held steady for many years until the recent fluctuations in the price of gold complicated international exchange. (By the way, the jewelry and nuggets presented to you as "special bargains" by itinerant hawkers are all fake, of course. The hawkers can become most unpleasant; they may annoy you continuously when you are walking in the street or sitting in a café. There is no sense in having any dealings with them whatsoever.)

For silver: The jewelers you find at the Artisans Village display and sell silver jewelry. But the specialists are the Mauritanian jewelers. They hold a silver market in the courtyard at 69 avenue Blaise Diagne that is well worth a look. They make handsome bangle and "slave" bracelets, filigree pieces, and splendid necklaces of wood-and-silver beads.

Fabrics and Clothes

Almost every kind of beautiful cloth in the world is available in Dakar; some of the finest of oriental and European fabrics end up here. On Avenue William Ponty and Avenue Lamine Guèye you can browse from shop to shop. Since you did bring your own clothes, what you are looking for are locally made goods that are beautiful and distinctive. For these you will look in the area around Sandaga Market.

Starting from the Place de l'Indépendance and walking crosstown on the main drag, Avenue William Ponty, the market is down to your right as you reach the intersection of Avenue Lamine Guèye. As you turn to face the market you can see that it is in the form of a triangle. On your right straight ahead is the continuation of Avenue Lamine Guèye—that doesn't interest you because it is a street of fruit and vegetable stands. You want to take the street to the left, Avenue Jaureguiberry. Before you, on either side, stretching for several blocks, are every manner of traditional material and tailoring for sale. You can buy dresses, *dashikis* and other shirts, and children's clothing in a wide range of colors and design. Any of the tailors will make up a simple shirt or skirt for you overnight.

As you continue farther down the street, you find the market for hand-dyed cloth. Trade in hand-dyed materials is lucrative; the merchants are refined and sophisticated; the women you rub shoulders with are fashionable and affluent. Cloth bought here will be an extremely satisfactory souvenir of your trip. It is sold in pieces 6 feet long and 4 feet wide, known as a *pagne*. They are usually sold in matching pairs, at about $10 for the two pieces.

Observation: Tie-Dye Cloth For several years now, West African women have chosen locally hand-dyed cloth as the most desirable and sought-after materials for making dress clothes. The wax prints of European, Japanese and African machine manufacture are for everyday wear. Some imported goods—the silks and brocades—have glamour. But the hands-down, absolute favorite is the individually made-by-hand, designed-and-crafted-by-local-African-women cotton cloth called "adire," "garra cloth," "tie-dye," "tioup," and other names.

The materials are made by women dyers; each one has a special "secret," a unique design, an unusual way of handling the cloth. With consummate calculation and artistry, using rice, stones, corn kernels, thread, raffia and sticks, she has twisted, tied and sewn in the design. Then, over a wood fire in her backyard, assisted by her children, the dyer boils up the brew of color. As the cloth is immersed in the bath, all her concentration and intensity are needed to assure a successful marriage of cloth, color and design.

The cloth is pure cotton. The process is a tie-and-dye, combined sometimes with a batik (wax print). The cloth is bathed in dyes of indigo for the blue and cola nut for the brown. With these two basic colors, the women have created a rainbow of shades from midnight-blue—black to navy, to royal, to clear, to pale, and from dark, dark brown to rust, to beige, with all the greens and olives in between. The women also know that colors change quality in contact with others, so that they arrange to get new "colors" through juxtaposition, and contrast. Further, there is a subtle interplay between the dyed design and the surface texture of the material.

Every year new techniques are tried and a new pattern becomes the highest fashion. Not long ago, damask dyed in very deep shades of brown and blue approaching black were the latest thing. At another point, a range of violet magenta was added in combination with the blue, and that became *de rigueur*. A free-form splatter was chic for a while, and now batik-on-top-of-tie-dye is immensely popular. There are the classic designs that appear year after year. One of those seen frequently is the blue sun-burst design; the other favorite is diamonds of cracked shading on a solid background.

Just as gold jewelry is sold by weight, not the workmanship, so hand-dyed cloth is sold by the *grade* of the cotton, not by the artistry of the design. The cheapest is muslin (think of the bed sheets), a rather coarse-surfaced material; percale (again think of bed sheets), which is a finer, smoother, softer material (costs more). The favorite, especially for use in designs of great subtlety, is "bazin" (this time think of tablecloths), a lightweight but sturdy, soft damask whose raised surface adds another magical dimension to the design. Cotton sateen is also popular because the hard, shiny surface reflects the light and adds brilliance to the colors.

There is no really effective way of setting the colors and making them permanent. You must rinse each piece in a salt solution, dry it, then rinse again—five times in all—but even so, the dyes will slowly fade in the wash. Dry-cleaning is one answer; so is having lots and lots of material so that you can wear and wash any particular one infrequently.

* * *

Antiques and Curios

The quality of authenticity of the pieces on sale vary widely. The dealers have wooden masks, and statuettes covered with a (real or fake) patina of age, bronzes, ivory and, for under $20, a tanned panther skin. Some of the most highly regarded merchants have shops in Old Dakar in the Pinet-Laprade area at the Central Post Office. One of these experts is **El Hadj Yonda Diop** at 9 rue de Thann, right behind the post office. Also look in at **Vacquerie,** 5 rue Dagorne, and at **Aux Souvenirs d'Afrique,** same address. Another interesting walk for shoppers is along the length of Rue Mohamed V from the corner of Avenue William Ponty. There are all manner of African and Moroccan shops along Rue Mohamed V, selling every sort of gift and art object.

Bookstores

Dakar is one of the leading cultural centers in all of West Africa. As part of the educational structure there are dozens of primary and secondary schools, a whole system of Islamic parochial schools, and a number of research institutes. There are seven bookstores in their service.

The best is **Clairafrique** at 2 rue Sandiniéry (the corner of the Place de l'Indépendance, just below the Chamber of Commerce). It has the most serious collection of books on African culture, politics and economics. They are official distributors for the scholarly publications of I.F.A.N., so you will be referred here if you wish to purchase the bulletins and monographs of this organization.

There are three bookstores along Avenue William Ponty. **Librarie Du ?** is at No. 8, **Librarie Universitaire** at No. 26, and **Africa** at No. 58. They sell popular books, cards, stationery, and that kind of thing. The place to look for records of African folklore is at **La Maison du Livre et du Disque** (13 avenue Roume). **Librairie Nouvelle de l'Ouest Africain** is in the Maginot Building on Rue Victor Hugo; **Le Sénégal** is at 117 avenue Blaise Diagne.

THEATER AND FILM

Daniel Sorrano National Theater, Boulevard de la République   The Sorrano Theater is one of the prides of Dakar. It is one of those places built to meet the specifications and requirements of a very modern, technically up-to-date comfortable theater . . . in France. But here it is in Dakar. Fine Senegalese theater troupes perform there, and it is the official theater of the National Ballet Company. During two weeks, there could be the following: a children's program of Bach and Vivaldi, a visiting French chorus singing madrigals and Mozart (its opening a benefit for the Rotary Club), a French musical comedy performed by a local amateur theater group, the dance company performing traditional ballets.

Film   Dakar is *the* film capital in West Africa; the *Dakarois* takes his film-going seriously. There are ten movie houses in downtown Dakar, all comfortable and plush; out in the neighborhoods conditions are more rudimentary. But it doesn't matter, because every theater is packed every night. Many films open here while they are still first-run in France, and others circulate as long as they please the fans.

The Senegalese are pioneers and leaders in making films in Africa on African subjects. Ousmane Sembene and Djibril Diop are two of Dakar's many distinguished cinematographers, whose works have received international acclaim. Also, recognizing the film-fervor of Dakar, a variety of countries have begun presenting week-long festivals of their national films at modest admission prices.

Visiting Stars   For quite some time a visit to Dakar has been *de rigueur* for a world of luminaries in the entertainment and sports fields. Practical reasons—nearness to Europe, being on the route to South America, presence of a large, enthusiastic and affluent group of fans—all make a stop in Dakar a favorite with performers. A French singer or an Afro-American basketball star may be in residence at the moment. Their visits are preceded by weeks of speculation and preparation, and followed by months of discussion.

Foreign Cultural Centers   Dakar has the largest number of foreign representatives of any other African city; many of these diplomatic missions organize cultural events that are announced in the press. The United States and France are most active in this regard—offering films, gallery displays of artists' work, and such.

BEACHES

Dakar is built on a peninsula, and is extended even farther into the sea by capes and promontories. The beaches are vast and beautiful. They are free and easy to get to, are frequented by enthusiastic Europeans and Senegalese, and offer very pleasant diversion.

West Corniche (West Marine Drive)

There are beaches to be found behind the university (**Fann Beach**) and another behind the Musée Dynamique. As you expect, the university beach is popular with all those stunningly built male students. (You choose between N'Gor and Fann depending on whether you like to feast your eyes on males or females.)

Madeline Beach on Madeline Cove is not as popular or developed, so it is more private. Beware of **Pasteur Institute Beach**;

it is fine for wading and sunbathing, but the gigantic waves make it dangerous for swimming. The scenery is beautiful, so take your camera. **Ouakam Beach** on the way to N'Gor is also good.

East Corniche (East Marine Drive)

The east seaside from the port in downtown Dakar all the way to Cape Manuel is beautifully developed for recreation. There are two calm beaches: **Children's Beach** (Plage des Enfants) and the beach of **Bernard Cove.** Many private persons and clubs own waterfront property along here. At Bernard Cove there is a good restaurant, **Chez Goguette**, with al fresco dining around a pool.

N'Gor

The best swimming is on **N'Gor Beach** and **N'Gor Island,** at the base of the N'Gor Hotel. The sand is clean and fine, and the sea is calm. On the shore you will find cabanas, parasols, cushions, showers and a snack bar. You can skin-dive among the fascinating rocks off the island. You can swim over to the island (Rosa Guy does) or take the little ferry.

Other Beaches

There are places for bathing at **Almadies Point,** not far from N'Gor. There is another beach near the International Airport at **Yoff.** The one at **Camberène** is not recommended, because the undertow is dangerous.

SPORTS

Another Dakar superlative. For a city of its size, Dakar has remarkable sports facilities. Sports are a mania with all the males of Senegal of all age groups. Senegalese athletes have long been famous in the Old World and the New World, and they excel in endurance and coordination.

Spectator Sports

The easiest way for a tourist to approach the folklore of Senegal is by spending a Sunday afternoon at the **wrestling** matches called "Luttes Sénégalaises." The tussle between the opponents is rather short; it's the preliminaries that are fascinating.

Minor bouts precede the major event, accompanied all the time by a series of chants and invocations that can go on for hours. The wrestlers move in very slow, studied motion. They preen and prance, posture and pose, and parade like the peacocks that they are. The rituals go on forever, so it seems. The crowd is fervent and resplendent—the ladies in the highest fashion bedecked in the heaviest gold.

Although European-oriented sport is favored by the government and students because it is associated with being "modern" and because it offers ambitious youngsters a chance for international competition and the government a chance to enhance its international prestige—despite all these points, traditional wrestling still attracts the dedication of talented athletes and a fanatic following. Boy Bambara is the current champion. (There is no better description of the matches in English than that given by Geoffrey Gorer in *Africa Dances*.) Matches every Sunday around 4 P.M. at the arena in the Fann area. Tourists are welcome, usually are given seats of honor, and are helped by a translator.

In attendance figures, **soccer** is number one in Senegal. There are many teams, organized into several leagues, playing very busy seasons. Also, there are often visiting teams from Europe and South America. They play in Dakar's well-appointed stadiums. The big one is called variously *Stade de l'Amitié* or *Stade Dembé Diop*, or more simply, *Grand Stade*. It has all the amenities and 15,000 seats; next to it is a smaller, 2,000-seat stadium where they hold **basketball, volleyball** and **boxing** matches. The others are: *Stade des Abattoirs*, Route de la Corniche; *Centre National des Sports*, Avenue Blaise Diagne; the *University Stadium*; *Omnisport Stadium*.

Horses fare very well in Dakar's cool, dry climate. The transport routes from North Africa bring in fine blooded Arabian steeds. **Horse races** are held on weekends at the *Cercle de l'Étrier* on Hann Beach, and at the *Cercle Hippique Sportif* at the 15-km mark on the road to Rufisque.

Participation Sports

To recap the facts: Dakar is built on a peninsula that has also several major promontories. It has miles and miles of beaches, and a climate of perfectly sunny, cool and mild weather (65 to 75 degrees) for nine months of the year, with hotter (80 to 90 degrees) damp weather for the other three months. Whites in Dakar are affluent and enthusiastic about vigorous outdoor activity. People come on vacation, and they regard Dakar as a heaven for a healthy, robust life. Furthermore, the Africans are crazy about sports, avid fans and participants, with a great personal pride in having a well-developed physique.

So, because of all these special factors, Dakar has a great range of participation-sports activity, much wider than the standard summer sports. There are good facilities for surfing, water-skiing, sailing, skin-diving, gliding, judo, fencing, sports-car racing, parachute jumping, flying, fishing, tennis, miniature golf, bareback riding, pelota, boccie bowling. The Tourist Office has listings of locations.

HOTELS

Senegal is making serious efforts to attract large numbers of tourists to Dakar; the government is planning on tourism as a major source of income and prestige. A wide selection of moderately priced package tours advertised and sold in Europe appeal to visitors whose basic interest is sunshine in an exotic atmosphere. Publicity for these tours emphasizes Dakar's clear balmy weather, good dining and abundance of varied recreational facilities.

Dakar is on the "sun, sea, sand and sex" circuit, attracting holiday travelers who barely stray from their seaside hotel from the day they arrive until the day they fly home. Readers of this book are interested in West Africa's culture and history and in getting to know African people; Dakar's tourists, in contrast, voyage to Africa *to go to the beach*. These holiday tourists fill the hotels during the "season" November through April, and now Dakar is also popular during the summer months.

The most recent building caters to this new-style tourist. The Méridien-Dakar Hotel Complex at N'Gor has expanded into a complete resort, and a large new vacation village is in full swing. In the center of town there is a major new businessmen's hotel, and there are more hotels on the drawing board. Besides these glittering new additions, Dakar has a goodly number of solid hotels offering good accommodations at modest cost.

International Class

Méridien-Dakar Hotel Complex, 10 miles from downtown Dakar at N'Gor (B.P. 8092, Dakar; tel. 455-35; telex 682)   The complex consists of the Hotel N'Gor, Hotel Diarama and N'Gor Village. The appeal of this resort is based on the beauty of its natural surroundings and the comfort of its accommodations. The air has purity and freshness, and the light dazzles and shimmers. The views are magnificent, and the atmosphere soft and sensuous. Vast gardens slope down to a fine beach, and there are many terraces where the visitor can enjoy refreshments. The complex offers tennis courts, a miniature golf range, and horseback riding; it also organizes big-game fishing trips to deep-sea waters, and tours to nearby sites.

Hotel N'Gor $20–30 single, $24–$35 double.   It's all a matter of taste, but for a short vacation stay, the N'Gor is the absolute favorite. Some of the rooms are outstanding in their design and structure. You enter a large, high-ceilinged room with white-washed walls and floors of shining marble tile. The furnishings are sparse: a desk, couch, coffee table and chairs. One wall opens onto a balcony overlooking the gardens of the hotel sloping down to the shore. On the other side of this room there is a sleeping loft that you reach via a short flight of winding stairs. Here is a bed and a night table, breakfast table and chair. A huge window reveals a lagoon, the thatched roofs of the chalets, and beyond to the Senegal landscape.

The hotel is so situated that in this room you see the rising sun from your bed. The sun is blocked overhead in the heat of day, and when it comes down to set in the evening you have the splash and vastness spread out before you. It is breath-taking.

When night comes, lie out on the balcony under the stars for a while—all very gentle and cradling. (If you are assigned a room that doesn't have windows and views it can be a real dud, so be sure to find out first.)

Hotel Diarama $20–$30 single, $24–$25 double. This new addition to the complex is more modern and efficient in design. The rooms are smaller and not nearly so charming, but they are very comfortable.

N'Gor Village (tel. 456-15) $20 single, $25 double. The Village is in the shadows of the big hotels on the hill. The rooms are in rustic style: thatched-roof, two-room chalets set in verdure near the lagoon. It is pleasant, but since the Village recently raised its prices 125 percent(!), it has lost its charm; for the money the bigger hotels are much better.

Hotel Croix du Sud, 20 avenue Albert Sarraut (center of town) (B.P. 8092 Dakar; tel. 229-17) $18 single, $25 double. This one has everything you'd expect in a modern place; it is centrally located, clean, neat and efficient. From the balconies you look onto the flower market and European-style shops of this area. The Croix du Sud is fashionably cool and restrained. You'll enjoy the international French ambiance and the elegant comings and goings. Even when those newer, more modern hotels are built and open, the Croix du Sud will certainly retain its chic.

Hotel Teranga (center of town) (B.P. 3380, Dakar; tel. 205-75) $28 single, $33 double. This shining new hotel (*teranga* means "welcome") is the last word in modernity and opulence. It meets the most stringent international, businessmen's standards of comfort and efficiency. The rooms are sumptuous and cool; the better rooms look out over the rooftops of Dakar on to the port and Gorée Island in the distance. The Teranga has every amenity within its walls—shops, cafés, restaurants, a beauty parlor and a barber—and it is right in the middle of plush Dakar boutiques and offices.

Tourist Class

Dakar has three good, inexpensive hotels, each of which is

clean, well maintained and centrally located. They each have a steady clientele of international travelers who are looking for value and convenience. Each room has a telephone, and a shower unit with hot water. They each offer air conditioning for a few dollars extra. Because the rooms are so spacious, a couple can be very comfortable for about $10 a night—an excellent value, especially for West Africa.

Hotel Vichy, 26 rue Félix Faure (B.P. 534, Dakar; tel. 231-32) $8–$10, all rooms double, with shower. Workaday, well located in the center of town, a good tourist hotel. Though there are few frills, every room is large and adequate, and has a small balcony. This is where many visiting United Nations staff and other international civil service personnel come when they pass through Dakar.

Hotel Clarice, 9 rue Jean Jaurès (B.P. 19, Dakar; tel. 320-90) $10 single, $13 double. Much the same as the Vichy, but the Clarice is in a much zippier part of town, near Sandaga Market. The street is alight most of the night as barbers, tailors and fruit vendors toil away. This is where many of the Senegalese *deputés* come to stay when the legislature is in session; it is also a favorite with international agencies.

Hotel Atlantic, 52 rue du Dr. Thèze (tel. 223-24) $6 single, $8 double. Run by an American woman, this is a small, clean, modest place.

Economy Hotels

Dakar has a wide selection of inexpensive hotels; you can count ten that are clean, well serviced and usually offer a private lavatory.

The **Hotel du Plateau** (6 rue Jules Ferry, tel. 337-74) is centrally located, cheap and popular. An air-conditioned double is about $12. At the **Hotel de la Paix** (38 rue Thiers, tel. 260-44) singles are $6, doubles $12. It looks pretty from the outside and the rooms are nice. The **Touring Hotel** (52 avenue Gambetta, tel. 363-55) is also very smart-looking; air-conditioned rooms run from $10 to $18. You'll like the **Hotel Farid** (B.P. 1511, Dakar; 51 rue Vincens, tel. 267-65) because the owner is hospitable and the rooms

($8, air-conditioned) are well kept. The **Continental** (10 rue Galandou Diouf, tel. 234-47) is adequate.

If you are planning to stay in Dakar for a long while, there are some clean, simple places that can serve your needs. For younger travelers, the best of this group is **Mon Logis** (57 rue Blanchot, tel. 364-11) because the rooms, each with a little balcony, are clean and comfortable. The regular rooms are less than $4 a night; in the student annex they are cheaper. You are advised to tell the management to take out the extra beds, or you will be charged for them.

Consider the **Coq Hardi** (34 rue Raffenel, tel. 330-12). At this place you can rent a room for $64 a month, $3.50 a night. The **Saint-Louis** (68 rue Félix Faure) is the same price. Quiet and comfortable is the **Provençal** (17 rue Malenfant, tel. 226-40) just off the Place de l'Indépendance. For about $3–$4 you have one of the individual "bungalows" grouped around a courtyard. The **Hotel Paradis** (54 rue Vincens, tel. 225-39) is another good buy.

There are still some others that you might want to find out more about. Your Senegalese friends can make recommendations. Ask their opinions of: **Hotel Océanic,** 9 rue de Thann; **Hotel des Fleurs,** 11 rue Escarfait; **Hotel Thérèse,** 9 rue Caille; **Hotel des Artistes,** 38 rue Galandou Diouf; **Hotel de France,** 114 rue Blanchot; and **Hotel du Marché,** 3 rue Parent.

VACATION VILLAGES

The popular new style in resorts is the "vacation village" featuring simple outdoor living in comfortable and self-contained romantic settings. These villages, modeled after the fantastically successful Club Méditerranée, offer the maximum of easygoing fun in the sun, at modest cost with a *soupçon* of adventure and novelty.

The newest and most inviting of these villages in Senegal is the **Club Aldiana,** on the oceanside at Nianing, an hour-and-a-half drive from Dakar. The complex consists of a hotel, 125 bungalows with 250 rooms, a night club, swimming pool, restaurants, cafés and boutiques, all set in lovely gardens, refreshed by the sea air and the sound of the surf. Cost is $13 a night for a room, $28 for complete pension. An attractive European bikini crowd comes to enjoy the space and the casual conviviality.

There is now a **Su-Nu-Gal** village located near the Dakar airport (B.P. 8066, Dakar-Yoff; tel. 456-30). Its bungalows are air-conditioned, it has a pool and an outdoor restaurant, and a jovial atmosphere. $17 a night for one person, $23 for two. (N'Gor Village has already been described.)

RESTAURANTS

Dakar is a cosmopolitan city, and if there is one thing it has, it is first-quality restaurants, the very best in West Africa. The large French and foreign population crowds into the excellent restaurants on the Plateau, both at dinner and lunch time. Each place has distinctive cooking and a devoted clientele. You have a wide choice of cuisine. There are a couple of good African restaurants as well as a large number of French ones. There are several places serving Chinese, Vietnamese, Italian and Lebanese food.

Remember, Senegal is not a lush tropical land; it has no rich agricultural bounty. Therefore, fresh fruits and vegetables are neither plentiful nor cheap and the whole cuisine is leaner in style than, say, Ghana's or the Ivory Coast's. You will enjoy dining out in Dakar only if you don't quibble over price. Every restaurant offers a daily menu special that is bargain-priced, but à la carte selections are generally high. *Bon appétit!*

Hotel Restaurants

Hotel N'Gor Restaurant   This is a big place in the grand old style: lots of crisp linen and shiny silver. The meals are fine French cuisine with good local specialties. And the costumed waiters are faultlessly gallant and patient. Everyone who is anyone shows up here—that whole mix of wealthy Africans, American foundation executives, French businessmen and the staffs of the Eastern and Western diplomatic corps, finance missions and cultural delegations.

La Madrague, at the N'Gor Hotel Beach   Open air, down on the beach, this place is an exciting change, though a bit chummy. You sit outside watching the sand and the waves and the bathing beauties. However, you have to keep your eyes delicately averted or else glazedly uninterested in the aggressive French display of flesh, body fur and protuberances. The food can't miss, because it is simply flipping fresh fish and lobster grilled on beds of coal, brushed with delicate oils and herbs. At night there is a barbecue of chicken and meats.

La Croix du Sud, in the Croix du Sud Hotel   As you might expect, one of the best hotels has one of the best restaurants. It is quite elegant and formal; the food is first-rate, and high-priced. They broil lobster over herbs magnificently.

Popenguine and Sabran, in the Hotel Teranga   The restaurants are exquisitely decorated and boast excellent kitchens. The food is *haute cuisine* and the prices match. The comings and goings are elegant indeed as the diplomatic corps and international firms use the restaurants and salons of the Teranga for an unending series of *soirées de gala*.

Folklore, in the Vichy Hotel   Everything prepared at the Folklore is scrumptious. This restaurant serves some of the best food in Dakar—chicken, fish, steaks, all cooked with style and imagination. They serve thick steaks of *dorade* and *thiof* fish, and they make good omelettes. For vegetarians they make a big plate of green beans, blanched, then sautéed in garlic and butter. You can't believe how delicious *haricots verts* can be. The prices are a bit high, but worth it!

African Specialties

Senegalese food tends to be simple, with flavors that are clean on the palate. Seafood is the staple protein source in Dakar; the day's catch of an enormous variety of fish and crustaceans in this port town gets distributed every evening when the fishermen return. The fish is brought to the table cooked in a variety of pepper sauces; with it, people usually eat steamed rice. Senegalese eat quantities of vegetables also.

The national dish is called *riz au poisson,* and it is delicious. It is a dish that is served to company; long-term visitors to Dakar who have to eat in restaurants learn the schedule when it is a special dish at their favorite restaurants—for example, Farid's serves *riz au poisson* on Friday, the Lagon on Thursday.

Riz au poisson is a bouillabaisse made by first browning sliced onions and fish fillets in oil. Tomato sauce, garlic, dry red pepper and fresh green pepper are added. After they've cooked together, a quart of water and diced vegetables are put in—pumpkin, cabbage, cauliflower, eggplant, sweet potato. When the vegetables are tender they are removed, along with the fish, and rice is cooked in the remaining broth. The dish is served as a platter of fish and vegetables with a savory rice and a side boat of sauce.

Le Baobab, 44 rue Jules Ferry   The place is very well appointed and nice to be in. The food is good and the menu interesting.

Le Tam-Tam, 34 boulevard de la République   The Senegalese specialties here are well prepared, and the atmosphere is pleasant. Meals start at $6 and spiral up.

Le Su-Nu-Gal, on the road to N'Gor   There is an air-conditioned inner restaurant, but it is better to be outside under the thatched-roof verandas. The décor is rustic "African," the food is Senegalese, the discotheque rock and soul.

Le Ramatou, on the road to N'Gor   The Ramatou is built of bamboo, in the style of the round African houses. The conical roof is intricately woven; the whole effect is stagy but pleasant. There's a piano, and two giant elephant tusks soaring to the ceiling. They serve Chicken Yassa (chicken marinated in a lemon sauce and simmered) and *mafé* (meat and vegetables in peanut-butter sauce served with rice).

Le Soumbedioune, West Corniche   The Soumbedioune gets high marks for everything but the food. Since it is in the Artisanal Village, it is convenient after a morning of shopping. Being on the shore, it has a lovely view. The fixed-price menu is only $2, the service is friendly, and there's an orchestra on Saturday and Sunday nights. It's just that the food is no good! Try it anyway, because maybe by now things have improved.

Le Cannibale II, 42 rue du Dr. Thèze   The name is regrettable, but the food is good. If they have it, try the brochette, the Lamb Soleil, or the couscous.

Le Saint-Louis, 68 rue Félix Faure   The prices are cheap and you eat outside in a garden. You have a choice of African and Caribbean dishes.

Gallard, Rue 6, at the corner of Rue 15, Médina.

M'Baye M'Barick, Niari Tali, Grand Dakar   These two are simple places, away from the Plateau. They both serve good African food at modest prices. The fish dishes are the very best.

French

Colisée, 34 avenue Lamine Guèye   This is a Dakar institution, and many things to many people. It is a good restaurant that serves a variety of French, Italian and English dishes. It has a good grill for steaks and chops, and an impressive selection of pastries. You can have snacks and drinks on the terrace, or dig into a big platter of oysters. But the Colisée is not about the food—it is about the atmosphere. Members of the French establishment come to the Colisée, drink in its bar and give banquets in its dining rooms. Its club room for retired French army colonels and for prosperous French businessmen offers the alienated visitor a clear view of some of the privileges and prerogatives of empire.

Victoria, 4 rue Parent   Located on a little street off Kermel Market, the Victoria has a firm reputation among Dakar restaurants. The specialties are steak, chops and brochettes charcoal-broiled. The hors d'oeuvres are good, and the Irish coffee is a treat. There is an English-style bar, and cozy leather chairs arranged for chatting.

La Taverne Alsacienne, 8 rue Sandiniéry   Marcel Schreiber is the chef of this long-famous Dakar restaurant. He cooks dishes from the Alsace for a flock of loyal customers in a room decorated just like those places in France. Expensive.

Seafood

Le Lagon, East Corniche   The Lagon is one of the most dramatic dining places you'll ever find. It is so attractive that it is on postcards, and serves as backdrop for movies—you'll see why. It is in the middle of town but set on a quiet seaside drive. You pass under an arch and then descend long flights of plank stairs down to the restaurant itself, and find yourself on a covered wharf, the surf pounding under you. It is full house here all the time. Businessmen entertain clients at lunch, and the diplomatic crowd comes regularly.

The food is straightforward and hearty. Every kind of shellfish is available, but it is the huge grilled lobsters ($12 each) that make your mouth water. They make an excellent *riz au poisson* one day a week (Thursday), and there is always a wide selection of superbly grilled and sautéed fish. The beer is cold, the wine is good, and the prices high.

An extension of the wharf where you dine is a pier jutting into the ocean. In the afternoon and evening the beach umbrellas are up and people are out in the air sipping drinks and eating snacks. Half of them are in bikinis or shorts, because the Lagon is also a club house for water sports. Athletic young men come here to water-ski and arrange for skin-diving trips.

The ambiance is compounded of air, sun, sky, sea and shore; good food, good wine, and supremely healthy, attractive, self-assured people basking in it all.

Au Virage, on the road to N'Gor   At the Virage they make charcoal-broiled chicken and lamb chops and brochettes that are very good, but everyone comes for the bouillabaisse. They combine the fish and seafood, vegetables and herbs into a wonderful, hearty bowl of textures, flavors and aromas.

Italian

La Pizzeria, 47 rue de Grammont   The Pizzeria serves pizzas, of course, but the difference is that they are cooked in wood-burning ovens. The Pizzeria has a full list of other Italian dishes and makes Neapolitan desserts. They serve gallons of chianti, and remain open practically all night, in case you get a 2 A.M. urge.

Le Vesuvio, 38 rue Vincens   Another place selling Italian food and staying open very late. People stop in for dinner after the movies.

L'Estérel, Maginot Building   In addition to the regular Italian fare, the Esterel prepares Sicilian specialties. They go in for all sorts of ice-cream dishes and special continental desserts.

Vietnamese

The story of the Vietnamese in French-speaking West Africa is long and complex. It has to do with French colonial administrative policy that could send West Indians to administer hospitals in Algeria, Guineans to teach in Saigon schools, and Vietnamese to work in the West African civil service. Sailors and merchants, wives and professionals—all of them traveled within the lines of the French language and the franc zone. So Dakar, like Paris, Cotonou and Abidjan, has its Vietnamese restaurants. The Vietnamese, like the Chinese and Japanese, cater to the insatiable Western appetite for Oriental food.

Baie d'Along, on the Route des Puits   This restaurant is a bit out of town on a minor road. They use chicken, mushrooms, almonds, beef, vegetables cooked together in magical ways. The room is dimly lit, and there is the usual Chinese calligraphy on the wall. Since most restaurants in Dakar are forthrightly public, you can use this place for your tête-à-têtes.

Jean Tam, Boulevard de l'Est   Both French and Vietnamese food is served here. If you order in advance, a group of four persons can have a variety of dishes for about $4 each.

La Tonkinoise, 6 avenue Albert Sarraut   Here you can have Chinese food as well as Vietnamese. Try one of each style and get more of an idea of what the differences are.

Kim Son, 61 rue Thiers   This is a place where the Chinese food is first-rate.

Eurasia, 16 avenue William Ponty   Right in the middle of things, the Eurasia doesn't look too promising at first. However, if you go into the back dining room, you enter a cool oasis where the Vietnamese food is well prepared and nicely served.

Hanoi, 85 rue de Bayeux; **Faidherbe-Saigon,** 27 avenue Faidherbe; **Van Loi,** 100 avenue Gambetta; **Dragon d'Or,** 35 rue Jules Ferry—a selection for you to try, all of them modest in price.

Lebanese

Le Farid, 51 rue Vincens   A homey place for lunch or dinner, this is author's choice because the food is simple, well prepared and consistently good. The shrimp brochettes are highly recommended, and are to be eaten with rich garlic or pepper dressing. The Lebanese salad (mint, parsley, tomato, herbs chopped together), *homos* (dip of crushed chickpeas and sesame oil) and grilled fish steaks are outstanding. Every day there is a different special dish of good quality quickly finished by Farid regulars. For a refreshing dessert, have a dish of their delicious, tart, homemade yogurt, no relation to that pudding we buy in U.S. supermarkets.

Adonis, 78 avenue William Ponty   Monsieur Farouk runs this easygoing place. All the Lebanese favorites are served here: stuffed lamb, *kafta* (lamb burgers), *kibbi* (patties of lamb mixed with cracked wheat), *felafel* (fried dumplings) and *homos*. Try the chicken and rice. The food is good and cheap, really your money's worth.

Baalbeck, 8 rue de Thiong   The decorations are Oriental, the food is Lebanese. Again, this one is a bargain.

Low-Cost Eating

There are still small, family-style restaurants in Dakar where you can eat very well for around $2 for a four-course meal. They are related to those restaurants you find in France where a limited number of simple, regional dishes are well prepared fresh every day by mom and pop.

The **Montparnasse** (rue de Valmy, next to the Clarice Hotel) has a small choice, but what they serve is excellent. The dishes are "Béarnaise" in style (i.e., Basque), and the atmosphere is amiable. At the **Coq Hardi** (34 rue Raffenel) the dinner is $2, the cooking is Provençal, and there is a nice garden. **Les Gourmets** (96 rue de Bayeux) bills itself as a "temple of fine cuisine." It is not that great but it is good, and again, you can eat for $2.

Just across the street from the Central Post Office is the **Cosmos** (12 boulevard Pinet-Laprade), a restaurant where the meal of the day costs only $1. If you look in this area and down near the port, you'll find other places just as inexpensive. Try **My Long** (8 boulevard Pinet-Laprade) for Oriental food at cheap prices. The **Kermel,** at the market place, makes bouillabaisse, paella and couscous.

The **Biarritz** (9 boulevard de la République) has Spanish, Italian and Russian food for about $1.50. Back to the big time, the posh hotel of the same name has **Snack Croix du Sud** (Rue Béranger-Ferraud), where $2 buys you a meal with a carafe of wine included. The **Sarraut** (8 avenue Albert Sarraut) has a daily $2 menu also.

In case you have no special restaurant in mind, you can always stroll along Avenue William Ponty and drop in at a place whose specialty of the day strikes your fancy. The **Rustique** (No. 53) has a relaxed atmosphere, and cheap food. **Le Paris** (No. 28), with its jaded crowd, is a bit honky-tonk, but that may fit your mood. It opens at 7 A.M. and doesn't close until midnight. Some people like the **Ponty** (No. 13) better. In all of them you may be bothered by street vendors who will nag you to buy their junk jewelry and broken watches.

Ice-Cream Parlors

As you stroll around Dakar, you can't help noticing the ice-cream parlors and pastry shops. They are usually small, there is a display of sweets in the window, and there are a few chairs and tiny tables where you can sit and relax.

Pâtisserie A. Gentina, 22 avenue Albert Sarraut   You'll enjoy this place; all Dakar does. There are two parts. The front is a large pastry and sweet shop selling a variety of local and imported ice creams and candies, and a large selection of pastries, pies and cakes made by the house. The second room is big and airy, crowded with tables and chairs. This is a tearoom serving cool bottled water, sodas and fruit drinks, beer, snacks and pastries. If you wish, you can choose cakes, pastries and tarts from the display area. This is a place to stop for a few minutes and refresh yourself. The company has been in business for seventy years!

Estérel, Galeries, Maginot Building   Remember that Senegal is a

Muslim country, so very few of its citizens drink alcohol. Instead they prefer fruit juices and sparkling waters. Estérel is a place where distinguished people often come for ice cream, tea, coffee, glazed fruits and pastries. (At night this is an Italian restaurant.)

La Marquise, 52 rue du Dr. Thèze   Located on a central side street, the Marquise is quiet, cool and nice.

La Chantilly, 45 boulevard de la République   It is interesting just to sit here and watch the privileged of Dakar come in for a bite to eat. The Chantilly is one of the thoroughly French places, busy being itself.

Pâtisserie Orientale A. Fakhoury, 59 avenue Lamine Guèye
Laetitia, 52 avenue Lamine Guèye
Marquisette, 44 avenue Lamine Guèye
Le Mont Dore, 58 avenue Lamine Guèye
La Parisienne, 77 avenue Lamine Guèye
La Pâtisserie Libanaise, 25 avenue Lamine Guèye

You've got the idea. Just walk along Avenue du Président Lamine Guèye and drop in anywhere for a bit of scrubbed-tile cleanliness, sweet buttery smells, and piles of gooey, creamy European and Oriental delights: honey with nuts, almond paste, chocolate icing, flaky crusts, custard fillings, meringue toppings, all spread out before you. Enjoying Africa?

CABARETS AND NIGHT CLUBS

Considering . . . considering the population of Dakar, and their sophistication, and love of elegance in body and in movement, and considering the large number of nationals from all over Africa and Europe, considering all this you'd think there would be great places to dance and socialize in Dakar, but there aren't. (That the country is almost 100 percent Muslim is no answer; they dance in Mali.) I think what happens is that the fun-lovers give parties *at home.* First there is a talk, then dancing, then a big feast of, say, a barbecued lamb, and then the guests dance on through the night.

For a while now, **Le Baobab** (44 rue Jules Ferry) has been the favorite for dancing, and for what passes in Dakar as café society.

It is the place where the first secretary of the embassy will bring the visiting foundation official to show him the bright side of Dakar night life. **Le Niani** (on the East Corniche) has a lovely terrace on the sea. **Le Soumbedioune** has some swinging moments, as does the **Su-Nu-Gal** (road to N'Gor). The **Africana-Club** (in the Hotel N'Gor) and **Play Boys** (in the Maginot Building) are cold, smoky, and for a European discotheque crowd. **Le Caveau du Rond-Point** (57 avenue Albert Sarraut) and **Le King** (30 rue Victor Hugo) are dignified. There are some gritty ones in the neighborhoods; first find out which ones are in style.

Outside of Dakar
The Island of Gorée

Gorée, an island off-shore in Dakar harbor, is the place where permanent European influence on West Africa began. Back in 1444 Portuguese sailors made contact with the Island of Gorée, and thus brought it into the stream of European history. From the beginnings of the slave trade in the 1600s to its end in the late 1800s, Gorée was the pivotal point of the triangular trade between Africa, the Caribbean and North America.

By conquest and treaty it passed over the decades from Portuguese hands to Dutch rule, to English to French, but its reason for being never changed—it was a point of departure for blacks going in chains to the New World. Then, when slavery was abolished, Gorée was used as a naval base for control and suppression of the trade.

It is from Gorée that the settlement of Dakar and the rest of Senegal began. Gorée was just too small to accommodate the number of people who came to work there—the governor, administrators, military men, merchants, businessmen. The crowding plus the disastrous effects of a yellow-fever epidemic prompted people to move to the mainland across the bay.

These days Gorée is a quiet, charming place where life is routine and peaceful. A ferryboat regularly plies the one and a half miles between Dakar and Gorée several times a day. The trip takes twenty minutes one way, and gives a nice view of the harbor and horizon. Frenchmen and Senegalese make their homes on Gorée because it is calm, away from the bustle of Dakar, in an atmosphere of old buildings recently renovated or refurbished.

You, the traveler, come to spend a day on Gorée because it is an essential part of your visit to Dakar. You can spend the morning visiting the sights, then have a late lunch in a good restaurant; then spend the afternoon on the beach, and go back to Dakar on one of the evening ferries.

There are commuter ferry services to Gorée during the week, but on Sundays and holidays there are twelve departures for the convenience of the picnickers and visitors who come to enjoy the day. Gradually Gorée is developing into a tourist center. Its pleasures are simple, and it has a rosy, archaic charm.

Places to Stay and Eat

Relais de l'Espadon $6 single, $10 double; air conditioning extra. Half pension with room, breakfast and dinner, $9 per person; full pension $12.   Formerly the governor's mansion, the Relais is dazzlingly whitewashed clean. You enter from a rustic street, pass through the hotel lobby, across a court to the open-air terraces built at the seaside. The light and air are glorious—you feel transported by the freshness and shimmer. The hotel itself was built on a grand scale and has a stately, cool ambiance. The restaurant serves a great assortment of fish and seafood in the court outside, under the shade of those ubiquitous Air Afrique beach umbrellas. One limpid, magical afternoon in May, the author spent convivial hours of conversation and fellowship with two of the world's finest men, Gilbert Pongault and Nicolas Songuémas.

Hostellerie du Chevalier de Boufflers,   right on the wharf, offers good food and a romantic atmosphere. It is named for a governor of Senegal, a dashing eighteenth-century character, libertine poet, lover and letter writer who made Gorée Island known throughout Europe as a place of sensuous adventure. **Les Boucaniers** is another place serving excellent food.

SIGHTS TO SEE AND THINGS TO DO

Big-Game Fishing

The big activity on Gorée is big-game fishing. Groups of very serious fishermen fly in from all over West Africa and Western Europe to spend a week deep-sea fishing. The catch is swordfish—the record was set in 1963 with one weighing 1,100 pounds!—and blue marlin, tuna, sharks, blue fish, barracuda, bass, cod. There is fishing for twenty species of fish recognized by the International Game Fishing Association, and another twenty-three varieties of local sport fish. Daily trips, sea voyages are organized on the fishing boats of the fleet of the **Center for Big-Game Fishing,** located at the Relais de l'Espadon Hotel. Air Afrique will give you all the details and make all the arrangements.

Historical Sightseeing

Gorée is perfect for long walks and sightseeing. The little streets on the low lands of the island, the forts and castles of the heights all make for interesting, thought-provoking climbs and strolls. If you are fortunate, you will be taken in hand by one of the sleek, self-confident, articulate twelve-year-old historians who were born and brought up on the island. When not in school mastering intricate dilemmas of French syntax, they guide tourists around for extra change. You will be shown the following: 1) The police station—the walls were erected in the 1600s on the site of a Portuguese church built in 1482; 2) le Jardin du Gouvernement; 3) two old schools—Faidherbe and the famous William Ponty—where so many leaders of French-speaking West Africa were educated; 4) the forts—Orange and Saint-Michel; 5) the little mosque that dates from 1859; 6) the remains of Fort Nassau; 7) the fortified hill castle.

Museums   Open 8:30 A.M.–12:30 P.M. and 2:30–6:30 P.M. Closed Wednesday morning and all day Monday. Hours subject to change, so check first.

There are three on the island, and each is distinctive. The

Musée Historique starts with the foundation of West African medieval kingdoms and then charts the development of West African political history. At the **Musée de la Mer** the visitor finds exhibits about all sorts of sea life: 750 species of fish, hundreds of mollusks and shellfish. Very educational. A guide will show you around the **Maison des Esclaves.**

Other Activities There is a tiny beach for swimming right at the port—it is good for sunbathing also. For shopping you have a good choice of the novel Gorée dolls, small vanity dolls dressed in Dakar *couture.*

Observation: Maison des Esclaves An aging French architect has come to town. He stands at the hotel reception desk, all dash and temperament and ease, modeled on Frank Lloyd Wright. You know immediately that he is an *artiste.* I want to make of Gorée a jewel, he says to the reporters. Rebuild the hotel, refurbish the museums, construct holiday cottages! It will be an island resort, a gem!

Since 1944 the whole of Gorée Island has been classed as a historical preserve. Now the President of Senegal wants to build on Gorée an "Acropolis of Negritude." An enormous project providing enlarged museums, archives for the preservation of the works of black writers, museums for collections of black art, meeting rooms and auditoriums for colloquiums on African philosophy, theaters, for the preservation of African music and dance. Memorials to the giants of Black history and Black culture. Ô Gorée. Ô bloody, bloody, bloody island!

You come to Gorée to see the famous, infamous slave trading house, Maison des Esclaves. The guide comes in a few minutes with the keys to the big wooden front door to show you around. It is said that the house was constructed around 1776. You enter into a courtyard with low stone buildings on each side and you face the "big house"; a curved flight of steps on each side leads up to a balcony supported by four square columns. Behind this balcony are a whole set of rooms that were the residence of the owners and visitors to the house.

Old prints show the picture of a few captured African women and children in the courtyard; other Africans were locked away, awaiting shipment. Scores were forced into tiny, airless cells. The more rebellious were chained and manacled and whipped. All were routinely starved, punished, abused. At any one time there were two hundred captives in the house waiting to be sent to the New World in ships ready at the little beach.

It is very difficult to figure out how many captives passed through this house. Professor Philip Curtin's very sober and carefully documented work, *The Atlantic Slave Trade*, puts the total number of black people actually reaching the New World at about ten million. But, as he concludes, "the cost of the slave trade in human life was many times the number of slaves landed in the Americas. For every slave landed alive, other people died in warfare, along the bush paths leading to the coast, awaiting shipment, or in the crowded and unsanitary conditions of the middle passage." Tens of thousands passed through Gorée, a central dispatch point for trade to the French colonies.

When it came time for the actual trading and sales, owners and prospective buyers would gather on the balcony as Africans were paraded and displayed below. How was the judging done? By what criteria were human beings bought and sold? What aspects of appearance were used to determine the best—the most profitable— choice?

Captive men were judged on their *musculature.* Black, shiny sinews, ropes of muscles, hard and glistening backs, supple pivoting waists. The women, next, by the amplitude and firmness of their *breasts.* And the children, the young children, a cluster of them, sweet and chocolaty, anonymous, jostling each other in front of the camera, smiling happily, grinning up at you—yes, the teeth, the teeth, the children were judged by their teeth.

Recall now, the pictures of Africans you have so often seen. There is continuous evidence of the same white fixations. All in all, there is a concentration not on the beauty and grace of black form and movement, nor on the creative intelligence of blackness, but rather on its elemental, primal force and power: the image of black males stripped to the waist, muscles rippling.

Recall the postcards of fishermen throwing their nets, or cutting the water with powerful thrusts of their paddles. Recall, too, the endless tourist photographs of young, bee-stung girls, melon-ripe adolescents, mature young women, nursing mothers, shriveled old women. Breasts budding, breasts heavy, breasts hanging, black mother, black mammy, black nurse. And those cute little black children, those darling little brown babies, those adorable colored kids, with their shiny button eyes and their pearly teeth, with no antagonisms, no problems. Not yet. Crinkly hair—a rub brings good luck.

You go out through the portals into the streets, outside those thick walls of the Maison des Esclaves. You imagine Gorée as a resort town, free people gamboling and partying, free people. But above the tumult and pleasure you continue to hear the cries of degradation, that sobbing of blood. You believe after all that angels are airy because, if not, certainly by now their weight would have sunk Gorée into the sea.

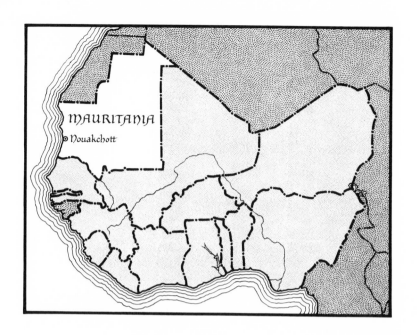

Mauritania

NOUAKCHOTT

My dear, hello. Hello, my dear. You are here now? Yes, I am here now. You have come back to us? Yes, I have come back. The voyage, was it fruitful? Yes, it was fruitful. Are things all right over there? Yes, they are all right over there. And are you well? Yes, I am well. And your wife, is she well? Yes, she is well. Your children, are they prospering? Yes, they are prospering. And your heart, is it happy? Yes, it is happy. And your body, is it strong? Yes, it is strong. And your mind, is it serene? Yes, it is serene. Your work, is it good? It is good. Your cattle, are they multiplying? They are multiplying. And their milk, is it sweet? Yes, it is sweet. Your garden, is it growing? Yes, it is growing. Your lands, are they blessed? Yes, they are blessed. And your house, does peace reign there? Yes, peace reigns there.

—Mauritanian greeting

The Atlantic Ocean forms the entire western boundary of Mauritania, from south to north. In this desert country of nomads and camels, dunes and tents, at the edge of this parched land runs four hundred and fifty miles of coastline—the purest, longest beach on the globe. Here and there a cove or a bay indents the shore, but otherwise it is one long, long stretch of sea, bordered with powder-smooth sands. As your plane approaches Mauritania you strain in your seat to see this startling shore. From the air it seems a passion of absolutes—the desert and the sea bearing hard on each other, meeting at every point, folding into each other's arms.

The ocean near Nouakchott, the capital city, is a blue-green aquamarine; it has the clear, pale look of an inland sea rather than an ocean. Near the shore the water is calm and fairly shallow; in many places you can walk out for yards and yards. You feel the ocean both as a link and as a barrier, because you know what lies just on the other side. This same ocean is the one that comes to the Caribbean: Mauritania is exactly opposite Jamaica and Haiti in latitude. You sense the direct line between the Old World and the New.

Nouakchott is back some three miles from the ocean. All the buildings are new, most of them built since 1960, all in a sand-and-concrete spectrum from gray-beige to ochre. Lacking the expected accessories of lawns, fences or sidewalks, each building seems to spring right out of the sand as though it has no foundation. Before long you become attuned to these seascape colors—a light brown, a sort of beige. And the persistent pale blue. It all becomes startling and mysterious, completely obvious and absolutely covert. The same colors. Ocean against beach; pale sand of concrete against the cloudless, endless blue of the sky. Streets of sand and people in their robes of blue.

In Nouakchott everybody wears blue every day. For the men, the outfit is a pajamalike shirt and loose pants, sandals and a loose outer garment called a *grand bubu*. The suit will be of pale-blue damask, probably embroidered at the neck and cuffs; the *bubu* will be embroidered at the front and back. Clothing is always blue. When it is windy, the folds of the *bubu* billow out, caught parachutelike by the air, taut and stretched against the wearer. The men may hold the cloth tight around them, then wrap their head in a turban of midnight-blue indigo and pull the ends across the face. For the women, the daily dress is a sari, yards of blue piqué or eyelet, wrapped around the body and over the head. They wear a pill-box affair or a fake chignon on top of the head over the brow so that when the cloth covers the head, the whole visage is lengthened and crowned.

(Blue, you ask, why does everyone wear blue? He answers, Blue is more natural. Why not something else? you ask. He replies, Because white dirties too quickly. No, not white, you continue, but what about another color, perhaps green? Green, green? he responds. Nobody would think of wearing green. Silence.)

Ten or fifteen years ago, what you see of Nouakchott today didn't exist. From the time it became a colony of France in 1903 until it obtained independence in 1960, Mauritania was governed from the town of Saint-Louis in Senegal. The site for this new capital for a new nation was chosen by the President and his council of ministers; it represents a point in space between the sandy lands of the northern nomad peoples and the tropical lands of the southern sedentary farmers.

In 1950 there was a flood for the first recorded time; a combination of rains and ocean turbulence sent a tidal wave raging onto the land. After detailed measuring and expert forecasting, it was decided to construct the town here, far enough away to save it from disaster but close enough to make the ocean easily accessible. Formerly this spot was a vast empty place covered with sand, bedded in the stuff of the bottom of the sea. Now it is a crossroads for these two worlds, and a symbol of the unity of this new country.

The buildings are as you would expect: squared off, rectangular, the sharp edges of industry, the repetitive patterns of the machine. It has all the regular angles of planning, like all the other anonymous "modern" buildings and towns built recently. In the west the straight enclosing shell of buildings matches the straight enclosing shell of men's clothing. But here, though the buildings are rigid and closed, the male dress flows and ripples, constantly wrapped and draped by the wearer. This fluid, changing garment seems to blend in better with the nomad's tents that dot the city; they too move with the wind and respond to the human touch.

Frankly, there isn't very much for a visitor to do in Nouakchott. You can visit old Nouakchott, now known as Luxur or Kasr; it is just a bit out of town. For centuries it was a trading settlement but it never grew to be big or important. The old town is there today—beaten clay houses and stores, wooden windows, sloping streets. If the wind or sand is blowing, the town is hushed, shuttered. When the air is calm the streets are crowded with a spill of children, chickens, goats, old taxis and small traders.

Back in town, there may be an exhibit of a local artist at the **French Cultural Center.** Or you may want to visit the **Artisans Center.** Lunch can be a meal in one of the hotels along the main strip, or you may simply eat some cheese and sardines in your room. You can just relax, because it doesn't much matter what you do. Without the drain of pressures, you feel yourself being energized. The afternoon you spend at the beach, basking in the sun, hanging around to watch the fishermen, or strolling and daydreaming. By four-thirty or five the men are in their gaming clubs, playing cards, draughts or chess. You feel like writing letters and postcards to tell your friends that you are here in Mauritania with Othello.

After a while you no longer feel ladylike in your short, print, American drip-dry dress. All the Mauritanian women you see glide and slip by quietly; they are wrapped and hidden; their look of privacy seems subtle and lively. In contrast you feel so *obvious* and vulnerable. You too want to be swathed in yards of blue cloth, so you go to the market.

Nouakchott Market is a very simple affair; it is rather austere and masculine. In the shops you are shown the bolts of cloth, on one side for the men, on the other side for the women, lined up neatly, little bargaining or discussing. Like an Eskimo, you begin to see designs in snowflakes. The monotone turns out to be damask of dramatic patterns muted in the monochrome of pale blue on pale blue. You see that there is a right side and a wrong side, an up side that catches the light, a down side that dulls it. You are fussy now—a colorless rainbow of designs. You inspect the swirls and rondelles and circles and sunbursts. The words "pale blue" are not exact enough. As the shopkeeper points out a bolt, you shake your head, no, it is too light. Just a while ago they were all the same color, but now they are on this tiny sky spectrum and you are sensitive to the shades, and very, very selective.

You want some kind of dress, long, something to cover you up. Here is a tailor shop; you stop in this one probably because the man at the sewing machine is so young and handsome and because there is another woman sitting in the shop. The tailor tells you how much cloth to buy; you go to make your purchase and then come back. He is nimble, dashing, refined, delicate (you measure your own hips and bust). He doesn't approve of the flimsy clothes you have on, doesn't think that they flatter you. Overnight this wizard makes you an embroidered caftan. You feel a sister to the women of ancient cultures, all of whom wear concealing, subtly draped clothing; you are at ease now, at home.

LEISURE AND PLEASURE

In the morning

—Visit the government Artisans Center and look at the jewelry and the chests.

—Walk around the camel market, and if you'd like, bargain for one.

In the afternoon

—Drive to the seashore and take a long stroll along the beach. Wait for the fishermen to return with their catch and admire the beauty of their painted wooden canoes.

—Browse in the old village of Kasr. Look around at the houses and people.

In the evening

—Dine with Mauritanian friends on a dish of couscous and lamb.

—Sit in at one of the local cinemas; movies are often American, dubbed in French, with Arabic subtitles. The incongruity of it all and the surprise of the reactions of the audience make the whole show.

SHOPPING

Traders from neighboring countries show their wares near the bank buildings, and on the streets of the arcades. In the market, the most interesting purchases can be made from the great variety of fine-quality blue damask cloth.

At the **Artisans Center** you can buy exquisite work in silver and wood. The necklaces made of wooden beads incised with silver filigree are extraordinarily elegant. The vogue in West Africa for men's silver slave bracelets started here, so naturally you can find the largest selection of sizes and styles at this center. The bracelets are made of very pure silver melted down from coins from Mecca, and they are well modeled and chiseled. A major purchase would be one of the gorgeous boxes and chests made of carved wood decorated with embossed silver appliqué. The intricate designs and superb craftsmanship make them costly ($50 and up for each, depending on size and workmanship) but they are treasures, made only in Mauritania. (They should be admitted duty-free as artifacts.)

Observation: The Teapot   Frequently during your travels in West Africa you will find men using an aluminum or porcelain teakettle. Muslims keep them by their side at all times. The taxi driver will keep his on the floor of the car next to the accelerator; the miller will have one on the shelf; and the barber will put his on a table. You get to appreciate the teapot and begin to realize how handy and practical it is.

Once it is filled, it can be bumped along the roughest roads with hardly a drop spilling. The spout is so small and curved that dirt and insects don't get in it to contaminate the contents. This same spout pours a judicious amount of liquid in your mouth; and it gives direction to the flow so that it can be controlled. You can keep fresh water, juice or milk in it. Put it on the fire and make yourself some tea. Before prayers, after a dusty journey, or when you are too hot, pour it over yourself in a cleansing, cool stream.

*   *   *

HOTELS

At the moment there are four hotels, and plans for another very big one to come. They are all clean, well run, and near one another on the main drag. Since there is seldom a crush of tourists, you will not find it difficult to find a room.

The government hotel, **Le Marahaba,** is a pretty place: nice rooms, new swimming pool, traditional tent serving Moorish tea. If there is a delegation of visiting dignitaries, all the rooms may be taken. International standing. $15 double.

L'Oasis, the oldest hotel in town, is right in the middle of things and next to L'Oasis cinema, so there are constant comings and goings, $7 per person. **El Amanne** is fresh and bright, part of a little shopping complex. **La Pergola** is all right, too.

RESTAURANTS

Mauritanians are not in the habit of eating out, so the restaurants are strictly for the convenience of travelers and expatriates. The restaurants are in the hotels. As you would expect, **Le Marahaba** is the most expensive and formal. The service is great; cuisine is simple French food. **L'Oasis** is the most crowded and bustling, and like **La Pergola** and **El Amanne**, it has a reasonably priced menu.

OUTSIDE OF NOUAKCHOTT

Though you're a confirmed town-lover, here in Mauritania you are urged to leave the capital and get out into the countryside. Imagine yourself on the trail: going north following the nomads, battling the sand, flying over the dunes; going south to the oases and the rivers. Since you have come as far as this, you are in the most remarkable place in West Africa for experiencing the ancient, the strange and the wonderful.

Mauritania is seldom visited by tourists, perhaps because it is one of those bridge lands linking northern Africa with sub-Saharan, and thus a bit off the main line of modern finance and politics. Also, admittedly, access to the most interesting sites has been difficult, so Mauritania is usually skipped by the charters and the tours. But this is a case where comfort varies in inverse ratio with the level of adventure and thrills.

If you can put aside two or three weeks at leisure for travel throughout Mauritania you are promised unique experiences. You will obtain a most extraordinary sense of removal from the mundane; the feeling of being transformed far beyond the usual. You will view some of the most beautiful scenery in the world as you journey through both time and space. The essentials are the sky and the sea, the desert and the river, sand dunes, lakes and oases. Palm groves, cliffs, rock formations, sky, sky, sky, and stars. All the cosmic vibrations, the spiritual stirrings, that communication with the firmament—all this is waiting for you.

From Nouakchott you can hop a plane to the northernmost end of the 450-mile Mauritanian seashore—the Cap Blanc peninsula, a politically divided finger of land whose Atlantic side is part of Río de Oro, the Spanish-owned Sahara, and whose eastern half belongs to Mauritania. The hard base of the country's financial wealth is centralized here: the fishing port of Nouadhibou, the terminus of the railroad that brings in the iron and phosphates from the desert mines, the mineral port of Cansado, and other installations of Miferma, the government mining corporation. You have an opportunity to see all sorts of energy and power production and mineral ingenuity up close.

This area has a sizable European population, gathered here to work in the fishing industry and in the mining operations. They live in Nouadhibou town or at the Cansado housing development, both little patches of expatriate luxury. The **Clupéa Hotel** ($17 double) in Nouadhibou is the social center; it has a restaurant featuring freshly caught lobster, grilled or flambé, and a desperate little night club called the Whisky à Go Go. (**Le Relais** is clean, and its rooms are cheaper.)

The waters off Nouadhibou are literally the richest fishing grounds in the entire world. Unfortunately for the Mauritanian economy, trawlers from four continents come here to benefit from

the bounty. To the professional fisherman this is a major fishing port, the center of a dried-, salted-, and frozen-fish industry; to the amateur, it is a dream-come-true of swarming, gullible whoppers waiting their turn to jump on your line. Some "Imraquen" fisherman have even trained dolphins to help round up the fish.

The coastline of this peninsula offers the traveler a most extraordinary range of sights. If you will rent a motorboat you can take an excursion to three of the wonders nearby. First you visit Île d'Oiseaux (Bird Island), a dot of land not far from Baie du Lévrier (Greyhound Bay). As its name implies, thousands and thousands of birds nest here, covering every inch of this small rock island. It can be eerie to find yourself in a small boat in open sea facing the shrieking and flapping of these hard-eyed creatures; they seem powerful and demonic while you feel human and frail.

Next, you can go to the strange and beautiful **Baie de l'Étoile,** a part of Greyhound Bay. Because of a very peculiar configuration of stone passages formed by natural erosion, the sea is channeled to resemble a river. You go through a small entrance that leads to calm waters and surroundings that resemble a hidden green valley. The third unusual attraction is **La Côte des Phoques** (Seal Bay). In a sheltered cove at the foot of gray cliffs live a multitude of huge monk seals, a phenomenon in Africa, and a rarity in the world.

The sea, the sand—if you want to really experience the desert, here is what you can do. At Cansado, book a seat on one of those passenger coaches that is hooked onto the freight train heading to the iron mines at **Zuerata,** 470 miles inland, away across the desert. After you have traveled for a while, ask to be let off somewhere, say, at PK 30. The returning train will pick you up ten hours later. Meanwhile, you find yourself, all alone in the midst of infinity. Nothing, nothing at all will happen, and the only moving objects will be the sun and your shadow on the sand. Here, and here only, will you feel that the earth is indeed a planet in space, and that you are a creature riding on it, and you will wonder whatever for. When you get back to town and rejoin your fellow-men, they will want to know what the desert was like; you will be silent because certain sights are beyond description.

Mauritania is ancient of days, fabled in history and legend. Scattered throughout the desert there are settlements and towns rooted in societies and civilizations of by-gone eras. At **Akjoujt** you see a modern copper-mining town built next to a traditional market center. Copper has been mined here for centuries, much of it going into the bronzework of ancient and medieval African kingdoms; you can visit the remains of these mines, and the cave paintings in the vicinity.

In medieval days, the walled town of **Atar** was the capital of the Moorish Almoravid empire before its soldiers crossed the Mediterranean to conquer Spain and rule from Grenada and Cordova. You can travel there by plane or by truck; there is the pretty **Hotel du Tourisme** where you can sleep comfortably and take your meals. There is an enormous, fascinating traditional market where camel caravans still pass carrying large slabs of salt, and packs of rugs and leather goods.

Atar can be your home base for excursions out to some of the most breath-taking sights in this part of the world. It is best to travel with a guide by camel, for otherwise these places are almost inaccessible. You ride to the palm groves at **Azougui.** Farther out in the desert you find the oasis of **Chinguetti,** a Muslim holy city at the end of a wilderness. Here there is a library housing ancient manuscripts, and a mosque dating from the thirteenth century. At **Ouadane** you find an oasis with rich green palm plantations; it too was once a major center of Islamic learning. All throughout your journey in this area you will find remains, ruins, archaeological sites of cave paintings and iron tools, and always the dazzling, rugged scenery and the hushed, ageless quiet.

As the Sahara dried, the Arabo-Berber people pushed the original black inhabitants of Mauritania farther and farther south. These black men settled around the banks of the Senegal River. In this area you can stay in the rest houses at **Rosso** and **Kaédi.** You journey to the landscapes surrounding **Aïoun-el-Atrouss**; then you push on to the caravan city of **Oulata** and walk through the ruins of **Koumbi-Saleh**, capital of the ancient empire of Ghana.

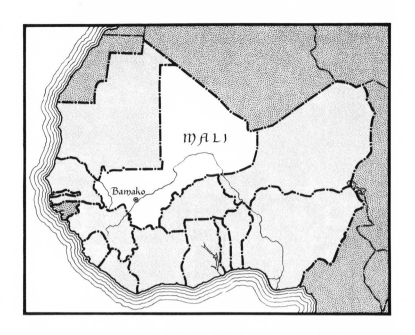

Mali

BAMAKO

Mali is huge, landlocked, and centered in the heart of West Africa. With no opening to the sea, surrounded by Senegal, Mauritania, Algeria, Upper Volta, the Ivory Coast and Guinea, Mali is completely continental, a residual, as Charles Cutter has called it, "of colonial nibblings at the coasts of Africa." A vast expanse of territory, Mali stretches from the deserts in the north to the intermittent lushness of grassy savannah in the south. Though it has no ocean frontage, Mali is not without water, for it is served by two of Africa's most important rivers—the Senegal and the Niger.

The two rivers have been the arteries, the life givers, of Mali, and the base of its remarkable history and culture.

The Niger is one of the great rivers of the world. Through time the fabled cities of West African history have developed along its banks. Bamako is the capital of today's Mali, as Kangaba was capital of ancient Ghana. Ségou was capital of the medieval Bambara kingdom. Beautiful Djenné, located on the tributary Bani River, has for centuries been a center of trade and religious learning. Farther along is Mopti, a modern commercial and fishing center. Timbuktu, the "mysterious," prospered as one of the great intellectual and cultural centers of medieval times, its schools of law and theology famed throughout the Muslim world. Today Gao is a small and slightly sleepy regional capital but it was once the seat of the greatest of all the West African empires, the empire of Songhai.

The history of Mali is long and fascinating. At various sites around the country and even in the capital of Bamako itself, there are preservations dating from prehistoric man and from earliest antiquity. The grottos of Korounkorakalé contained objects from the Mesolithic and Neolithic periods of human development. Tombs in the Bandiagara hills date from the latter part of the Iron Age (about the time of Plato), around 400 B.C.

In antiquity and in medieval times the area stretching from Western Sudan to the Atlantic was the site of the great West African empires of Ghana, Mali and Songhai, and the caliphate of Hamdullahi. The story begins around A.D. 200 with the first organizing of the Ghana state. By 600 Ghana was a thriving, powerful country; by 800 it had attracted the attention of the rest of Africa and the Muslim world. Drawing on accounts of ancient Ghana from Muslim accounts, the historian Basil Davidson writes:

> The origins of ancient Ghana lay among West African peoples, mainly Soninke of the Mande-speaking group who lived at a crossroads of trade between the oasis peoples of the Sahara and the gold and ivory producers of the grassland and forest country to the South. . . . North African demand for gold and ivory was one side of the picture. West African demand for salt was the other. Then as now salt was indispensable to the comforts of life. But salt was a rare commodity beyond the Sahara. Much of it came from deposits like

Taghasa far into or across the desert. The salt trade was no less important than the gold trade, and was probably much older. This means that ancient Ghana, approaching maturity in the Western Sudan at about the same time as the Franks were organizing their empire in Western Europe, could draw strength and revenue from the movement of two precious minerals: gold from the south and salt from the north. Other commodities were of course added as the years went by: copper and cotton goods, fine tools and swords from Arabian workshops and afterwards from Italy and Germany, horses from Barbary and Egypt, ivory and kola nuts and household slaves from the south; but the staples of the trade, in earlier times and later, were always salt and gold. These were the prize of political success. These were the means by which the new states and empires could support their soldiers, their governors, craftsmen, courtiers, singers of songs. And the power of these empires became legendary as the years flowed by: writing in the twelfth century at the court of the Norman King Roger II of Sicily, Al-Idrisi described how the lords of Ghana would often feed thousands at a time, spreading banquets more lavish than any man had ever seen before.

When the empire of Ghana fell apart into small states, it was succeeded by the empire of Mali, founded in the eleventh century. Islam was introduced at this time. African rulers adopting Islam had access to new administrative techniques and the assistance of Muslim clerics whose bureaucratic skills would facilitate the development of imperial organization. Islam also provided access to Arabic scientific knowledge and new ideas of architecture, planning and design.

This empire knew glorious beginnings in the military triumphs of Soundiata Keïta and came to glittering heights under his grandson, Mansa Moussa (1307–1332). At that time his realm stretched from the Atlantic Ocean to the Niger, down to the rain forests, up into present-day Algeria. In the fifteenth century the Mali empire was eclipsed by the rise of Songhai, under the leadership of the great Sunni Ali. Sunni Ali was a successful ruler who gained control over his weaker neighbors, enlarging the empire and increasing its influence. A gifted, innovative executive and administrator, he organized the empire into malleable provinces headed by regional governors, created a civil service, and developed a standing army and river navy. Through his control of agriculture, commerce and precious metals, Songhai reached a pinnacle of medieval power and wealth.

Following Sunni Ali, the Askia dynasty ruled Songhai for a century (1492–1591) until Songhai was defeated by an invasion of Moroccan mercenaries, ending the period of great empires and the political unity of Western Sudan. For the next two hundred and fifty years the Mali area knew a variety of smaller city-states that flourished and maintained separate forms of government, trade and culture. The fame and wealth of this West African land waxed and waned through twelve centuries of proud statehood until France's armies invaded in the 1890s. The French unseated the last great African leaders, then went on to wider military conquests. Under the name of French Sudan, this area was controlled by France until 1960, when it regained its independence and resumed the name of Mali.

From the earliest times there has been a place named Bamako, but it was never more than a tiny town of less than one thousand population until the French colonial government established an administrative center there. It is still possible to see this old Bamako in a fishermen's district called Bozola; the narrow twisted streets and tiny houses are still intact. The town grew in stages, each area received a particular name that it maintains even today. Dar Salam was the area where the domestic servants of the French lived; Médina-Koura was founded by the vanquished troops of Samori Touré; Ouolofo-Bougou was the residence of the Senegalese workers brought in to work on the railroad.

Bamako has its special character because it is an all-African city. That is, the black residents are in complete possession of the city. There is no large European population living in sumptuous isolation. There is no foreign merchant group running the downtown shops and living near their stores. Africans are not segregated in any way. The city is genuinely African.

Bamako invites you to walk and to stroll: the pace is slow, and the air is gentle. This is one city that you explore on foot, taking your time to savor the originality of the various neighborhoods and areas. By walking you will be able to enjoy the good looks of the Malians, the colorful movement in the shops, the design of the buildings, the shape of the streets. You can best enjoy the authentic African flavor by taking it all in slowly.

Bamako is romantic, with a relaxing, seductive air. It has its own kind of style and beauty—all of it on a human scale, never threatening, never brusque. The city has a unity and saneness about it, and it is meshed together with a coherence which the visitor experiences as reassuring and alluring. Most other cities in Africa are shiny-new or dilapidated-old. Bamako alone seems to have its own equilibrium and a personality of place; it has a charm and attractiveness that make it endearing and memorable.

Observation: The Merchant The merchants of Mali are to be found in business all over West Africa; a merchant is an entrepreneur, a wholesale distributor. They are talented men who combine enormous business acumen with patience, determination and the ability to endure hardships. A merchant starts out as a trader, and after a long apprenticeship he will be able to move up to a position where he controls a large store of goods and an important capital.

These men are the "rich merchants" storied in the Bible and *Arabian Nights*; known as Dyula traders, these very men play a role and bear a heritage that stretches back unbroken for centuries. Their history as a guild goes back to the fourteenth century, a period of commercial expansion. Professor Davidson tells us that much of it was the result of Dyula enterprise. "These Dyula traders penetrated southward into the forest country, travelling the roads with their own armed escorts, establishing themselves at regular relay-stations, patiently linking one zone of production with another. In the course of time they accomplished for the western regions of West Africa what the Hausa and Yoruba traders achieved for the eastern regions; and the story of Dyula enterprise runs like a vivid threat through the records of West Africa from the early times of Mali to the present day."

Traditionally the merchants are Muslim; they are educated in Koranic schools, read and write in Arabic, and manage to speak some English, French and all the vernacular languages in the vicinity. Their personal style is lean, devout and absteminous. No drinking. Only an occasional smoke. No stimulants or medications. Only a light evening meal. Regular praying on schedule.

You have made the acquaintance of a company of men who deal in fabrics. The senior partner is a distinguished-looking older man; the two other partners are close friends, both in their early forties. They are reputedly very wealthy. At their invitation you come to visit their offices on a crowded commercial street near the central market.

From the street you enter a run-down shop where a few bolts of cloth are propped against the wall. Five or six men are sitting engaged in serious conversation. One of them shows you to the inner office. The place is dark and grimy. Dirt blackens the walls and cobwebs lace the ceilings. The one electric light, a single dim and dusty bulb, dangles at the end of a hanging wire; the main light comes from the doorway to the shop. Just inside this door is the boss's desk. It is an old, beat-up teacher's desk, on it a telephone and piles of papers. Across from the desk is a large table, holding an adding machine, a few pens, a stapler. The only ventilation comes from a barred cell window high up on the wall. The room, huge, leads off into piles of burlap-wrapped bundles, stacked twelve feet high. All sorts of creatures must be scuttling around in there—better not think about it.

From here the company does a million-dollar business in import and export. Nothing is spent on appearances. With the profits, a fleet of trucks grows, apartment buildings go up in Dakar, sons are sent to France to study medicine, European cars waiting at the curb. Be careful, one merchant says to the driver as we go home; remember we are *pères de famille.* That is certainly so. Each of them supports a troupe of fifty or sixty people in the family compound. Each buys one hundred pounds of meat at a time, gallons of yogurt, bushels of vegetables, the fisherman's whole catch.

Being Muslims, they are polygamous—the first wife was the choice of the families and has now become a tender bosom friend; the second wife a younger beauty chosen in passion and desire. One of them was planning on marrying a third, a girl whom he had known and loved since she was a toddler whom he had watched grow and mature to her present seventeen years. With the two wives come two sets of in-laws: mothers, fathers, brothers, sisters, aunts, uncles, nieces, nephews, cousins without number. Plus his *own* mother and father. As the merchant grows in prosperity more relatives come to live under his protection; the family compound grows to be half a city block. He, his two wives and six children are a small unit in the household that spreads and extends, interweaves and interlocks.

The merchant does not grumble about his burdens. Allah has been good to him, his work is blessed, he enjoys prosperity and respect. His body is strong and his mind clear. His name is honored because he is a truly good man.

*   *   *

Here in Bamako a new friend invites you for dinner. You have met him by chance while downtown. Your friendship has gradually grown, and now he invites you to visit at his home.

The house is on a corner in one of the traditional wards. Once you turn off the main road into one of these residential areas the road is no longer tarred or paved; instead, it is rocky and rutted. Your lightweight taxi kicks and bucks along, skirting potholes and easing through puddles as goats and children scatter. By now you have learned to enjoy it all. There is a kind of amusement-park air about it—a slow, safe ride with just a touch of adventure. You think ruefully of the straight, smooth and wide American highway of rapid, sudden death. Here, with all the obstacles in its path, the automobile seems a ridiculous, bumbling carriage, barely able to cope with an addle-brained chicken. It hardly seems a death-dealing demon, demanding, as it does in the United States, the sacrifice of fifty-thousand human lives in a year. Here it seems under human control, possessed by the human situation.

The house is surrounded by a flat wall on three sides of the block, its façade broken only by small shuttered windows high above the ground. The wall is made of *banco*, a mixture of water and claylike laterite soil. This hardens into a tough, solid mass that maintains its integrity for years.

The actual entrance, a small arched doorway, is on the side street. You must watch your step because the opening is narrow and the pathway is studded with stones and puddles. Once you pass through that eight feet of passageway, you are in the compound. It is closed in on all four sides. There are three long houses, an animal shelter and a variety of sheds, all facing onto a central courtyard. The major houses are made of thick concrete and stone. A veranda runs the length of each house, permitting all the rooms an opening on the courtyard. At the far end of each building is a shower and a john. Every house has five large rooms, each is large, square, thick-walled, and receives air from the entrance door and small, high windows.

The courtyard is a center of activity. Goats and chickens wander about. Two little girls take their baths—hopping playfully out of zinc tubs of sudsy water, scrubbing, rinsing, rubbing, splashing. Two women chat as they cook at the hibachi stoves. In another corner stands a blazing fire where another woman of the family prepares batik by dipping the waxed-and-tied material into indigo dye contained in a huge boiling vat.

Your host shows you around from room to room. "This is an auntie's room; my mother's sister lives here. This next room is for another auntie, the second wife of my uncle. This third belongs to still another auntie. The adjacent one is my uncle's. All the little children use this fifth room as a dormitory." In the building at a right angle to the one you have just seen he shows you more. "This is the room for me and my wife, and next to it is my sitting room. Then a room for my mother when she comes, and one for her old friend who stays with us. Across in the third building, that is my uncle's door; he is a cantankerous old man who lives alone. That one is for the first cousin of my mother and her husband. My wife's sister lives here because her husband is always away trading. The rooms up to the back are for the domestics. The concrete house near the entrance is a dormitory for the older boys to use when they are home from school—they like to be near the street so they can come and go and have their friends over to visit. That shelter over there is for the animals, but we keep the he-goat tied to the tree. The turkey was a gift my mother brought when she came. That space over there is where my aunt does her craft work." Graciously he has shown you everything, satisfied your curiosity about the arrangement of things.

Soft drinks are served in the host's sitting room. By now you know what to expect. The room is crowded with big, heavy furniture—dark, lacquered wood surfaces, chrome trim, felty coverings. Dainty lace doilies, tiny coffee table; a huge German cabinet shortwave radio set; lots of knickknacks, souvenirs of a trip taken abroad for a training program. And something every West African seems to love—a portrait of himself. A full or three-quarter view, formal, posed, a big 9″ by 11″ size, in a frame, hanging by itself on the wall. Supper is on the veranda—a delicious assortment of fish and chicken dishes. You laugh a lot, talk, listen to the radio; the evening ends in a glow, a warmth of companionship.

Your host's compound faces the local cinema. Upon leaving, you find the road crowded with bicycles and motor scooters; it is show time. Along the street sit his aunts, each woman at a lantern-lit table selling small things to the moviegoers—mangoes, oranges, peanuts, homemade skewers of meat. They laugh and greet you, offer you gifts of fruit. Your host sees you to a taxi. You return to your hotel.

A few days later your friend invites you for a spin on the Niger; there is a place not far from Bamako to rent boats. You buckle and bump along washboard roads until you come to a nondescript village at the river's edge. It is dusty and brown—its houses of *banco,* the ground trampled and bare. The only building of note is the local mosque, built in the Sudanese style that Labelle Prussin has studied in such detail. The village is quiet, almost deserted; men and women are away working at their farms. Down at the riverside there are a few women washing clothes, some children wading around, and a few idle teen-age boys. One is delighted to rent you a dugout canoe; your friend is rowing.

Not that far from shore is a small island where a few reeds grow sparsely and where tiny fish swim in pools. You walk and play, sit on the boulders and talk. Surrounded by the past, you fantasize an idyllic future. You will marry each other and have four beautiful babies. He and his friends will rise in government and lead Mali to new strength and power. You will work to promote national cultural expression. Together you will create and build for prosperity and peace. A romantic daydream on another gentle Bamako afternoon, dabbled in sunlight, blessed with mystery. Time now to return to the canoe, across the Niger-River-of-History, back to town. A deep breath of clean air, the cradling in spiritual warmth, hands washed in the waters of time.

LEISURE AND PLEASURE

In the morning

—Plan to spend at least one morning getting your legal things straightened out at "Securité" (see "Legal Matters," below).

—Pretend that you are planning to buy a horse and so get a chance to see people's stables.

—Listen for the sound of drumming at Place de la République. Maybe you'll be lucky and get a chance to see Mali's excellent National Theater Troupe.

In the afternoon

—Spend the time comparison-shopping along the long streets of gold and silver smiths.

—Hire a taxi at sunset, drive up to Point G to see the inspiring view.

—Relax at the end of the day with a cold tamarind juice on the terrace of the Grand Hotel.

In the evening

—Drive out to the Lido for an evening of dinner and dalliance under the stars.

—Try sitting in the cheapest seats at the movies, right in the midst of the fervently participating audience.

—Round off your evening with a romantic stroll in the Botanical Gardens.

Legal Matters

1. Before you arrive in Mali, you must obtain a visa; be sure it is still valid. The visa stamped in your passport is only for *entrance* to the country; you will need to have an extension.

2. You are not allowed to take pictures in Mali without a permit. The permit gives you leave to photograph places and people of cultural interest, but you must not take pictures of industrial or military establishments. You will need to know the make and number of your camera.

3. For both a visa extension and a photo permit, go to the Tourist Office. There you obtain two forms and pay a small fee (25 cents). Then on to the Central Post Office to buy a tax stamp (another 25 cents).

4. Take the two completed forms, tax stamp and an identification photo to the Securité Office; Securité issues the actual permits, usually the same day if you leave your forms in the morning.
5. If you are planning to take the train to Dakar when you leave, go to Securité to have your visa stamped and to the Police de Chemin de Fer for another stamp. When you go to buy your ticket, ask for exit instructions.
6. You can obtain a tourist card at the Tourist Office. It is free and it is a nice thing to show at bus stations and hotels and tourist offices in different parts of the country. It is good for identification purposes, and entitles you to special consideration.
7. Just to be on the safe side, stop at Securité for an exit visa before you attempt to leave.
8. Regulations change often, so be sure to find out the latest information from the U.S. embassy or from the Tourist Office.

Mali is certainly one of the most stimulating countries in Africa, and Bamako is the author's choice as one of the most pleasant and enjoyable cities to be found. Bamako has a way of getting a hold on you and haunting your memories. There is so much to do and so much to see that you are tempted to daydream about staying for months on end, basking in the human climate and learning from the spiritual and material culture of the country.

After settling into your hotel, you make your first stop a visit to the **Office Malien du Tourisme.** Directed by the wise Mr. Sy, this office will give you sound and gracious advice on how to make the best of your time and fulfill your interests. The pace of life in Bamako is relaxed, so you cannot expect to do a lot at a time. Rather, you should plan to do one thing in the morning, go back to home base for lunch and a siesta, and then make another excursion in the afternoon.

Note: A little Citroën "2CV" (*deux chevaux*) rents for only $7 a day in Bamako. Since traffic is courteous and quiet, it is recommended this once that you get a car. Or you may rent any street cab for about $9 for the morning.

PLACES TO VISIT

Botanical Gardens Area

Musée National du Mali   The National Museum has a small but choice collection of the arts of Mali's peoples. Upstairs in the offices you may ask for assistance; if you are in luck you can be accompanied by the English-speaking guide who will explain all the objects on display.

Botanical Gardens   The gardens are planted with trees and shrubs typical of Mali and West Africa; the style is free-form and spacious. For many years, the gardens have been the cavorting and courting grounds of the young *lycée* students. The atmosphere is very gentle and cool and conducive to leisurely strolls.

The Zoo   Lions, zebras, crocodiles, antelopes, and other animals, are displayed in very spacious grounds, with enclosures designed to resemble their natural habitat. Again, a visit makes a very agreeable walk.

Koulouba Area

You will need a car in order to enjoy these scenic drives. For about $5, most taxi drivers will be pleased for the opportunity to show you around all morning.

First you take the **Koulouba Tourist Road.** Leave the paved road, and take up the pebbled scrap road that rises along the Koulouba hills. You will come to a parking place near the water tower. From here you have a breath-taking view of the whole of Bamako and beyond. It is easy to understand why young people climb to this point all the time to enjoy the panorama—you surely feel like the king on the hill. Hopefully you are accompanied by a Malian who can point out to you the fairy-tale castles and gardens that spread out below you. The **Point G Tourist Road** rises through a woods, and all the way you have stunning views of the town and its surroundings.

On the **Koulouba Plateau** are located the government offices and ministries. Here also you will see the residence of the chief of state. Tucked away on the side streets are some very attractive private and diplomatic residencies. Go as far as the Point G Hospital, leave the car. Off to the right you'll see a path that will lead you to another beautiful panorama. There is also a prehistoric grotto whose walls are covered with paintings and signs.

The "Villages"

The city of Bamako is divided into a number of self-contained wards, known as "villages." Each one has its own distinctive ethnic flavor and self-contained social life. It is here that the majority of the population lives in houses protected from view by high stucco walls. Their names are wonderful: Dar Salam, Dravéla, Bagadadji, Missira. Visit the area your friend recommends. Wander through the streets—you'll find children at play, craftsmen at work, women selling home-cooked food. In one of these villages, Médina-Koura, you will even be shown another prehistoric grotto.

Piscine Omnisport

Bamako boasts a beautiful, well-maintained Olympic-sized swimming pool. It is open all day from 8 A.M. to 6 P.M. The character of the crowd changes as the day passes: athletes in the morning, the diplomatic corps in the early afternoon, schoolchildren near closing time.

Horses and Races

Mali is an important source of horses and livestock for all of West Africa, so naturally Malians have the most thoroughbred horses and are the most expert trainers and jockeys. Races are held at an attractive race course; the newspapers and radio announce the time of the meets. Also, there are several stables in town where you can rent a horse for the afternoon.

THE VICINITY OF BAMAKO

Road to the Barrage des Aïgrettes

This is a lovely six-mile trip out of Bamako, past the industrial area (match factory, etc.) and onto a lovely shady road. After a distance you arrive at a roadway that crosses the Niger River rapids. When the rains come, this roadway is submerged by the river; but before then this dry riverbed is a haunting moonscape of black, smooth, shiny rock formations, polished and sculptured over the millennia by the currents of the Niger. Climb over the rocks to the edge of the river, gaze at the waters, and feel the sense of heightened awareness, and a oneness with nature and time.

Farther on you come to the Pont des Hirondelles, so named because thousands of swallows make their nests under this part of the bridge over the river. They chirp, dip and dart. You climb down from the roadway onto the rocks again, then onto the sandbanks under the sides of the bridge, along the river. You remember the game Katherine plays in the Truffaut film *Jules and Jim*: what you do is look for the last traces of civilization. On a May afternoon you and your friend could only find a bottle cap, a discarded shirt, and evidence that someone had made a fire. It is not hard to guess that this road is a favorite trysting place with lovers. Cars park along the roadway, and the couples disappear into the night to some one of the sandy mattresses.

SHOPPING

How can you choose when confronted with the art and the handicrafts of Mali! The sculptors of Mali have created some of the world's most perfect art, and the skilled craftsmen have few peers in the fineness of their work and the personality of their products. Mind you, the emphasis is on extreme restraint, subtlety, elegance and spirituality. You won't find the exuberance and flamboyance of Central African arts; here everything is austere and intelligent.

Central Market

A good place to start is in the shops of the Central Market. The atmosphere is very low-key, so you can browse at leisure; no one will be after you to buy. One place sells handmade sandals; they come in a variety of styles and colors. Another stall displays a pile of classic desert *couvertures,* translated to mean a heavyweight blanket or a lightweight rug or wall hanging. These are handwoven of wool or cotton in the narrow palette of black, gray and maroon on a white background; the designs are spare and geometric. In former days, the cotton ones were worn by the women, but now they are used to decorate the bed, and to sit on and under during long nights of conversation and conviviality.

The weavers also make a special kind of cotton coverlet that is very popular as a wall hanging in Malian homes. They come in vivid shades of yellow, green, red, black and are in step-checkered patterns with a variety of symbols woven into the designs. In addition, the weavers make up women's skirt material. At the moment stylish colors are in the purple spectrum of mauve, lavender, purple and black stripes. Very beautiful.

An old man will be selling a collection of beads and semiprecious stones; another will have a treasury of silver coins. The beads—associated with immortality and divinity—will become parts of necklaces and waistlets; silver coins will be adorning the hair and veils of the northern women. You can find the delicate golden-straw woven jewelry from Timbuktu selling for a teeny price.

Handbags made of leather and alligator, hand-thrown pottery, indigo-dyed materials, ready-made *bubus* and *dashikis,* calabashes, sculptured boxes, ceremonial swords—you'll find all of them in the market. Give over a morning for leisurely browsing and chatting.

Tourist Office Shop

The government keeps a boutique that is very interesting, selling crafts of great quality. Occasionally they stock lengths of *bokolanfini,* called "mud cloth" in English. This beautiful, deeply spiritual cloth is handwoven from locally grown and spun cotton; then it is dyed in a complicated manner with seasoned mud scooped from the bottom of select ponds. The designs are abstract: ideograms relating to Mandingo history and philosophy.

In another exposition room they show a collection of masks and statuettes—examples of Bambara and Dogon art. They have pieces typical of the various styles made by those two divinely artistic groups; the shop will certify that the piece you buy is authentic. They charge moderate prices; you may leave standing orders if you wish, and they will ship your purchases carefully packed.

Artisanat

Across from the Tourist Office, in the Place de la République, you will find the handicraft stalls. Artisans sell cloth, blankets, handbags, rugs, leather goods, jewelry and clothing. You may order from samples, or buy from what is at hand.

Curio Shops

Right downtown near the Printania general store you will find several shops selling a variety of locally made crafts, and pieces of (mostly fake) sculpture. The selection is much better elsewhere, but here you get a chance for some jovial exchange with the middleman.

Jewelry Shops

The boutiques and ateliers of the goldsmiths line the sides of Avenue de la Nation. Some shops are larger than others, but every one of them seems to be offering superb work. The price and quality of the gold is controlled and must bear the seal of the Ministry of Mines. Malian goldsmiths specialize in delicate and intricate filigree. They make lovely necklaces, and the V-shaped Liberian bracelets are the current mode (see "Shopping" in Liberia, below).

Tapisserie Artisanat Tissage

You will be impressed by this small factory where Malians weave rugs, coverlets, table settings and yard goods. The work is first-quality. You can buy what is available or you can leave an order. Plan enough time for a tour of the place. It is located next to the American embassy.

HOTELS

Grand Hotel (B.P. 104, Bamako; tel. 225-81)   Double with air conditioning, $16; without, with overhead fan, $10.   The Grand Hotel is centrally located in a lovely residential area, and everybody stays here or comes in the evening for drinks and meals. The rooms are large and well kept, each one with a shower and a large balcony. The restaurant is only so-so, but always crowded. You will enjoy the little garden bar with its porch-swing chairs.

Le Motel (B.P. 911, Bamako; tel. 236-22 or 24)   Entirely air-conditioned. $12 single, $15 double.   The Motel is a newer place, located about a mile out of town. It is pretty; chalets arranged around a large garden. It is popular with businessmen who like "privacy," and with some foreign delegations.

Hotel Majestic (B.P. 153, Bamako; tel. 229-20)   Double with air conditioning, $16; without, $10.   Located right in the commercial center, this small hotel is always fully booked with the old-style French who make it their headquarters.

Le Lido (B.P. 133, Bamako; tel. 221-88)   All air-conditioned rooms from $9 to $12.   What a lovely place—truly charming in appearance. It has ten nice rooms, gardens, a bridge over an enormous waterfall, a good swimming pool, fine service and an aura of graciousness. Come here for a relaxing time: since it is three miles out of town, transportation in and out can be a bother, though.

Buffet de la Gare (B.P. 466, Bamako; tel. 20-88)   Rooms $4 to $6. Right next to the train station, built in old style, this is a cheap, clean, convenient place—so expect to find it fully booked.

Bar Mali (near the Vox Theater)   Rooms $4 to $6.   Can be dingy, dirty and noisy, and there's an odd sweet smell in the air. Popular with "dropping-out" crowd.

Observation: Hotel de l'Amitié   Right on the edge of the Niger River, at a spot where the air is fresh and the view is wide, stands this seventeen-story rectangular-shaped hotel called **Hotel de l'Amitié**, Friendship Hotel. It is anonymous and impersonal-looking; it could just as easily be overlooking the Hudson River, or better, Orly Airport. It has a swimming pool, a cinema, conference rooms, and all the amenities. Rather, it *will* have all these things, one of these days when it finally opens. Its picture is on the new 100 franc Malian notes, and it should be functioning by now. A lofty project for Bamako, planned as a gift from a rich neighboring country—it has stood unfinished for years.

As explained elsewhere, these "modern" air-conditioned, closed-in marvels are terribly expensive in money and manpower for a small city to maintain. The mechanic who might be better employed keeping the municipal buses in repair is kept busy looking after the elevator. Many of the manufactured goods imported from the West are designed with built-in "planned obsolescence." Add to these defects the strain put on motors by the West African climate (in which metals greatly expand, sweat and rust), the irregularities of electrical currents, the lack of experience on the part of many of the users—put all these things together and you see why machinery is always breaking down. Broken, the machine sits a long time until the expensive spare part can be imported, and the man skilled in repairing this particular item flown in. The shoddy construction of much that comes out of the developed countries these days (remember your consumer indignation at cars that are lemons, appliances that soon break down) helps out the rich countries but further cripples the poor ones.

Today's travelers suffer all year in overheated or overchilled indoor air; they work in offices where the temperature and humidity never varies for 365 days of the year, regardless of what is happening out-of-doors. There the air is often "unsatisfactory" with high levels of "pollutants." Africa, on the other hand, has fresh pure air and glorious evening and night skies—but you can't breathe that air or dig those heavens if you are shut away in a closed, sharp-edged, refrigerated box. Since it has often been demonstrated that by clever design and engineering, rooms can be cooled with (free) natural ventilation, expensive refrigeration plants that tax an African city's resources are just not necessary.

Feeling enervated and desperate from the tensions of a clanging machine society, sophisticated New Yorkers will go any distance to find

114

a place that has individuality and charm, pay any rent to live in a town house. What a letdown to come to Africa and find these impersonal, anonymous blocks. How ironic that in Africa they are built in the name of "modernity," while in the States they are put up as monuments to the astronomical costs of prime commercial land, workmen and building materials, combined with cold-hearted greed and sterility of imagination. Since none of these conditions apply in Africa—land is plentiful, local workmen and local building materials are relatively inexpensive, and the Black spirit is endlessly innovative—why these boring boxes? Another example of Africa's inheriting the West's problems by being sold the West's discards.

It would be lovely to see smaller hotels of climbable height (just in case) inspired by traditional African forms, designed to enhance the originality of their location. The comforts are desirable, of course, but the emphasis should be on projecting the pleasures of the unique and unexpected in African surroundings, not on duplicating the dreary excretions of the Western war societies.

* * *

RESTAURANTS

Hotel Restaurants

If you are fortunate you may be invited to a dinner ordered in advance at the **Lido** (at about $3 or $4 a person). The pretty garden setting, the flowers on the table, the thoughtful service and the good food will put you in a mellow mood. This place has a charm all its own. The food at the **Motel** is good but you have to eat indoors in a dining room; same as at the **Grand Hotel,** where the food is only so-so. **Bar Mali** has good steaks and chicken at cheap prices (a meal for $1); **Buffet de la Gare** is a few cents more, but surroundings are much nicer. The restaurant at the **Majestic,** called The Aquarium, serves hamburgers and cheeseburgers to America's hungry (for their own type of soul food) children, omelettes to France's.

Other Restaurants

La Gondole, located on Avenue de la Nation, enjoys great popularity. It is a favorite with Malian big shots and with the diplomatic community. You eat out-of-doors in a pleasant garden, seated on those terrible small-bottomed chairs. The food is so good (try the brochette and the *capitaine,* a salt-water carp) and the ambiance so agreeable that you'll soon forget your initial discomfort.

Les Trois Caïmans charges more than $6 for dinner, an outrageous price in budget-heaven Bamako. **Chez Koumba** (Avenue de la Nation) is one place where you can order good African dishes as well as European fare, for the usual $2 a meal. **La Bonbonnière** is a newer place, serving both French and Vietnamese food.

At the **Restaurant Central** (first right turn after Printania on the left-hand side) you should order their delicious, inexpensive *plat du jour.* **Restaurant du Souvenir** (across from the Place de Taxi) and **Restaurant Oriental Gandone** (near the Banque de Développement du Mali) are both adequate.

Chop Bars

Bamako has a couple of restaurants that offer local-style food at tiny cost (80 cents a meal). Though not very appealing to international tourists, they are quite safe and suitable for students. Their names: **Chez Kassout, Chez Jean, Restaurant de la Paix** and **Chez Bakari.** Find out from your friends which ones they recommend.

Refreshments

There are a couple of places downtown that offer the hot shopper cooling drinks. You can always order cold sodas and beers, but why not try the excellent canned fruit drinks—guava, tamarind and mango, made in Mali. You can stop at the counter outside of Printania, or at **Socoma** (in front of the Place de Taxi). **Le Berry-Café Brasserie,** right in the center of town, has a terrace where you can sit and watch the rest of Bamako go by. For stuffing with creamy goodies, it's the **Pâtisserie Kamouh.** Sturdier stuff can be found at **Le Chantilly, Le Bambou** and **Le Fanion;** all three are bars that serve soft and hard drinks, and peanuts.

Note on food in Mali: Food to be found in Bamako's markets is abundant, of excellent quality and moderate price. Feast on the fruits—they are great. Look for the excellent mangoes, papayas and pineapples. (There is an especially luscious mango called *musca*—it costs more and is harder to find, but it is incredibly delicious.)

Water: Long suffering from chronic drought, Mali is—sinister irony—on top of a vast underground lake of some of the world's purest water, free of DDT, radioactivity and the usual pollutants. Tap water and water from artesian wells is of excellent quality.

NIGHT CLUBS

In Bamako, as in other places, the rules for night-club going are the same. Here are some reminders. Check always to see if they are still in operation. Night clubs have notorious reputations and notoriously short lives. Many places shut down during the months of June, July and August, when their foreign owners are off to Europe because it is raining in Bamako, shining in Rome. As a general rule, the places where there is dancing to a live band out-of-doors appeal to the elegant African youths who come immaculately dressed to show off their formidable suppleness, indefatigability and talent for auto-choreography. Rather than be shamed off the floor, whites (male technicians and teachers) often prefer to cluster in the low-temperature, high-proof, smoky night clubs where the dance floor is tiny and crowded, and where the girls are impressed by a display of cash rather than a display of virtuosity. Taxi drivers know the way; prices go up on weekends and holidays; and things don't really start to jump until around 11 P.M.

The best bands are to be found near the riverside at the out-of-doors **Les Trois Caïmans.** (Yes, they have three horrid little alligators in decorated pools!) On a good night the dancing can be spectacular—light, intricate and warm. Drinks cost around $1.50; ambiance and rustling night skies are free. **Le Jardin,** next door to the Grand Hotel, and **Hotel de la Gare** both have al fresco music and dancing, with drinks a bit less than at *Trois Caïmans.*

For a lungful of Gauloises, go to **Le Village** in the Grand Hotel, **Le Motel** night club, and **Le Dalton** out at the Lido. Drinks are about $1.50. **Le Club Sportif et Cultural** is a youth center, open on weekends for dancing. Not far away is **Jour et Nuit,** a discotheque.

BEYOND BAMAKO

Many of Mali's towns have an interesting history going back to medieval times. Each of them is rewarding to visit because they offer a variety of encounters and surroundings. The traveler's path follows the curves of the Niger River, and the Mali Tourist Office will arrange excellent trips at modest cost.

Ségou Situated on the right bank of the Niger River, 120 miles from Bamako, Ségou is a handsome town, well laid out, shaded by lanes of towering trees. In the early nineteenth century Ségou was the capital of the theocratic state of El Hadj Omar, a leader in Mali history. Today it is the cultural center for the Bambara people, a group famed for their poetry, sculpture, and dance. This is a picturesque area with lovely scenery, interesting festivals, and numerous historical sites. Ségou is easy to reach by group taxi from the station in Bamako, and there is a small, comfortable rest house.

Mopti Mopti is a high-spirited, prosperous fishing port on the Niger River, 175 miles from Ségou; it is a commercial center where people of many different backgrounds meet, trade and celebrate. The town is built on three little islands linked by an incessant movement of canoes. Mopti has such a fascinating mixture and variety of sights and scenes, and such a raucous charm, that expatriates have nicknamed it "New York." Easy to reach by river boat, plane or taxi; a comfortable rest house and an up-to-date motel.

Djenné The central attraction for visitors and pilgrims in this religious city is the mosque, a remarkably beautiful example of true Sudanese architecture. The town, 70 miles from Mopti, has a sort of Biblical atmosphere—gentle, introspective and holy.

Bandiagara Bandiagara is the gateway to Dogon country. The Dogon, a people of great originality, inhabit the nearby cliffs. Dogon history and culture are well documented by ethnographers, and Dogon art is enjoying a tremendous vogue among art collectors and connoisseurs. The religion and cosmology inspiring the art works are described in an important book in African studies, *Conversations with Ogotelmmeli: An Introduction to Dogon Religious Ideas*, by Marcel Griaule (Oxford University Press). Bandiagara is reached from Mopti over 60 miles of rocky road.

Timbuktu The ancient, elusive, mysterious, veiled city of Timbuktu has become synonymous with "the ends of the earth." From the fourteenth century until its decline in the seventeenth, Timbuktu was a famous center of learning; its renowned scholars and professors attracted brilliant students from the whole Muslim world. Now this is just a reserved, dusty town, haunted by its past, jealously guarding its secrets. Regular plane service from Bamako, and a small rest house.

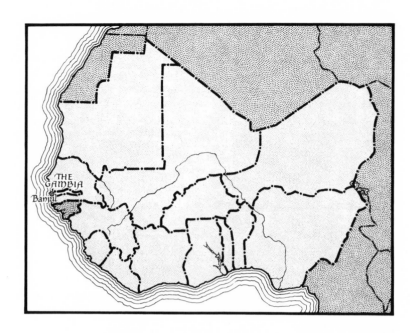

The Gambia

BANJUL

There is a man in The Gambia, a widower, who has set up his office in Banjul. He travels a great deal, often staying away for two and three weeks at a time. He leaves his suburban home, his two children (a girl aged twelve and a boy aged ten), plus a barnyard of chickens, turkeys and pigeons, all in the care of a nonchalant domestic who comes in the morning and goes home after supper. But, you protest in concern, who looks after the children? The father explains, "That is easy. The children are in school all day from eight A.M. to six P.M. In the evening they come home, eat, do their lessons, then go to bed. Nothing can happen to them."

Of course, in Banjul, he is right. There is very very little in the way of trouble for one to get into even if he should go out looking for it. Banjul, formerly Bathurst, is a quiet, sedate, reserved place. Gambians are pleased that it is calm and peaceful. In a hotel when you accidentally tip over a glass, three people jump forward to see "what has happened," and the telephone directory reminds you, at the bottom of some of its sixty wide-spaced pages, to "speak softly."

Banjul is probably very unimportant as a place, and quite unconcerned about that unimportance. There are about 30,000 souls in Banjul and they make up 10 percent of the entire population of The Gambia. Banjul is at once the only city, the largest settlement and the capital of the country (none of the country's towns has more than 5,000 people). Banjul manages with one dentist, one hospital, one pharmacy, one bookstore and one bank. And one fire engine. These facilities are not strained; they are able to handle most things quite nicely.

The Gambia boasts that geographically it is the closest to Europe of all the English-speaking tropical African countries, but the feeling you get is more like being *sur la lune.* The news comes in a government-published compact fact sheet, rather the size of a college newspaper, to keep citizens abreast of Gambian and outside news; the other papers are mimeographed political squabble sheets. The radio is on for three or four hours a day, but you didn't come to The Gambia to get the latest world happenings. You came to change gears and to be in a place whose personality is charming and stimulating.

On a Friday afternoon in Banjul you and your friends go hunting—not safari hunting, but dumb country hunting—to get some fowl for the table, pigeons and guinea hens, and to shoot some monkeys for meat for the dogs. The whole expedition is organized in less than an hour: one shotgun, some rounds of ammunition, a taxi, and off you go. A mile or so out and you are in scrub country, the thicket having been burned away so that the land can be planted. The car creeps along the road as everyone watches for a sign of game. Suddenly one of the men spies a monkey in a tree. Amidst a lot of shouting discussion he grabs the gun and runs across the field in pursuit. He spots the monkey, shoots him and returns to the car triumphant. Then another monkey is hit, but as he falls his leg is caught in the branches; before long the buzzards will be there to pick him off.

Then one of the company spots yet another monkey; however, it is obvious that a little baby is clinging to her back. The driver is told to continue on, but one of the men has not had a turn to shoot yet. He rationalizes that there must be a male monkey nearby. The others urge him to "leave her alone. She has a baby; there are other monkeys." "No," he responds, "I just want to see." He runs off with the gun. In the meantime the city girl still can't see *any* monkey anywhere; nature, she thinks appreciatively, does an excellent job of camouflaging her creatures.

Then . . . a shot! As the company watches in disbelief, the mother monkey tumbles to the ground. Nobody wants to talk to the gunman when he returns to the car carrying the dead beast. Instead the conversation turns to general comments on man's inhumanity. To lighten the gloom, the driver tells the story of two Americans whom he took out hunting one day. Frustrated after a fruitless two-hour wait to spot some game, one of them saw some goats ahead of the car. "But you *can't* shoot goats," the driver protested, "they are tame, and besides, they belong to somebody." The Americans just *had* to bag *something*, so the goats met their end as hunting trophies. Everyone laughs and the car heads back to the house.

A couple of years ago, into this peaceable kingdom came the Swedes—big and blond and looking for a place under the tropical sun. The heat, the verdure, the surf and the wide, cloudless blue skies transported them worlds away from the miseries of the Stockholm winter. At first they came in small organized groups for a vacation spent swimming, sailing, hunting and fishing. Now tourism is the fastest-growing industry in The Gambia; it is planned to have eight thousand hotel beds by 1978 to accommodate increasingly larger groups from Sweden, Germany and Britain.

The Gambians speak darkly of the flood of whites. In small, trusting, traditional Banjul, where everyone knows each other and the tone of life is especially quiet and refined, the presence of thousands of huge Vikings galumphing around is a shock to the town's nervous system. The stranger's comfort causes the Gambians annoying deprivations: the imported luxury goods are soon sold out; all the tradesmen cater to the visitors first, leaving the regulars' needs aside; for the first time parts of the beach are restricted and private. The Swedes are "ruining the country's morals," you hear. Their bold nudity and penchant for sexual novelty is disturbing. A story circulates about pubescent Gambian girls being paid to pose for postcard collections, and about the peculiar appetites of the Swedish women. The most prudish society is assaulted by the world's most libertine. "Of course," an official explains, "it is understandable that some of the Swedes will want to make love with our Gambian boys and girls, but they should be *respectable* about it."

On Thursday afternoon you go to an exhibition at the Banjul City Council. There is no museum in Banjul, so a committee has been organized to try to raise funds for one. The show is in a large hall; it is filled with groups of schoolchildren, there on their own initiative it seems, wearing their blue-and-white school uniforms. The displays are varied: local agricultural products, farming implements, crafts.

At the center of the exhibit is a table featuring dresses of one hundred years ago. There are examples of the Victorian Mother Hubbard dresses in which the missionaries clothed the local converts. High-necked dresses with long sleeves, hemlines to the floor and yards of crinkly stiff materials. You are reminded of Gauguin's paintings: those young South Sea–island women likewise shrouded from head to toe, similarly victims of the Christian impulse to modesty.

Resting lightly on a swath of old yellowed silk is a group of photographs from a church's archives. One photograph shows the personal portrait of a stunning young beauty. Though her body is submerged under piles of Victorian taffeta and lace, her face is aware, but private, and self-contained. There is another photograph of another woman; she is not so beautiful or so self-confident; the heaviness of the crinoline and the wool weights down her spirit.

The photographs lie casually. You yearn to be able to take them with you, or somehow make a copy. You want to be able to look again and again at those black women and learn from their faces. You will always wonder about that proud beauty, the first in this land to be Christianized, free, detribalized, present as her fettered sisters went off into slavery; that proud beauty, witness at the beginning, mouth wide and closed, eyes inward.

LEISURE AND PLEASURE

In the morning
—Go to Lancaster Road to see a goldsmith at work on his forge, fashioning traditional Wolof jewelry.
—Visit the bottle designer on East Hamilton Street.
—Stroll through the town and market, saying good morning to the many people who will greet you.
In the afternoon
—Get yourself invited to the Gambia Sailing Club and go out on a dinghy.
—Walk along the Bund Road on the oceanside to see the boats and the profusion of birds.
In the evening
—Drink a frosty Heineken's (or Carlsberg) in the lounge at the Atlantic Hotel.
—Dance to the music of the fabulous Congolese band that has been cooling it in Banjul for the past couple of years.

PLACES TO VISIT

James Island

A tiny place in the estuary of the Gambia River about twenty miles upstream where you find remains of the trading post set up by one of the English Merchant Adventurers companies in 1618. You can charter a boat to go there and to **Albreda,** just opposite, formerly a French trading station.

Barra

Just opposite Banjul, is accessible by a pleasant thirty-minute ferry ride. Visit **Fort Bullen,** swim and picnic. Boats leave lackadaisically every hour.

Boats go up the Gambia River, one of the best waterways in West Africa. The scenery along the way fits Hollywood stereotypes of tropical "Africa." There are villages and trading posts along the banks, thick forest vines and verdure, aquatic animals alongside your boat, and arboreal ones overhead. Usually the boats leave on the weekends and take five days for the round trip. The cost is nominal, maybe around $25 for the accommodations and meals. You may also pick up a small ocean vessel going upstream to load peanuts at Kuntaur, Jaur and Balingbo.

Stone Circles

Pat McNaughton thinks that as each area of Africa is studied with a view to establishing its early history, monuments and remains will be found of numerous great and mysterious lost civilizations. Nigeria is known now as the land of the elegant 400 B.C. Nok culture because workmen building an iron mine found some distinguished works of art. Archaeologists in Mauritania now work on the antiquity of that area because of the cave paintings found when engineers were establishing a copper mine.

The Gambia too has mysterious monuments that suggest a lost civilization—the stone circles along the Gambia River. What people made these circles? Why are the stones arranged as they are? What is the political, social, economic and cultural history embodied in the monuments? All these questions are still unanswered. Scientific investigations were carried out in 1964–1965 by the official Anglo-Gambian Stone Circles Expedition. The circles are described as being made from local stone. The stones contained in each circle are uniform in size but the dimensions vary from circle to circle—some are only two feet high, others tower eight and a half feet; some are one foot in diameter, others three and a half feet across. Investigators conjecture that the stones mark burial mounds and that the circles represent royal cemeteries dating back to antiquity; radiocarbon testing gives the year A.D. 750.

To see the circles you can take the regular Gambia River boat; the major sites are at **Kaur** and **Georgetown.** *Note:* A Color film about the circles, entitled *African Stonehenge,* is available for loan from F. A. Evans, Duke of Edinburgh's Award Scheme, 2 Old Queen Street, Westminster, London.

SHOPPING

There is a **Craftsman's Center** on the beach not far from the Atlantic Hotel. Its hours are erratic.

Gambians make a beautiful hand-blocked batik cloth that is difficult to obtain elsewhere in Africa. The prints are soft-edged geometric, in those lively shades of blue. They are on sale on **Sawjack Street.**

Naturally, on this Wolof coast, they make gorgeous jewelry of government-controlled quality. Get names from your hotel—just about any jeweler you find will be excellent.

RESTAURANTS

There are no really interesting places for meals, so just forget about it. You can eat in the hotels—bad British at the **Atlantic,** Lebanese at the **Adonis** and European at the **Wadner.** The **Caribbean Restaurant** has copious dishes of African food at very cheap prices. (*Student note:* You can get a steak, salad and soup dinner for about 50 cents here.)

HOTELS

Banjul is in the middle of a hotel-building boom, so the facts change monthly; the Tourist Bureau will have the most up-to-date information. Remember that during the height of the tourist season, from November through March, every single room in town may be booked by the hordes of holiday travelers from Sweden,

Denmark and England. During the summer months, rooms are always available. Prices below include breakfast.

Atlantic Hotel $19 single, $26 double.   Well located near the center of town on a broad, pretty beach. Rooms are large, air-conditioned and adequate, and there is a bar where Banjul comes for conversation and conviviality. Food is strictly canned-colonial, and expensive, but the cook will make you tasty African dishes if you cajole.

Uncle Joe's $8 single, $12 double.   In the center of town, the least expensive rooms available; clean but rustic.

Adonis Hotel $16 single, $26 double.   In the commercial area, its bar is the center for what passes in Banjul for intrigue and big deals. The nearby **Banjul Hotel** ($10 single, $16 double) is also lively, run by the same company. They also own the **Carlton** ($13 single, $20 double) on the edge of town, quiet and agreeable.

Fajara Hotel $19 single, $26 double.   Some ten miles outside of Banjul, this is a new tourist hotel built to accommodate European guests.

Sunwing Hotel $19 single, $26 double.   Built with English, Swedish and Gambian investment, this large new hotel is on a glorious beach peninsula and features a swimming pool.

Wadner Beach Hotel $10 single, $16 double.   Another seaside hotel, large and attractively furnished, congenial atmosphere. Better food than most places.

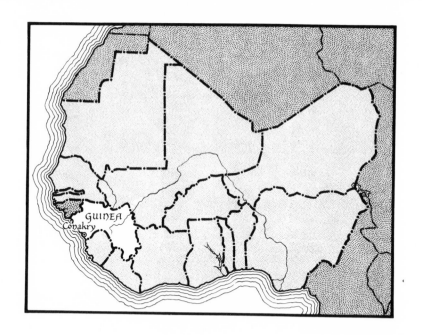

Guinea

CONAKRY

West Africa has in great abundance what vacationers are seeking: pure air, sun, sea, sand and space. A leisurely tempo, and interesting things to see and do. Now that many people are bored with the same old places in Europe, they look to Africa for new experiences, new learning and new feelings, and Africa welcomes them with open arms. Everyone has a friend who has returned from visiting or working in Africa with glowing reports. As the social concerns of the world are changing, more and more people are interested in witnessing the evolution of the political, social and cultural life in Africa's developing countries. Africa's wealth, culture and heritage make her future of compelling concern.

The travel boom is caused mainly by the increasing volume of student and young-adult travel. Where, formerly, travel in Africa was a province of only the very wealthy, now more and more younger people of modest means are going. Reduced air fares and charter flight plans have greatly reduced transportation costs, and if one doesn't mind some discomfort, it is possible to live and travel around quite cheaply.

Tourism would seem to be an easy moneymaker for West Africa's financially strapped governments. A nation doesn't have to do very much to profit from it: the basic tropical ambiance of sunny warmth and out-of-doors recreation doesn't cost a country anything; nature gives her best for free. Once the administration or private capital provides for some hotels and basic facilities, the rest seems automatic. People will come, and the money the country earns from their visits is in foreign, hard currencies. Both The Gambia and the Ivory Coast look at it this way, and they are basing much of their economic planning on the revenue they expect from tourism.

But there is one country that most emphatically does not welcome the tourist. That country is Guinea. Already Guinea is beginning to disappear from the tourist maps. If you take a look at some pretty travel brochures you will see that where Guinea should be, the illustrator has placed some decorative little palm trees. That's O.K. with Guinea because she is not interested in receiving any visitors, and in her planning, income from tourism is not given any kind of mention.

It isn't that Guinea is anti-West or anti-American. On the contrary, late trade figures show that most of Guinea's imported supplies come from the United States—more, in fact, than from all other countries combined. The bulk of her exports go to the United States and France. The hard-cash figures show the intensely close economic ties between Guinea and the United States. Despite the dreadful economic reverses it suffered in the early 1960s, Guinea now has a highly favorable balance of trade, mainly due to the consistent help of the United States and foreign private investment. Guinea has modern shipping ports and airports, a fair transport system and good telecommunications, just the kind of infra-structure needed to meet the most complicated tourist demands.

Still, to repeat, Guinea does not want any tourists. It is almost impossible to obtain an entry visa. You may try of course, but you should expect disappointment. You are *not* advised to show up at the Conakry airport without one—some people have tried and have been put right back on the plane, or worse, jailed. Guinea has decided that she can better develop and prosper without tourists, thank you. The explanation of why Guinea does not welcome vacationing foreigners gives a perspective on some of the negative aspects of tourism; it shows why a young country would decide that the harmful effects of travel far outweigh any short-range financial advantages. The reasons are many.

In the light of past history, Africans surely have the right to be dubious about an influx of whites. Europeans have been visiting Africa for the past five hundred years, almost always with the intent to control the land and exploit the people. During the seventy years of the colonial era from about 1890 to 1960, West African countries were under European military rule; they were governed by white dictatorships; their wealth was stolen, to build the power and affluence of Europe. Who is to say that the new crop of pale faces has more benign interests and more comradely notions?

Socially, many of the African countries have rather closed class systems. The local traditional elites and the new national elites all want to enjoy the prerogatives of their status. So they are upset when tourists arrive expecting to be part of the upper strata, and demanding that they be waited on first. It means also that many scarce, expensive resources must go into what is essentially a service sector of the economy to meet the comforts of strangers. Foods and delicacies must be imported to please the foreign palate; the radio has to play some of the latest in metropolitan pop music. The electrical plant must be able to support demands of the air conditioners, elevator and ice machine. Entertaining the visitors uses up some good people who should better be doing other, more economically and socially productive things. Educated citizens who speak European languages are induced into becoming guides, hostesses, barmen, hotel managers.

Tourism means greater enhancement of the attraction of life in the cities, to the further impoverishment of the countryside. As the glistening hotels multiply, the small earthen cottage becomes not traditional but squalid. The urban areas become even more alluring and glamorous, and the administration's attempts to keep the population "down on the farm" more fruitless. The stream of people in from the country only brings with it multitudes of familiar urban problems.

There are even greater dangers in what happens to a population's psyche. A tourism of whites means encounters of a racialist nature that are painful and infuriating to the local population. Unless an African is wealthy or prominent, he simply is not welcome in the new hotels and restaurants. The beaches, lovely promenades and other public pleasures are increasingly out of the domain of the average citizen, and the prices of luxuries spiral upwards completely out of reach of the local population. Also, because of the whole color thing, Africans are easily transformed into anonymous "boys," shadowy servants, waiting on their "superiors" from abroad as if it were the natural thing.

For young people, the presence of glossy, well-heeled tourists with radically different world views can be extraordinarily confusing. In societies as morally, financially and socially straight-laced as African ones, a large contingent of highly visible foreigners which is there for the pleasures of vacation self-indulgence can be very upsetting. The young African does not always understand that the money spent on this tropical fling may have been saved from years of earnings, or that it may be a gift out of an accumulation of capital. All that *shows* is his white contemporaries living in a prosperity and luxury that is not only galling but also misleading.

In order to please visitors who come with a different perspective and always an attitude of superiority, the African is always having to abuse his own cultural personality and system of social values. Therefore a country may well decide that the encouragement of tourism reflects only a preoccupation with immediate profits, not with any long-term goals. A country may decide that a reliance on income from tourism ties it even more to the whims and fashions of Europe. It may decide that having a lot of former colonial masters around on vacation does not make for the best climate in the struggle for true economic and political independence. So when a country considers all these factors it may decide, as Guinea has decided, that tourism is of low priority.

YOUR STAY IN CONAKRY

First of all, try and find out just what the general political situation is at the moment. Guinea has been under constant siege for years; it has been invaded, and the fabric of the country has been rent by the frequency of political trials.

Visitors are regarded with suspicion and you will find it very difficult to move about freely. There are so many rules and regulations controlling every aspect of the Guinean's life. If the taxi driver tells you he "can't stop here," believe him. Your insistence can cause him a heavy fine.

Foreigners are not allowed to leave Conakry town without travel permits. The American embassy will do its best, but bring extra photos for the applications, and lots of extra time for the waiting. Also, you will not be allowed to take pictures unless you have first received written authorization from the Ministry of Information. These two rules are very strictly enforced by young guardians of the peace—don't try to get away with it, unless you are prepared to be incarcerated as punishment for your indiscretion. Life in Guinea is harsh.

When a diplomat learns that he is assigned to Guinea he feels challenged, while his wife goes into a fit of despair. Really, though, a stay in Guinea has many compensations. For one thing, you will be meeting the whole of the expatriate community, a small, tightly knit one. You are sure to learn all the gossip and feel very much a part of international skulduggery.

During a long stay, Guinea can have some enforced salutary effects. Let's say you drink too much, eat too much or smoke too much, or you are profligate or promiscuous. You sober up fast when liquor is $40 a bottle; food and cigarettes are scarce; there are no consumer goods around for you to waste money on; and once your womanizing is restricted to your immediate social circle, your old wife may begin to look pretty good again.

Guinea is a very isolated place—news takes so long to reach you that you feel "out of sync" with the times, experiencing a funny lapse between something "happening" in the world and your finding out about it. Actually, you may find this rather relaxing. If you are going to be in Conakry for a while, you can go to the movies all the time, go to a tennis club or a sailing club, or go fishing. The various embassies sponsor cultural programs, and once a year, without much prior notice, the Guinean Information Secretariat organizes its annual tourist trip to the interior.

Also, be aware that the Conakry rainy season is very, very hard on people. From around the middle of June until the middle of October it rains in *sheets.* Everyone stays indoors and turns green like his shoes. So if you can, time your visit for the dry months. There was once a French girl who was teaching in Guinea. As the end of the spring term approached she asked the principal to tell her the date when school was officially ended. The principal replied that there was no definite date; school just ended when the rains started and the pupils stopped coming. Sure enough, the second week of June started out cloudy. A few children stayed home Tuesday when it drizzled; some more were out on Wednesday when it showered. By Thursday it was pouring, and by Friday afternoon school was out, the term was over.

LEISURE AND PLEASURE

In the morning
   —Starting out from the Hotel de France, stroll along the shady streets.
   —Walk out to the museum.
In the afternoon
   —Go for a swim at the Plage Péronne.
   —Get yourself invited out for a spin at the Nautical Club.
In the evening
   —Dance at the G'Bessia night club.
   —Take a walk along the Corniche.

PLACES TO VISIT

Conakry Museum

You reach the museum after a walk down from the Boulbinet (near Hotel de France), between two cemeteries and gardens. The museum is located on a peninsula whose rocks are constantly being pounded by the surf. It contains a fine collection of masks and a good research library. This is one of the lovely spots in Conakry.

Îles de Los

The Los Islands lie in Conakry harbor. They are made of bauxite, and thus form a great part of Guinea's wealth. Unless you get a ride on a private boat, you can only get to one, **Kassa Island;** for Kassa there is a regular ferry service. Go and enjoy the idyllic beaches.

Beaches

The **Plage Péronne** is located near the Hotel de France, behind the Club Cinéma. Sometimes it is crowded with children who go there for athletics. When the tide is low the water is shallow for a long distance out, but it is all very pleasant. There are also beautiful beaches at **Camayenne** and **Dixinn.**

Buildings

You will of course want to see the large hotels, the large schools and mosques and the **Palais du Peuple** (conference hall).

HOTELS

Hotel de France   For many years the **Hotel de France** ($20 double, $26 air-conditioned) was considered to be the loveliest hotel in all of tropical Africa. Though much of its former glory is gone, and it is run down and out of order, you can still see its charm.
Its entrance is set at the end of a shady residential street, in the

center of town, near the ocean drive. The elevators don't work, the lights are broken, it's not clean, but the best of the Hotel de France (like a woman's face with good bones) has beauty built into its very structure. The rooms are large, airy and well laid out. And their louver doors slide to open a whole wall onto a gorgeous garden, arustle with the taffeta of palm trees. Just beyond is the sea, and in the evening, the sunsets startle and soothe with their palette of pink, orange and purple.

At the time this hotel was built, a few French architects were experimenting with notions about "modern tropical architecture" for Africa. They had some good ideas: they designed for the site, utilized many local materials in construction, and used angles and designs to take advantage of the natural movement of light and air. The Hotel de France and the nearby apartment buildings, called "Boulbinet," were built on these principles. At the Boulbinet, for example, the arrangements of open grillwork, louver doors and room shape makes so extraordinary use of natural air currents that even in sweltering Conakry the apartments are always comfortable and breezy.

There are several other sorts of modern designs, base plans using a combination of the oldest and the latest in concepts, that have solved many of the problems for hot climates. If one is indeed going to have to work indoors for long periods of time, one needs a refreshing coolness in order to produce at an optimal level—a coolness not dependent upon the expenditures of huge sums for temperamental air-conditioning systems. So the architects made their plans. The experiments were built. They worked just perfectly. The concepts were *proven* correct. But they were *doomed;* they were never put into widespread use. Why? Because they did not *cost enough,* because they depended on ingenuity rather than expenditure, and could be managed on the local market rather than imported.

In the heyday of the early days of independence of Guinea, the bar of the Hotel de France was called "little United Nations." Sékou Touré and Patrice Lumumba, CBS journalists, scholars, diplomats, politicians from every country in Europe, Africa and Asia—everyone at some time or other was sitting there, involved in intrigues and big deals. About ten years ago, there was no more exciting spot in Africa.

The world has gone around in circles many times since then, but if you can, rent a room at the hotel (remember, it is always jammed with international personnel posted in Guinea who stay there while they try to find a house in town).

Hotel Camayenne $15 single, $23 double. This is in town on a very pretty beach. It is built block-style, and most of the rooms have a pleasant view.

Hotel G'Bessia $15 single, $23 double. This newest place in Conakry is out near the airport. It is built motel-style and offers air conditioning and other comforts.

RESTAURANTS

For a while now, food has been scarce in Guinea. The staples are strictly rationed and it is difficult to find meat and produce. The only places where you can be sure of finding meals available are in the restaurants of the three major hotels—**Hotel de France, Hotel Camayenne** and **Hotel G'Bessia.** No matter how dire the situation, they each manage to put together some kind of dinner every day. Prices are very high, so you should plan to spend on an average of $8 to $10 per person for an ordinary meal with beverage; that is, around $15 to $20 per day.

The other restaurants in town are the **Paradis,** the **Djoliba,** the **Royal Saint-Germain,** the **Grillon** and the **Oasis**—although they may no longer be in business.

Note: Conakry is the one place where you *cannot* hope to save money by living on fruits, bread, sardines and peanuts. These things have not been regularly available in local markets for a long time. So plan to spend money for eating unless you can find some kind of "deal." See what the embassy suggests (probably that you leave!).

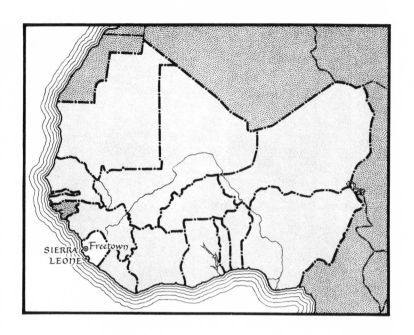

Sierra Leone

FREETOWN

A friend writes from Freetown that a recent Lantern Parade is the most beautiful he has seen in the last ten years there. The parade celebrates the Feast of the Fast-Breaking, Id al-Fitr, marking the end of Ramadan. Ramadan, the ninth month of the Islamic calendar, is observed with strict fasting; the friend, a Muslim, has abstained from taking all manner of food and drink from sunup to sundown. He has done more than the usual amount of praying; he has gone frequently to the mosque to mingle with the congregation and receive instruction from the elders.

The Lantern Parade is an Islamic religious pageant, but

everyone in town takes part. Muslims now outnumber Christians among the 132,000 population of Freetown, although the city was founded by hymn-singing converts and first financed by Protestant philanthropists. The Christians of the town join wholeheartedly in the festivities, and the followers of animist religions all turn out in numbers. They all live in Freetown, intermingling casually without antagonisms across religious and ethnic lines; so Lantern Parade becomes a symbol of the city's cohesion and its long history of inter-group cooperation and mutual support.

Work pressures mount during Ramadan as people begin to prepare for the holiday season that comes after the month of deprivation. All during the month, artisans have been coming into Freetown at the invitation of various "Lantern Clubs." These clubs, sponsored both privately and by various commercial interests, are formed in the manner of other carnival clubs around the world: people practice music and dancing all year, and then spend months planning elaborate floats and processions for the grand spectacle. (Lantern Parade comes at the *end* of a fast; the ones you are most familiar with—Carnival in Rio, Mardi Gras in New Orleans and Nice—come at the *beginning* of a fast time.)

Everyone joins in the Freetown parade, a sprawling affair that lasts all day and all night. Children carry candles and kerosene lamps, schools and companies have displays, and the clubs try to outdo one another in the artistry of their presentations. The large lanterns are big, intricate floats made of a kind of rice paper colored and cut into beautiful patterns, then pasted onto a wooden framework—in the manner of the festive Japanese lanterns so popular in the States. They then are lit from within by candles, and moved slowly through the streets—a fantasy of horses and houses, mosques, ships, magical birds, coconut and cotton trees, lambs and flowers.

Lantern Parade will be talked about for weeks, until the next big event. Because if there is anything that the citizens of Freetown love, it is pageantry and social events! Though the town itself looks shabby and drab, the life that goes on in Freetown is exciting and colorful. The fascinating nature of Freetown society springs from the incredible mélange of people and cultures to be found there, and from the uniqueness of its history.

The area that is now the city of Freetown has probably been populated for more than three thousand years. When the first Europeans ventured there in 1462 they found an active, enterprising group of people. Christopher Fyfe, an historian specializing in West Africa, tells us that

> the inhabitants of the villages along the shore of the estuary lived by fishing, farming, and making salt, which they traded with their neighbors inland for cattle, leather goods, or woven cloths. When, in the 15th century, they made contact with Europeans, their country became an important centre for import-export trade. European ships called in regularly at the bays along the peninsula, particularly at King Jimmy, to get drinking water and to trade. So people were attracted to come and live there, and more small towns and villages grew up along the shore. The Freetown site was, therefore, inhabited long before any settlement from Europe was founded.

Freetown has its particular name because it was the point of settlement for Africans released from slavery. These alien Africans came at first from across the Atlantic Ocean. Today's older elite families are descendants of black people who had fled to Nova Scotia, Canada, after fighting in the American Revolutionary War on the side of the British (Nova Scotians); other black people returned from Jamaica plantations (Maroons), and still others from London. Later on the Nova Scotians, Maroons and Londoners were joined (and greatly outnumbered) by men and women, originally from Senegal, Nigeria and the Congo, who had been rescued from slave ships before crossing the Atlantic.

At first the hostility of the indigenous people and the inclement living conditions succeeded in routing the fragile coastside settlements. But later the newcomers drove the original population back to the hinterland and established themselves as residents in Freetown and in nearby areas. After a while the original residents moved back again, mixing and mingling in this new thing, the new West Coast cosmopolitan African town, with its privacy, flexibility and social mobility. They all interrelated and accommodated to one another. It produced a new language, Krio, and a new kind of society, Sierra Leone Creole.

Today, add to this base the upcountry people who come down

to the coast to live and trade, the Nigerians who come to make a permanent home, the young people from all over English-speaking Africa who come to attend Sierra Leone's well-reputed schools, the sizable East Indian and Lebanese populations engaged in commerce, the English who are businessmen, officials, teachers and missionaries, the Peace Corps volunteers, and the Germans on holiday. It makes a heady brew that is endlessly bubbling.

Freetown is the capital and largest city of Sierra Leone, a small coastal country of 2,600,000 people geographically tucked under the wing of the much larger Guinea, wedged next to Liberia. Besides agriculture and fishing, Sierra Leone's wealth is founded on a goodly quantity of industrial diamonds. They lie right under the surface of the soil, are easily gathered and concealed and easily smuggled. It is a sad but true *Almanac* fact that the huge export trade in diamonds in neighboring Liberia is based on diamonds smuggled there from Sierra Leone! Occasionally some gorgeous gems of jewelry quality show up; the most recent spectacular example is the "Star of Sierra Leone," a huge 968.9-carat stone purchased by the New York firm of Harry Winston and on display for a while at the American Museum of Natural History.

For some time now the government has been talking about the name Sierra Leone: the officials feel it should be changed to something more African in origin. The words "Sierra Leone," meaning "lion mountain" in Portuguese, were given it by Pedro de Sintra, a navigator from Portugal who reached these shores in 1462. But long before he arrived, the inhabitants had been calling it Romaron, meaning "the place of the mountain." Several other countries have chosen new names that break from the old colonial titles: the Gold Coast to Ghana, French Sudan to Mali, the Congo to Zaïre; it is a sign of greater pride and an aspiration for greater self-determination; perhaps Sierra Leone will yet follow the same course.

Freetown's natural setting is very beautiful, and its citizens are politely friendly; you are introduced to both as soon as you arrive at the airport. You go through formalities quickly because chances are there are a few other people arriving at the same time, and because the staff is efficient and welcoming. You board the waiting bus and drive around for twenty minutes through the rural areas to the town of Tagrin, where you and the bus get on the ferry for the hour's crossing of the estuary to Freetown. The boat ride is memorable—before you rises the vista of Sierra Leone's glory. You see the dappled shore, the verdure, the misty peaks. Freetown is a city of streams and valleys; it is lushly green all year round, and the flowering trees blaze. With its hills and its bays—Cline Bay, Fourah Bay, Whiteman's Bay, Destruction Bay, Kroo Bay and Susan's Bay—the affluent denizens of the mountainsides have views to be compared in magnificence with those of Rio de Janeiro.

Once you get to the middle of town you may not find Freetown appealing. Most of the city was built a long time ago; a great many buildings are more than one hundred years old. The residents treasure their old houses, though to American eyes the houses seem ramshackle and moldy. Freetown was a planned city, designed in accord with nineteenth-century European philosophical and colonial ideas, with straight, square blocks. Then, within these rectangles, Africans often jumbled things up to suit themselves.

The social life in Freetown is much like the physical city, planned on a European model, but irrepressibly African. At first the British influences seem striking—Fourah Bay College students going to class in black academic robes; folks dancing the waltz at a formal-dress ball; judges in their white wigs. Sierra Leoneans were dismissed as being "black Englishmen" as the Anglicisms of daily life were noted and scorned. Freetown just is *not black enough* for those whites and blacks who are looking for a more *African* Africa. Though the start of the establishment of the Christian religion and the formal Christian church were both in Africa (in Ethiopia), visitors are put off by the large number of churches in Freetown. Though Beethoven had African blood, they are disturbed when Sierra Leone choirs sing Bach and Mozart. It is too easy to fasten on Freetown's old ways. But if the visitor will retain an open mind and a willingness to go beyond superficialities, he can begin to approach the truer spirit and ethos of this land.

Observation: The *Lappa* It is called a *lappa* in Freetown, a *pagne* in French-speaking countries, "cloth" in Accra, "wrapper" in Lagos. The fabric may vary; the name, though, refers to the size of the cloth—6 feet long, 4 feet wide, used as a skirt by African women. Buy one as soon as you can; make it one of your first purchases. A *lappa* is a very handy thing to have.

You use the *lappa* to drape around your shoulders as a stole when you feel chilly. Wrap it around your chest and walk around the house in your sarong. If you need a quick skirt, you wrap it around your waist. If your hair looks awful, you can fold the *lappa* in half lengthwise, then use it as a *ghele* to tie around your head.

In a hotel room when you lie on the top of the bed, cover yourself with it. If your bunk is only rudimentarily furnished, it makes a ravishing bedspread. If you find that the sheet is less than clean, use it to stretch out on. If your room has no curtains, up it goes, pinned at the window. Spread it on the ground to picnic on. If you are sleeping on a straw mat, use it as a bottom sheet. When you travel in a car, roll it up tightly and use it as a small pillow or neck rest.

*   *   *

To get to the heart of Freetown, you must know someone who lives there. It is extremely important that you have contacts, for otherwise you will be impatient and miserable. Once you are attached to someone, stay in close contact with him or her and begin to circulate in Freetown. Be he a Muslim or a Christian, a merchant, physician, clerk, United Nations staff member, carpenter, student, dock worker, teacher—just let him know that you want to get to know his life. Then just let yourself flow with the rhythm and beat of the town. It is not landmarks and monuments that your host will be showing you, but rather you will be seeing the circle of his community—his family, co-workers, clubs, church, hideaway. You will begin to see that Sierra Leone is not imitation anything; it is truly itself. It has its own style of religion, its own kind of dress, its own way of expression, all to suit itself.

LEISURE AND PLEASURE

In the morning
   —Wander around downtown looking at all posters an-

146

nouncing social events. Here's one: "Funky Nobles (the above named club of Kissy Street) will be staging a Grand Ball Dance on Friday, 28 May. The Main Motive of the Dance is to select Miss Funky Noble of Kissy Street."

—Poke your head into a street barbershop and get a look at the names and illustrations of the haircuts: Baby Face, Three Friends, King on Board, Barley Style. Try to get the barber to sell you the painted sign board. He won't.

In the afternoon

—Get on a double-decker bus, any one you see coming, anywhere, and ride around to your heart's content.

—Have a beer at the City, Paramount or Brookfields and just listen to the conversation, or join in.

In the evening

—Attend a theater production given by one of the numerous amateur dramatic groups—the Sierra Leone Players, Drama Circle, National Theater League or the Western Dramatic Society. Or, better yet, go to a performance of the soulful Sierra Leone Dance Troupe if they are in town.

GETTING AROUND

Freetown is the center of Sierra Leone's good state transportation system. Buses take you all through the city and to neighboring areas. Bus transport is regular, scheduled, frequent, convenient and extremely cheap. Check at the Road Transport Department, Blackhall Road, Freetown, for information. They will tell you how to get to the beaches, up the mountains and around the peninsula on your own at minimum expense. Train and airline service takes you to farther spots within the country.

Note: If you enjoy collecting West African wisdom from the sayings on the back of lorries, don't be disappointed here in Freetown. The place to look for the sayings is inside the taxis on the dashboard. Look for: "Money Hard to Get but Easy to Spend," "Women Like to Engineer Words," "People Must Say Against You."

SIGHTS TO SEE

Churches and Mosques

Freetown has been described as a city of churches and mosques. The towers and steeples of the churches and the minarets of the mosques dominate the skyline. In Freetown there are sixty-five churches and Christian meeting places, and seventeen mosques. Make them your hobby if you wish, while in Freetown. St. John's Maroon Church (on Westmoreland Street), more than a hundred and fifty years old, is tiny and quaint. The Fourah Mosque is a confection of whitewashed, blue-trimmed cupolas, minarets, steps and balustrades.

Cotton Tree

Standing in the center of town, on Westmoreland Street at the junction of Walpole Street, Westmoreland Street and Independence Avenue, Cotton Tree is the main landmark of Freetown. The tree is huge, its roots forming a carousel around the trunk. It certainly is more than five hundred years old, and it continues to have thick foliage. Legend has it that a slave market was held at the base, and that later, men in bondage were brought here to be freed of their chains.

Sierra Leone National Museum

Located under the Cotton Tree, run by the Educational Department of the government, this is a historical, archaeological and ethnological museum. Everything on display is indigenous to Sierra Leone. A fine collection of ceremonial carvings.

Fourah Bay University College

The college, built on the top of Mount Aureol, can occupy a morning or afternoon of your time. (Take a taxi or a bus.) The college was established at Fourah Bay waterside in 1827, then later moved to the mountain. It is the oldest university institution in West Africa. As members of Sierra Leone's educated elite have gone to work in other countries of West Africa, so a great many English-speaking Africans have been trained at Fourah Bay College. Look around at the classrooms, dormitories, library, gardens, museum and bookshop, and do not miss the view over the east end of Freetown. Fourah Bay College's Botany Department has a **Botanical Garden** and also a small **Ethnological Museum** with objects drawn from the peoples of Sierra Leone.

House of Representatives Building

This is an attractive example of modern architecture—as anonymous and handsome as one can imagine. Check the current political situation to know if you can tour and listen in on debates.

King's Yard

Water Street (at Connaught Hospital Medical Stores) was the area where liberated Africans taken from intercepted slave ships were housed before they were dispersed, free, to villages in the Freetown area. With all the interest in slave ports where black men were shipped *out* in bondage, here in King's Yard you will find a place that is *freedom ground.*

BEACHES

Freetown beaches are, simply, among the finest in the world, and certainly they are the finest in Africa. What you have is a gorgeous thirty-mile stretch of sand, interspersed with quiet, shady bays and coves, all of it easily accessible by car or public transportation along the scenic marine drive. It is all perfect—fine white sand, pure water, warmth and clear air.

Hans Zell has given us detailed information on Freetown beaches, of which the best are (distances from Cotton Tree in the center of town):

1. **Lumley.** The favorite—exposed two-mile stretch of sand linking the rock islands of Cape Sierra Leone and Aberdeen Point with the mainland. Cold drinks available on the beach

(sometimes) or at the Cape Club (near the Aberdeen end). Turn right at Shell filling station 150 yards beyond junction of Hill Road and Wilkinson Road at the Lumley Police Station. 6 miles.

2. **Juba.** Good for children. Small cliff-backed cove, access to which is through Juba military barracks. 6 miles.

3. **Goderich.** Attractive, wide, rock-flanked, and steeply shelving beach of coarse yellow sand. Turn off along the road to the Milton Margai Training College, continuing several hundred yards beyond it (and turning right). 9 miles.

4. **Lakka.** Fine, little-used beach. Two access roads, near the Lakka Hospital, both in bad condition. 11 miles.

5. **Hamilton.** Small tree-fringed cove. Good for children. Very popular. Turn off at Hamilton bus stop, and ask way in village. 12 miles.

6. **Sussex.** Small rocky cove, excellent for children. Turn off main road at the first public road right beyond Guma Valley, and take second turn left. 15 miles.

7. **No. 2 River.** Fine beach of brilliant white sand, backed by lagoon. Take sunglasses to moderate glare! Turn off at No. 2 bus stop, and take first right. 17 miles.

8. **Tokeh.** Another excellent, little-used beach. Look out for the Tokeh bus shelter, and turn right along the track toward the village, turning for the sea before the village is reached. Take care to avoid becoming stuck in sand. 21 miles.

9. **York.** Turn right in village where main road turns sharp left for small beach. Rocky, and rather dirty sand. The Government Resthouse at York (top of hill on way out of village) has a magnificent view south across Whale Bay to the Banana Islands. Worth the climb off the road. Approximately 23 miles.

10. **Black Johnson Beach.** Most beaches have villages close by, or on them. This one is quite isolated. Delightful palm-fringed beach, excellent for skin diving (the best beaches for this are in the southern part of the peninsula where the water is clearest: this is one of the best). Three miles beyond York; look for crude signpost "Beach. To car park." Fifteen minutes' walk through trees to the beach, but porters usually available. Approximately 26 miles.

11. **Bure Town.** Very popular. A short walk down the road leading off the main peninsula road to Kent. Porters and watchmen available on weekends. Excellent beach with magnificent views north. Approximately 30 miles.

SHOPPING

Garra Cloth

Serious shopping in Freetown means searching for *garra* cloth, the Sierra Leone name for tie-dye material. Some of the finest examples of this craft technique come from here, made by artisan women to exacting standards. (There is no comparison between what you make at home with a box of Rit and what these women are able to create and design.) They work in poplin, percale, damask, sateen and velour. Some patterns are the more ordinary rectangular/repeat designs of popular tie-dye, but the more adventurous one-of-a-kind lengths are art pieces of free-form design with a rich palette of color—truly an African form of painting.

Ask around where you may find the sellers. In the lobby of the Paramount Hotel you will usually find a display of extremely fine cloth; the receptionist will tell you how to contact the artisans. Maybe the following will help you:

Mrs. A. Williams, 7 Ross Road
Mrs. Fatima Kabia, Liverpool Street
Mrs. K. Adams, c/o J. Kaloko, Fourah Bay College Bookstore

Also, look at "country" cloth—the traditional cloth woven in strips that are then sewn into one piece of cloth.

Souvenirs

Try the **Sierra Leone Arts and Crafts Centre** at the Government Wharf (below Water Street) for country cloth, *garra* cloth, carvings and masks, and baskets. The **Sierra Leone Small Industries** has a workshop at Tower Hill which sells fabric, baskets and wax prints. *Note:* Among the displays at the **Sierra Leone Museum** are some very fine crafts. Perhaps the museum lady will give you an idea of where to find the craftsmen.

Books

It so happens that Freetown is a very good place to buy books. **Fourah Bay College Bookshop** on the college campus is a truly first-rate bookstore that specializes in Africana. Oh, how you'll long to be back there once you are home in the States and trying to collect some books about West Africa! The **CMS Bookshop** on Oxford Street is also well stocked. If by this time you are interested in improving yourself, they have lots of how-to books. On Upper East Street, the **Islam Book Depot** has a good selection of Muslim works. Look here for the Islamic prints—designs in black-and-white made of the names of Allah, and the colored comic-book-cartoon pictures of Biblical scenes. They cost only pennies and you can use them for a while to embellish your room and then leave them behind, or manage to get them back home.

Curios

Most of the things for sale in Freetown shops were made elsewhere, most likely in Nigeria. The **Nigerian Stores** (6 Glouces-ter Street, opposite the City Hotel) probably has the nicest display and some fine ceremonial pieces. Look in at **Musa Saccoh Brothers** (4 Walpole Street), **Jana's Art Store** (30 Westmoreland Street, opposite Barclays Bank), **New African Curios Store** (14 Pademba Road), **Usman Na'Maijada and Sons** (5 Howe Street, opposite Kingsway Stores), and **A. B. Karo and Sons** (32 Rawdon Street)—all at your own risk. Keep a sharp eye and a silent tongue until you are convinced.

Stamps

Sierra Leone stamps have some of the most daring designs in the world. They are free-form (not bound by the usual perforated rectangular shape) with the stamp on a backing that sports advertisements (only the best—Harry Winston, the jeweler, for example). You can have a wide selection for a few pennies; they are a lovely acquisition—cheap, good-looking, lightweight and educational.

Tailors

Freetown women are smartly dressed, in part because they have good tailors who fit well and embellish the garments with beautiful embroidery. Author's high recommendation is **Ousmane Leigh and Bros., Tailors** (14 Free Street). In their crowded, jumbled workshops they turn out clothes of imagination and taste. The work is done rapidly and the prices are reasonable.

HOTELS

Paramount Hotel, Independence Avenue (P.O.B. 574, Freetown; tel. 35-31) All rooms air-conditoned. International standing. $17 single, $30 double. Price includes breakfast. The Paramount Hotel is pleasant enough. Food in their dining room is usual English-dreary, but there is a good, festive curry lunch on Saturday, and on Sunday a good buffet lunch—roast suckling pig, roast turkey, and other hearty dishes—that is a delicious bargain. This is that place in town for meeting expatriates and sitting around sipping drinks.

Brookfields Hotel, Government Resthouse (tel. 20-00) Out of town a bit. $9 for single with air-conditioning, less without. British colonial style—big barny rooms, heavy furniture, thick concrete walls. The rooms are great, the food is bad. Eat elsewhere.

Lamar Hotel, 21 Howe Street (P.O.B. 748, Freetown; tel. 42-06) $9 single, air-conditioned. Clean, new, in the center of town, very odd design, but OK really.

Cape Sierra Hotel, Lumley Beach New, beautiful modern hotel on the beach with a casino nearby.

Other Hotels

Freetown has a clutch of old, seedy hotels in which living

conditions are very bad. Take a look and decide for yourself. The oldest and most famous is the **City Hotel** because it is the setting for Graham Greene's novel *The Heart of the Matter*. Its bar is still *the* place for lively conversation and murky intrigue. The **Lido Hotel** and the **Riviera** are in poor shape. The **Vicky Hotel** across from the City is cramped but pretty clean and very cheap, $3 a night. You have been warned.

Note: **Fourah Bay College** has a number of comfortable and inexpensive rooms available for traveling students and educators. Contact the Bursar, Fourah Bay College, University of Sierra Leone, Freetown.

RESTAURANTS

The Lebanese restaurants in Freetown are quite good. **Khadra National Restaurant** on Rawdon Street has steaks, chicken and hamburgers, as well as Levantine specialties. They serve pastry and ice cream, and they have a take-out service. **Lamar Restaurant** (21 Howe Street) has *homos, kafta, felafel,* and more of Middle East favorites. Both are recommended for hearty meals, reasonable prices and pleasant atmosphere.

Cathay Chinese Restaurant (in the Couma Valley Building on Trelawney Street) is excellent for Chinese food. **La Tropicana Bar and Restaurant** (Walpole Street) is highly reputed in Freetown for its châteaubriand steaks and its peppered chicken. **Lucy's Bar Restaurant** (38 Somerset Street, Murray Town), is popular for French and African dishes.

For a good, cheap African place, try the luncheonette on the same street as Barclays Bank, at No. 17A. For 40 to 50 cents you can get a large serving of rice, meat and vegetables. The chicken and fish are also delicious.

NIGHT CLUBS

You can have a great time at the variety of Freetown night clubs. The open-air **Cape Club** at the far end of Lumley Beach has a beautiful Tahitian setting right on the sands. There is food, drinking and dancing. **La Tropicana Bar and Restaurant,** air-conditioned, is extremely popular with the expatriate community for steaks and for dancing. The **Pasarice Club** (Government Wharf) has many attractions and great music; **La Gondole Restaurant and Bar** has dancing to live music daily. Most popular with Sierra Leoneans is the very attractive **Kit-Kat Bar and Night Club** (opposite Odeon Cinema). You have to be a member to get into the **Moulin Rouge Club.**

The place in town that jumps and that is especially recommended for younger tourists is the **Yellow Diamond Club** (at the corner of Guy Street and Krootown Road). It is right in the center of Freetown life and offers a hearty, informal atmosphere, good live music and general bright humor. Sit inside if you want to see the latest in Highlife dance steps; from the balcony outside you hear the latest in good-humored banter. There are also tables outside on the balcony—from here you overlook a yeasty, raucous scene of street dancing, eating and a hilarious exchange of badinage—a close-up tableau of modern West African town life.

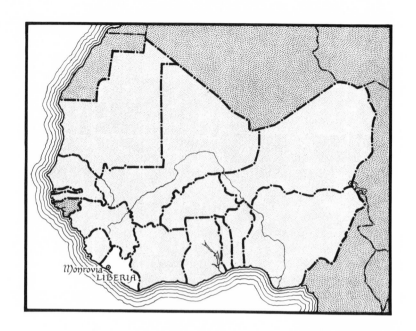

Liberia

MONROVIA

The Liberian handshake starts with the two people grasping each other's hands, a short pump, then a slide to the tips of the fingers with a loud snap of the two middle fingers. It is complicated, expressive and jolly, and like so many other things in Monrovia, it is done with nonchalant ease, a good introduction to this country.

Robertsfield International Airport, where you will land, is a full fifty miles from the capital, so you must be prepared for a long hour's drive through the countryside. The air is heavy and still. The vegetation is thick, its deep green color contrasting with the hard red soil. There are a few scattered dwellings. The outer reaches of the city present a picture of solid houses interspersed with flimsy dwellings, but it is when you get into the town center, known as "Monrovia" (the same way that Manhattan is known as New York City), that you first sense some of the special, sometimes disturbing quality of Monrovia. There are extreme differences in housing all bunched together: you will find "modern" square-lined business offices, tiny cottages made of earthen clay, storied stone mansions and lean-tos made of tar paper and mats. Most striking, however, is the old-style architecture of houses built more than one hundred years ago in the "Liberian style." It looks ante-bellum, and gives the feeling some observers compare to a humid American Southern city—say, old Natchez or Memphis.

Because Monrovia is hilly, many of the houses are built on piles, keeping them level though the terrain is uneven. Some of the piles are in the form of classical columns, others are just heaps of stones. During the day the area under the house is put to good use—it shades petty traders selling small items to supplement the household income. At night it forms a roof for the domestics. In the typically Liberian house you come up first to a large veranda that serves as a living room and as a place for receiving guests. Bedrooms and family rooms open off behind this veranda, and the kitchen is all the way in the back. As in several other African towns, the more modern houses front on the street, while cheap, ramshackle shelters pile up in the backyards. Because of the rain, everything gets a bit of mold, but also because of the rain, the most run-down street may be ablaze with towering, flowering trees.

Liberia is one of the smaller countries in West Africa; its population of 1,200,000 is next to the lowest. It hugs the Atlantic Ocean, having a long coastline, and has a shallow interior. Monrovia, the capital city, was named for U.S. President James Monroe; its population is now 125,000. Liberia's flag, patterned on the American, has eleven red and white stripes, and a blue field in the upper left corner with a single large white star. The government has a President, a Congress and a Supreme Court, affirming the historical closeness of Liberia with America.

The U.S. dollar is the currency used in Liberia. After the confusion of pence and pesewas, leones and francs, and never being able to *feel* what something costs, it is nice to be handling good old American dollars again; it is reassuring to get prices back into perspective. When you listen to the Liberian radio you hear the talk shows in an American cadence, and the long stretches of the very best black soul music. At first it is all a relief, so familiar and comfortable, then you start to feel uneasy because Liberia seems "so American." You are challenged by your foreign friends. If you are white and on your way to Liberia, a Frenchman has told you that "If you think what we did in Senegal is bad, wait until you see what you Americans have done in Liberia." If you are black, a Nigerian tells you that it is those Afro-Americans who returned to settle in Liberia who have been oppressing the local people over the years. But if you are thinking of Liberia as an American colony, don't expect the Liberians to agree with you. In fact, it isn't and never was. Liberia's history is much more complex and grim.

The story begins in the 1600s when slaves were being taken from the Grain Coast (today's Liberia), as they were from all along the West Coast. By the late 1700s in the United States, quite a few of these blacks had gained their freedom (some because they had fought in the American Revolutionary War, or because they had bought their freedom). This class of free Negroes—educated and capable—were vocally restive about their lowly place in society and were seen as a source of trouble for slave owners. There was great discussion then, as now, about "what to do with the discontented blacks." One answer was to return them to Africa, in a settlement similar to that in Freetown. The American Colonization Society, sponsored mainly by Protestant churches, sent about 16,000 of America's Africans back to the Grain Coast and in 1847 those settlers who had survived the hostile atmosphere proclaimed the sovereignty and independence of Liberia. They called themselves "Americo-Liberian," established Monrovia as a seaport, and gradually gained influence over the interior.

At first Liberia did well. The settlers engaged in trade and commerce. The Liberians were great shipbuilders and soon had a fleet of more than fifty merchant vessels moving goods. Liberia traded in rice, cotton, coffee and sugar cane from her flourishing plantations. She was oriented toward Europe and did the bulk of her business with Germany and Britain. But this prosperity was short-lived: competition from European shipyards and South

American raw materials proved too much for the Americo-Liberians. By 1900 Liberia was stricken with poverty; she was in debt to foreign governments and her commerce was controlled by European interests.

Marcus Garvey, the great popular leader of black Americans, stirred interest in Liberia again in 1920 when he visited the coast looking for a place of settlement where Afro-Americans could build a strong modern state. The progressive, egalitarian Garvey was appalled by the ruling Americo-Liberian aristocracy and their exploitation of the indigenous population. The Liberian government in turn was dubious about Garvey, suspecting that a wave of vigorous immigrants with a radical ideology would oust the establishment and completely change the shape of Liberian internal and foreign relations. In 1923 Liberia ceded a huge tract of land, 40,000 acres, to Garvey's United Negro Improvement Association, but it was soon withdrawn because of foreign pressure and Liberian disapproval of the iconoclasm of the group. Ironically, that same land was leased a few years later to the Firestone Company and formed the area of the first of the huge rubber plantations, the beginning of foreign exploitation of Liberia's natural resources.

It was only after World War II that the United States *government* began to take an interest in Liberia, both because of her strategic location and because of her rubber and huge, pure mineral deposits. American agricultural and mining firms then began investing in Liberia, and some Point-Four postwar reconstruction funds were allocated to Liberia to raise the levels of health, education, agriculture and transportation.

All of this history helped create the unique situation in Liberia. Though things are changing, there are still obvious, piercing class distinctions between the descendants of the original immigrants—the Americo-Liberians—and the rest of the population. This group, one percent of the population, is firmly in charge of the political and business life of the country. They usually distinguish themselves by the formality of their dress: men wear strict suit-and-tie business attire; women are in Western dresses, rarely in long, wrapped African clothing. For generations, they have set the standards of approved demeanor. Clever, attractive and cosmopolitan, the elite Americo-Liberian lives a life of privilege and power, similar to family-based oligarchies in South America and elsewhere.

With all the advantages they enjoy has come the Americo-Liberians' stern hostility to a white presence. There are many places in West Africa where the former colonists still retain special prerogatives; European educational and religious training, and European economic and political power have sometimes convinced Africans of the advantages of having a white skin, and of the superiority of European ways. Not so in Liberia. The upper crust is exclusively black, and although alien whites control much of the economy, they certainly are not made to feel welcome. Whites are forbidden to own land and cannot be extended Liberian citizenship. Most surprisingly, Monrovia is the only city in West Africa where whites in the diplomatic corps and the business firms complain that they are socially isolated, that they have no high status, and that they have no entrée to their peers in upper-class Liberian life. Research has found that Liberians of a poorer background are most sympathetic to whites; and as you rise on the socioeconomic scale, people display increasingly hostile attitudes to whites. Black Americans, in contrast, are welcomed warmly by all levels of society.

This history also explains something about the look of Monrovia. It is an all-black town with widely divergent housing, but there is little economic segregation, so big houses stand next to shanties. Unlike French-speaking countries where you find branches of metropolitan French companies, there are no readily visible American traders—no A & P, no Woolworth's, only the English, French, German and Dutch trading firms you find all over West Africa, along with the usual Lebanese shops. If the waterside trading warehouses are in bad condition, it is mainly because the Liberians do not allow foreigners (black or white) to own land, and foreign corporations refuse to invest in building on rented lots.

Liberia's development has begun to move more rapidly. When she was a destitute country, Liberia entered into many unfavorable agreements that used her resources and milked the land of profits, but now these contracts are being reworked and renegotiated. Long a heavy financial contributor to a variety of West African independence and liberation movements, Liberia enjoys good relations with her neighbors. She has a favorable balance of trade, and regular budget surpluses. Liberia welcomes investments and encourages strong relations with Afro-Americans. It will be interesting to watch the changes. In Liberia the situation never lends itself to easy assumptions.

Observation: The Guinean Dressmaker Our peripatetic friend from The Gambia, the gentleman who has been *everywhere,* says that the very best place in West Africa for buying clothes in Monrovia! Again, given preconceived notions about Liberia, it sounds so unlikely. But as it turns out, he is right.

For one thing, the choice of fabrics in Liberia is remarkable. The finest of Swiss cottons comes in along with the best of the Dutch wax prints; Japanese materials and cloth manufactured in other African nations all land here. Woolens, damasks, brocades and silks are available in profusion, as is every kind of sewing notion. Remember, Liberia is a free port, and unlike other African countries, it has practically no restrictions on imports. Also, there is every kind of dressmaker/tailor for every taste; more than one Americo-Liberian woman has studied dressmaking in Europe and makes high-fashion Western-style clothing for a well-heeled clientele.

But as always in black fashions, what's happening is in the streets. Here several trends meet to produce the marvelous clothes you see around you. First, the younger indigenous Liberians from the hinterland have come in numbers to Monrovia looking for education and jobs. During the last years of the Tubman administration, opportunities opened up for a wide range of the population, giving them some power, and some money. In Liberia, also for the first time, the social climate has shifted a bit, so that it is respectable, not shameful, to have traditional origins. Then, all over the world, *including* Africa, the African style of appearance has growing glamour and appeal. American blacks have projected it into an international fashion. So, instead of wanting to emulate the starchy, Western-style clothing of the Americo-Liberian aristocracy, local young people wanted the typically African modes of contemporary dress.

At the same time as this upsurgence of pride was manifesting itself, refugees fleeing from the hard times in Guinea began coming to

Monrovia in number. Guineans are justly famed in Africa for their handsomeness and their extraordinary good taste and feeling for beauty. Using their good advance publicity, Guineans started making clothes. By grit and good luck, they began supplying a service in Monrovia that was not in competition with any existing Liberian enterprise. Now, downtown Monrovia is studded with Guinean tailor workshops.

The Guineans produce quantities of excellent *dashikis*—well cut, well embroidered—and then send brothers and cousins out to sell them on the market streets. But they really shine when it comes to dressing women. They can make any dress from your own design, but they show their skills in making the styles called "Apollo" (a shift) and the *lappa*. They will design flamboyant sleeves, and fit you perfectly. The inside will be lined and sewn as perfectly as the outside. They love heavy embroidery and dramatic necklines. Within the confines of the traditional design, they come up with beautiful, imaginative innovations.

Young, style-conscious Liberians keep the tailors busy. They flaunt their gorgeous African creations, knowing they are projecting their own special beauty and their own special heritage. Their triumph—lately the Liberian president himself has taken off his tuxedo, and now sports the clothes of the people.

*   *   *

LEISURE AND PLEASURE

In the morning
—Mingle with the crowds shopping on Water Street. Buy some materials from one of the large trading companies or from one of the men passing by.
—Take a cruise boat around in Monrovian waters.
In the afternoon
—Visit the Monrovia Free Port. At any one time there are vessels in from all parts of the world.
—Swim in the rooftop pool at the Ducor Hotel, where, as you climb out of the water, you have a great view of the entire city.

GETTING AROUND

There is no public transportation in Monrovia, and no mode of getting into the interior except by robust automobile over very bad roads. Those buses you see in Monrovia are privately owned, and erratic. There are a variety of taxi categories at all kinds of prices. Be prepared to pay out for cabs in order to get around; 25 cents has long been the rate for trips in town, more to residential areas. You may want to hire a car, or better, a taxi, for a day.

SIGHTS TO SEE AND THINGS TO DO

In Town

Fort Norris, right below the Ducor Hotel, is one of the most famous sites in Monrovia. You will see the monument dedicated to J. J. Roberts, the first President of Liberia, and the Monrovia lighthouse. The view over the town and port is great.

Monrovia has some outstanding public buildings: the **Capitol Building,** the **City Hall,** the **Temple of Justice** and the **Masonic Temple.** If the **New Executive Mansion** is still as open and as accessible as it has been, apply for a tour of the public areas. The **National Museum** has a small collection of historic and ethnographic materials well labeled and nicely displayed.

Outside of Town

The **National Cultural Center** is a distance out of town, 20 miles away in Paynesville, but it is worth the visit. Under the direction of the Cultural Bureau of the Department of Information and Cultural Affairs, Liberia has constructed a center for the encouragement of traditional arts and crafts. The Center is on thirteen acres of beachfront land, and it features the actual dwellings of Liberia's sixteen major ethnic groups, made by traditional master builders.

Organized Tours

The **Division of Tourism** of the Department of Information and Cultural Affairs organizes tours of Monrovia. The most interesting is the three-hour-cruise boat tour: it leaves from the Monrovia Free Port and passes several of the townships. At Providence Island you see the spot where the first immigrants from America landed, and the trip ends up at the New Market Place, a farmers' produce market. Another tour is by land and takes in each and every one of the historical sights of Monrovia. You will also be shown the finer residential areas, cultural and social institutions (government departments, the University of Liberia, the stadium, etc.), and there are stops in scenic spots for picture taking. Contact the Division of Tourism on Capitol Hill for details.

Beaches

Bernard's Beach at Sinkor and **Cooper's Beach** at Kenema are sheltered for swimming. **Elwa Beach** at Paynesville is safe, so you might want to stop there after a visit to the National Cultural Center. Otherwise, beware of all other Monrovia beaches. They are *not safe for swimming* because of the treacherous undertow. They are beautiful to look at with their spotless white sand, but be *most careful.*

SHOPPING

The Liberian Ring Liberia gets the credit for the V-shaped ring (made of two V's joined at the wide tips) that is so popular all over West Africa. It is worn with the V point away from you; the effect is dramatic. The jewelry shops on Broad Street (and the overpriced gift shop at the Ducor) sell a large variety of this design. Those made in gold filigree are especially beautiful; they also come plain, studded and in silver. The smiths make a bracelet in this pattern also; the bracelets are a bit "hard to wear," so be sure it fits comfortably first, before you buy.

Clothing and Materials It will be easy for you to find the shops selling the *dashiki* shirts. The Guinean shops cut from fine tie-dye indigo prints and do the most fanciful embroidery—some of the shirts are truly beautiful. Many times you will find men on the street selling shirts also. In any case, look to see that the material design is even; sometimes scraps are fitted in, spoiling the symmetry. The cheaper-quality shirts are embroidered with cardboard as a backing; avoid them in favor of the ones made of double material. In forty-eight hours the tailors will prepare you a custom-made outfit from the material you bring, in the design you want.

Along Water Street you will find a fabulous array of wax prints. Everything seems to show up in Liberia, so you can have a great time just looking around. The United Africa Company (U.A.C.) has the most serious collection of authentic Dutch wax prints. You can tell the important merchant stores by the number of Liberian and Nigerian trading women who are there haggling, resting or chatting with one another. These places are like warehouses and have long planks where the 12-yard pieces of the same design are all piled a yard high. (Any woman out shopping will show you where the better stores are.)

Wanderers' Wares Poor people come to Monrovia from the rural areas to seek their fortunes, carrying with them a capital of handicrafts from the village or odd pieces of material off a ship. Men walk around with garlands of sandals around their necks, or with stacks of indigo cloth on their heads. If there is something you see that you like, buy it right away. You'll never see the vendor again, and chances are you'll never see as nice an article of that type again either.

HOTELS

Ducor Inter-Continental (end of Broad Street; tel. 22-200)   International standing. Fully air-conditioned. $14–$25 single, $23–$31 double. The Ducor is an impressive place—large, well appointed. It has a marvelous location on a hill that gives a remarkable view of the sea and the countryside. It has a swimming pool, roof garden, night club and tennis court.

Carlton Hotel (Broad Street; tel. 27-247) Fully air-conditioned. $12 single, $16 double. This is the place where the international staffs stay. It is located in the center of town, well kept up and lively.

Studer Hotel (top of Benson Street) Air-conditioned. $8 single, $10 double. This is author's choice because it is such a peculiar place for a hotel. There is no reception desk or office, but it is immaculate and everything runs smoothly. Rooms are huge, with big bathrooms, excellent mattresses, and every room has a refrigerator! You can cook in the gigantic kitchen or take Austrian specialties in its little restaurant. A find. (By the way, this place is a big secret—used for assignations, no doubt—and never listed in any official listing of hotels.)

Other Hotels

The **Viscount** on Randall Street ($10 single, $16 double) is a popular place that has a restaurant serving Lebanese dishes. **Heinz and Maria** (it has a German restaurant) on Carey Street and the **Capitol** rent singles at $7 and doubles at $10. Look at the rooms first—some are run-down, but most are adequate. The fortunes of the **Ambassadors Hotel** on United Nations Drive, once a great favorite, don't seem good, but it may rise again, taking advantage of its great location and atmosphere.

RESTAURANTS

There are three leading restaurants in Monrovia at this writing, each one a pleasure in its class.

First, **Roseline's** (on Carey Street), where the food is the best in Liberian cooking—which is good indeed. You'll not find better palm-butter or peanut-butter stew anywhere. They are both freshly made and flavorful, meaty and hearty. They also make excellent *palaver* sauce and Joloff rice. Come to stuff, washing it down with ice-cold beer. At Roseline's you'll be seeing (and probably meeting) the chic set of Monrovia—politicians, businessmen and their friends come here every day. The atmosphere is informal, friendly, and jolly. A true enjoyment.

Next on the list is **Diana's Restaurant** on Broad Street. They serve European dishes, and they make a variety of Middle Eastern specialties as the mood hits them. Crowded with whoever is in town at the moment, it has a relaxed, easygoing atmosphere. The broiled chicken is the most succulent you'll find anywhere.

For an evening of elegant dining in a continental atmosphere, the recommended place is **Salvatore's Restaurant** on Benson Street. Veal, chicken and fish are prepared the French way. The salads are good, and the wine selection varied. The guests are cool and well dressed, foreign and rich.

Of course, the **Ducor Hotel** restaurants are all pretty good, but not outstanding. Still, if the food lacks, you can feast your eyes on the glorious scenery. Other places in town are **Maxim's,** the **California,** and the **Country Club,** all on Courley Street, and **Oscar's Chalet** and **Hotel de France.** Things keep changing, of course, so ask around. For a late hamburger or scrambled eggs, try the Ducor at any hour.

NIGHT CLUBS

Across from the Studer Hotel is one of those West African beer bars. A barbershop by day, at night it turns into a dancing spot. That's easily done. There is a refrigerator where the beer and soda are iced; they serve cupcakes and tins of sardines. The manager moves a couple of tables and chairs onto the sidewalk, turns on a blue fluorescent light and puts blaring blues records on a phonograph. A couple of girls and some guys get together, and soon everyone is laughing and dancing and the mood is set for the night. There are dozens of these beer bars in Monrovia, all acting as places of entertainment for the local young people. The beer doesn't cost much; neither do the girls.

At the **Coconut Lounge,** the setting is sedate and air-conditioned. Drinks are Scotch, girls are white, and an evening is much more expensive. **Maxim's** and **Cava de Roy** were functioning, with a variety of music and floor shows. The **Ducor** has one or two clubs in operation all the time, and their **Press Bar** stays open very late.

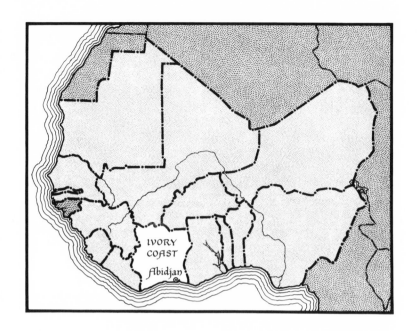

Ivory Coast

ABIDJAN

"Si nous voulons transformer l'Afrique en une nouvelle Europe, l'Amérique en nouvelle Europe, alors confions à des Européens les destinées de nos pays. Ils sauront mieux faire que les mieux doués d'entre nous." One of the leading philosophers of the Black Liberation struggle is Franz Fanon. Wise and nearly infallible, he advised Africans to rely upon Europeans if they wanted to build European-style developments in Africa. He pointed out that naturally, Europeans know best how to construct a copy of European life.

Well, the leaders of the Ivory Coast thought about it for a

while, decided that Fanon was right—they took his advice very much to heart. The Ivorians asked Europeans to come and build the Ivory Coast to resemble Europe; Europeans eagerly answered the call. There were an estimated 12,000 Frenchmen in the Ivory Coast at the moment of independence in 1960. In ten years that figure has tripled—there are now 36,000 and the number grows daily.

Most of the industry is owned by foreign interests whose companies and employees return much of the capital to France each year in the form of repatriated business profits and salaries. Expatriates hold from 60 to 90 percent of the middle and top management jobs in such key areas of the economy as construction, transportation, commerce and industry. As the economy grows, more and more foreigners will be needed to make it work.

You can expect to see predominantly white faces in downtown Abidjan. While the men are out of view in offices and bureaus, their wives and children fill the streets during the day, and the whole family appears at lunchtime and in the evening. Most of the small French businesses hire only white personnel: in a pharmacy you will pay your money to a French cashier; in a dress shop a French woman will wait on you; in a sports shop a French man. It goes without saying that the vast majority of the primary-, secondary- and technical-school teachers are French, as are the college professors; the whole educational establishment is firmly in French hands.

Frenchmen are not the only foreigners who flock to the Ivory Coast. There are businessmen from all over Western Europe, the United States and Japan. There is also a large Levantine population of Lebanese and Syrians who work in small commerce. With Europeans around you still need someone to do the work. So, in search of jobs, from Mali have come 250,000 people, mostly men, and from Upper Volta have come another 350,000. A whopping 35 to 40 percent of male African labor comes from these neighboring countries, and is concentrated in Abidjan and other urban centers. Mainly, they are in service jobs, in lower-level clerical work, and in larger stores and businesses. This means that your hotel clerk is from Ouagadougou in Upper Volta and the waiter comes from Guinea. At the bank, the teller is a Congolese from Brazzaville; in the bookstore you are waited on by a Dogon from Mali. Your airline reservations are taken by a Cameroonian, you buy cloth from Nigerian women, a Ghanaian band makes music for dancing in a restaurant owned by a Togolese.

At a glance it is clear that the Ivory Coast has a very special make-up. A substantial proportion of its population is foreign-born, and these foreign-born people have great weight in the business and production affairs of the country.

Out of a population of 4.5 million, there are around 3.9 million indigenous Ivorians; most of them live in the rural areas. They are the farmers and planters who grow the Ivory Coast's remarkable agricultural bounty. They raise crops and keep cattle, fish the local waters and work in the mines. One unusual characteristic of Ivorian people is their enjoyment of small-town life; though most live on farms, fully 25 percent of them live in urban areas. The large number of small towns scattered throughout the country are centers of trade, manufacturing, construction and food processing.

At the turn of the century one of the smaller ethnic groups, the Ébrié, was living in the area of today's Abidjan. The land was declared a colony of France in 1893, but the French did not establish secure control until the 1930s. The great West African military strategist Samori Touré valiantly fought the French for seven years, until his defeat and capture in 1898. With Touré sent to die in exile and his armies vanquished, the French could extend their hegemony for the next ten years through coercive but peaceful negotiations. Then the local populations rallied, and warfare broke out again. It took another ten years of continuous and bitter military clashes, until around the time of World War I, for the French to be firmly in control.

The self-confident, conservative, French-oriented Ivory Coast you see today has had the bloodiest and most turbulent colonial history of any country in West Africa. The French used the whole racist arsenal of military occupation: conscription, forced labor, chain gangs, torture, imprisonment and murder. The unarmed Ivorians countered with passive resistance, strikes, sabotage and subterfuge. Railroad workers stopped work in demand for their human rights. Farmers organized to protest the fact that they were paid half of what the white planter was paid for a sack of cocoa.

173

The prize for which the French fought was the remarkable rich land of the Ivory Coast. Although there is a bit of manganese and some industrial diamonds underground, the major wealth of the Ivory Coast comes from its fertile topsoil. It is agriculture that provides the backbone for the exuberant expansion of the Ivorian economy and its continually favorable balance of trade. It is agriculture that is the livelihood for 85 percent of its population, furnishes 85 percent of the exports and 65 percent of the hard-currency income. Today the Ivory Coast's cash-crop exports are coffee, timber, cocoa, bananas, cotton, palm products, pineapples, avocados and rubber. Almost half of the agricultural production is in maize, millet, sorghum, yams, sweet potatoes, and other foodstuffs. There is abundant produce for all the country's population, and ample feed for the large number of livestock. The Ivory Coast also is able to supply the food needs of its nearby neighbors.

Abidjan began to grow from 1893, once the decision was made that this area should be the site for the headquarters and terminal of the new railroad. By 1903 there were administrative offices, workshops and lodgings. Then, in 1934, Abidjan was chosen as the residence of the governor of the colony. The offices formerly in Bingerville and Grand-Bassam were moved to Abidjan.

Abidjan is created by four peninsulas whose tips converge near one point in a network of lagoons. The city was cut off from the sea by a Long Island–like littoral until the opening of the Vridi Canal in 1950. This engineering feat sliced a passage through the land, linking the Abidjan lagoons with the Gulf of Guinea and the Atlantic Ocean, thus setting the stage for Abidjan's phenomenal development. Abidjan now has a major deep-water port, almost as large as Dakar's, handling more cargo tonnage than any other French-speaking country. Large grants of French development aid have made Abidjan the center of the Ivory Coast's communications and transportation system.

Abidjan, then, is a comparatively new city; in the space of twenty-five years it has mushroomed from small town to major city. You see the building all around you, the rapid expansion of a boom town. New factories are opened, businesses are enlarged, construction continues—right before your eyes. The furious activity and the vast fortunes at stake make you feel ill at ease in this city. There is nothing polite or friendly about Abidjan. The pace is hard, and the race is to the swift. Money is god, king, balm and carrot. Everyone is out for lucre; and competition is fierce. There is little time for the graces and the amenities. Language is crude; the words are barked or shouted; sarcasm and one-up-manship set the tone. Back home in France, the French are often reprimanded by their leaders for the anger and tension of their voices and the graspiness of their manner. Exacerbate this French irritability and rudeness by a miserable climate; add the hustling-to-make-it of underpaid Ivorian urban workers, and you get an idea of the harsh, grating nature of this city.

The divisions of the city itself are a case in point. Abidjan is separated into five principal areas. The **Plateau,** built on one of the peninsulas, is the downtown center. Every inch is developed with stylish buildings, wide avenues, spacious lawns and modern conveniences. This is where you find the embassies and delegations, the corporation offices, businesses, shops and movies, restaurants and supermarkets, governmental and administrative bureaus.

The peninsula across the lagoon from the Plateau is a residential area called **Cocody.** It stands on gently rising hills, where the air is as fresh as it gets in Abidjan. The houses are fine structures, large and spacious, tastefully designed, open to lush, flower-filled gardens. The area is quiet, exclusive and strictly upper-class: ambassadors and business tycoons make their homes here. Most important, Cocody is the residence of the chief-of-state. The presidential mansion is a wonder of fountains, chandeliers, gardens, marble, rugs, statuary and salons. It is extravagant on a grand scale—matched dinner service for one thousand.

The other landmark in Cocody is the Hotel Ivoire, the most luxurious and magnificent hotel in Africa. It is gorgeous, a Hollywood, movie-set kind of hotel. Everything about it is lavish and showy. Through its rooms pass a constant stream of businessmen, diplomats and international *bons vivants.* Hundreds of townspeople come every day to see the sporting facilities, to eat or drink, and to ogle the splendors.

Cocody is wealthy, almost all-white, pleasing in a Beverly Hills sort of way. From the Hotel Ivoire you can take a ferry across the lagoon to **Treichville,** 100 percent black, a town whose population is drawn from a dozen different African countries. In this vast popular district live 150,000 souls, and at times it seems that every one of them is on the streets at once! The streets, by the way, are perfectly straight, "planned" and all that, but Treichville is a Harlem. It is solid and well built, but crowded, noisy, busy, active. So is Lagos. So is Accra, but the difference is that in those places there is no overpowering white-face Plateau, no snooty Cocody, no all-European club policies that force segregation and create Harlems. And like Harlem, like any place where black people congregate, Treichville is night-town. As you'd expect, there is life, vitality: Treichville is filled with interesting restaurants, night clubs, small dancing spots and the red-light district. It is the place to go to relax and unwind, to let your hair down, swing, enjoy.

Treichville is also an area of a thousand small shops, both Lebanese and African, that sell every practical and luxury article imaginable. The stores stay open until all hours, and there are always customers. Treichville is at its very African best on Sunday nights near the beginning of the month (after payday), when the various nationality groups set up loudspeakers for dancing in the festive streets. For the visit of a foreign dignitary or a national holiday, the area around the market is roped off, and there are wonderful performances of dancing and drumming by people from the various regions of the Ivory Coast.

Adjamé, another all-African section, is at the other end of Abidjan, on the same peninsula as the Plateau. Adjamé is more rural, less slick and smart. Many of its inhabitants are newly arrived from the farms and small towns of the interior. They come to stay near people from the same region, with relatives of the same ethnic group. So the flavor is much more provincial, the pace slower and more dignified. There are many housing projects in the middle of large stretches of empty land; the outskirts blend into the hinterland.

In Adjamé there are only country-style distractions. The high-pressure market in Treichville closes at 2 P.M., but here the market bustles all day long. Pipers and drummers circulate through the crowds, while poor people search through the worn items in the flea markets. Magicians and stunt men stand below the windows of apartment houses doing their tricks for coins from adults and applause from children.

Observation: The Church of William Wade Harris   One of the biggest attractions in Adjamé is the evangelical church of the sect called *"Harrisme,"* founded by the prophet William Wade Harris. At congregation time the devotees parade through the streets in long, shining white clothes, singing, playing castanets and rattling maracas. They dance into church, read from the Protestant Bible, and spend the meeting in fervent, loud praying. After the service they dance out into the courtyard and begin singing again—all in the enjoyment of religious fellowship. The dances are village dances, the songs are village melodies recast with religious words.

Harrisme is one of the many indigenous African sects that flourish in West Coast cities. All of their histories are similar. They were founded by African prophets, not by European or American missionaries. Such a prophet, usually a local man of great intellect and compassion, felt called by the Lord to establish a Christian Church adapted to the African personality. Thus it is not the usual gloomy, austere Christian church dominated by sorrow for a dead Saviour. Instead, these churches are gay and high-spirited, the meetings filled with rousing music and dance. The disciples participate wholeheartedly in the proceedings, responding joyfully to sermon and prayers, for *as always,* African religion is communal and participatory.

There is no liturgy copied from the strict forms of a mother church somewhere in Europe; instead the services use traditional cultural forms of country people, infusing them with new texts and meanings. Healing and blessing services are a high point of the religious activities, and the members find intense satisfaction in the emotional release they experience. The churches form a number of social and benevolent clubs that care for members and assure them some measure of social security. Polygamy is encouraged and worship is a family affair.

It is easy to see why these churches are categorized as "syncretic," for indeed they take all manner of faith and worship, of tenets and rites from a variety of religions, then mix them into something new and creative. Among the *Harristes,* you see this blend. The Protestant Bible, Catholic holidays, Christian cross (*not* crucifix), the African chief's cane,

177

long white robes on the style of Catholic nuns and priests, traditional dance steps, olden tunes with new, modern lyrics, storytelling sermons, group praying, miracles, cures in psychic medicine.

These new churches are among the most interesting phenomena on the contemporary African scene. Through them people transplanted to urban areas beyond the protection and control of their traditional communities, find new fellowship and learn new city ways.

* * *

In comparison with all the personality-plus areas of the city, **Marcory** seems tame and unimaginative. Built on a fourth peninsula, it is simply a good middle-class residential area. Whites, blacks and Lebanese live here in modest, comfortable homes. There are several additional sections within the city limits. **New Koumassi** is an area dominated by Akan people and named for their ancestral capital, Kumasi, in Ghana. Many of the residents here are fishermen and laborers in nearby industrial zones. The housing and life style are traditional. **Port-Bouët** is a fishing village that still possesses a gentleness and charm. **Vridi** is a seaside resort area; the **Parc National du Banco**, on the mainland, is a forest reserve.

The Ivory Coast is one of the most prosperous countries in West Africa, and its capital is probably the most beautiful and most modern West African city. But the sky hangs gray over Abidjan; the air is sweltering and close. The elaborate, intense divisions of the city are disquieting: they have the look of apartheid, the sharp color lines, the ostentation of wealth, the rasping push for money and goods. For some, the city is an example of progress and development; for others it seems antagonistic and dangerously divided, a sacrifice of the human for the material. At the moment Abidjan continues to expand exuberantly, while its critics wait and see.

LEISURE AND PLEASURE

In the morning
—Explore the spacious streets of Cocody, looking at the homes.

—Take the ferry to the Plateau and catch the late morning hubbub at the market, as the salesmen become even more persuasive.

In the afternoon
—Order a half pineapple or a glass of cold beer at the Hotel du Parc sidewalk café, settle in and watch the world go by.

—Go ice skating or bowling at the Hotel Ivoire, or have a sauna.

In the evening
—Dine in a West African or North African restaurant.

Observation: *Complications* Anything planned and engineered by us imperfect human beings is bound to contain many obvious, sometimes overwhelming flaws. Among the things that will be marred by all sorts of shortcomings will be this, your long-awaited trip to Africa. So maybe one of your days will go like this:

In the morning
—Check anxiously at the bank to find out if that remittance you sent for from home has finally come.

—Spend the next hour getting the money in American travelers checks and then the travelers checks changed into local money.

—Brood a bit after inquiring at the embassy and finding that the *important letter* you are expecting from your lover, mother, university, boss, secretary or friend still has not come.

In the afternoon
—Hear on the radio that there has been a coup d'état in the country you were planning to visit next, or that the borders have closed for some complex, political reason.

—Go to the airline office and try to get a place on another plane going somewhere else.

—Look for a photographer who will take your pictures for that new set of visas and permits you need.

In the evening

——Get all dressed up and then wait around impatiently for a date who never shows up as promised, and never calls.

——Realize that you are being eaten alive by mosquitoes in this outdoor restaurant where you are eating.

——Rant and rave because you just can't stand being hassled one more time by your roommate, tour leader, hotel clerk, taxi driver, whatever.

*   *   *

GETTING AROUND

Taxis

If you didn't bring your Mercedes-Benz with you, you are going to have to rely on the little red Abidjan taxis. They are fast, cheap, plentiful, but very hard to find when you need one.

Ferry

You are not in a rush, so why not get around by ferryboat. Just below the Hotel Ivoire there is a ferry that goes to Avenue I in Treichville (not far from the market). From the same place you can catch a ferry to the Plateau. There is no schedule; boats leave when they are full. Fare: 3 cents.

Buses

There are numerous bus routes lacing through the city. For 5 or 10 cents you can ride all over Abidjan. Buses on the popular routes run very frequently, but they are jam-packed every hour of the day.

Railroads

The city of Abidjan grew originally as a railroad center; it is the terminus for the great Abidjan–Niger Railroad. The cars are clean and well maintained; the schedules are kept faithfully. You can travel the length of the Ivory Coast by rail, and then go farther to Upper Volta. A first-class ticket to the second-largest city in the Ivory Coast, Bouaké, a distance of about 200 miles, costs about $6.50. There are dining and sleeping cars on the long runs.

Automobiles

Hertz (B.P. 4091, Abidjan) will have a Fiat or a Rambler waiting for you at the airport. Rates are $8.50 to $20 a day, plus 9–16 cents a mile.

SIGHTS TO SEE

National Museum (Boulevard Carde, Adjamé) Open daily except Tuesday 9 A.M.–12 noon and 2:30 P.M.–6 P.M.

The sculpture collection contains treasures of extraordinary refinement and beauty. The rural populations of the Ivory Coast produce sculptural art of remarkable repose and power that especially appeals to European and American tastes. Baulé, Dan, Senufo, Ngere, Guro, and a half-dozen more groups, forest dwellers, fishers in the lagoons, all create a visual heritage that has influence in art circles the world over. Some fine representative pieces are on display here.

Abidjan University (in the Cocody area)

The university is a complex of modern buildings. It is a large campus, set in lush gardens of flowering trees and vines.

The Port and Fishing Port

The sights at the Abidjan port are the kinds that are difficult to get near back home in the States. You are free to walk all through this area; there are no restrictions. The scene is hectic: there are a dozen ships from all over the world, docking to discharge and receive cargo. There are areas for shipping of fruits, minerals and timber. At the end of the regular port is the **Port de Pêche,** center of commercial fish distribution. It is an interesting place to visit and even to purchase some seafood, should you be in the mood. Most of the time it looks like a large version of a familiar fish market—lobster, shrimp, sole, bass, cod and red snapper, but on some days you will be startled by a sudden display of huge sea turtles, sharks, stingrays, and frightening-looking glumps called, for want of a better word, "monsters."

Aquarium (Boulevard Pelieu)

This is a clean recreation center that attracts a young, handsome crowd. You can swim in a pool overlooking the lagoon, water-ski, skin-dive, or rent a canoe or sailboat.

Hotel Ivoire (Cocody)

The Hotel Ivoire has everything you need in a resort to keep you active and healthy. For about $1 you can use the pool, have snacks poolside and play ping-pong. You've heard of the famous only-one-in Africa ice-skating rink, of course. Remember there is also a bowling alley, a sauna, slot machines, and little motorboats for riding around the lake.

Air Afrique Building

One of Abidjan's more outstanding buildings is the headquarters of the multinational company Air Afrique. Aside from the good design of the building, its huge doors are decorated with sculpture of traditional Akan religious symbols; really quite stunning.

TOURS AND EXCURSIONS

Abidjan is so located that the tourist can find an enormous variety of scenery and experience within easy distance. Air Afrique or the Tourist Office can arrange full-day trips for you that cover nearby appealing spots.

Parc National du Banco

This 7,500-acre park, right on the edge of developed Abidjan, is a thriving example of a true African tropical forest. It is a shock to go deep into the dark thickness to see the shadows of camouflaged animals and the glint of yellow birds. You feel very close to origins, to the primeval. There are clearings where visitors may picnic, an arboretum with hundreds of different marked trees, and a small forestry school that you are welcome to visit. **La Chaumière du Banco** is a restaurant on the premises which is pleasant but expensive.

Bingerville

All Abidjan drives out to the small town of Bingerville for fresh air and unusual scenery. Among its attractions is a botanical garden, a lagoon and charming, flower-covered houses. Bingerville is an educational center with several important schools—a boys' technical high school, an agricultural training school, an orphanage, a *lycée*, a coffee and cocoa research center, a military technical school, and a civil service training center. The most important institution is the African Art School, a place where Ivorian youngsters are taught to sculpt in wood.

Eloka Ferry

The road from Bingerville leads to the Eloka Ferry through forest and flat lands. By the time you arrive at the ferry you and your friends are suddenly on holiday and special things are happening. There will be a wait for the ferry and new people to talk with. The ferry has a quality out of the ordinary.

Grand-Bassam

Before 1933, Grand-Bassam was the colonial capital of the Ivory Coast; it retains evidence of its former glory. The tree-lined avenues are wide, and sadly empty. The old houses were built on a big scale, with balconies and "verandas" popular during that era. Grand-Bassam has the storybook character of places belonging to a different era but now anachronistic. This gives it a look of ease and timelessness that charms the visitor. Nearby there are sites where one can enjoy seaside and beach. At **Azuretti Beach** there is a hotel-restaurant, and a bit farther on a fishing village.

Note: The most popular tourist trip is a circular drive to Bingerville and Grand-Bassam. You leave by the Adjamé road, passing the university and an orchid plantation. You visit Bingerville, then ride through palm-tree plantations and take the Eloka Ferry across the lagoon. You drive until you come to Grand-Bassam. There you may relax over a meal or drinks at one of the restaurants, and afterward explore the town and visit the seashore. On the road back to Abidjan you pass through coconut-tree plantations. Then you arrive near the Abidjan fishing port, for a stop there if you wish, before returning to the center of town. This is an especially easy trip that offers a multitude of surprises and pleasures.

Vridi Beach

Vridi Beach is miles and miles of beautiful tropical beach: fine white sand, coconut trees, gentle breezes. But beware of the water—the undertow is rough and the swimming dangerous. There is a bus to Vridi Beach leaving from the Fonction Publique du Port in Treichville.

Jacqueville

Here is a beach where you can swim. Jacqueville is a picturesque island village where there is a restaurant and comfortable facilities. It is around forty miles from Abidjan, between the littoral and the Ebrié Lagoon; a ferry links it to the littoral.

Grand-Lahou

The best way to get here is by the small boats that leave from the foot of the old bridge in Treichville. The boats travel slowly down lagoon in a leisurely voyage.

SHOPPING

The Ivory Coast is rich, rich, rich. The cultures of her people are deep, profound; the products of these cultures are extraordinarily beautiful. Because there is so much hard cash floating around, dealers from all over West Africa come here to sell their wares, knowing that they can command a stiff price. So you can expect to find a dizzying variety of goods mostly of fine quality at reasonable prices.

The patterns and colors of Ivorian crafts are gayer, more complex than those you'll find to the north in Senegal and Mali, or to the east in Nigeria. The dominant ethnic group, the Akan, likes its colors vivid and hot: reds, gold, royal blue, green. Everything is brighter and brisker, more flamboyant and dashing.

Treichville Market Open from early morning to 2 P.M. daily

Just as Abidjan is one of the most attractive cities in West Africa, its main market is one of the best you'll find. In Treichville it is a two-story market with a large courtyard. At 2 P.M. it is scrubbed and hosed down. On show is a sampling of all the produce and crafts of the country. The best time to come is on Sunday morning, when the whole town turns out in a festive mood to buy and sell, to talk and be social.

On the ground floor is a vast display of fruits, vegetables, tubers, nuts, cereals, meats, seafood, condiments, spices, medicinal plants and cooked food. Six live crabs are stood edge-to-edge, woven into a clawing tower. Tasty stews boil in cauldrons, and a little girl sells a small pile of dried red peppers.

Upstairs is the domain of the traders in dry goods. Stalls are jammed next to one another with special sections for each type of item. As you come up the main stairs you will see rows of beads, necklaces, bracelets, all manner of antique and traditional craft jewelry. Then you plow through the dense forest of overhanging wax-print cloth to come to tables and tables of costume jewelry all in gold plate in contemporary styles. Farther back are men selling hand-dyed cloth. There are Yoruba head scarves, Akan *adinkra* cloth, ready-made children's clothes. And there are women who sell jewelry of heavily alloyed, low-carat "gold." (Be very dubious about the gold jewelry on sale near the back. Some men have their attaché cases outfitted as display cases for well-designed, light-weight gold jewelry. For your protection, ask to see the govern-ment-stamp guarantee of quality gold.)

As part of your Sunday morning shopping in Treichville, go over to the Hausa mosque on Avenue 7. There, on Sunday mornings only, you'll find an outdoor flea market. Most of the stuff is old and rusty. But if you take the time to plow through it, you may come up with some surprises: one tourist discovered a grouping of huge keys, the kind that open the big locks in castle doors.

Adjamé Market   Open all day, every day

Vivid, colorful, crowded, this is the author's choice for the most interesting place in Abidjan to shop for fabric. The traders show a wide range of manufactured wax prints. A number of them commemorate Ivory Coast events—the visit of Mr. Pompidou and of Mrs. Nixon, for example. The skills of the Ivorian dyers are in the batik work: moons slide through their circles, suns burst into tears, and waves wash on the shore. Fire and water, and air and earth are all there, in motion. Then you turn a corner and the mood changes: the prints are in brooding gray and black, very dark and dense, the making of a stunning "dark cotton" for stateside city wear.

Adjamé Market stays open all day, except for a siesta break. It is homier, more neighborhood-y than the other markets. Prices are lower, people are friendlier; there is less of a hustle, mainly because few Europeans come here to shop.

Plateau Market   Open from early morning to 1 P.M.

Plateau Market is a big food exchange, where Ivorian and French housewives come to do their grocery shopping, so in general, there is less variety, things are more select, and prices are higher than in other sections of town. Nonetheless, there are some good items for sale. The variety of flowers is stunning: magnificent bouquets of perfumed, wildly colorful tropical flowers in full bloom, selling for a song. To live well during your stay in Abidjan, buy some of these beautiful flowers for your room. You will have days to admire their hues and savor their fragrance. Their graceful presence will delight you and enrich your trip.

Men from Niger and Upper Volta bring down finely detailed leather goods—handbags, belts and boots. Other fellows are selling long dresses made from batik fabrics. The vendors can overwhelm the hesitant with their cheerful persistence. These very self-con-

fident young men flatter you in a variety of languages and melt
your resistance with dazzling African smiles. Flirtation and bargaining are part of the fun.

Marché Artisanal (Boulevard de la République)

Across from the Hotel du Parc is a large park, a portion of
which is given over to a maze of trading stalls, open all day. To
repeat, the money is here in Abidjan, so traders bring in wares from
all over Africa. You can't expect to find authentic traditional wood
sculpture here: the good pieces are sold by art dealers to their
high-paying, discerning clients. This market only offers copies of
sacred works, or standard carved heads and busts. The best choices
can be made among the craft items. There are first-quality rugs and
wall hangings for sale. Some of the ironwork is worthwhile, and
there are good buys in leather.

Hotel Ivoire Gift Shops

Go to the Hotel Ivoire for hassle-free shopping in a pleasant
atmosphere; you will find good-quality tourist items, chosen with
taste. The prices are marked and there is no bargaining, but the
costs are really quite reasonable. In fact, before braving the hustle
and bustle of market shopping, you might want to come here first
and get a leisured look at select, interesting objects. This is the best
source for authentic traditional sculpture at modern inflated prices.

Jewelry   The fashionable ladies of Abidjan adorn themselves in
baubles, and the whole world knows that the French population
tends to hoard great quantities of gold. So, naturally, the sale of
jewelry in Abidjan is a big and serious business. Shop along **Avenue
Franchet d'Esperey,** along **Rue Gourges** (the square block from the
corner of the Hotel du Parc, down to the market, under the arcades
and down, back across and up); all the boutiques have an
extravagant display of glitter, all dutifully certified to be 18-carat
gold. For more authentically African styles of good taste and high
quality, visit the workshop of **Seck Mamadou,** on Avenue 3 Rue 5
(not far from Chez Tante Sally—see below).

HOTELS

Abidjan hotels are just superb: they are beautiful, comfortable, clean, well maintained, well located. Generally, the staffs are helpful, too. All the places listed are completely air-conditioned, with private bath, radio and telephone in each room. Because of the large capacity of the hotels, you should have no trouble finding a place, but still, you are advised to wire ahead or to have Air Afrique make arrangements for you.

International Class

Hotel Ivoire Intercontinental, in Cocody, 3 miles from the center of town (B.P. 8001, Abidjan; tel. 34-94-81) $15 to $28 single, $23 to $33 double; $38 to $75 for a suite.   The story is often told of the club of twelve people (six couples) who came on a ten-day holiday to Abidjan. They booked into the Hotel Ivoire and lived in the luxurious rooms. During the day they swam in the Olympic-sized pool wearing the new bathing suits they bought in the hotel's boutiques, took motorboats around the artificial lake, and went sailing and water-skiing at the hotel's own marina. They played tennis on the three tennis courts, bowled in the ten-lane bowling alley, and clambered around in the gymnasium. They took saunas and had sybaritic massages, and when all else paled, they went ice-skating. They ate and drank in the hotel's seven different restaurants and cocktail lounges; they had breakfast omelettes in the coffee shop, lunch entrees at the poolside café, and dainty sandwiches at the tearoom. In the evening they had cocktails in the piano bar, and dinner in the penthouse restaurant, Le Toit d'Abidjan, serenaded by the orchestra; then they went dancing. Later at night they went to the casino and played at the machines and tables.

When it was time for them to go back to Paris they bought gorgeous gifts for their relatives and friends from the hotel's curio shops. They had never set foot out of the hotel's grounds. At home in Europe they described their vacation in ecstatic terms, and just raved about the pleasures of "Africa."

Relais de Cocody (Relais Aériens Français, B.P. 767, Abidjan; tel. 34-94-61) $16 single, $19 double; $23 for a bungalow; $30 for an apartment.   The Relais, another hotel in the international luxury class, is also in the residential Cocody area, a bit outside of town. The hotel is all quiet luxury, with a good deal of charm. Its rooms overlook the bay; it has a French restaurant reputed to be the best in the country, a good night club, comfortable public rooms and a fine pool, and boats for rent.

Hotel du Parc, Plateau area (B.P. 1775, Abidjan; tel. 22-23-86) $15 single, $17 double; $25 for a suite.   The Hotel du Parc is located at the absolute center of town, and part of what is happening happens here. The rooms are very nice and all that, but what this hotel has is its location and with-it atmosphere. At the heart of the Plateau, the hotel is across the street from the park, next door to the chic shopping area, near the commercial and government establishments, right near what is going on. Its sidewalk café is the spot in town for watching the white-settler world go by.

Palm Beach, Vridi Beach (B.P. 2704, Abidjan; tel. 36-81-16) $13 single, $14 double; $15 single bungalow, $17 double bungalow.   Located not far from the airport, this is a luxury motel-style resort, built on the beautiful Vridi Beach. It has tennis courts, a splendid salt-water pool and a seaside restaurant.

Tourist Class

Grand Hotel, Plateau (B.P. 1785, Abidjan; tel. 22-28-91) $10 single, $14 double.   Author's choice because of the value for its modest price, the Grand Hotel is located on a quiet Plateau street, nonetheless in the center of town. Ask for the rooms that have a view of the lagoon—a cooling sight during the day, lovelier at night. Economy-minded travelers should request the basement rooms—air-conditioned, but without a view.

Hotel de France, Treichville (B.P. 690, Abidjan; tel. 22-78-37) $10 single, $15 double.   This is a small, clean, good hotel. Being in Treichville, it is in the center of things, and is half a mile from the Plateau. A good bargain.

Lower-Cost Places

Abidjan offers budget travelers a choice of reasonably priced hotels. The quality of the accommodations vary, but in general there is no air-conditioning, and you share the john.

Hotel Terminus (Boulevard de Marseille, Treichville), across from the railroad station, has rooms for $10. Not far away is the **Hotel Palmyre** (Avenue 16, Treichville), where rooms cost around $10, are clean, and have hot water and showers. On the road to the airport you'll find the **Hotel International.** The rooms cost $12, have hot water and showers, and the hotel's restaurant serves a good $4 dinner. **Les Tourelles** (on the Bassam road) is a little place where the rooms ($5) are on the beach or surround the salt-water swimming pool.

Note: The **Mission Biblique** (in Cocody, across from the Institut National des Arts) offers the traveler a bunk bed for $3 a night in a clean, pleasant hostel. The missionaries are friendly people, who will welcome you if you have written ahead.

RESTAURANTS

Food in Abidjan is excellent. There is an abundance of locally grown produce, freshly available fish and meat, and a large selection of imported foodstuffs, so cooks have all the ingredients for delicious dishes. Rich Frenchmen and rich Africans fill the higher-priced restaurants at both lunchtime and dinnertime. The hotels offer French cooking and there are many individual French restaurants, but every sort of ethnic cuisine is also available.

Note: Nobody knows why, but in supposedly sophisticated Abidjan, all conversation stops dead each time the restaurant doors open; and everybody stops eating and talking in order to turn and stare at the newest patron. Terribly gauche, *non?* But don't let it bother you. Look around you, unseeing, until the host comes to seat you.

Hotel Restaurants

The traveler's friend, **Hotel Ivoire,** has a wide variety of eateries for your choice. They serve hamburgers and milkshakes in the bowling alley, sandwiches in the coffee shop, and full meals at the pool. A full-course dinner with wine for two in the penthouse casino can run you $30. But the bargain is a sumptuous luncheon buffet served by the pool on Sundays for $3.50 per person. Plan on paying about $6–$8 for a modest meal here, $2–$3 for snacks.

The **Relais** is famed for the excellent cuisine of its restaurant, and you can also eat at poolside. **Hotel du Parc** has a good restaurant called "Le Parc," a lower-priced cafeteria ("Le Calao"), an American-style bar, and an outdoor terrace café, where good snacks are served (try the pineapple boats). The restaurant at the **Grand Hotel** opens into a verdant courtyard; it is always popular, and serves a range of specialties of Périgord. It is worth a trip to the **Palm Beach** restaurant for the lovely oceanside location.

African Specialties

It is difficult for the traveler to find good African food in Africa. Generally, Africans are very finicky about food and prefer to eat at home. Almost all the restaurants depend on expatriate patronage, so they try to please their customers by offering familiar, European-style meals. Only here in Abidjan will you find a selection of well-located, nicely decorated African restaurants, run by Africans, catering to an international clientele.

West African

Attoungblan "Chez Tante Sally," Boulevard Delafosse, corner of Avenue 4, Treichville   Author's choice because the atmosphere is so chic and comfortable at the same time, because the clientele is so attractive, and the food so delicious. Attoungblan opens at 10 A.M. and keeps serving until midnight in this air-conditioned, charming place. All the dishes are African food. The menu features specialties from several West Coast countries: Chicken Yassa (lemon chicken with rice) is a big favorite. Everything here is great, but the beginner will especially enjoy the palm-oil sauce, the peanut-butter sauce (*mafé*), the stuffed crab and the lamb brochettes. They serve chilled palm wine (the real thing—fresh and frothy) in calebashes.

Le 421-Calalou, Avenue 2, Treichville, near the market   The Calalou is operated by a Togolese who speaks English; he will help you choose from the extensive menu. The food is first-rate, and the back room is where you want to sit.

   La Bonne Auberge (Rue 7, Avenue 5, Treichville) is not in the same class with the other two, but nonetheless serves a good meal for only $1. **Au Bon Repos** (Rue 11, Avenue 5, Treichville) is only so-so.

North African

Chez Babouilla, Rue 9, Avenue 12, Treichville   This place is so popular you will need a reservation. The Mauritanian chef prepares Moroccan dishes in the grand style. You sit on cushions on the floor, are served on chiseled brass trays, sip from wee cups of tea.

Chez Mikou, Rue 38, Avenue 8, Treichville   (*Note:* This is on the spot where the famous Nanan Yamousso's restaurant used to be; taxi drivers know it by that old name.) Delicious food in an *Arabian Nights* setting. You can eat here alone very comfortably; couples loll on the low couches. The cold Algerian salad is a winner, and their Chicken Tagine dishes are great.

Le Marrakech, Avenue 21, Treichville   Those in the know call a day ahead and order sumptuous Moroccan specialties: *méchoui farci* (a whole stuffed, roasted baby lamb), or Chicken Pastilla (a flaky, nutty, meaty pastry-crust layered confection for which the word "pie" is not adequate). Since you can't have any of these extravagences unless you have planned in advance, content yourself with the good *mouton vapeur.*

   Chez Victor (Rue 12, across from the Pharmacie Nouvelle, Plateau) serves couscous. **L'Algeria** (72 boulevard de Marseille) specializes in great Oriental pastries and a full line of Algerian wines.

Italian Food

Pizza di Sorrento, Boulevard de Marseille, across from the lagoon $4 buys a large, well-coated pizza pie that will automati-
cally put you in a good mood. You eat outdoors in a continental
atmosphere, and the food is excellent.

La Pergola, Boulevard de Marseille More good food, in a casual
atmosphere, with high prices. Try their barbecues, and their daily
specials: couscous on Sundays, paella on Thursdays.

Vietnamese and Chinese

There are more than twelve Oriental restaurants in Abidjan,
all of them good; however, portions in the Vietnamese restaurants
tend to be small.

La Baie d'Along, Boulevard Achalme, Marcory Author's choice
because the Vietnamese-style food is so good and the atmosphere so romantic. The tables are set in a garden bordering the
lagoon decorated with plants and lanterns; very pretty.

Le Dragon, next to the Paris movie theater, Plateau The chefs
come from Hong Kong and they cook excellent Chinese food.
The service is good and the portions huge, so go with a friend or
a big appetite.

Also try these places, all on the Plateau: **Le Meh Kong** (next to
the American Cultural Center), **Le Jonque d'Or** (across from the
French Cultural Center), and **Le Dalat** (12 rue Paris Village). All
are air-conditioned, fairly expensive, with good food.

French, of course

Chez Valentin, Avenue 16, Rue 23, Treichville (tel 32-47-16) The
most notable French meals are to be had at this little place. The
atmosphere is intimate and the excellent cuisine is definitely
haute. Such divine tastes and smells don't come easily or cheaply,
so remember that you must make a reservation and be prepared
to spend Paris-type prices ($20 for two with wine) for dinner.

Au Coq d'Alsace, 24 avenue Chardy, Plateau (tel. 32-10-
88) Highly recommended for good food and a bright am-

biance. There is a regular jovial crowd which comes to enjoy the hearty Alsacian specialties: pork chops, sausages and sauerkraut.

Also on the Plateau: **Au Vieux Strasbourg** (Avenue Noguès) opens at 9 A.M. and serves gourmet meals all day. **La Petite Auberge** (Rue des Dragages) offers a fixed-price menu at $8 per person(!), **La Brasserie Abidjanaise** (a few doors down from the Hotel du Parc) is very good and popular.

Other Nationalities

You can eat Lebanese style at **L'Horizon,** a good place, located at the corner of Avenue Nogues and Boulevard Botreau Roussel on the Plateau. In Treichville try the **Phonecia** (Boulevard Delafosse and Avenue 7). On the Plateau there are Spanish specialties served at **Le Méditerranée** and Greek specialties "chez Zorba" at **Le Monaco.**

Seafood

Try **Les Halles Brétonnes** (Rue 5, Avenue 16, on the road to Port-Bouët). They feature seafood, some of it air-mailed in! **La Marée** in the Plateau has a large variety of shore specialties. However, the best of the lot is the **Bar des Pêcheurs** located in Treichville near the fishing port. It is hearty, good-humored, and the seafood is sparkling fresh and well prepared.

Pastries and Sweets

If it's just pastries you want, you can buy them to take out at the **Printania** department store, but for the best ice cream with the best atmosphere, go to the **Hotel du Parc** sidewalk café. **Pâtisserie Central** on Avenue Delafosse is chock-full of delicacies. The **Brioche** is next to the Air Afrique Building, and **Mimosa** is near Pam-Pam.

Snacks and Quick Foods

At the moment the American favorite is the **Pam-Pam** (corner Avenue Chardy and Rue le Coeur, Plateau) where they serve quick sandwiches and good crepes and waffles. **Marcory Snack Bar** in Marcory has good food, inexpensive prices, and an outdoor terrace for your enjoyment. **Bar des Sports** (Avenue Général de Gaulle) has delicious, inexpensive prime steaks of Argentine beef, served in a casual atmosphere.

Feed Yourself

After all this enumeration of restaurants, the author really advises that you feed yourself! Food in Abidjan is abundant, fresh and very reasonably priced. All the markets sell a dazzling variety of fruits: melons, papayas, bananas, pineapples, grapefruit, oranges, lemons, limes, mangoes and avocados. You find greens, cucumbers, onions, tomatoes, cabbage and green beans. Certainly you should go to the excellent Abidjan restaurants—that is part of the fun of the trip—but you will be missing something if you don't rely on the markets for many of your meals. It is a good idea to eat in a casual, economical manner during the day, and then in the evening make a special occasion of a visit to a choice restaurant.

Ready-cooked: The hippest place for buying meals is at **O.N.U.** near the Treichville market. This is a cooperative of African women who sell homemade food on the street. A brochette costs about 15 cents, a barbequed chicken about $1.50. Everyone comes by here—the big cars line up at the curb and out step the fancy ladies or their chauffeurs, come to buy food to be eaten in the house later. The solitary bachelors take their plates next door to the rudimentary bar. Children spend their pennies on hot cakes, or their mothers send them to bring home a bowl of peppery stew. This is a place you can depend on.

All the supermarkets on the Plateau have excellent imported cheese, bottled water and canned goods. **Printania** has a good Parisian-style delicatessen, where they sell all manner of cold cuts, patés, salads and barbequed chicken. **Le Froid Industriel** and **Nour el Hayat** sell cooked foods, and an A & P selection of marshmallows, pickles and cake mixes.

NIGHT CLUBS

What is there to say that isn't negative? Understand these remarks as a kind of general summing up. Night-time Abidjan is corrupt, not bright and colorful. Outside of the large hotels there is no casual, informal dancing time to be had; the emphasis is on the exchange of money for certain kinds of "entertainment." All of the European *bar de nuits* are overpriced; drinks start at $3 for a shot of whiskey, and the bill mounts from there. A drink in a European cabaret is more—$4; the tab at the end of an evening is criminal. Bored Europeans are paying for white-hand service, for pitiful performers in acts called, most kindly, camp, and for an easy approach to white prostitutes.

Having said all that, here is a guide to Abidjan nightclubs:

The places on the Plateau cater to very stuffy rich Frenchmen and well-heeled visitors. The **In Club** (at Nour el Hayat) features imported French and American entertainers. At the **Submarine,** moored on the lagoon, you go down in a (real) submarine to a discotheque. The **Pussycat** is a Lebanese strip joint.

You can probably have a better time in Cocody at the **Hi-Fi** night club in the Hotel Relais and at the **Toit d'Abidjan** in the Hotel Ivoire. **L'Aiglon** and the **Country-Club** are some more names.

Things are a little better over in Treichville; at least you do have more choice, though again the rule is $4 per drink. The music tends to be better; there are often live bands, and the general atmosphere is chummier. Try the places along Avenue 16 for a variety of entertainment, and the taverns along Rue 12 for those red lights (or, as they say in those guidebooks to Paris—for a good time, tell the taxi driver to take you to "A-ven-noo Sez" or "Roo Dooz").

The **Boule Noire** is an African-style place that is visited by partying Abidjan couples. The **Fraternité Bar** and **Bar Bracodi** are considered nicer than most. The **Happy-Club** is another place, also the **Quartier Latin,** the **Kit-Kat** and the **Jour et Nuit.** Local girls who speak English and are willing to keep men company hang around the **Calypso,** the **Night-Club** and the **Emporator.** Good luck!

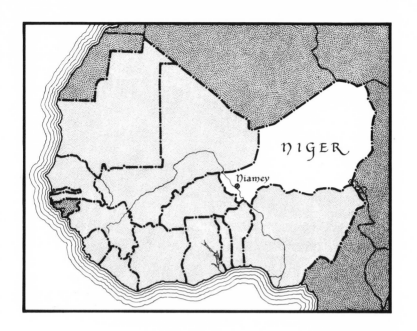

Niger

NIAMEY

In Niamey—this parched city in a country looking for water—the Niger River is a throbbing artery of movement and life. The headwaters of this 2,600 mile long river are in Guinea. From there it courses northward into Mali through Bamako and by Timbuktu; then it curves to the southeast through Gao, crossing the border into Niger. The Niger River flows three hundred miles through the southwest corner of the country. At Niamey the river is slow and muddy, carrying with it the nutrients and richness that make its delta in Nigeria an area of great prosperity.

Throughout the history of Niger, its sovereignty has been

disputed by waves of settlers and kings. In the eighth century the Toubou and Kanembou empires were founded on the shores of Lake Chad. In the sixteenth century the empire of Songhai dominated the Aïr region, and the Kanembou kingdom extended from the lake over to Zinder country. Early in the seventeenth century, the decline of the Mali empire made way for the Hausa sultanates, and the Tuareg principalities; Bornou supplanted Kanembou and established itself to the west. In the eighteenth century, the sultanate of Sokoto invaded the Hausa country and came into conflict with the Tuaregs.

European penetration by explorers began in the nineteenth century, followed by French military occupation. The country became independent in 1960 as a presidential republican regime. For a long time the country's development has lagged behind that of the rest of West Africa, due in part to colonial neglect, its location far from any coast, and the difficulty of locating viable mineral deposits. There is some tin, some iron, and some uranium, but still, external trade has only a minor influence on the economic and political structure of the country.

The country of Niger is named for the river. It is the largest country in West Africa—a huge 490,000 square miles, almost twice the size of Texas. It is completely landlocked, sharing borders with seven countries—Algeria, Libya, Mali, Upper Volta, Dahomey, Nigeria and Chad. Niger has three distinct climactic zones. In the northeastern area, an immense stretch of the Sahara desert, almost all sand and clay without oases, almost completely uninhabited. The northcentral area is characterized by the Aïr mountain range, renowned for its scenic beauty: rugged peaks with palm trees at the base, haunting rock formations and the strange *koris,* rivers which are impermanent but whose banks are lush with verdure—narrow green ribbons across the sands. Cave paintings tell of a time when the climate was more clement and the area was filled with wild life. The third area is the monotonous flat plateau of the south, where Niamey stands.

The Niger River is an implacable presence in Niamey. You get to know the river by going to it at different times of the day, and to different locations along its length. During the day it is sluggish and stolid, as brown as the soil it leaches. This river, the same color as the earth, seems as firm as its banks. As sunset approaches, the river is a palette of deep reds and purples, browns and golds. The view changes from minute to minute and seems to flood the spirit and psyche. Sky and river, then buildings and vegetation take up each nuance of color, play with it, turn it, then absorb it the instant a new shade emerges and shines. The effect is hypnotic, a spell cast by the play of light.

Walking or riding along the riverside for a couple of miles, you can see the variety of life. By day, the river is hyperactive. It is filled with canoes transporting fruits and vegetables from the truck gardens on the other side of the river. At one spot a large number of men come every day to wash the clothes and linens of private homes and institutions. Soaped clothes are slapped against the rocks to loosen the dirt, rinsed and wrung out. Then they are laid upon the banks, a Klee painting of vivid colored squares, spreading for blocks along the river. The washermen are boisterous and teasing. A joke will convulse the whole group, or they may shout and sing back and forth. How does the brown water give white sheets? Somehow, it does.

The John F. Kennedy Bridge spans the river right in the center of town; before it opened in 1971 all traffic crossed the river by boat or ferry. Following the riverside road you can get close to the villages along the bank, with their small gardens and mango trees. The road then rises and doubles back and mounts to the Plateau area of governmental and diplomatic buildings.

Estimates vary of the population of Niamey, but it is probably about 42,000, with more people arriving every day from the vast hinterlands. The newcomers tend to move into an urban agglomeration with houses made of woven straw, known as Boukouki—an area on the edge of town. Here for the first time different ethnic groups meet and mix: Djermas, Tuaregs, Hausas, Bellas and Foulahs all live together. They come from the countryside and settle among their own people until they can adjust to life in the city.

In Boukouki absolutely no vegetation can be seen and animals outnumber men. There are tens of thousands of camels, horses, sheep and bullocks. Life here revolves around the care of the animals. If you come during the morning the whole place seems deserted, but comes alive in the later afternoon as the animals return; in the evening the whole area is animated by the trade and exchange in beasts and cattle. It is a brown and dusty world in Boukouki, with attachment to family and livestock.

After you have gone along the riverside and after you have visited Boukouki, you may want to see the market place in the center of town. Niamey is a lean city, so its market is far from opulent. The wealthy merchants are magnificent in appearance: enviably resplendent in their immaculate, starched robes; serenely serious about their property. Desert blankets woven in geometric patterns are the most substantial items for sale, but if you wish you can buy a Niger-made bed, a confection of iron, painted in blue and gold, decorated with flowers and adorned with little mirrors.

Among the more conspicuous groups at the market are the Yoruba engaged in selling pomades and talcum powder, storm lamps and padlocks. They have done well in Niamey because they are careful to develop businesses that serve a definite need and do not compete with older established groups. They come from the poorest of the Yoruba people, pushed by the overcrowding and unemployment at home in neighboring Nigeria, and by the competition from their better educated, more affluent countrymen. They come to Niger for opportunity, to earn money, to save and to build a substantial cement house in their hometowns in Nigeria, as a symbol of their industry and success.

Technically, only the central state banks can make financial transfers, and at this writing neither the currency of Niger nor of Nigeria is easily convertible on the open market. The interested parties have a system, illegal, that works well, benignly overlooked by the authorities. The key man is the cattle broker, called the *dillali,* who moves freely back and forth across the Niger/Nigeria border. He is at once trader, moneychanger and banker. This is how it works: a Yoruba in Niamey gives the Niger francs he has earned to the broker; a Niger shepherd walks his cattle over the border to Nigeria and sells them to the broker, who then sells his newly acquired cattle to northern Nigerian slaughterhouses for Nigerian money. The broker pays the shepherd in francs—the francs he got from the Yoruba man—and gives the Nigerian money to the Yoruba trader. The broker makes his profit, the Niger shepherd has his money in francs, and the Yoruba has his money in pounds (niara) he can use back home in Nigeria. It is profitable for everyone involved; transactions and all businesses have been conducted in a "climate of total and reciprocal confidence" among people who for the most part can neither read nor write.

*   *   *

*The stars have guided your steps to
the right place.
Your presence among us lightens our
hearts.
You are our friend.
Our towns and villages open their
arms to you.*

This is the poem that greets the traveler when he arrives at the airport. It prepares you for all the lovely people you will meet. Stated simply, the people in Niamey are very, very nice. Even in Africa, where men and women are usually courteous and hospitable, the people of Niger are known to be especially gracious and especially refined.

You ask your desk clerk if you have received a letter. He will never give you a straight negative answer; rather, he will say that the letter isn't there yet but surely it is on its way. Did you get a phone call while you were out? Well, there's no message in your box, but sometimes it is hard to get a dial tone, or else probably the person who was trying to call you found the line busy, so he will surely *call again.*

A person keeps appointments, and on time. Someone is always there with a pleasant word or a helping hand. No one will ask you prying questions or comment on your figure or your suitcase. No one is eying your travelers checks or your wrinkled pants. With any indication at all that you are coming, the hotel car will be waiting for you, no hard hustling or being pushed around.

Honestly, no one is going to try to cheat you or take advantage of you. But do *you* know how to behave? The tourist is in the store to buy some fruit and is vexed to find that prices are so high. When she asks why fruit is so expensive, the clerk replies that all of them are imported, from Dahomey, the Ivory Coast or France. So, she asks, where are the fruits from Niger?—a land without water, land of dry-bottomed wells, land of thorns. He explains that there are none; she insists that there must be *something* from Niger. He tells her no again. What, no fruit!—but now she stops. He has turned away in pain, embarrassed for the country's deficiencies, sorry about the exhorbitant prices; she has actually hurt his feelings—he is not defiant, only sad to have no answer.

The most beautiful attraction of Niamey is the **Niger National Museum,** a 60-acre cultural park sprawling in the center of town. All of the Niger National Museum is a marvel; it is simply the best in its class. The way the Museo de Antropología of Mexico City is a star, so the Niamey museum is a model for all other African museums, an unsurpassed example of what can be accomplished with imagination and a clear philosophy of beauty and goodness, even when times are hard and money scarce. As a tourist you can roller-skate through the Louvre, or you can take it easy. This once, here in Niamey, give a museum a lot of time.

The Niger National Museum is a microcosm of life in this huge land of half a million square miles. The museum is an immense park containing all manner of gardens and exhibitions. The director has gathered all the traditional and popular arts of the Niger people—their clothing, jewelry, tools, musical instruments, architecture—and displayed them to show their value and beauty and potential. Everyone goes to the museum all the time. Townspeople come every day; the young splash in the pools and showers of the children's park and attend outdoor classes to learn the history and culture of their land; older people stroll through the exhibits. Hundreds of young boys come in groups by themselves, grave and respectful, dazzled and fascinated by the spectacles. When there are important visitors, or on the occasion of national holidays, dignitaries hold receptions and parties on the museum grounds because the setting is so lovely.

Once you have been close to a giraffe out in the open and once the giraffe has actually looked at you, *noticed you* and puzzled over you, you may feel different about your approach to things. Even though all your life you have sneered at all that East African safari bunkum—here, being stared at by a giraffe, you may feel a thrill of

204

a certain primacy, of the acknowledgment of your own "creature-ness" and the volatility of the power in front of you. For wild animals *are* powerful, their reflexes are sharp and their muscles are coiled to spring. They are bigger and stronger and swifter than we are, and just as unpredictable.

At the museum you can ask the gamekeeper to take you into the twelve-acre area where gentler animals—antelope, giraffe, ostriches, buffalo—range free. Instead of looking at them from a safe distance across a protective barrier, you are *with* them—it's a whole new sensation. And it all makes you yearn finally to go to a game park, without camera and without gun, to *be* there only, relying on the nobility of the beasts to allow your presence.

Aside from the unusual animal enclosure, the other most striking exhibits are the various habitations of the people of Niger: a traditional Songhai compound, a rural habitat of the Djerma, a Hausa country dwelling and a town house made of adobe and painted in different colors, homes of the Foulah and the Bilma. You can also see the tents of the nomadic people—the Kourtei, Wogo, Tuareg. Each dwelling is true and authentic and complete, and you can enter each one and poke around to your heart's content.

Admission is free, and though the exhibition halls close at 5 P.M., the grounds stay open until dark. The average number of visitors is 360,000 per year, eight times the population of Niamey itself! Every day it has a crowd. People come from every corner of the country because they are made to feel that the museum is *theirs*, and it is about them and their lives. The tourist thus has the added experience of seeing a broad cross section of the Niger's citizens as they learn about the diversity and unity of their own country. The boy from the sand dunes stands spellbound by the water sport of the hippos; the shepherd stares at his enemies—the jackal and the hyena; and the city mother listens to the recordings of the tales and songs of the river. Together they visit their nation's museum, and together they develop a sense of a new national community, proud of its diverse heritage.

Observation: The Curio Shop   In West Africa there are tractors stalled because fuel hasn't come, and there are markets unwashed because a part of a pipe is missing. Schools whose books have never arrived stand next to hospitals awaiting necessary equipment and medication. But wherever you go in West Africa, from Dakar to Lagos, you find the trader's display of the rug made in Mali, the mask made in the Ivory Coast, the ironwork made in Upper Volta, distributed efficiently, silently, across a span of six thousand miles.

Avocados rot in the harbor, rice piles up on the shore, typewriters still crated lie in a corner, and penicillin boils in the sun. Yet, down the road bumps the latest shipment from Senegal of crocodile handbags, lizard wallets, seed-bead necklaces and cowrie-shell belts—unmarred from the journey, never forgotten, never misplaced.

Whenever you go to a souvenir shop or stall, stand and conjecture for a moment about the savvy and sweat that went into bringing this whole collection together. Fake Senufo masks from the Ivory Coast, small iron Mossi figures, Malian prayer rugs, painted Mauritanian pouches, charms and amulets from Senegal, horn birds from Guinea, Dahomean appliqué work, gold weights from Ghana, leather purses, metal medallions, gray-and-black paintings of village scenes, pipe-cleaner dancers sketched in colored paint on black art paper, huge slave anklets, Nigerian bronzes, along with, of course, the ivory tobacco holders—all of them laid out artfully for your selection.

As you approach you will be greeted, depending on the cut of your clothes, in French, English, maybe German. "Come and see, nice lady," they implore. "Look here, look here." If your eye so much as lights on a particular purse, or ashtray or fur rug, the trader grabs it and comes running. You will be cajoled, wheedled, flattered and conned. "The price one thousand francs; pay eight hundred, seven hundred for you, don't walk away, tell me what you pay."

Most of the merchants are partners in a company, formed usually in collaboration with a family member, brother or cousin. This small company is part of a larger ethnic trade organization in that particular town and is joined to a West Coast–wide network of importers and exporters. Take time to chat with some traders. They are usually men of charm and sophistication who have a sharp eye for subtleties of feeling and behavior. They enjoy good conversation and spirited bargaining and have a sense of the sardonic and the wry.

In addition to all the skills you bring to bargaining, and no matter how triumphant you feel about your purchase, be gracious. The merchant's margin of profit is small, and the number of his dependents is large.

* · * *

GETTING AROUND

No public transportation or railroads, so expect to get around by taxi in the city; they charge a flat rate of about 35 cents. You can rent airplanes and all manner of cars with or without chauffeur. There are only a few hundred miles of asphalted roads in Niger, so long trips are made over sand or laterite tracks and require a robust vehicle. The Tourist Office has Land-Rovers for rough trips into the interior.

THINGS TO DO

Swimming

Yes, you're on the edge of the desert, and yes, water is precious, and yes, there are five swimming pools in Niamey! There is one at the **Grand Hotel,** at the **Terminus Hotel,** and at the **Roniers.** There is an Olympic-sized municipal pool near the **Hotel du Sahel,** and a military pool on the banks of the Niger open to tourists.

Horseback Riding

There are three riding clubs in town, and you can rent a horse for about $1.50 an hour.

Flying Club

The flying club has two Jodels (seating three passengers) that Mr. Dahout will rent to you for about $50 per flying hour.

Horse Racing

The races, attended by prosperous merchants and a colorful gambling crowd, are usually held on Sunday afternoon. It's a stimulating event with some good-looking horses.

Sailing Club

You'll have to know someone to get invited. They have water-skiing and sailing on the Niger for members and guests.

Movies

At the French and American cultural centers practically every night in the week.

EXCURSIONS

Say

You can spend a very nice day on a visit to this village, 36 miles south of the capital. There is a good ali-weather road from Niamey, and in an hour you are there. Go on a Friday morning to visit the market. If you have reserved beforehand you can have a delicious lunch of Nigerian couscous waiting at the rest house. In the afternoon you can take a boat ride on the Niger. At this part of the river there are numerous wooded islets where you can stop. You will be astounded by the aquatic life—herons, storks, pelicans, ducks and geese.

Tillabéri

Tillabéri is about 90 miles to the north of Niamey on good road that touches the river along the way. The town itself is the center of a grain-growing area, but you came to see the animals: the road leads to a large stretch of savannah where great numbers of giraffes wander freely, pay no attention to tourists and let themselves be approached and photographed, especially in the morning and evening when they go to the river to drink.

Ayorou

Air Afrique or the Tourist Office will help you arrange a two-day excursion to Ayorou, an attractive village 25 miles north on the Tillabéri Road, beyond Tillabéri, near the Mali border. You drive there on a Saturday afternoon in a comfortable car, and upon your arrival you will find a well-appointed camp with a fine table ($3.50 a night for a bed, $3.50 a meal). The camp is situated on the banks of the Niger River, and from its terrace at sundown you enjoy the extraordinary skies of this part of the world. (If it is a fine night, why not sleep out under the stars—the camp will arrange it for you.)

In the morning you can take a canoe or a motorboat on the Niger from a nearby post and go looking for the hippopotami that bathe in the river. On the way back, visit the island of Firgoun and its Songhai village. The main attraction of the trip is the Sunday afternoon market. All the desert ethnic groups are represented— Tuaregs, Djermas, Foulahs. They travel great distances on donkey and camel, on foot and horseback for a weekly festival of trade, food, stories, contests and gossip.

W National Park

This territory, 100 miles south of Niamey, is a 3,800-square-mile national game park named for the shape of the double bend of the Niger River which meanders through. This is a very picturesque region: the topography varies from scrubland to mountain range; there are jagged gorges and raging torrents; elephants, gazelles, lions, buffalo and monkeys wander freely, and a world of big and small birds walk, swim, ride or fly by. Air Afrique or the Tourist Office will help you plan your excursion, but you will need three days to really look around. Comfortable living accommodations are available on the site.

Agadès

Anyway you look at it, a trip to this town in the middle of the desert requires planning and forethought. The easiest way to get there is by combining it with your trip to Niamey. If you are planning on flying from Niamey, the fare alone will come to around $200 round trip—remember, the distances are immense. Or, like Ama McHardy, you may find yourself there after crossing the desert, for Agadès is one of the stations on Trans-Saharan Route Three, the Hoggar Route; it starts at Algiers, continues through Agadès to Zinder, then ends at Niamey. In fact, when you are in Agadès you may find some young adventurers waiting to get on a truck that will take them north up to the Mediterranean.

Agadès is charming and strange. It is an ancient site whose documented history goes back to time immemorial, to the dim past when the area was not yet desert but a humid steppe inhabited by abundant game and strong hunters. As the land dried, cattle became the way of life. Now it is full Sahara, a difficult challenge to its denizens. The Agadès you see now dates from medieval days. Its mosque, first built in the 1500s, still stands, a sugar loaf eighty-eight feet high. See the market, its picturesque square and the sultan's palace. There are two hotels: 1) **Hotel de l'Air** (tel. 347), facing the mosque. Several of its twelve rooms are air-conditioned and will cost you around $12 a night; 2) the older, **Hotel Boudon,** has non-air-conditioned rooms for $4 a night.

At Agadès you are at the gateway to the whole Aïr mountain region. Air Afrique will help you arrange a Land-Rover trip that will take you to see the magnificent countryside with its rock paintings thousands of years old, ancient mosques, desert-palm groves and caravans of hospitable nomads.

SHOPPING

National Museum Shop—Niamey

Make this your first stop, because if they don't have the article you need, it can be made to your order in a few days by the men you see at work in the open-air studios. The shop has a beautiful display of local handicrafts: silver jewelry, sandals, handbags, musical instruments. They show the famous *croix d'Agadès,* a cross in silver. Author's choices are the gorgeous complicated Niger chest locks and the beautiful riding boots. Everything here is of government-controlled quality and fine taste.

Hotel Stalls

Traders set up shop outside all the hotels—at the **Grand Hotel** there is a large shelter for the tables. Remember that the things they sell all come from outside Niger, so if you are traveling back to the coast you will be better off buying there. Still, good for bargaining and conversation. If you've grown to love giraffes, buy a little brass one as a souvenir.

HOTELS

The hotels in Niamey are generally good. Because the Nigeriens have this remarkable graciousness, the service is generally patient and warm-spirited. (*Note:* Niamey hotels all give breakfast included in base price.)

Grand Hotel du Niger (B.P. 471, Niamey; tel. 26-41, 42)   Fully air-conditioned, $22 single, $24 double, with private shower or bath. International standing.   This is a beautifully designed place, part of the Relais Aériens chain. It is clean, well kept, the gardens are lovely, the view over the river is spellbinding and the restaurant has fine French food (expensive, though—$8 a meal).

Hotel du Sahel (B.P. 627, Niamey; tel. 30-31)   All rooms have twin beds and are centrally air-conditioned. $17 single, $19 double.   The Sahel is an interesting little hotel on the river. Author's choice. The design is simple and in good taste; the staff is remarkably accommodating. The Sahel comes alive at night when its terrace hosts the most popular restaurant in town. It serves delicious, cheap ($1.80) pizza pies and good barbecue, and the crowds come in on weekends. Close to the municipal swimming pool.

Hotel Terminus (B.P. 882, Niamey; tel. 22-52) $10–$15 for air-conditioned rooms; $7–$9 for non-air-conditioned.   Everything about this hotel is good but the rooms. The restaurant is regarded as the best French restaurant in town; its prices are reasonable. The hotel has a good pool, a garden featuring an artificial waterfall(!), and a location in the center of town. But the rooms leave much to be desired, because they are dark.

Hotel Rivoli (B.P. 87, Niamey; tel. 25-09) Completely air-conditioned. $12 single, $17 double. Downtown in the middle of things, near the museum.

Hotel les Roniers (B.P. 795, Niamey, tel. 31-38 and 34-32) Bungalows and air-conditioned rooms, $17 single, $20 double. A clubby old French atmosphere in this small, impeccable hotel that is a bit out of town. Features a small gymnasium and facilities for tennis, riding and swimming; this is a resort spot. French cooking.

RESTAURANTS

The best food is served in the hotels, but there is still a good selection in town. Several places serve Vietnamese specialities: the **Baie d'Along** has the best reputation and the highest prices; **Au Saïgon, La Pagode** and **Le Viet-Nam** also serve Asian food. **La Flotille** has Russian dishes, and the *Tip-Top* has brochettes and hot dogs. The **Épi d'Or** has hamburgers and banana splits and **Chez Nelly** is popular for its good dinners at $2.50.

Note: The U.S. Embassy canteen for local staff serves lunches of good African food made by a temperamental Nigerian chef; you get a generous serving of meat, sauce and rice for about 50 cents. He also makes hamburgers, and other stateside stuff.

NIGHT CLUBS

Downstairs at the Sahel Hotel you'll find the **Fo-Fo Club.** Good stereo system, loud music, low temperatures, teeny dance floor, good-looking expatriate crowd paying $3 a drink. **Harry's Club** is well decorated, and like the **Hi-Fi Club,** it is in the middle of town. They both feature recorded music, light shows, and drinks at $2.50.

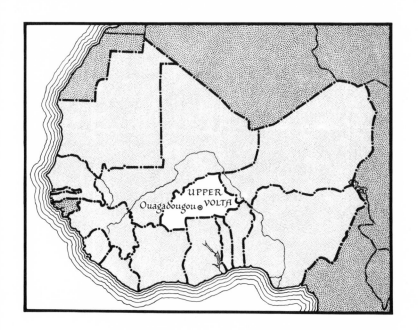

Upper Volta

OUAGADOUGOU

Tradition has it that many years ago when the Mossi were about to go to war with a neighboring people, the king (called the *Moro-Naba*) was asked by his favorite wife for permission to visit her family a distance away. The king agreed, giving her instructions to return no later than a given date. When the time was up—it was a Thursday—the beloved one still had not returned home. The next morning at sunrise the *Moro-Naba* ordered his horse to be saddled, for he intended to set out to bring her back. However, the war was about to break out and his people begged him not to leave them. In his heart he yearned to recover his wife; instead he descended from his horse and stayed in his castle: his first duty was to protect his subjects.

At 7 A.M. on Fridays, the *Moro-Naba,* ruler of the Mossi, re-enacts this ritual of the monarch's commitment to matters of state over those of the heart. Robed in red, he leaves his room just before sunrise. He then re-enters the house and comes out again, dressed in white, as soon as dawn breaks. His captains surround his horse, and he climbs into the saddle despite their tears and supplications. But at the very last minute, he renounces his desires and makes his way sadly back into the house.

The *Moro-Naba* is selected by the elders from the outstanding men of the royal family. And today's *Naba* continues a kingly line of rulers unbroken by a thousand years. Two and a half million of his subjects live around him in an area fanning out from Ouagadougou (pronounced waa-ga-*doo*-goo). A million more live in Niger, Dahomey, the Ivory Coast and Guinea. In olden days the crown was immensely wealthy and the king lived in splendor and pomp. Today his circumstances are more modest, but he remains the undisputed traditional ruler of great spiritual influence.

Founded around A.D. 1000, the Mossi kingdom is distinguished for its remarkable cohesion and unique longevity in West African history. Since early medieval days its states have been famed for their high degree of internal, political and social organization, and for their military art. Their earlier wealth was based on very profitable and extensive foreign trade, for their strategic position on the savannah allowed the Mossi kings to act as intermediaries between the northern deserts and the southern forest regions. Salt was imported from the north to be exchanged for kola nuts, cowrie shells and gold from the south. Skilled Mossi blacksmiths manufactured iron farm implements and axes which were sent south to Dahomey, the Ivory Coast and Ghana; and their herdsmen exported horses, cattle, donkeys and sheep. The king himself had a firm control over the trade routes, and for centuries the state coffers were filled by duty on goods passing through the country and by tolls guaranteeing secure, unobstructed passage along the roadways.

The young men of the *Moro-Naba*'s court are great horsemen, but they appear publicly only on ceremonial occasions, when horses and the riders are outfitted in medieval splendor. Depending on rank, the men wear embroidered tunics studded with ritual amulets, wide pants and richly ornamented leather riding boots. They wear helmets encircled with cowrie shells, and they carry unsheathed swords. Their horses are richly caparisoned in quilted clothes; saddles are decorated with metals and with designs pyro-etched in leather. Their display-in-movement is dramatic and colorful. They parade the colors in formation, then perform a series of feats. Beautifully trained horses dance and prance to the music of horns and drums. They walk on their hind legs, doing all manner of fancy stops and turns to the delight of the crowd, finally bowing in appreciation of applause. Others are sport horses that carry their riders in competition in dueling and jousting, racing and jumping. It is a show for today rooted in the pageantry of the Middle Ages.

Upper Volta is another of the landlocked West African countries. It is bordered by Mali to the west and Niger to the east, and by the Ivory Coast, Ghana, Togo and Dahomey to the south. It is named for the three Volta rivers that creep too slowly through the land—the Black, White and Red Voltas. The population is estimated at 5,250,000, on 100,000 square miles, making Upper Volta one of the most densely populated countries in West Africa. Most of its citizens are subsistance farmers, raising grain crops in small villages. Only a few farmers raise cotton crops for export. A large group of pastoralists raises livestock—horses, cattle, sheep and goats—some of which is for export too.

Economic experts make studies that statistically "prove" that Upper Volta simply should not exist! Areas created by European power politics and kept dependent on European economics are now criticized because they don't have sufficient resources to go it alone. Its poverty? Its "viability" as a state? A sure-of-himself political scientist thinks this country "a joke," an entity that was never meant to be self-supporting. It isn't. Upper Volta is poor, it is without a seaboard and without river connections to the coast. Its lands are dry and unyielding, the conditions of life are harsh. It depends on aid from a variety of foreign sources and from the money sent back by Voltains who work abroad. Its cattle by the thousands, its men by the hundreds of thousands annually take the road to Ghana and to the Ivory Coast; they are Upper Volta's "main exports." Strange, but in the world that preceded colonial and neocolonial domination, the area of Ouagadougou was renowned for its statecraft and prosperity.

Today's downtown Ouagadougou has a peculiar kind of institutional emptiness. Administrative buildings march up the central boulevard, alike in their hard-edged anonymity. Behind the straight lines and right angles of the main avenue, you'll find the Africa you came looking for if you head for the market place. It pulsates, it moves; it has those hot colors and savory smells that will forever be associated in your mind with the word "Africa." You move toward the glass box of cakes—little orange pound, homemade and baked in an outdoor stone oven; the chubby woman selling them is aglow with delight at meeting you.

Certainly in Ouaga you sense the structure, the order, the cohesion. That shock of colors and textures mixed with the reserve. The shiny eyes, ready smiles and gracious manners combined with the dignified aloofness. Traditional society in its strength and spiritual depth survived in this area, and you do feel yourself to be in a strong, black land.

Because the country's desperate young men, forced to leave their villages for economic reasons, have gone south to seek their fortune—to Accra, Abidjan or Kumasi—you don't see those youngsters, so common elsewhere in West Africa, who are the wanderers of the city, living on handouts, chasing after small jobs. Everything here is much more under control.

If you will pay a visit to the Tourist Office in the row of offices at the Hotel Indépendance, you will be given maps and directions on how to get around. While you are at the office you get the chance to stare up close at some Voltaic beauties. The personnel keeps changing, of course, but at one time they had a *bijou* behind the counter. Her face was embroidered with tattoos—there were four fine black lines from under her lip to the edge of her chin, four more at the two corners of her mouth, more between her eyes. The effect was devastating, articulating the expressive parts of the face—the eyes and mouth, enhancing their brown roundness with black exclamation points. Most African peoples have traditions of beautifying the body with markings, tattoos and scars as well as a huge variety of beads and bangles. But Voltaic people are known for the extraordinary markings in their faces—fine-lined and intricate designs.

Observation: The Crocodile Pool at Sabou   At the suggestion of the beauty in the Tourist Office, you are off to the town of Sabou to see the pool of sacred crocodiles. In a poem to his mother in his book *The African Child,* Camara Laye tells of his mother's calm wading among the crocodiles in their home village in Guinea. In northern Ghana too, at Paga, there is a pool of tame crocodiles. So there are a few places where men and beast live in some sort of equilibrium.

At Sabou you find the pool, fishermen are working in the water, and there are children playing and splashing on the side. The crocodiles are venerated by the villagers. Legend says the spirits of the villagers reside in the crocodiles: for every man in the village there is one crodocile; when a man is born a crocodile is born, and when a man passes away a crocodile dies.

An older boy knows best how to handle the crocodiles for the wonderment of visitors. He ties a baby chick into a string and carries it with him into the water. When he is out a distance he beats the water with the frantic little bird, until, in a little while, it happens. Up from the bottom of the pool, up from near where the boy is standing surfaces the crocodile. Yes, they look just like they do in cages in zoos, only this one is *here*—huge, scaly, long spiked tail, fierce steel-trap jaws. The boy backs out of the water, teasing and enticing him with the chick; the crocodile follows to the shore, snapping his monstrous mouth at the dangling bait. The game is over; you have seen the show; the boy throws the morsel to the clanging teeth. The crocodile rears up, grunts his satisfaction, then slowly backs into the water and once again sinks out of sight.

Personal reflection: You really have to be game for this kind of thing. My conviction in dealing with all fauna—from bug to beast—is that *everything bites,* and that every bite is somewhat poisonous. (A healthy man can go into a coma after a bee sting!) Now, also, by nature, I believe in *everything* (without looking for a "scientific explanation"), and I'm sure that everything is true for *someone.* So tell me it's a sacred pool of sacred crocodiles and I will go along with you. Inconsistencies we all have plenty. But something happens to us all on a trip; we become fearless and sure-footed, more willing to take a fling, to gamble with danger, to shrug off the possibility of disaster. It follows, then, that there are pictures of my holding a huge python because the herpetologist assured the group I was with that it was OK. And, yes, I've actually patted a holy croco. However, *never* in my wildest moments would I ever *wade* into a lake, no matter how sacred. One, I don't know the condition of the water, and two, I might accidentally go *walking* on something, or I might kick a reptile inadvertently, and he might take offense.

* * *

Unfortunately, few tourists think of coming to Upper Volta despite the perspective it offers on the history and personality of the powerful savannah states. If you are on one of the many study tours and chartered planes that go to Ghana every year, it is easy to make the trip to Upper Volta. Once you are in Ghana you invariably travel to Kumasi. Well, the trip from Kumasi to Ouaga is only a few hours over good roads. At the Kumasi bus depot there is comfortable government transport to the town of Paga (with its pool of sacred crocodiles!), and from Paga over the border to Ouaga it is $5 per person in a group taxi. As simple and direct as that.

Upper Volta is different from Ghana or Dahomey, or any other coastal nations. It is the heart of the land, on the crossroads of the old World. The country is dry and open, the atmosphere less dense, more spacious. The tall slimness, the horses, Islam, vibrant artistic traditions—all give it a different look, that elegance of "the North."

LEISURE AND PLEASURE

In the morning
—Get invited to the Aéro-Club (telephone 21-03, or write ahead to B.P. 61) and get an aerial view.
—Find the riding club, and see things from horseback.
In the afternoon
—Swim in the pool at the Buffet Hotel or play bumper pool (water volleyball).

—Play tennis at the Hotel Indépendance.

In the evening

—Go to the Marché du Soir (Koulouba Market)—a stroll among the lantern lights.

GETTING AROUND

Taxis

There is no public transportation in Ouaga, but taxis are cheap (around 20 cents a ride) and plentiful, and the drivers are unusually courteous and obliging. You can even make appointments to be picked up if you wish. If you are traveling alone, the Tourist Office will help you by giving the driver directions and working out a price for you. (Roads, by the way, get pretty bad during the July-to-September rainy season.)

Planes

Air Volta will rent you a six-seater Cherokee at about $150 per flying hour to take you to the small landing strips near hunting areas.

Railroads

There is an excellent train service from Ouagadougou. You can go to Bobo-Dioulasso for about $9 in first class, to Bouaké in the central Ivory Coast for $22 and to the capital of the Ivory Coast, Abidjan, for $29, or $43 in a sleeper.

PLACES TO VISIT

Bois de Bologne Area

Right on the edge of town, two miles from the center, is a large wooded area known as the Bois de Bologne, named for the park in Paris. It is an oasis in a dry city. There are nice winding walks and a coolness from the reservoir lakes it contains. At night before you are taken to your hotel your host may drive you around the lake for a look at the reflections and for the evening breeze—it is the kind of place where people cruise for a few minutes of refreshment and air.

Ethnographic Museum

The Mossi, the Bobo and the other ethnic groups of Upper Volta cultivate and train excellent artists. Even the poorest villages conduct dancing, drumming and masquerade performances and ceremonies as part of the year-round cycle of religious and social assemblies and festivals. The sculpture used—statues, marionettes, trophies, masks, musical instruments—is of great artistry and profound meaning. The museum has a small but fine collection.

Moro-Naba Ceremony

Admission is by appointment *only* (telephone 22-39 or inquire at the Tourist Office). The ceremony is held Friday mornings at seven o'clock. This is not a tourist attraction, but a meeting of the king's court and an opportunity for him to see his subjects. (The ceremony is not held *every* Friday, and may no longer be open to the public.)

Central Market

Ouagadougou Market is one of the best you'll see. It is clean, well organized, filled with a wide variety of goods, frequented by courteous crowds.

Cultural Centers

The **Centre Cultural Américain** and the **Centre Cultural Franco-Voltaïque,** both on Avenue Binger, show movies at night during the week, and maintain the usual reading rooms and range of activities.

The National **Maison du Peuple** is the scene of big-deal happenings: sporting events, visiting orchestras and performers.

EXCURSIONS

Sabou and Koudougou

Sabou you know about. Koudougou is the center of a religious sect known for its harsh puritanism and the intricacy of its rites and rituals. At certain times of the year they display some peculiar artifacts, new sacred buildings and organized dancing.

Po Hunting Reserve

This 120-mile trip takes you right into big-game territory—elephant, lion, buffalo, boar and antelope. If you are fortunate you may come at the right time to see some local dancing in the neighboring villages. Ask to see the pottery made by local craftsmen. You leave Ouaga early in the morning and are back by nightfall. Air Afrique or the Tourist Office will help you plan the trip.

Arly Park

The Arly Camp, 320 miles east of Ouagadougou, is near a pass through which the Arly River crosses the Gobnangu range of sandstone mountains. It includes one of Africa's most extraordinary zoological and botanical parks. Huge watering holes are scattered far apart, and the animals are free to wander as they wish. This is the real thing; a rich game area abounding in gazelles, water buffaloes, wild boars, giant horse-antelopes, and lions, lions and more lions.

Inspired by the traditional housing of the neighboring Gurmanché farmers, the camp itself is a model of fine simple design, rustic but clean and comfortable. There is also a completely air-conditioned hotel nearby.

This trip takes two days. You leave on an Air Volta Cherokee that takes you to the park. The fee of $120 covers the plane trip, room and meals, and cost of admission to the park. Alas, teachers, you can make this trip only from December through April.

SHOPPING

Upper Volta crafts are outstanding and its ethnic arts are consistent masterpieces. Everything is good. Even the fakes are first quality! Admittedly that supermarket mentality (otherwise known as Mexican silver malaise) does go to work on you: you see so many things that are alike that their impact is dulled and their specialness obscured. So keep imagining how extraordinary they will look as choice possessions, well highlighted and displayed.

Centre de Formation Féminine et Artisanale, on the Bobo road, near the *château d'eau* (water tower)

Author's choice as the first stop on any shopping tour of Ouaga. This is a school and training center for young women who produce a variety of handcrafted articles. The extraordinary finds here are the thick pile rugs made entirely by hand. Only natural vegetable dyes are used to obtain the rich earth colors; the patterns are adaptations of traditional designs; and the rugs are woven on the school looms. The rugs are deep and have that "sensuous something," all at low prices for high quality. The young girls also make handwoven cotton tablecloth sets embroidered with traditional motifs, and exquisitely finished outfits for baby rajahs. This is where the government usually comes to buy presentation gifts for visiting dignitaries. Shipping is a bit of a problem, but they will do their best. (This was formerly a private school run by nuns, so your taxi driver may know the spot as the *"mission catholique."*)

Stalls at the Buffet Hotel

These are permanent booths extending around the corner of the hotel. Take your time, look, savor, appreciate. Admire the masks, statues, craft objects. Sure, many things look alike, but some may nevertheless be authentic, i.e., made for use in traditional religious ceremonies. Look at the bronzes and the baskets. One of the specialties of this area is the series of charming little painted bronze statuettes made to represent each of the crafts—carpentry, ironwork, etc.

Hotel Indépendance Bloc

There are three shopping places here: the Government Tourist Office, a private antique dealer (this man and his nephew also run the stall at the airport)—both entrances on the street; and a gift counter in the lobby of the hotel proper.

The Tourist Office has a small but choice collection of crafts. They are an outlet for a leatherworking cooperative, so they sell the fire-engraved leather skins made into game boards. You may find some original batik tableaux here—ask; and they have lots of information on where else to go for what. The antique/craft store has its ups and downs, depending on the season and the shipments. Should you spy something you like, this is the place and time to use all your bargaining skills. Haggle mercilessly. Play it to the hilt. The merchant never loses. The gift counter in the hotel has mediocre, overpriced stuff. Maybe it's better by now, so take a look for yourself.

Strolling around

The scared young man carried the five-foot-high Bobo sculpture into the office of the museum director, offering it for sale for $100. The museum didn't even have that much in its coffers so the young man went out into the street with his treasure. The piece was remarkable, a masterpiece, sneaked out of the village, out onto the open market. If you should happen to see a beautiful piece go by, it is probably the real thing, taken from the rich caches of traditional art in use in the villages. A great purchase if you can afford it.

Near the market place you'll see all kinds of things. If someone offers you a pair of embroidered riding boots and they fit, consider buying them because they are sure to give you great pleasure.

HOTELS

Hotel Indépendance, Avenue Ouezzin Coulibaly (B.P. 127, Ouagadougou; tel. 27-20)   Completely air-conditioned. $15 single, $20 double; $30 for bungalows.   Sorry, but there just are too many structural flaws in this building, and the furnishings are flimsy, so this hotel never meets international standards as intended. The public rooms, pool, etc., are pleasant and good to visit. But check your room before moving in.

Buffet Hotel, Avenue Binger (B.P. 62, Ouagadougou; tel. 23-80)   All rooms have two beds and bath. $15.   Excellent small hotel, best of its type. Well-designed rooms, fine service, spotless and pleasant. Pretty pool, a nice bar and central location.

Hotel Riccardo (B.P. 439, Ouagadougou; tel. 21-75)   Located at the side of Dam #2. All air-conditioned; pool. $10. A pleasant little place located in a lovely wooded setting. The atmosphere is festive and the rooms comfortable. They offer a motorboat service across the lake into town.

Pavillon Vert, Avenue de la Liberté. $2.50 for room with no fan or air conditioner; $6 with a fan, $7 with airconditioner.   A favorite with visiting soccer teams. Some rooms are kind of crummy, others adequate. Look first.

Hotel Central, northwest corner of the market (B.P. 56, Ouagadougou; tel. 23-66) $9 single, $10 double, $7 non-air-conditioned double.   Right on Times Square. Bustling, busy, interesting.

Note: **Assembly of God Mission,** one mile from the center of town on Bobo Road, has a clean, bare hotel. On occasion they accept travelers.

PLACES TO EAT

Hotel Restaurants

The **Hotel Indépendance** restaurant charges around $4 for a good and fairly substantial four-course lunch or dinner; à la carte is higher. Very good and very expensive Sunday cold buffet lunch. You can have drinks at the outdoor bar or at poolside. The **Buffet Hotel** restaurant—on Avenue Binger—has good, plain French food served in an immaculate colonial atmosphere. Your first game of bumper pool is free with any meal or drink. The **Riccardo** bar-restaurant serves a variety of good meals available to order: tender steaks, good omelettes, clean salads, Spanish specialties, all in large servings and all inexpensive ($2 for a full meal), with a $1 daily special; couscous served on Sundays usually. Drinks are cheap and cold; filtered cold water if you ask for it. Pleasant, cool, with talkative clientele. The **Hotel Central** restaurant can't be recommended. Prices are high for poor quality, but it may have improved.

Other Restaurants

Eau Vive Voltaïque, on north side of the market square Large variety of good meals. The lunch menu for the day is usually around $2 for three courses, dinner menu similar, à la carte quite reasonable. Good, quick, cheap lunches and dinners available in front section. Very pleasant and cool inside at lunch (air-conditioned) or outside at dinner (under the stars, with fountain, etc.), with music (classical) and good service.

Palace Restaurant, on Avenue Yannenga, near the Princesse Bar Wide variety of cheap food, average meal not more than $1, including very good couscous.

La Bonbonnière, Avenue Yannenga This is a good bakery shop, selling a large variety of rolls, breads and cakes. They make an excellent loaf of French bread that you might want to eat with cheese for a light lunch in your room. At the small tables you can be served coffee, croissants, good Italian ice cream and rich pastries.

PLACES TO DANCE

There are several places in town that feature bands on the weekend for dancing. Most of them serve kebabs of marinated beef and barbecued chicken for snacks and the usual fruit juices, soda pop, beer and whiskey. Inquire about the **Jeunesse Bar** (near the Pavillon Vert), the **Jeunesse Club** (a very clean, pleasant place out past the water tower on the Po road), **Sport Bar** (near the market).

The places with the best reputation are the following: **Oasis**

Bar, next door to the Riccardo restaurant; run by Madame Riccardo. Beer is $1.25, other drinks $2 and up. Dancing and crowds usually begin around 11 P.M. on Fridays and Saturdays; not very swinging on other nights unless you bring your own crowd. **Scotch Club,** on Avenue Yannenga south of the Bonbonnière. Entrance is on the side street. This bar always has some of the best music. Drinks are about the same as at the Oasis, but it is just a bit more sedate, except when the jazz is playing.

Cabane Bamboo is quite lively on weekend nights, with very recent and swinging records, lots of lively dancing and once in a while an entertainer. There is a cover of $1, but with the first beer free when there is entertainment, otherwise the usual prices.

SEEING THE COUNTRY

BOBO-DIOULASSO

Bobo-Dioulasso, called "Bobo" for short, is 216 miles from Ouagadougou. It is a town of 78,000, located on a plateau that is a crossroads for the major routes to Abidjan, Bamako and Niamey. It is an important commercial center, and a thriving town to visit.

The European section of town is made up of bungalows set back in lushly flamboyant gardens; thick shade trees line the streets. The African areas by contrast are dry, without greenery, the red-brown color of the laterite soil used in building the thick walls that enclose family compounds.

Observation: No African Lawns   It is evident when you look at the two parts of Bobo, the European and the African, that the two groups have different ideas about what constitutes pleasant urban living conditions. For the European it is an individual house set in verdure: a lawn bordered with flowers and bushes, shade trees and flowering vines. Non-Africans find the greenery to be cooling and soothing. Luxuriant gardens stir feelings of contentment in the Western psyche and make for relaxation and refreshment. Gardens are remembered as places of play and pleasure, designed to delight the eye and give the spirit a place for joyful expansion. In the Western creation myth, human life itself began in a garden, and gardens are forever synonymous with Paradise. Houses in the country, summer camps in the woods, parks in the middle of the city, suburban lawns, rose-growing clubs—there is no end to the evidence that everything to do with woods and decorative plants is beautiful and deeply satisfying.

To the African, the opposite is the case—he doesn't like gardens because, as in Eden, gardens come with snakes. The African sections of Bobo, typical of all traditional West African urban areas, look harsh and inhospitable to our eyes; there is not a blade of grass in sight, no greenery of any kind anywhere near the house, only perhaps an isolated tree for shade. To the African mind, living areas should ideally be swept bare of "nature"; the expanse of bare, packed earth indicates that human society is here established and firmly in control. Austere barrenness proclaims (temporary, limited) triumph over the relentless and hostile forces of nature. It demonstrates that men have succeeded in cutting back the forest, in clearing away bush and brambles, in routing wild animals, in banishing insects, in leaving no spot for the hated snake to hide.

*   *   *

Places to Stay and Eat

The **Royan Hotel,** located in the center of town, has eleven comfortable, clean air-conditioned rooms, about $10 a night. The **Buffet Hotel** has twelve comfortable, clean air-conditioned rooms, also about $10 a night. The Buffet Hotel is an architecturally striking building not far from the railroad depot. Both hotels have pleasant, small dining rooms where a large clientele comes nightly for the well-prepared meals.

A Visit to Koro Village   Only 10 miles from Bobo on the Ouagadougou Road is a site of remarkable originality. Near the P.K. 9 road marker, just beyond a tiny culvert bridge, there is a turn to the right. Drive in for about a third of a mile; the road is just a track. To your right rise the cliffs of Koro. Leaving the car, you walk through the scrub grass toward the rocks. You are being

observed from above—all strangers are—so by the time you reach the base of the cliffs, there will probably be an old man waiting solemnly. You approach and exchange greetings; neither you nor your Voltaic host speaks the village language, but your driver and the old man find a common means of communication and he translates for you. The villager is dry and leathery, agile and sure-footed as a mountain ram. He casually climbs ahead, turning to guide you with patience. You follow in his path, some carved steps hacked out of stone, other narrow toe holds, expanses of sheer, inclined rock. There is no time for talk; it takes all your concentration to keep up with the climb.

At the pinnacle you sit on a table rock from which you can see the view across the plains in a circle. During the rainy season there is a waterfall tumbling down the cliffs, but in June it is dry. You follow your guide down through Koro village, an extraordinary sight. The homes are of stone and clay, built on the flat tables of the mountain. They are like eagle's nests, perched on the edge of the cliffs. The men and most of the women are away in the fields; some women are left behind to prepare the meals. Legend says that these people fled to this lofty, isolated place in order to escape the harassment of the religious and political struggles of medieval kingdoms. Here they eke out a meager living in peace. You stare, awed by the self-contained austerity of these cliff dwellings. Then you realize you are being loudly scolded by a withered old lady who is gesturing menacingly. Then you catch on; you have stepped dangerously near to her vegetable garden—a patch of earth the size of a postcard in which a tiny corn plant has managed to take root.

By the time you reach the bottom and stand on flat land again, your mind is momentarily as wobbly as your legs. Your life seems so easy in comparison. You feel humbled by the precariousness of the cliff dwellers' existence, respectful of the attention, cooperation and care their life demands of each of them. You admire their integrity and solidarity. You have seen a bit of life whole unto itself; it has been a trip through time and space.

PHOTO: SARITA HENRY

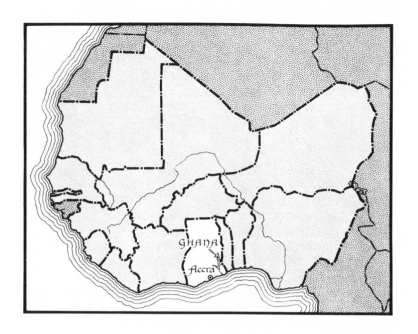

Ghana

ACCRA

A visit to Accra means going to see your friends in Ghana. You have friends in Ghana "because your college roommate used to date a Ghanaian guy" or because you "have a pen pal" or because you were once invited to an embassy reception, or because you met a Ghanaian student at a party, or the Ghanaian public relations man came to your school to show slides, or because when you went to get your visa at the consulate you struck up an acquaintance with one of the young men in the office, or because your friend went last year and can give you a lot of names.

Everybody knows at least one Ghanaian. Gather names and

addresses, and when you get to Accra, look people up. Before you go, be sure to drop them a note letting them know you are coming, because the indispensable key to enjoying Accra is the company of Ghanaians.

You can't help but come away singing the praises of Ghana and Ghanaians because their good humor, high spirits and outgoing friendliness carry the day. Ghanaians enjoy themselves; they know how to work hard and play hard. Because you have Ghanaian friends you are invited to participate in Ghanaian social events: an "out-dooring" (party for a newborn baby), a wedding or a funeral. On these occasions, crowds come lavishly dressed, jolly in mood, ready for conversation, laughter, flirting and feasting. If you are included in the continuous festivities you will have a ball.

When you have friends in Ghana you also get to eat their marvelous home cooking. Again, if you are lucky, you will be treated night after night to two or three different dishes—stews and sauces, roasts and garnishes, all delicious. Their names: *palaver* sauce, palm-nut stew, groundnut stew, light soup, Joloff rice, curry, garden-egg (eggplant) stew. Ingredients: chicken, fish, turkey, crab, lamb, tomatoes, onions, peppers, greens, beans, eggplant, oil. Some are rich and savory, others light and sharp, others thick and peppery. Even the grains and staples have great personality in the hands of a Ghanaian cook. Rice you know already. *Kenkey* is a corn-meal dough, lightly fermented so that it has a sharp, adult taste; *aboloo* is mild; *fufu* is—well, interesting.

Observation: *Fufu* *Fufu,* also *foo-foo* and *foo-too,* is famous. Everybody has heard of it. Not everyone, however, relishes it the way Ghanaians do. *Fufu* is a gelatinous dumpling ball formed by pounding cassava or plantain with a mortar and pestle. It is always served with some sort of gravy or stew. It is gummy in consistency, so it has to be dipped in a liquid to make it palatable. The secret of eating *fufu* is—*don't chew.* Break off a small piece, dunk it so that it is well coated with sauce, then swallow it whole.

Personally I never developed a taste for *fufu.* One: Who needs *fufu* when the world is full of long-grain, short-grain, white, brown and wild rice? Two: When made from plantain, *fufu* is nutritious, but made from cassava, a root vegetable, it is pure starch, so I don't approve. Three:

Kenkey, with its slightly bitter beer taste, has so much more character; *aboloo* is so bland and light that it has meaning all its own. Four: I like to chew my food; I don't go for something sliding down my throat. Five: It just doesn't seem right for two women out in the kitchen—one pounding with the long heavy mortar, the other turning the ball—to be working more than half an hour to make one dumpling of *fufu* for me to eat in a few minutes, unappreciatively distracted by conversation and conviviality; it doesn't seem worth it; it's a waste.

But Ghanaians are positively religious about *fufu;* they eat it all the time with deep satisfaction. When they travel abroad they make cunning substitutes—from Cream of Wheat! Anyway, you must try some. You may like it. If you don't, refuse further offers graciously and stand firm. Your hosts really won't push you that much: they know *fufu* is an acquired taste. And besides, whatever you don't take means either a lot less work for the household, or even more *fufu* for *them.*

*   *   *

Sorry that it is not very romantic: the word "Accra" means "ant hill." And as a visitor you'll find these red clay piles along the sides of the road. They come in weird, convoluted shapes, architectural wonders. Considering the height of an ant, they must be like Empire State Buildings, relatively. Accra is on the Atlantic Coast, but since it is not designed to incorporate the shore into the city's presence, you hardly realize that you are right at the ocean's edge. Accra is built on a plain, almost totally without hills. Reflecting British tastes, the more affluent sections of Accra are built far away from the shore on higher ground, considered "healthier." The weather is warm and sunny almost all year round. It stays within the 75- to 85-degree range most of the time, and humidity is generally low.

The population of Accra is around 700,000, with not more than a couple of thousand Europeans and North Americans, Lebanese and Indians. During the Nkrumah regime (1958–1966), Ghana established itself as a prominent and important country, one whose foreign policy was of world-wide importance. Consequently, around sixty countries set up embassies and consulates in Accra. Ceylon, Bulgaria, Brazil and Iraq, Saudi Arabia, Turkey,

235

Switzerland, Finland and Spain all have diplomats in Accra. The United Nations and UNESCO have regional offices here. Airlines of fourteen different nations, and twenty-two shipping lines, keep offices in Accra. Though these numbers are not great, they are impressive for a modest sized city. With such an august and ceremonial foreign population, Accra has an unusually cosmopolitan flavor.

The size seems ideal because Accra is small enough for you to know almost all the people doing the same things you are, and at the same time it is big enough for a measure of privacy. Small enough for you to meet many fascinating new people, big enough for it not to be narrow-minded and provincial.

Strange but true, both white people and black people find Accra cordial, open and welcoming. For whites it is a friendly city where they can easily get to swing with Africans. To them Accra is like a prosperous, cheerful Harlem. Here people are warm and accepting rather than cold and hostile. There is an obvious coherence, order and purpose in this Harlem, unlike the disorganization and anger they know in the one back home. Whites, who are uncomfortable around America's home-grown Africans because they can often be negative, argumentative and hard to know, are surprised and pleased by the easygoing, chatty exchange they can have with the average Ghanaians. At last you can sit down and talk freely with a black man who is not tense and "thin-skinned"; you can get close to a black person and just enjoy the jocular, relaxed company.

For Afro-Americans, Accra is a dream come true, for here is a city in a country that is *black* up and down. In fact, the city and the administration are African, up and down, in and out. If you have already visited a French-speaking country and found white men making decisions, you will be relieved to be in Accra, where Ghanaians are in control. Every person you see has a black skin, and that's a whole, huge, self-identity trip. Shop clerks are black, carpenters are black, teachers, auto mechanics, radio announcers, policemen, taxi drivers, nurses and bartenders are black. The director of the Bank of Ghana is black, as is the president of the National Insurance Corporation, the vice-chancellor of the university and the newspaper editor. The doctors are black, the dentists, the professors, the lawyers and judges are black too. The Attorney General is black; the admiral, the chief of police and the chief of state are black. All the faces on television are black; all the people in the bus are black; all the kids in the schools are black; all the women in the market are black; and all the men in the factories are black.

I remember the butcher at Kingsway. I could never get over my delight that the *butcher* was a *black* man. There I would stand, glad for the long line so that I could stare at him in appreciative wonderment. Somehow just seeing him cut the lamb chops or package the chickens gave me a thrill! How long could I hang around, after all, with a silly smile on my face? How could I ever explain why his presence, his being in the world, made me feel so much better inside?

There is one point that strikes everyone the same—the general good looks of Ghanaians. They tend to be medium in height, with even features, and a rich brown color. Ghanaians describe this look by the word "plumpy," meaning a symmetrical roundness of the body, a good shape, a full head of healthy hair, and soft, even-textured skin polished and glowing from prosperity. Their personal cleanliness is amazing. The "bath"—whether standing in a shower, sitting in a tub, stooping at a bucket—is a twice-daily ritual of soaping, scrubbing, rinsing, rubbing, cologning, powdering and dressing in fresh, immaculate clothes.

Ghanaians love to dress; their clothes are beautiful, and they can afford it. A whole range of styles are in fashion at once. Ghanaians have always dressed in the African mode, and have gradually developed classical styles extremely flattering to black body shape and skin coloring. If you want to get the full enjoyment of seeing Ghanaians at their shining best, take yourself to any of Accra's middle-class churches on a Sunday morning and wait as the congregation spills out around twelve-thirty. The individual beauty, the group handsomeness—moving and memorable.

There is usually an ebullience and optimism in the air in Accra, a never-ending badinage about politics, foreign trade, economic development and social problems. Ghanaians are unusually well informed about current affairs and take a lively interest in all matters of public policy. Since everybody seems related to everybody else, everyone has some sort of personal stake in the latest government decisions and debates.

Ghanaians consciously try to project their "personality" and image—one of self-confidence, self-sufficiency, progressive ideas and bold action. Ghanaians are doers, builders. They enjoy challenges and constantly take on difficult projects. Ghanaians feel that Ghana is a *very important place* and are justly proud of it. They are always ready to negotiate with foreign governments and corporations on a sovereign basis, and are always ready to plunge into international power plays. Ghanaians may be exploited and oppressed in reality, but they don't seem to feel or act that way. Sometimes outmaneuvered at the conference table, outsmarted at the negotiations, outvoted on the committee, yes, but that happens to every country, every people; it's just part of the hard knocks of being independent and sovereign in a world where others have greater might or greater experience or greater influence.

Because Ghanaians are so handsome and because they don't especially reproach and blame whites for the hardships they have endured, whites don't have to feel guilty. Because they don't feel guilty, whites don't call upon the venal arsenal of defenses (prejudice, exclusion, coercion) to secure psychological relief. Afro-Americans are enormously heartened by these same features of Ghanaian character. The bright sense of freedom that Ghanaians display comes as a surprise. Their spunkiness on the international scene makes the Afro-American feel proud and strong. Their unabashed admiration for black Americans and the friendly welcome they give newcomers makes everything seem right.

Perhaps you think this is "Africa." Not so. No other place in West Africa is quite like Accra. Dakar's plateau is handsome and its surroundings scenically gorgeous, but it is also clear that Frenchmen are still very much in charge, still running things. Lagos is exciting, but very rough on the meek; Abidjan has a climate like an oven, and a coarse, colonized atmosphere. Beautiful Bamako is reserved and self-contained; gentle Niamey is quiet. No, only Accra has this relaxing, urbane, black and vibrant ambiance.

Some Background for Understanding Ghana

Ghana derives its name from the first of the ancient empires that developed in Western Sudan during the early Middle Ages. It seems likely that the Akan peoples are in fact descendants of those who were driven south from the area of the Niger bend into the forest regions of West Africa following the breakup of the old Ghana empire. Other migrants followed from the north and east, especially from what are now Dahomey and Nigeria.

The first Europeans to arrive were the Portuguese around the year 1469. They were followed by the Dutch, English, Danish, Swedish, French, Spanish and Germans. For several centuries they came to trade and coerce a bounty and booty of gold and slaves. Black bodies were shipped by the thousands to New World plantations in the southern United States, Jamaica, Santo Domingo, Cuba, Brazil and the Guianas.

During the nineteenth century the British gained control over the coastline, moved inland, and by 1901 administered the old Gold Coast Colony, Ashanti and the Northern Territories. After World War I, the former German colony of Togoland was added as a mandated territory, and the entire country became known as Gold Coast.

The Gold Coast obtained internal self-government in April 1954, and declared its independence on March 6, 1957, with Dr. Kwame Nkrumah as its first prime minister. On July 1, 1960, when Ghana became a republic, Nkrumah became the country's first President. In 1966, while President Nkrumah was traveling abroad, the police and armed forces seized the government and placed it in the hands of the National Liberation Council, consisting of senior officers from both services. On October 1, 1969, the Second Republic of Ghana was inaugurated, led by Dr. Kofi A. Busia as prime minister, but in 1972 there was another coup, again by the armed forces, which now created a National Redemption Council to govern the country.

Ghana is a nation of 9 million people, about 20 percent of whom live in the urban areas. The other 80 percent are farmers, fishermen or miners. Ghana is one of the richest countries in tropical Africa, deriving its wealth mainly from the enterprises of its rural population. The farmers produce the hundreds of thousands of tons of cocoa, Ghana's main export, to provide more than half of the country's foreign-exchange earnings. Ghana's agricultural products include maize, rice, millet, yams, plantains and

239

beans for local consumption; palm oil, coffee, peanuts and rubber for export. Mining constitutes Ghana's second industry, with gold, bauxite and diamonds as the main earners of foreign exchange. Precious timber and hardwood from Ghana's forest reserves are another valuable resource. In the industrial field Ghanaian factories are still small but are developing rapidly; there is a wide range of articles produced locally—cotton cloth and piece goods, canned fruits and vegetables, beer and spirits, cigarettes, soap, motor vehicles, furniture, plastics goods, and the like.

Geographically Ghana is bounded on the east by Togo, on the north by Upper Volta, and on the west by the Ivory Coast; the southern boundary is the Gulf of Guinea. The country is divided into nine regions: the Upper, Northern, Western, Central and Eastern, as well as Brong-Ahafo, Ashanti, Volta, and Accra-Tema. As you travel inland, coastal plains of scrub and grassland change to the high forest that covers about one third of the land—and produces much of the agricultural and mineral riches. The remainder of the country, lying to the north of the forest zone, is mostly savannah—arid plains covered with short, widely spaced trees and high grass. Ghana is well watered by a number of rivers. The damming of one of them, the Volta River, has created a vast reservoir of water, Volta Lake at Akosombo, with an area of 3,500 square miles, extending over 200 miles upstream.

Ghanaian cultural style is set by the Akan people, a large ethnic group spread from the coast through the forest regions of Ghana over into the Ivory Coast. Accra is the home of the Ga people, and the Ewe (pronounced *ev*-vay) people live in the east. The most important groups in the north speak Hausa and Dagbani.

LEISURE AND PLEASURE

In the morning
   —Buy all the Ghanaian newspapers and look them over from cover to cover, to get a feel for what is happening.
   —Make a tour of Accra's landmarks and monuments.
   —Browse in Makola Market.

In the afternoon
—Find out the program at the Arts Centre or at the Drama Studio.

—Spend some time at the beach.

—Take a walk in the Botanical Gardens at the university.

In the evening
—Jump to the music in one of the local hotels or dance halls.

—Go to a production of one of the popular vaudeville "concerts" in the vernacular; your Ghanaian host will translate.

GETTING AROUND

Ghanaians travel fast and light. Ghana has the best transportation network of any other country in West Africa, and everything is always crowded with customers. In the major cities *taxicabs* cruise during the day and the early evening. As it gets later they wait for customers near bars and hotels. They will keep appointments you arrange in advance. Before you get in, make sure the driver knows your destination, and that you agree on a price (cabs with hotel stickers charge more). *Municipal buses* don't run frequently, and they are crowded and slow. *Lorries* and *Benz buses* go up and down the main thoroughfares.

Intercity Travel

State Transport Corporation Buses
The STC runs bus services between Ghana's cities and towns. The buses are cheap, clean, fast, reliable, punctual and jam-packed. You *must* buy your ticket a day in advance if you are leaving from Accra, and you must plan to arrive a good half-hour before the bus is scheduled to leave. Although seats are usually reserved, people come early, and the buses tend to leave as soon as everyone is seated.

In no other African country can the independent tourist cover so much ground on his own. There are buses to absolutely everywhere. Up-to-date information and schedules are available from the Corporation's main terminal, on Ring Road West, Accra (tel. 21912). You can plan to use State Transport for intercity travel, and then, when you arrive, rely on local taxis for short trips.

Planes

Ghana Airways connects Accra, Kumasi, Takoradi and Tamale on a regularly scheduled daily basis. Contact Ghana Airways (Cocoa House, Liberty Avenue; tel. 21921) for the current schedule.

Railroads

They are there—slow and not very well maintained. There are new trains on the Accra–Kumasi–Takoradi line, and a night sleeper service between Takoradi and Kumasi. Inquire at the railway station at the foot of Liberty Avenue.

Private Transport

The author has found short- and long-distance travel by Peugeot station wagon (taxi shared with seven other passengers) very satisfactory; the cars are fast and the conversation is lively. Benz buses are also adequate. Private transport for Tema leaves from Tema Lorry Station at Kiribu and Independence Avenue; for Kumasi and Cape Coast–Takoradi they leave from the Shell gas station at Kaneshie Circle. All other departures are from the Central Lorry Park. Private transport is *not* recommended for travel on the dangerous Accra–Kumasi road.

Lorries

Justly famous for their rakish self-confidence and philosophical bent, the lorry drivers of Ghana ply every highway and byway of the nation. Wherever you want to go there is a lorry leaving for there in a few minutes, carrying a cargo of people, hardware, animals and produce. The lorry is the backbone of Ghana's internal distribution system, a stalwart component of national development, but recommended only for student travelers in a pinch.

Observation: Lorries They are called ''tro-tros,'' ''poto-potos,'' ''mammy wagons'' or lorries. They are the passenger and freight trucks that travel the West African roads and provide for the mobility of people and the distribution of goods. Romantically, they may be considered a way of being "with the people," but why anyone in his right mind would take one if not necessary is a mystery.

The best part of them is their slogans. The sayings are pithy and profound. They have been analyzed by ethno-psychiatrists, used as book titles and studied by sociologists. The latest crop is always a conversation piece. You are bound to have your favorites. (Mine? The old ones: POOR NO FRIEND and BLACK MAN TROUBLE. Translated: If you are *poor* [in money and/or in spirit] you can have *no friend;* and wherever I see *black man,* I see *trouble-o!*)

But the point is that you can only appreciate the saying from the *outside.* Once you are inside a lorry you can't see *anything.* You can ride sideways, backward or forward, but in any case you will be crowded without a view because the lorry *won't start* until there is not a square inch left for man, chicken or plantain.

It is hard to find a good word for lorries. Usually the cost is the same as for the faster, more comfortable station wagons. True, lorries do leave often, but don't be misled—your taxi will speed past a lorry that left half an hour earlier.

Your journey will be slow. The lorries are stopped at dozens of checkpoints along the way by all manner of policeman and soldier. And then, of course, the drivers are a chummy lot: they stop each other on the road to borrow cigarettes, ask for change and chat—sometimes interminably. You can also be sure there is something wrong with the truck: a weak axle that will groan and collapse, a burned-out headlight as the gloom approaches, or nonfunctioning windshield wipers as the rain pours down.

Get to know people this way? Hardly. Passengers close their eyes New York City–subway style; they have developed a whole set of ruses for avoiding the gaze of others. And besides, the art is to suffer patiently in silence; there is no energy left over for any friendly stuff.

If you happen to be driving your car behind a lorry (inevitably), you can be certain the driver will not let you overtake him, will not give hand signals and will maneuver capriciously. He doesn't have taillights or even brake lights, so you have to outguess him. He may break down on the road and neglect to place twigs behind him as a warning. Lorries can be a menace; always be careful and give them a wide berth.

Lorries do have a couple of good points. Let's say you make a cool move—like buying a motorbike for about $200 at the beginning of your six-week summer-session course at the University of Ghana. (It is convenient for traveling around town and you'll easily sell it at the end of your stay.) Now, if you want to go any long distance you can take a lorry, pay a little bit more to have your bike strapped to the top, and you're off. If you are on a road looking for a ride, a lorry will almost always stop and pick you up if there is any possible way of fitting in another body.

* * *

PLACES AND WALKS OF INTEREST

Ghana National Museum, Barnes Road, near Museum Circle. Open daily from 9 A.M. to 6 P.M. Closed Mondays.

As you come into the entryway of the museum you should walk straight ahead into the circle of displays of Ghanaian ethnology. The exhibits are well laid out and the labels very informative. Then you can move to the outside of the circle and see the displays from northern Ghana.

From there you come to the displays that rivet my attention every time—the collection of historical documentation and memorabilia. They date from a time before Africa was subjugated and carved into colonies. At this point Africans are still pictured and drawn in the fullness of their humanity and majesty, before Europeans felt the need to develop the popular image of an inferior, subject creature, less than human and devoid of nobility. Here you will see the original T. E. Bowdich 1819 drawings of Ashanti court life, and the John William Wright paintings, made in 1831, of two hostage Ashanti princes sent to live in London to secure a peace treaty. It's all there—graphic representation of the whole bloody struggle, Africa's defeat and subsequent resurgence in the modern period.

If your interest in Ghanaian history has been aroused, you can learn more by going around the corner to the **Ghana National Archives** (Castle Road, near the YWCA). *Suggestion:* You might want to get to the museum about 10 A.M. or so; look around there, head over to the Archives, then finish the morning with luncheon at the YWCA.

Accra Arts Centre, across from Parliament House.
Open daily.

The Arts Centre setting is lovely—right by the seaside. The building acts as a center of Ghanaian cultural activity and is the headquarters of the Arts Council of Ghana. The Centre has a theater which hosts visiting theatrical productions and local amateur groups. The Arts Centre Dance Troupe performs there, as does the National Symphony Orchestra and Choir. Look in on the Gallery and the curio shop; there is always an exhibit of artwork by local artists and craftsmen.

One of the nicest programs in Accra takes place here on Saturdays from 12 noon to 2 P.M. when the Centre offers poetry readings, music and dance in the garden. If you are creative or artistic, why not contact them in advance and arrange to read your poetry there, or show some of your artwork? Write the Executive Secretary, Arts Council of Ghana, P. O. Box 2738, Accra.

Flagstaff House Zoo, Liberation Road

Behind the Army Headquarters at Flagstaff House, the visitor will find a well-kept zoo. Many of the more exotic and valuable animals were obtained as gifts from other countries, or in exchange for Ghanaian fauna. You can have refreshments here, or you can go to the **Star Hotel**. If you have decided to take a trip to Upper Volta or to Dahomey, this is a good time to visit the nearby **French embassy,** where they handle the visas for these two countries.

Jamestown

This old oceanside section of Accra is not scenic or nice; it is rough and harsh. The air is salty from the spray; the houses are crowded together. Its old buildings are interesting, many bearing dates from the early 1800s. **James Fort** was built by the English in 1673 as a trading post. Now, three hundred years later, it is still in use, grievously, as a prison. Even older is nearby **Ussher Fort,** dating from 1652, built by the Dutch, now also a prison. Down below James Fort is the lighthouse and farther along Cleland Road and the Old Wineba Road (both extensions of High Street) is a long stretch of turbulent sea, easy to approach and look at. Plan to be in the area around 4 P.M. so you can see the fishing boats returning to the beach.

Black Star Square

The square is a huge parade ground graced with *two* triumphant arches. It is the scene of military and national spectacles. Combine your visit with a stroll along the **Marine Drive** through the lovely beach and park area past the government hospitality center, and approach the **Castle,** the residence of the head of state.

University of Ghana, Legon

Certainly one of the loveliest campuses anywhere in Africa, the University of Ghana was built lavishly and lovingly, a shrine to the country's pride in higher education for her sons and daughters. Almost all the buildings are low and rambling, built of white stucco, and roofed with red-clay tile.

As you enter the grounds from Liberation Road, the **Institute of African Studies** with its School of Music and Drama is to your left. If you continue straight ahead, you pass the colleges and classroom buildings on each side, all set in lawns and gardens and rising on a gentle hill. From the top you look down over the university complex and onto the Accra Plains.

You'd be dismayed by the number of visitors from abroad who feel that the University of Ghana is "too good" for Ghana, a mere "developing" country. They are accustomed to crowded classrooms combined with the gloom, slush, cold and misery of European and American winters. The University of Ghana, all spread out in the brilliant sun, just doesn't seem puritan enough somehow, not *oppressive* enough to build character and develop intellect. Californians are a bit more tolerant.

Visit the library and spend some time shopping at the bookstore. By all means, see the colleges and have lunch in the visitors' section of the cafeteria. It is a bit of a walk, but the university's **Botanical Gardens** are worth a visit, especially in the cool of the evening. If you go to the Institute, you may be lucky enough to catch a rehearsal of the Ghana Dance Ensemble.

SHOPPING

Craft Cloth

Ghanaian craftsmen specialize in making two outstanding types of cloth: *kente* and *adinkra*. They are worn on festive and ceremonial occasions and are both artistic creations of unusual beauty. They form an important element in Ghana's great cultural heritage.

Kente is a cloth of silk or heavy cotton woven in strips on a traditional handloom. These strips are then sewn together to make a large cloth, so that geometric patterns are formed. The colors are strong and rich: red, royal blue, yellow, gold, green. Men wear the large, uncut cloth draped around the body and over the shoulder as a toga; women have a piece cut to make a wrapped skirt and a fitted bodice.

Good-quality *kente* is expensive. Before a Ghanaian man makes such an investment (several hundred dollars), he shops around for a long time. Young men just starting out will buy one by installments over a year's time. They are treasures and heirlooms.

Kente cloth comes in several popular (small) forms. You can buy *kente* neckties, cummerbunds and place mats. You can wear a strip of *kente* as a belt around your waist, or as a border (collar, lapel, inset) for a simple garment.

Writing and calligraphy have a long and intriguing history in West Africa. One example is to be found in the designs stamped on *adinkra* cloth. These long cloths are hand-printed with ideograms— symbols representing philosophical ideas and religious concepts. *Adinkra* cloths are worn by men, draped as a toga. (A fine poster explaining *adinkra* symbolism is available from the Glo Art Gallery.)

247

The envy of all your friends will be the wax-print cloth you bring back from Ghana. Go to Makola Market and browse among the hundreds of designs.

Boutiques

Shop One, Liberty Avenue near Liberation Circle   For years now, the enterprising Mrs. Harriet Jones has run a boutique that is something of a gallery of fine crafted African wares. She sells *kente* and carvings, neckties and bracelets, clothing, jewelry and accessories, wall hangings and pottery, all made by local artisans. Every item is of excellent quality, selected for its refinement and suitability for contemporary dressing and decorating. Shop One also features the work of artists resident in Ghana. Author's choice for the first stop in browsing and gift shopping.

The Loom, opposite Shop One

Africa House, Castle Road, opposite YWCA

La Boutique Africaine, in the Washington Hotel   These three shops feature a varied selection of local crafts. Quality is uneven, but you must take a look.

Art Galleries

The **Arts Centre** (near Parliament House, 28th February Road) has an exhibition hall for the display of sculpture and painting by Ghanaian and foreign artists. The **Glo Art Gallery** is a lively place, showing all sorts of traditional and contemporary art. Many pieces for sale.

Craft and Curio Shops, along High Street

Here you will find stall after stall selling the favorite souvenirs —most of it is obvious and corny tourist junk; some other things are of good quality and design. You can find spears, bows and arrows, strips of *kente* cloth, ivory ornaments, metal figurines, leather handbags, snakeskin wallets, Akan-style stools, beads and necklaces, wood carvings and sculpture, sandals and belts, grigris, amulets and bracelets. For a better selection, look into the shops behind the open stalls. Take your time—part of the pleasure is in the conversation and bargaining.

Books and Newspapers

Probably the best buy in Ghana is books, and the best place to shop for them is the **University Bookshop,** Legon. The hardcover books in the front shop cover every aspect of African affairs and African culture. They also sell postcards, West African periodicals, scholarly journals and technical workbooks. In the back they have a great selection of paperback books on all subjects, again the specialty is Africa. The books come in irregular shipments, so while they may be out of what you are seeking, they may have every one of Shaw's plays for sale, or a dozen P. G. Wodehouse novels. Sometimes there are hundreds of books in French, other times all of the Penguin "African Writer Series." It remains one of the best in-print African collections anywhere.

Buy the daily papers from street newsstands and newsboys. Kingsway department store has the best selection of imported newspapers and periodicals. It also has a bookshop, whose selections vary greatly. The **Atlas Bookshop** at the Ambassador Hotel also has newspapers and a small selection of books. There were few titles at the **Methodist Book Depot** and **Presbyterian Book Depot** (both on Makola Market Square) but try anyway; maybe things have improved.

EXCURSIONS

Tema

Tema, 18 miles from Accra, grew up as a planned industrial area, designed by teams of international experts to include factories, industrial complexes, housing estates and a large harbor. One of the most impressive achievements of modern Ghana, Tema is the heart of the country's development: more than sixty factories and industries have been established in the Tema industrial area. These include a vehicle assembly plant, a soap factory, a cocoa-products factory, factories for producing aluminum sheets and utensils, textile factories and plastics works.

Of greater importance is the oil refinery owned jointly by the Ghana government and an Italian company. There are also aluminum smelters, built by the Ghanaian-American firm Valco, which use power from the Volta hydro-electric project for processing aluminum. Tema harbor itself is one of the largest artificial harbors in the world. It is the base for the growing Ghanaian fishing industry and a port of call for ships from around the world.

Plan your trip to Tema for the afternoon. Tour the harbor area, the residential communities, and if you arrange in advance, one of the factories. You may want to have supper or spend the night ($10 to $15) at the **Meridian Hotel,** so named because Tema is situated exactly on the Greenwich meridian line. You get a panoramic view of the town from the roof. The **Mariner's Club** in the harbor area and the **Top Hat** in Community Two are places to stop for rest and food. **The Point**, at the junction of the Nungua–Tema Road, is open until midnight serving barbequed chicken, sandwiches and salads. Plan to stay in Tema until nightfall to see the lights of the plants ablaze. At night Tema has a sci-fi beauty that is compelling.

Travel from Accra: public bus.

Aburi

Everything about Aburi, 20 miles north of Accra in the Akwapim mountain ranges, is delightful, including the roller-coaster hills and scarps that lead to it. Check to see if **Peduasi Lodge,** a mansion used for government and international gatherings, is still open to the public. Farther up the hills are the **Aburi Botanical Gardens,** arranged in a series of graceful walks which present the visitor with a sampling of all of Ghana's flora. The Aburi gardens are a cool retreat, a place for relaxing, strolling, exploring, for taking deep breaths, gazing at horizons and learning a little botany. Did you know, for example, that there is a male and a female papaya tree; only the female produces fruit. (Lady palm trees, on the other hand, are so designated because they are short, and their nuts accessible without resort to an unladylike climb.) On the grounds there is a snack bar and a rest house, and a greenhouse where you may purchase plants. *Note:* Across from Aburi Girls Secondary School is the Swiss-run **Restaurant May.**

Travel from Accra: State Transport, 40 cents, right to the entrance of the gardens.

Akosombo

Fifty-four miles inland from Accra stands the mighty dam across the gorge of the Volta River. The water behind it forms a lake that is the largest man-made lake in the world (3,500 square miles). Lake waters feed the four generators of an electric power plant under the dam. The electricity generated is transmitted to aluminum smelters and industrial complexes in Tema and along a 500-mile transmission grid to Ghana's major towns and cities.

There are dozens of fascinating stories told about the development of the dam and formation of the lake. As an electrical- and civil-engineering feat, it is a project of enormous proportions with considerable impact on world trade and finance. As a project in social engineering, it ranks as a major forced resettlement of a population in the most patient, humane manner possible, a too infrequent example of persuasion, not coercion, in human affairs. No fewer than 80,000 people had to be evacuated from their homes as their ancestral lands were flooded by the lake waters. After an enormous amount of social engineering and planning, the former inhabitants of the area were moved into fifty-two resettlement townships.

The **Volta Hotel** stands on a hill overlooking the dam and the lake. Its resemblance to a Swiss chalet is intentional; it was built out of nostalgia for a European architectural form but is somehow incongruously harmonious in Ghana. In the early sixties the hotel was the meeting place for confrontations, "palavers," between the Ghanaian officials and the chiefs of communities about to be inundated. At daybreak, a time signifying the importance of the mission, the chiefs and their elders would walk in stately procession up the winding road to the hotel. The Minister of Social Welfare and Community Development was up from Accra to meet with them and resolve the problems that couldn't be handled by underlings. The proceedings were marked by their formality, politeness and restraint. For the chiefs, the concern was not solely the moving of people but also the moving of the gods. Protective, prosperity-giving deities, long resident in sacred portions of earth, forest and river, spiritual founders of villages, belonging from time immemorial to that spot and those folk—all would be lost to the waters unless they too could be moved.

There were sacred ceremonies, known only to the priests, whereby the gods could be propitiated, moved and gently resettled in a new site. But rituals of such weight and seriousness are expensive and demand a lengthy series of sacrifices and consecrations. What was the government willing to contribute toward these costs? The discussions were amiable and solemn, the two sides speaking in proverbs and parables. When finally the agreements were complete there was time for laughing, jokes and a bit of relaxation before the next group came, with the similar story, repeated over and over, yet special in each case.

From the window of your room at the hotel (around $6 a night) you look out over the dam and the lake. There is an Olympic-sized pool and charming gardens and terraces. You can arrange to tour the dam site and resettlement townships by contacting the Publicity Section, Chief Executive's Office, Volta River Authority, P.O. Box M. 77, Accra, or by telephoning them at 65421.

Travel from Accra: State Transport from the Central Lorry Park to Adomi Bridge stop; from there, taxi to the hotel.

Visit to Cape Coast and Trading Forts

Cape Coast, capital of the Central Region, is a famous old coastal town ninety miles west of Accra. It is built on a range of hills that slant down to the sea; its streets are narrow and winding; its houses from an earlier era. The most venerable secondary schools are to be found in Cape Coast. Of these, Mfantsipim School, founded in 1876, and Wesley Girls' High School (1835) are two of the country's oldest educational institutions. The University of Cape Coast and a large number of other schools make this town a center of learning and influence throughout West Africa.

Cape Coast Castle   One major historical landmark is Cape Coast Castle, one of the greatest castles in Ghana, and one of the first (1662) British establishments in West Africa. From this castle the British established their first contacts along the coast and gradually extended their power over the region.

Elmina Castle   Eight miles farther down the coast is Elmina Castle, built by the Portuguese in 1482. Named "The Mine" because the Portuguese were so impressed by the quantities of gold being worn by the inhabitants of the region, Elmina has been in continuous use for nearly five hundred years. It is thought to be the oldest building standing in the tropics, a witness to the flux and change of coastal politics. In 1637 it was captured by the Dutch and later bought by the British, in 1872.

The historian Sean Kelly has explained the castle system in operation. First the Portuguese came looking for gold:

> This was nearly a generation before Columbus and Cortez were to open the treasures of America, to Europe. . . . Gold and ivory found their way down to the coast from Ghana's interior, usually carried on the heads of African porters. The tsetse-fly ruled out the use of pack animals. But quantities of gold large enough to be carried by a half-dozen inland porters produced at Elmina a vast cargo of the trinkets, brass, and cheap cloth that the Portuguese bartered in exchange. It frequently happened that there were simply not enough porters available on the coast to carry such loads back into the interior. The Portuguese solved this by importing "labor" to Elmina. . . . They brought slaves to Elmina from other parts of Africa and sold them as porters to the Ghanaian gold traders who, incidentally, paid more for them than the Portuguese could get in Europe. Slave-pens were needed at Elmina, and the castle's dungeons were put to use.

So the story unfolds. It was not long before the main demand was for slaves for the plantations of the New World. Through Elmina Castle would pass thousands of black captives, branded, then chained and packed into ship bottoms heading for the West Indies and South America.

Elmina Castle is a square fort with round towers at two opposite corners containing a small courtyard (now called the female slave yard); a large outer courtyard is enclosed by walls running down to the sea. The whole landward site was once surrounded by a moat (now dry) cut in the rock from which stone for the wall was obtained. Stone was imported from Portugal ready cut for doors and windows, as were bricks for the vaulting. A church at the seaward end of the large courtyard was completed just before 1600. A third courtyard was built by the Portuguese, but it was the Dutch who built rooms within it. The east part of the central block became the Dutch chapel, and an upper floor was inserted in the Portuguese church which was converted (strikingly) into a slave salesroom. Two small towers were raised on the seaward ramparts. In one, the king (the *asantehene*) of the Ashanti, Prempeh I, was imprisoned before he was exiled in 1899 by the British, symbolically marking a proud people's loss of sovereignty.

You can visit the castle, now used as a police headquarters. Across the road on the top of Iago Hill is **Fort Conraadsburg,** built by the Dutch in 1637 as a defense for Elmina. It is still in use today and is very well maintained. Because its history is less bloody, it is easier to enjoy its whitewashed brightness and fairy-tale construction.

Fort Amsterdam   About 20 miles east of Cape Coast, atop Kromantine Hill, stands Fort Amsterdam. It was built by the British in 1631—of red bricks from Virginia—and captured by the Dutch some years later, in 1665. For two hundred years it functioned as a slave shipping center. Today it is being restored by black Americans under the leadership of Drs. Robert and Sara Lee, long residents of Ghana.

Accomodations—Cape Coast

The **Catering Resthouse** offers comfortable rooms for $5 a night, but they are in great demand. Write P.O. Box 305, Cape Coast, or telephone 2594 to reserve a room. The **U.S.T. Motel** on the Elmina beach, near the Elmina junction of the Cape Coast–Takoradi Road, has pleasant rooms in chalets ($5) and an adequate restaurant (tel. 20, Elmina). There is also a restaurant in **Cape Coast Castle,** and a number of good snack bars in town.

SPORTS

Swimming

Riviera Beach Club, on beach behind State Farms Corporation, west of Black Star Square The center attraction here is the huge, Olympic-sized salt-water pool. There is a diving tower with different heights, and usually some swimming star to put on a display. It is fully equipped with showers and changing facilities. Along one length of the pool there are lounges for sunbathers. Opposite is a restaurant serving drab European food. Admission is inexpensive. Even if you don't want to swim, this is a pleasant, breezy setting for early evening relaxation.

Ambassador Beach Club, near Riviera Beach Club Free for the hotel's guests, about 50 cents for visitors, the Ambassador Beach Club offers complete amenities for an afternoon at the seaside. There are cabanas, showers, a sun deck, beach umbrellas, lounges, and a (so-so) restaurant for refreshments and food.

Labadi Beach and Black Star Square Beach These are the only two public beaches where it is really safe to bathe; the undertow at the others makes them dangerous. Labadi is the most popular of the two; in fact there is a faithful crowd that comes several times a week. The fresh air, the sea, and the swaying palm trees are idyllic. You can buy fruit from the ladies who pass by.

Note: Out of town there is good swimming at the **Acapulco Beach Club** in Teshie, at **Paradise Beach** in Tema, and at **Prampram Beach** (31 miles from Accra).

Soccer

Ghanaians are crazy about soccer. Each of the larger towns has a team and they play in competition for a variety of cups and championships much of the year. The **Sports Stadium,** opposite Black Star Square, is crowded every Sunday when there's a match. Your host or the desk clerk will help you get tickets.

255

Horse Racing

African Unity, Black Is Best, Shabazz, Timbuctou, Champion Ali, Lagos Calling and Soul Music go through their paces at the **Accra Turf Club.** There are races Saturday afternoons during the season, and a fascinating cross section of Accra turns up to see the contests. Many VIP Ghanaians and foreigners are members of the club, thus privileged to sit in the members' enclosure and enjoy that particular set of amenities. Traders and merchants from northern lands and Lebanese merchants (many of whom own horses) are there in number.

HOTELS

At any time, but especially during the summer months, you may find all the hotel rooms in Accra occupied, so you must wire ahead. Prices include breakfast.

Star Hotel, off Switchback Road (Box 3094, Accra) $15 single, $20 double.   As the years go by, the Star Hotel just mellows and ages gracefully. The rooms are well maintained and pleasant. The chalets are rented on a long-term basis, and even the regular rooms are usually booked solid. The Star's reputation is built on the continuing glamour of its outdoor night club and indoor café. Author's choice, and still the favorite with most Ghanaians.

Ambassador Hotel, Independence Road (P.O. Box 3034, Accra) $20 single, $25 double.   The rooms at the Ambassador are not so good—they are getting run-down; design is routine and stodgy. But, again, nobody goes to the Ambassador for the rooms. The point is to visit the café, lounge, restaurant, rooftop dance floor, zoo, pool, bookstore, curio shop, and the rest.

Continental Hotel, Liberation Road (P.O. Box 5252, Accra) $20 single, $25 double.   This is the newest place at the moment, and the brightest and shiniest. The rooms are OK, but the service is indifferent. *Again,* the whole point is in the restaurant, night club, crowds and casino.

Avenida Hotel, Kojo Thompson Road, Adabraka (P.O. Box 756, Accra) $12 single, $18 double.   Author's choice, assuming you can't get into the Star. The Avenida is centrally located, near downtown. The rooms are good for the price and you'll meet lots of people.

Washington Hotel, Tudu Road (P.O. Box 4295, Accra) $12 single, $18 double.   The one good thing about the Washington Hotel is its location downtown. Otherwise, it's third-class.

Kob Lodge, Ring Road Central (P.O. Box 1191, Accra) $12 to $18.   This place is much off the beaten track but quite nice. It is set in a quiet residential area, off one of the main thoroughfares. Service is good, and the atmosphere is pleasant.

Cheap Hotels

The best of Accra's hotels can be scruffy at times, so you can imagine the condition of the ones that are frankly fourth-rate. A couple are semi-brothels, while others are quite decent. Their virtue lies in the price, $5 a night; and also, they all have convenient locations. You may not find them suitable, but lots of other people do (at least for a few hours), so you may find these hotels fully booked, too.

The **Ghana Airport Hotel** (Accra International Airport) is good to remember in an emergency. The **Cosy Inn** offers small, air-conditioned rooms in a quiet residential area (Ring Road Central; P.O. Box 2547, Accra). **Ringway Hotel** (Ring Road Central) and the **Aams Hotel** (Nsawam Road near the Orion Cinema) are pretty grimy.

Inexpensive Residences

Students and others on a very tight budget have a choice of very good accommodations in Accra for less than $3 a night! Several charitable and governmental institutions maintain dormitory-style residences in good locations. The rooms are uniformly clean and adequate, and the atmosphere is cheerful and wholesome. Of course, they are always, always fully booked, but one of them may try to squeeze you in. You *must* write well in advance, stating clearly when you will be arriving. Even then you may find all rooms taken—because the first obligation of these residences is to accommodate visiting groups from their religious and cultural sponsors. But do try; the residences are a bargain, and they are great places for getting to know young people from many nations.

Methodist Hostel, on Liberia Road, one block east of T.U.C. Building   This hostel is part of the private living quarters of the Methodist church complex. It is comfortable, and the one place whose rooms are suitable for couples. The $2 charge includes breakfast.

YMCA, Castle Road (P.O. Box 738, Accra)   This newish building is well kept, and the rooms are good. You sleep four to a room, and the $2 charge includes breakfast *and* dinner. As you'd expect, it's hard to find a room here; and the last time the author inquired, there was a touring German student symphony orchestra taking up every single bed! So write ahead in plenty of time.

YWCA, Castle Road (P.O. Box 1504, Accra)   At this Y there are some double rooms, and some dormitories sleeping eight. The Y is so dowdy it's positively chic to stay there. It has long had a reputation as being a home-away-from-home for a cast of international beauties. Thus you will meet all kinds of fascinating people here. Breakfast not included. Double room residence $3 a night, $20 a month.

Ministry of Education Hostel—go north on Kojo Thompson Road, turn right at stop light at Farrar Avenue, continue up hill and follow the blue signs on your right.   The atmosphere in this hostel is free and informal; there are no locks on the doors, and people come and go casually. It is clean, neat and convenient. Breakfast included.

International Students Hostel—Airport Residential Area (write to the Warden, Students' Hostel, P.O. Box M.95, Accra)   The rooms here are clean, comfortable and spacious. The hostel is located in a choice residential area, and is set in a garden. It has good Ghanaian-style food, and recreation facilities. The only drawback is that an individual just doesn't have a chance to get in here during the months of July and August. Student groups come from all over the world, and use up every inch of space. Still, you should write anyway. It's worth a try.

University of Ghana, Legon   The university graciously allots a number of rooms to visitors associated with education. The guest houses are the most comfortable places to stay; price is around $7 a day. The rooms are in great demand, so you must inquire well in advance by writing to University Guest House, University of Ghana, Legon, Accra, Ghana; give the dates you require and ask for written confirmation.

Mensah Sarbah Hall rents student vacation rooms for $3 per day single, $4 double. It is usually not necessary to make advance reservations, but to be on the safe side you may write: Bursar, Mensah Sarbah Hall, University of Ghana, Legon, Accra, Ghana.

RESTAURANTS

Ghanaian home food is extraordinarily good, while public dining is pretty dismal. Ghanaians proudly print the recipes for groundnut stew, *palaver* sauce, palm-nut soup; in order to eat this hearty fare, however, it is necessary to wangle an invitation to a Ghanaian home. Otherwise the best you can do is order the "Ghanaian dish" at hotel or cafeteria luncheons. There you have no choice—only one offered at a time.

Generally, restaurant and hotel food is dreary, British, unimaginative, pallid and greasy. When the dining rooms prepare their menus they seem to ignore the bounties of Ghana's harvests as well as the traditions of Ghanaian and other tropical cuisines. For example, Accra is on the seacoast: its famous fishermen bring in a fresh catch every evening—pompano, mullet, red snapper, bluefish, butterfish and sole. Crab, crawfish, lobster, prawn and shrimp are in the market all year. But in the restaurants you'll only get a slice of stale fried fillet. No rich fish stews, no sautéed crabs, no grilled whole fish or barbequed shrimp, just flat, bland, meager little bits. Ghanaian gardens produce every manner of vegetable, but the carrots served are from a can. Ghanaian trees bend under their burden of fruits, but you look in vain for mango pie or pineapple sherbet.

On Sundays, though, all the restaurants try to do something special. The smaller places serve curry with trimmings and the hotels spread a lavish buffet. No matter what day it is, however, the service is generally atrocious; waiters disappear for months at a time.

Ghanaian Food

The enterprising person who opens up a first-class restaurant serving Ghanaian home-style food will make a million cedis. In the meantime you can have Ghanaian food (for lunch only) in a couple of places.

YWCA Cafeteria   Probably on a day-to-day, year-in, year-out basis, the Ghanaian dishes served at the Y are the best in the city. Under the direction of Miss Barbara Baeta, the cafeteria reached standards of consistently high quality, all for a cost of less than $1 a meal. The best part of the "Y" dining room is the exhilarating atmosphere at lunch. Afro-Americans in town have lunch there, as do many of Accra's young intellectual community and visiting students. For a while the YWCA was an intellectual café, and I could make a case for saying that a whole literary movement was generated there—but that's another book.

Joy Advanced Cafeteria, Liberia Road, two blocks east of Liberty Avenue   This is one of the most enjoyable places in town. Their Ghanaian food is excellent; the roast chicken is good too. They also serve a nice curry. Like the "Y," Joy is inexpensive; you can eat for less than $1.

Black Pot, Ring Road East, next to UNESCO   The Black Pot is owned by James Moxon, an Englishman, who has played a checkered role in Ghana's history and has managed to survive it all; you'll hear the stories. Food here is good Ghanaian-ish, meant to please its European and continental clientele. Portions are small; prices medium. Open for lunch *only,* from noon to 3 P.M.

Biscay, Cantonments Road at Lokko Road   It takes a bit of stretching to put the Biscay on this list, because it's mainly a Chinese restaurant, but it is one place that has Ghanaian dishes both at lunch and supper.

Hotel Restaurants

The **Star Hotel** always has a good Ghanaian dish at lunch, but it's quickly finished. At night the outdoor restaurant has a certain glamour. Try the pepper steak. If you are in the outdoor café of the **Ambassador Hotel,** order the club sandwich. The outdoor **Palm Wine Bar** is fun at lunch and the kebabs are good. The **Avenida Hotel** has a café that sells barbequed chicken accompanied by a pepper sauce. The **Continental Hotel** serves the usual thing, except on Sunday, when it has a good buffet, as does the Ambassador. The **Kob Lodge** has a genuinely quiet and comfortable atmosphere, and the food, such as it is, is served well.

There are two restaurants in the Washington Hotel on Tudo Road: **George's Chicken Bar** has an unsavory-looking entrance but it makes good roast chicken, kebabs, *kafta,* and other Lebanese and continental specialties. **Casanova,** on the top floor of the hotel, has very good seafood and steaks.

Expensive Restaurants

There are two restaurants in Accra which cater exclusively to an affluent expatriate community—diplomats, UN representatives and businessmen take every table. They offer good European food in an air-conditioned, refined atmosphere that meets international standards. Reservations are essential; a meal with drinks can easily run $10 per person.

Le Chevalier, Nsawam Road, Kokolemle (tel. 24088) Closed Sundays. The Chevalier is generally considered to be the best place in town. It offers Swiss cuisine in an intimate candlelight atmosphere; Italian specialties at lunch and a curry lunch on Saturday. Good meals, heavenly pastries.

Chez Maxim, on Achimota Road near Kotobabi Junction (tel. 27144) Excellent French cuisine in elegant surroundings.

Medium-Priced Restaurants

The **Mandarin** (Ring Road East, opposite UNESCO) is Accra's Chinese restaurant; the food is pretty good, and it has the advantage of staying open and serving meals continuously from noon to midnight. The **Maharaja** (on Pagan Road, in the Glamour Building) offers Indian cuisine. Though it is in decline, there is a steady clientele for lunch and dinner. Both of them make some attempt at "atmosphere." **Le Rêve** (Liberty Avenue near Pioneer Tobacco House) and **Uncle Sam's** (Kojo Thompson Avenue, Adabraka) both are modest restaurants selling French-style food. In Republic House on Liberty Road is the **Diplomat,** another one of the nicer places. It has good meat. **Edward's** (Cantonments Road, Osu) has continental and Lebanese dishes.

Snacks

Dan's Milk Bar, Liberty Avenue, near Farrar   One of those tightly shut, cool, antiseptic, pretty ice-cream parlors you find in West Africa, where you go to forget your tropical-type hassles. It sells all sorts of ice cream and pastries, and serves light meals.

Talal's, Liberty Avenue and North Liberia Road junction   Popular place where young expatriate crowd gets together for Lebanese meals and sweets.

Wato Café, Salaga Market Street off Salaga Market Circle   Fried chicken most days, made by a Ghanaian woman who has figured out how to do it American style, so Americans come here.

Glyco Confectionery, Liberty Avenue, north of North Liberia Road   There are a few tables where you can sit and eat the cakes and ice cream and drink the sodas.

Department Stores   Kingsway, U.T.C. and **G.N.T.C.** department stores all have a variety of packaged groceries and ready-to-eat foods. The best buy is the whole barbequed chicken available in the meat section. Each store also has a snack bar where soda, cakes and sandwiches are for sale.

NIGHT LIFE

For gaiety, bounce, energy, humor and artistry, Accra night life can't be beat. Ghanaians love to go out to dance, listen to music, see plays, hear the latest anecdotes, drink beer and laugh. The big hotels have combos playing a couple of nights a week and people come simply dressed for a casual evening of dancing and storytelling. The weekends begin to swing at noon on Saturday when people leave their jobs. They go straight from work to the cafés to eat and drink together, learn the latest political and society gossip, and, of course, to dance. Ghanaians know how to have rollicking good times, and the visitor is invited to join in.

Dancing

Dancing is what it is all about, and the dances are Highlife, and Afro-Soul. Highlife has its origins in African court music and in the music of Africans returned from the New World. It began as a dance for the urbane and sophisticated; it now enjoys mass popularity throughout all of West Africa. Black musical creativity is endlessly innovative, so there are new steps and new fads in Highlife every couple of months.

The dance spots are perfect for visitors. The atmosphere is relaxed and accepting. Regardless of proficiency, *anyone* can manage to move to the rhythms. And if you feel like watching, just sit back and frankly stare at the dancers; no one will mind. Men and women change dance partners easily; there is no uptightness about it. If you are a woman, expect your escort to dance with others, and be prepared to graciously accept invitations to dance from the gentlemen who come over.

Dance Halls   The **Star Hotel** reigns year after year as the liveliest, happiest place in town. It has a big, open-air dance floor decorated with colored lights and set in a garden; and also has an indoor café dance floor. The best bands play here and the skies are always glorious. The weekend crowds come from the ranks of civil servants, teachers, business people, students, expatriates, visitors— a gathering of handsome people who dress well and dance with style; there is no place nicer anywhere. **Tip Toe Gardens** has a reputation all over English-speaking Africa for its good bands and great dancing. The crowds, mostly Ghanaian, are younger, more intense, very involved with the latest steps. It all hangs out at the **Lido.** This huge open-air dance hall is jammed on the weekends and popular during the week too. It is a little unsavory around the edges, however, and located in a tough neighborhood; a single man can easily have a good time.

This listing of dance halls is just the tip of an iceberg. Tell your Ghanaian host what you'd like to see and hear and he'll take you there. The **Ambassador Hotel** and the **Continental Hotel** have resident bands that play for more sedate dancing and simple outdoor cafés where the music is hot and the crowds know how to swing. At the other end of the spectrum is the **Pan African Hotel** in Nima where the dancing goes down to the nitty-gritty. Somewhere in the middle is the **Apollo Theater,** where the dancers only want to hear Afro-American soul.

Discotheques   Discotheques, new on the Ghanaian scene, are not terribly popular, cater mainly to Europeans who like to drink hard liquor, smoke and kind of dance indoors in air conditioning under dim lights. The only one that attracts Ghanaians is **Sainte Nitouche** in Asylum Down. The music is good and the atmosphere is casual. The **Stereo Club** at the Washington Hotel is the latest in a series of "continental-style" attractions offered in this particular room. **Piccolo Mundo,** behind Republic House, is another you might try.

Night Clubs and Casinos

The only really Western-style night club in Accra is the **Bukom** in the Continental Hotel. Why you have come to Ghana to watch a third-rate acid rock group and some "interpretive dancers" is hard to fathom, but if you want it, there it is. Expensive, of course. Both the **Continental** and the **Ambassador** have casinos.

TOURING THE COUNTRY

KUMASI

While Accra is flat and dry, Kumasi (170 miles from Accra) in the high forest region is hilly and wet. While Accra has thorny bushes, Kumasi has lush greenery. Accra people look to the sea; Kumasi people look to the land. If Accra soil is meager, the soil of Kumasi gives gold and cocoa. With about 200,000 inhabitants, Kumasi is the second largest city of Ghana. And the richest.

"Koomasie" is a name to be reckoned with—the cultural, economic and political center of the Akan people. Always the seat of government for the Ashanti chief of state, Kumasi has been a prosperous, influential town for hundreds of years. Ashanti emerged as a unified state in the late 1600s. By the early 1700s it had developed into the most powerful state in the forest belt, controlling, from its strategic location, the traditional exchange of gold, salt, produce and slaves between north and south. Ashanti grew very wealthy, extending its influence to the coast to do business directly with Dutch and English trading forts; gold was diverted from the Sahara routes to the coasts in order to meet the challenge of European demands. The historian Basil Davidson tells us that

> Asante upheld its widespread peace and power for nearly two centuries. Safe and busy trading trails went out westward through Bondiku and Kong to the cities of the Middle and Upper Niger, eastward through Salaga to Hausaland, southward to the Europeans on the coast; and all these made Kumasi, the capital established "under the shade of the *kuma* tree," into a market of far-reaching influence and a place of majesty and sure protection, when European agents were allowed to come here [in 1817–1820] . . . they were impressed by the king's liberal trading policies, the city's comfortable urban spread, and the agreeable condition of the people there.

The attraction for imperialist powers was obvious, and the British were determined to rule this wealth-producing section of West Africa. The Ashanti battled them by diplomacy, politics and warfare, but ultimately lost to a combination of technological superiority and cultural arrogance. In the second British-Ashanti war, from 1873 to 1874, Kumasi was burned to the ground and Britain annexed all the states of southern Ghana, but Ashanti rallied under the leadership of King Prempeh I.

Political and economic strife continued between the two nations until 1901, when Ashanti finally came under British domination, a rule that was to continue for sixty years. The fight was long and bitter because Ghana was a prize; it was, with India and Malaya (rubber), the richest of Great Britain's colonies—in those sixty years, gold, cocoa, manganese, diamonds and manpower flowed into England, a source of great wealth for its crown and its businesses.

As part of modern Ghana, Kumasi is a center for mining, agricultural trade and transport. Vast earnings from growing cocoa, from gold and manganese, from trade in livestock and foodstuffs are the bases for Kumasi's wealth and power.

Note: The road between Accra and Kumasi is very hazardous. The author strongly suggests that you try to secure a place on State Transport, or that you travel by plane. Avoid private commercial transport and lorries at all cost.

Sights to See and Things to Do

National Cultural Centre   Open daily 9 A.M. to 6 P.M., Sundays 1 P.M. to 6 P.M.

The National Cultural Centre is the site of the *Prempeh II Jubilee Museum*, also known as the *Asante Cultural Centre*. This is a museum that highlights the Akan cultural heritage: a whole range of magnificent objects that are part of the chief's regalia, examples of sculpture, personal ornaments, handcrafted traditional home furnishings, weaponry and musical instruments. Certain extremely important and valuable items of Ashanti culture and history are on reserve here, among them the treasure bag of the founding priest of Ashanti which has not been opened in nearly three hundred years.

The museum is set in beautiful, terraced gardens that welcome visitors and strollers. In the middle there is a plaza where open-air entertainment and receptions are held. Musical and dramatic presentations are frequently presented in the auditorium, and in a building housing the library and archives. A short walk away is the small zoo. It has a terrifying exhibition of snakes: the keepers put all of the same species in a big box, so they get all intertwined into one scaly, twisting mass with a hundred horrible, hissing heads.

Ghana Military Museum   The history of Ashanti military might, the force that fought off Britain for decades, is on display here. You can see weapons, documents, trophies and photographs. The museum is housed in Kumasi Fort, was built in 1816. by King Osei Tutu, and reconstructed at the turn of the century.

Grounds of Kumasi Hospital   On the grounds of the Kumasi Hospital are two landmarks of historical importance to Ashanti. One is the tree marking the spot where the Golden Stool, symbol of the divine rulership of Ashanti kings, descended from heaven. Another feature is the Sword of Okomfo Anokye, the founding priest of Ashanti. This sword was planted in the ground by the great priest as a symbol of the unity of the Ashanti people. Said to be impervious to all attempts to pull it out, it is a symbol of divine protection given Ashanti.

Kumasi Market   Giant and sprawling, Kumasi Market is the largest in Africa. It is a world unto itself—blocks of tomatoes, streets of yam, acres of pots and pans. It is exhausting and fascinating—too overwhelming for any economist's study, a focal point of striving and exchange.

University of Science and Technology   A beautiful place, built on tumbling hills, this is the center for the study of science, art and technology. They have a superb swimming pool that you may get permission to use.

Places to Stay and Eat

City Hotel $7 to $15.   A modern hotel, with considerable personality; the rooms are nice and well kept, and the restaurant is good. Whole families come to take refreshments in the lounges. For a while they had an open-air bar on the roof with charming swinging settees.

Government Catering Resthouse $6 to $8.   Built in the old, rambling colonial style, the Catering Resthouse is perpetually popular with visitors because it is so clean and comfortable. Cost of the room includes a sumptuous breakfast. The bar is a lively meeting place serving snacks and cold beer. In the restaurant the daily Ghanaian dish is quickly sold out and you are left with the usual English miserables.

Laundry Street Resthouse $2 single.   The price is very reasonable, and the facilities meager. No meals served.

Hotel de Kingsway $2 to $6   Right in the center of town, the Hotel de Kingsway is now quite notorious. The rooms are in bad shape. The restaurant, bar and night club are always jumping.

University of Science and Technology   If you have academic affiliations you can rent clean nice rooms at the university for around $1.50 a night. Though it's a good distance from town center, there are always taxis and lorries going in.

Tourist Cottage Club $4 single, $6 double.   Located off Ahinsan Road, near the East Sports Stadium, this place is quite satisfactory. There is a garden and a restaurant.

The Cabin Restaurant; The Chicken Bar   Both quiet places selling Western food and refreshments.

Excursions from Kumasi

Craft Villages   From Kumasi the tourist can visit nearby craft villages. **Bonwire,** on the Kintampo Road, is the *kente*-weaving village. Visitors have the opportunity to see many weavers at work, and to choose from a large selection of beautiful cloth, in whole pieces, strips and smaller items. The place to buy stools is at **Awhia** on the Mampong Road. There are several shops, all selling a variety of designs and shapes in a range of prices. For background and symbolism of the stools read the book by the Reverend Dr. Peter Sarpong, the Catholic bishop of Kumasi: *The Sacred Stools of the Akan.* Five miles farther along the same road is the **Adinkra Cloth Village,** where craftsmen offer splendid examples of these fabrics for sale.

Natural sites   It is only seventeen miles to **Lake Bosumtwi,** on a road that passes through a forest of hauntingly strange trees. It is the only natural lake in Ghana. The lake, which is about two hundred feet above sea level, lies in what appears to be a perfect bowl or cup, and is surrounded by thickly wooded hills rising seven hundred feet. Shrouded in myth and mystery, the lake is a sacred place; there is always a young guide on hand who will lead you down to its edge and tell you its legends.

When you travel to **Obuasi,** 40 miles south of Kumasi, take time to observe the richness of Ashanti's landscape. With its hills, and ridges and valleys, the surface is endlessly varied. The forests are thick and shadowy. This is where cocoa grows, the black gold of modern Ghana. The gold of Obuasi is yellow, from Ghana's richest mines.

Northern and Upper Regions

Ghanaians use the term "the North" to refer to the large, sparsely populated northern regions of the country. Part of this area belonged to the great medieval kingdoms of Mali and Songhai of Western Sudan. When these Sudanic empires broke up, some of the people, mostly Muslims, moved south and west into the area bordering the Ashanti kingdom.

For the traveler who can spare the time, a trip to the North can be extremely rewarding. The people of northern Ghana differ greatly in religion, culture and tradition from those of the south, so the visitor sees another whole world of artistic expression, another whole range of economic and social activities. The people look different: they are taller, slimmer, more restrained in character than the outgoing people you have been meeting. Southern Ghana can be frenetic, jarring to the nerves, overripe; in contrast, the North is austere and serene. After the density and funkiness of Accra and Kumasi, you will appreciate the spacious calm of Tamale and Bolgatanga.

The climate is hot and dry, except for the rainy months of June and July when the earth turns green. The countryside is open and undulating, its vegetation a low savannah-grassland. Though no cash crops grow there, the area produces grain and livestock. There is little prosperity; life is more difficult. Water often is scarce and people at home or on their farms wear only the barest of clothing.

The traditional houses of the North are of great beauty and utility. They represent masterpieces of "anonymous architecture," forms developed over time to cope most efficiently with the natural environment and to satisfy the occupants' sense of grace and symmetry. The better homes in the North are built of dark clay, the walls richly ornamented, the rooms cool and comfortable.

Tamale Tamale, 240 miles north of Kumasi, is the capital of the Northern Region. The northeast road out of Kumasi through Mampong is an excellent paved road. Flying, however, is advisable. For good lodgings and good meals, go to the **Catering Resthouse** (P.O. Box 100, Tamale; $5). Next to the Assembly of God Church there is also a chop bar selling hot meals for around 50 cents. There are several places of interest: the **Gulkpe Na's Palace** and the **Tolon Na's Palace,** both traditional residences for important local chiefs (the word *"Na"* means "Chief"); the **Central Mosque;** and the beer breweries. The best shopping is for the popular Ghana men's smock, *batakari* made of handspun, handwoven country cloth. The selection is huge, the prices cheap, and the market amiable.

Bolgatanga This is another 100 miles north, right near Ghana's border with Upper Volta. The landscape here is unusual. There are long empty stretches, then suddenly a mountain. In the crystal-clear air the sunsets are a remarkable play of light and color. The **Black Star Motel** (Box 18, Bolgatanga) and the **Hotel de Bull** both have comfortable, air-conditioned rooms for about $7 a night; they both have restaurants. There are many snack bars in town where you can get light meals. The great attraction of Bolgatanga is the **central market.** A wide selection of craft work of high quality is on sale here for very low prices: camel's-hair blankets, leather goods, smocks and the handsomely woven baskets. The atmosphere is lively and friendly. For entertainment, there are often performances by itinerant snake charmers and by sword dancer–acrobats.

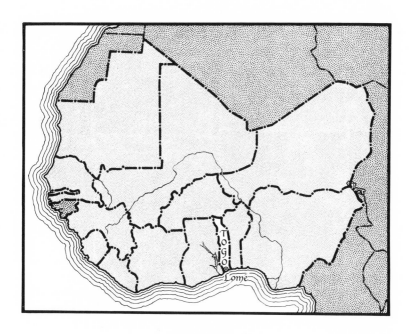

Togo
LOMÉ

Togo is a sliver of land sandwiched between Ghana on the west and Dahomey on the east, the second smallest republic in West Africa. With a 31-mile coastline, it is only 93 miles across at its widest point. While narrow, Togo is quite long, plunging 370 miles into the African interior. As a consequence, it has an extraordinary range of topography for so small a country. Togo is divided diagonally from the northeast to the southwest by a range of mountains, but on both sides of this diagonal line are large plains well watered by Togo's rivers. Only 2 million people live in this tiny land.

273

The capital, Lomé—120,000 population—is a swinging little town located on the coastal road linking Accra and Lagos, by way of Togo and Dahomey. The journey from Accra to Lagos is as beautiful and educational a tour as you can take in West Africa, and easy to do. In a space of less than one hundred miles the traveler touches four different countries: the scenery is glorious, the cultures rich and fascinating, the people gracious and hospitable. When American summer-vacation planes land in West Africa they discharge passengers in Accra and pick them up in Lagos for the trip back, assuming rightly that the travelers will want to visit the four different countries.

During the "season" from November through May, scores of European vacationers arrive in Lomé to enjoy the sun and seashore. Many are Germans who have all sorts of package tours coming to Lomé. Before World War I, Togo was a colony of Germany, and there is still a great deal of German influence here. While in possession of Togo, the Germans set out to make it a model, showcase colony; in the early 1900s they built the telecommunications system, good roads, wharves, a railway system and a large Protestant cathedral.

In 1918, after four years of British administration, Togo was divided and placed under a League of Nations mandate. The western section was allotted to Great Britain, and following a United Nations plebiscite, became part of Ghana in 1956, shortly before the latter's independence. The larger eastern area was placed under French tutelage, becoming an autonomous republic within the French Union in 1956. It became fully independent in 1960.

For the visitor, Lomé seems to have a frivolous, resort quality about it. Eating and drinking, sleeping and swimming seem to be the important things here. Perhaps because of its obscurity, Lomé is a delightful place to come for a breather. Ghanaians, Ivorians and Dahomeans all come to relax: it is one of those few places in West Africa that is a holiday spot for other Africans.

For a couple of dollars the visitor can rent a taxicab for the entire morning to see the sights. You will want to take a look at the beach, the wharf, the harbor, the old presidential palace built by the German governors seventy years ago. At the new executive residence you can see the pure lines of the symbolic marble sculpture by the Togolese artist Paul Akyi. Then on to Independence Park with its monument, the Kponton Museum (a private, historical museum containing photographs and mementoes of the German colonial period), the cathedral, the Protestant church, the high school, the Central Market. That's it.

Observation: Lake Togo A short drive from Lomé—around 15 miles—is Lake Togo, a vast triangle of fresh water about seven miles long on each side, fed slowly by four different rivers. It is only about six or seven feet deep; it is filled with fish and crustaceans, as well as clumps and tangles of aquatic reeds and vines. The lake is so serene and inviting that a small resort complex has been built on its shores—a hotel (comfortable chalets for $6), a fine restaurant serving excellent seafood and wine, a small outdoor café, facilities for public and water sports, and a yachting club. On Sunday afternoon the French of Lomé come in crowds to enjoy fine cuisine and outdoor recreation, but during the week the spot is quiet, fully staffed and almost deserted.

Even if you have a car at your disposal, you should take the trip by public transportation and by foot to enjoy the full color of the area and be open for pleasant surprises. The more leisurely pace and meandering route gives the open-minded traveler a chance to get close to West African life. From the lorry park you take a station-wagon taxi going to the lake. The drive along the coastal road is picture-book pretty: miles of coconut palms, small fishing villages, beaches of fine white sand, graceful canoes, foaming surf.

The stop for the lake is under a large, weather-beaten billboard marking the village of Porto-Séguro; an arrow on the sign points to the side road on the left that you have to take next. (*Attention:* the taxi reaches this point quickly, so you must keep saying "Lac Togo" and "Porto-Séguro" to remind the driver of your stop.) The way to the lake is nearly a mile more, but if you walk at a comfortable pace you will find that you can cover the distance easily. There is much to see along the way.

In days gone by, Porto-Séguro knew a brief prosperity and historical significance as a trading center for palm oil; now its two thousand inhabitants are fishermen and artisans. There is still evidence of its former importance: abandoned warehouses falling into decay, and big two-story Brazilian-style houses, built by Africans returned from South America. Along the way there are rows of tables where patient women and children sell salt, sugar, pepper, vegetables, rice and delicious ears of roasted corn.

The road crosses some railroad tracks and continues right through the gate of "Le Lac," the lakeside resort that is the traveler's destination. Straight ahead is the expanse of Lake Togo, after which the country of Togo itself is named. One of the villages across from the hotel is Togoville, where the treaty was signed in 1884 between Germany and the chief of Togoville, placing Togo under German "protection," a euphemism for colonization.

We, a couple from New York, took this route one afternoon. By the time we arrived at the café we were thirsty and tired, grateful for the shade and cool drinks. No one was around except the bartender and waitress. We talked of this being a sacred lake surrounded by sacred forests; perhaps we just imagined a special aura. We decided to go out for a tour on the water and the barman beckoned one of the dugout canoes cruising on the lake. The rower was a slight, serious young lad about ten years old. The barman explained in their language that he was to take us out in the boat. We entered, pushing off from the sandy shore; we were afloat.

With his long pole braced on the lake bottom, the boy guided the craft over the water; his demeanor was solemn; his pet crab perched unobtrusively on the stern. We soon reached the middle of the lake where the only sounds to be heard were the cries of birds overhead and the rustle of the wind in the sheaves of water rushes. We skimmed silently around the tangles of lake lotus, and suddenly we felt unnerved . . . the grave child at the helm, the silence, the distances, the unfamiliar craft, the slender pole.

The boy continued calmly on, poling his way to a small landing where a little friend was waiting. With that same studied cool the other boy joined us and together we glided toward a farther shore. The boat was beached on a tiny slip of sand for the benefit of the second boy, who now went off without a word while we got out to stretch our legs. Nearby we noticed the hulk of an abandoned boat, several people standing silent, a small clearing, and then a dense forest, the sacred forest. Something mysterious was in the air.

As we stood there we suddenly heard and glimpsed a chanting

procession, twenty women in their thirties and forties, devotées of the lake. With sarongs wrapped under their arms, they walked barefoot and bareheaded. Their faces were covered with white powder and they had adorned themselves with necklaces, bracelets and anklets of gold and old beads. Heading the line was the priestess; her eyes glared at the interlopers, but she never missed a beat of the rhythm. The women gathered at the edge of the lake, moving in patterns, singing to the waters, communing with the spirits. Their ritual over, they turned and danced back into the forest.

The boy was being scolded by the Africans standing nearby for the faux pas of landing at the time of a sacred ceremony. We were curious and fascinated, wanting to know what was going on, but we could only converse in English with a wave-watcher who, alas, was only interested in talking about my gold bracelets. The mystery remained. It was time to return to the café, so far away in time and space from this holy beach. The journey on the lake seemed as menacing as before, but so much faster now. Whatever we paid, the lad was pleased enough to smile his thanks, then push off again.

At the café there were several people laughing and talking. Minutes before, we had been gliding over baptismal waters; now, suddenly, we were returned to the world of Western tourists. We went to the hotel's tiny zoo to look at the captive monkeys and alligators and birds. We were once again outside nature, able to stand, safe and protected, observing energy and dynamism captured and caged. Out on the lake we had felt the continuity between ourselves and all other living things and natural phenomena, but here we were severed from the stars again, looking at God's creatures with distant amusement.

We returned to Porto-Séguro, over the tracks, onto the direct road. It was about six o'clock. From afar we heard drumbeats, and as we approached we saw the crowds. It was festival time. We learned that twice a year religiously inclined women of the area retreat to a traditional convent for several days of spiritual renewal. Before they leave their families and friends, they stage an evening of music and dance, attended by hundreds of people from neighboring villages. The women at the lake were part of the group.

The women, thirty or forty of them now, danced around and around in a circle and occasionally one, then another, would break into a fancy individual step. The crowd watched the bawdy antics of a heavyset woman who was dressed like a male circus tramp. She harassed the drummers, pantomimed lewd intentions and chased after the religious women with a stick. The "victim" would shriek and flee until the "man" would break into a boisterous dance and the circle would form again, drumbeats rocking steadily.

All the spectators were splendidly dressed and the air was filled with the smells of roasting lambs and simmering stews. The man standing next to us, like so many others in the crowd, we learned, made it a point to come home to this village twice a year in time for this festival. The feasting and merrymaking, he told us, would go on long into the night. It was getting dark—we were hoping he would invite us home with him, but he didn't. So, regrettably, it was time to head back to our hotel in Lomé.

* * *

LEISURE AND PLEASURE

In the morning
—Take a tour of the Benin Brewery, tasting the product as you go along.
—Play mini-golf on the grounds in the Hotel Bénin, because you would never, never play mini-golf at home.
In the afternoon
—Try to be at the beach in the late afternoon when the Ewe fishermen return, greeted by the trading women.
—Enjoy the beautiful promenades of the city: the Freau Gardens, Marine Boulevard, the residential areas, the harbors.
In the evening
—Choose a restaurant for a superb French dinner.
—Dance the waltz at the Edelweiss night club.

GETTING AROUND

The price for a taxi ride within the city limits is 75 francs (around 30 cents); at night it goes up to 100 francs. It is a regular taxi ride to the Ghana border, only about five minutes away. The taxi to Cotonou in Dahomey is about $2 per person, leaving from the lorry park. Cars are for rent at Tele-Taxi and at the Garage du Centre.

THINGS TO DO

If you are planning to stay in Lomé more than a few days, be sure to find out about the activities sponsored by the various national cultural centers. The French organize evenings of dance, theater and music, and they present art exhibits. The German Goethe Institute also has a full program of events; and the U.S. center offers American movies on Wednesday and Sunday nights for 60 cents' admission.

American Cultural Center, corner of Rue Pelletier and Rue Vauhan, across from the U.S. embassy
Centre Culturel Français, Rue des Alliés
British Council, Rue d'Amoutivé
Goethe Institute, Rue de l'Église

SHOPPING

Objects made by craftsmen of Togo are hard to come by; instead, you will find here the usual West African display of tourist art pieces. Since everything you see is imported from neighboring states, you are better off buying them *there,* not here. If you must buy, bargain hard.

Les Arts Nègres is on Rue de Maréchal Foch. Gallerie Africaine and Sculpture Africaine are both on Rue de Maréchal Galliéni; and the **Maison Historique** . . . they all sell African art. As you'll see, they are all within walking distance of one another.

The Lomé airport has a *tax-free shop* where you can buy perfume, whiskey, and other imported luxury items at a very low price. Look through the large Central Market (cloth is on the second floor; sandals and such on the third); it is most animated on Wednesday and Saturday.

EXCURSIONS

The Tourist Office will help you arrange full-day excursions to nearby places of interest.

Visit to Anécho

Anécho is a town of 12,000 people about 27 miles from Lomé along the beautiful coastal road. In the 1800s Anécho shipped gold and ivory and was a notorious slave center. After the suppression of the slave trade and the establishment of outright European colonial control in West Africa, Anécho became the capital of German Togo for a couple of years, from 1885 to 1887. Under the French regime it was the capital from 1914 to 1920. During these periods, Anécho developed into a prosperous town. It is significant today as Togo's leading commercial city. All the major European trading companies have branch offices here. It is an important agricultural center (palm kernels, copra, manioc and castor seeds) and it is located close to rich phosphate deposits now being actively and profitably exploited. The visitor will enjoy a trip to the town and to its lagoon.

Visit to Palimé

Palimé is 72 miles north of Lomé in the Akposso hills, a two-hour drive over good roads. It is the center of the coffee- and cocoa-growing region, and near several pleasant tourist spots. Palimé is a pretty little town of 14,000 souls set in park-like groves of flowering trees. Monday is market day, and on Sunday there is drumming and dancing in the streets—so both are especially good days for a visit. There is a Benedictine monastery, an artisans center and a dam in town. Not far away is **Château Viale,** a German castle built on a hill, harking back to the time when the Germans used Palimé as a commercial and administrative center.

Just a few minutes from Palimé is the remarkable **Kpimé waterfall,** three hundred feet high, whose cliffs are covered with thick verdure. The torrents plunge in short distances, then hit a rock table; from there they spray out and fall furiously into the circular hollow in the side of the hill, all amid a tangle of trees, vines and bushes. A glimpse of the primeval.

On this trip, the Tourist Office arranges for you to stop at an experimental agricultural and animal-breeding farm. Before you make a face, consider that such visits can be educational and fascinating. (A friend still recalls his visit to the research station in Guinea that had supplied Able and Baker, the two monkeys sent up in an American satellite. You remember things like that!)

PLACES TO STAY AND EAT

Hotel Bénin (B.P. 128, Lomé; tel. 44-85) International Standing. $10 single, $20 double. This is a good hotel, set in gardens and centrally located in a residential area right on the seashore. All the rooms and suites are air-conditioned, clean and comfortable. Each has a large balcony, and the best ones overlook the beach. There is a fine swimming pool and facilities for miniature golf and volleyball. Boring French and continental food is the best the large dining room can manage. Meals about $5.

The Bénin's outdoor terrace café and indoor cocktail lounge (there is also a bar) are the chic places to come to sit and meet people. French-style sandwiches and steins of icy beer are served. The lounge is bright and open, with chairs and sofas arranged for conversation. A continental pianist sometimes plays in the early evening.

Edith's Inn, on Rue Van Lare (B.P. 1703, Lomé) Screened bunk rooms at $3 per bed; $5 single, $10 double. Author's choice for one of the most enjoyable places an American traveler will find in West Africa. It is owned and operated by Edith Simpson, a black American woman who manages to run a "tight ship" and at the same time create a warm, informal atmosphere.

The restaurant has all the regular American favorites—hamburgers, pizza, ice-cream sundaes and such, and on Wednesday night they serve Chinese-style food. Every day, though, you'll find dishes cooked with a touch of soul: fried or roast chicken, ribs, rice and gravy, greens, cornbread and delicious cobblers and pies—all at reasonable prices. Sunday morning Edith makes fresh doughnuts for breakfast. There is great jazz on the stereo and a display of paintings by Ted Pontiflet, an outstanding black American artist.

Sure, you'll meet lots of Americans here. In fact, no one from this area would think of passing through without checking to see the Simpsons. So it's a good place to catch up on the latest happenings and get into some good discussions. Don't miss this place; write ahead for reservations.

L'Auberge Provençale, Avenue de la République (B.P. 1.138, Lomé; tel. 44-79) $15 for an air-conditioned single, $18 for a double. Though it is one of the most expensive places in town, the Auberge is always crowded. That's because   serve excellent meals in pleasant surroundings. In the open-air restaurant on the ground floor, there is a huge outdoor fireplace where the chef grills the steaks and the fish. The air-conditioned dining room upstairs is more formal. Meals start at $6. This place has truly fine food and a loyal clientele of diplomats, pilots and old-style *colons.* Nice rooms also.

Hotel du Golfe, 5 rue du Commerce (B.P. 36, Lomé; tel. 41-41). Rooms $10; $15 air-conditioned, all doubles. This is the most popular hotel with visitors to Lomé because it is clean, quiet and located in the commercial center. All the rooms are big enough for two, so the non-air-conditioned ones are really bargains. The air-conditioned restaurant features fine French cuisine. They are famous for the best escargots, frog's legs and such, and for a superb omelette. Meals around $4–$6. The place is spotless, simply furnished, set in a garden on a quiet street. The price range of the rooms attracts the thriftiest student and the most seasoned traveler.

Foyer des Marins, Route d'Anécho, just before the port. Rooms $3; $6 air-conditioned. Built as a recreational area for visiting sailors, the Foyer offers a pool, game room, films, etc. The comfortable and breezy rooms are available to outsiders if they are unoccupied. Like the rooms, the food is a bargain. A full meal with a bottle of beer can be less than $1.

Hotel de la Plage, Avenue de la République. Only non-air-conditioned rooms. $6 to $10. Clean, well situated across the road from a lively beach, this is for budget travelers who won't mind the awful beds and rudimentary furnishings. Popular restaurant serving Lebanese food ($3–$5 for a full meal). A live band on Saturday nights.

Hotel Miramar, Route d'Anécho (B.P. 502, Lomé; tel. 61-41) International class. Building entirely air-conditioned. $24 double. This is one of those glistening new "ocean liners," one of those very exclusive places that is expensive and cocooned in luxury. It is near the beach and has a good pool and a fine restaurant. All that is beside the point—the place is strictly for gambling and gaming. There is a casino (part of the "La Frisco" international chain) where you may play baccarat, blackjack, roulette and chemin de fer, plus an assortment of slot machines. No innocent pleasures here.

RESTAURANTS

Togolese Food Try the **Café Tabac** ("airport road," three blocks after Boulevard Circulaire, on the right). Varied menu of local specialties, plus steak and chips for $1. **Café Nazar** (turn left off Rue l'Église at Bata Shoes—café on the right) is much the same.

In Town:

Las Vegas Snack, Avenue des Alliés Lebanese food and attempted hamburgers; slow service, noisy, especially when air conditioner is off; also service outside on sidewalk under awning. Full meal, $4.

Mini Brasserie, Rue de la Gare Always active and full of people; attractive décor of small wooden tables and copper ornaments; you can also eat out back. Fast service. Good German sausages, goulash. Full meal about $3.

Paris Snack, Rue de la Gare, across the street from the Mini Brasserie Small, quiet restaurant in front; nice bar with records and dance floor in back. Good steaks. Full meal about $5.

4ᵉ Zone, Boulevard Circulaire, eastern end   Vietnamese food in generous quantities with large choice. Served outside under a festively lit tree.

At the Port:

La Provençale   This casual establishment consists of several small thatched *rondelles,* and a main one where you can sit at the bar. All outdoors and very relaxing.

Mini Beach   Small, casual, breezy. Swim and then eat in your bathing suit. Very crowded at Sunday lunch, with incredibly slow service. Good food; full meal about $4. Tends to get hectic.

Ramatou   Newest of all. Big *rondelle* with several smaller ones. Good food.

More Goodies

Milk Bar, off Boulevard Circulaire, eastern end; look for a small black-and-white sign with arrow   Great homemade ice cream! Lots of flavors; largest variety on weekends. A medium bowl costs about 20 cents. Frequent additions of favorites like mint chocolate chip and plain chocolate chip.

Souper Boulangerie, corner of Rue de Commerce and Rue de la Gare   French pastry shop with bread, croissants, lots of pastries; the ice cream comes from France. Several tables, so you can stuff yourself right on the spot.

Romeo's, Rue d'Amoutivé   Self-service. Selection of gourmet goods from all over the world. British jams, French wines and cheeses, Italian sausages, Mexican food, and cornflakes. There is a bar that is always busy with congenial, jovial company.

NIGHT CLUBS

For a town its size, Lomé has an outstanding collection of places offering the visitor a relaxed, enjoyable time. These are the night clubs frequented by an international clientele (drinks around $1–$1.50):

Maquina Loca, Ancien Boulevard Circulaire (now named Avenue de Calais) Frequented by the Togolese beautiful people, this is a place to go for the whole evening, not just to hop in and out of on your swing around town. There is usually a live band on Saturday nights, which adds a cover charge at the door. Air-conditioned.

Ambiance A rough place that visiting sailors are warned not to frequent when their ship is in, and not surprisingly it is generally packed whenever a naval ship has docked. Bar and dance floor. Live band is usually in evidence on weekends. No air conditioning. Drinks $1.

Le Rêve, corner of Rue d'Amoutivé and Avenue des Alliés Large dance floor, French records, mainly European clientele, not favored by faithful night-clubbing regulars.

Watusi, corner of Rue de l'Église and Rue de Chemin de Fer Here is the club with perhaps more soul than any other in town. The establishment, small and dark, is well patronized by young members of the American and Togolese jet sets; usually jammed tight on Saturdays. Modern American records and modern dances. Helpful staff. Precarious bar stools. Disgusting urinal.

Edelweiss, Rue de Palimé Lomé's French and Lebanese businessmen come here to clinch their latest deals, and sometimes to relax. Modern décor and comfortable seating with a well-stocked bar. Mostly French music, not all of the "pop" variety—in deference to those numerous clients whose expert glides and turns around the floor to the lilting strains of the waltz are a joy to behold. Effective air conditioning, but smoke gets in your eyes on Saturday evenings—not a bad thing if asphyxiation by Gauloises fumes tends to bring back memories of Paris. Drinks $2.

Club 421, Rue de l'Église, across from Goethe Institute A dimly lit, thoroughly air-conditioned night club catering mainly to Europeans. The bar is well stocked and the barman knows how to make your favorite drinks. Music is French (American discotheque). Upstairs there is a nice restaurant. Though the décor is Chinese, the food is French, very good and quite reasonably priced.

Le Pussy-Cat, Boulevard Circulaire, eastern end   A large dance floor bordered with tiny tables. Low lighting in the night club and low temperatures at the bar. A good restaurant also. Though not known as a hotel, Le Pussy-Cat also has a few rooms for $10–$15.

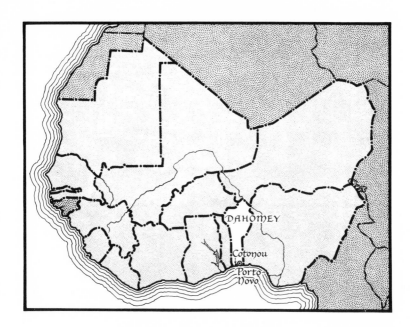

Dahomey
COTONOU and PORTO-NOVO

Modern crusaders from Europe and America are digging and poking all over West Africa. Where formerly white knights sought the Holy Grail, they now search for minerals. Long-abandoned reaches of sand turn to battlegrounds as soon as oil is discovered under the dunes. Sweltering, bug-ridden swamps become prized land once bauxite is found a few feet down. Uranium, diamonds, copper and gold below the ground; skins, timber, cocoa, palm oil above: Africa is rich. Alas, Dahomey *isn't*.

Two and a half million people live in Dahomey, a small country between Togo and Nigeria. It is one of the most densely populated African countries. Dahomey is self-sufficient in food, but she simply has yet to find any resource for export that has any great value on the international market. Her only cash export is palm oil. As world prices of raw materials continue to fall, Dahomey can only thrash about, searching for some way to afford the enormous carrying charges involved in maintaining the trappings of contemporary nationhood, little of which can be exchanged for oranges and bananas; United Nations membership fees are payable in hard currency only.

Dahomey is no "new African nation"; this is an old land where life has always been intricate and complicated, overlayed and entangled. The kings of Dahomey (known formerly as Danhomé) have no match in African history. The ruling dynasties consolidated their power in the 1600s, and continued until defeated by the French and British in the 1890s. They were absolute rulers of highly centralized states.

Today's Dahomey seems as complicated as the old. It is impossible to consider Dahomey without noting its recent turbulent political history. Since its independence from France in 1960, Dahomey has had the largest number of political crises and changes of government of any African country. The most remarkable, though of course temporary, solution was the three-man presidential council, one member of which was chief of state for a rotating two-year term. It worked for a while—there was even a smooth turnover in order from the first President to the regime of the second. Then the whole thing broke down, another military coup, another government.

The troika was an attempt to achieve some harmony in this unstable situation. It was composed of the three leading civilian political leaders who represented Dahomey's three rival centers of power—Porto-Novo in the southeast, Abomey in the southwest, and Parakou in the north. Governments past, present and yet to come now all face the same, probably unsolvable problems: there simply is not enough money to meet government expenses, and not enough opportunity for Dahomey's brilliant, energetic population.

During the colonial administration, Dahomeans were noted for their intelligence and high level of education. They did extremely well under the French system and moved into responsible positions throughout the French West African territories where local people had fewer educational opportunities. Many Dahomeans still work in France, Canada, Senegal, Nigeria, Gabon, Zaïre, Ethiopia—wherever there is a place for their skills. Tens of thousands of others, however, have returned home after losing their jobs to newly qualified nationals of their host countries, while thousands more have fled back, refugees from anti-Dahomean persecution. In the Ivory Coast and Ghana, for example, pressures to provide employment for fully trained local citizens meant that Dahomeans were forced sometimes unceremoniously to leave their jobs and flee the country.

The presence of this remarkable intelligentsia, along with a large and sophisticated military, powerful traditional chiefs and rulers, foreign intervention, well-organized unions, long-suffering rural dwellers—all make for rollicking, often bitter rivalries in politics, economics and culture, periodic violence and coups. It all tends to bewilder and astonish the visitor, but is balanced and understood by a wise population that somehow, with dignity and graciousness, manages to cope.

Every inch of Dahomean soil has its history. Every bit of land has been fought over and has changed hands many times between different Africans and Europeans. Cotonou today is a quiet town with shady streets and slow traffic, but this calm was not always so. Twice before, a town had grown on this site and twice was destroyed by warfare; the present Cotonou is Cotonou *Three*.

It was thought that Cotonou was first founded through the amalgamation of two neighboring villages. The great and terrible warrior-king Agadja of Abomey, pushed his way to the coast from a hundred miles inland in order to profit directly from the growing coastal trade with Europeans, and Cotonou was destroyed in the battles of 1732. After a time the town came back to life, only to be leveled again by one of Agadja's descendants.

When the slave trade was interrupted by some European powers, the king of Abomey looked for waters not policed by foreign soldiers to continue the illegal trade. Cotonou was rediscovered and re-established in the 1800s as an alternate slaving port, but gradually slave trading came to have so many risks that the king looked for other uses for Cotonou. One of his ministers developed palm-nut plantations, using the captives as laborers, and began this important Dahomean industry. (The export of palm kernels and oil accounts for 75 percent of Dahomey's foreign earnings today.) Trading treaties were signed between the king and the French, and branches of French merchant houses were constructed along the coast, but soon foreign merchants began to exercise such influence that the sovereignty of the Dahomean kingdom was seriously threatened. When the last king of the Abomey dynasty, Béhanzin, mounted the throne, he resolved to expel the French. He nullified the agreements signed by his predecessors and mounted a campaign to regain control of Cotonou and its commerce. He attacked twice in 1889 but lost both battles and was forced to withdraw. Cotonou came firmly under French control. From this beachhead they spread their influence and by 1892 Dahomey was under French dominion, not to regain its political independence until 1960.

Cotonou is the economic and administrative center of modern Dahomey, although Porto-Novo, eighteen miles away, is the official capital. While Porto-Novo becomes more and more a suburb, Cotonou grows steadily. The huge, gaudy presidential mansion is located in Cotonou, as are most of the ministries, government operations, foreign embassies, large merchant firms, the airport, railroad and central post office—a concentration of administrative, commercial and industrial life. Because it is outside the political spheres controlled by the big three regional factions, Cotonou is perennially a district in dispute; in order to take control of Dahomey, a faction must first rule Cotonou. To be buffeted by a succession of clashing interests seems to be Cotonou's fate—seven changes since independence, a continuation of its early history.

Visually, Cotonou displays the divisions typical of a French-developed town. There are posh residential districts, a solid commercial area, nice greenery and spacious landscaping. A walk along the beach and harbor provides a view of Dahomey's modern economy: the warehouses hug the harbor; the railroad lines reach to their doors. Workers are handling palm kernels, coffee, peanuts and cotton. The newly enlarged harbor is prospering, and Cotonou is now the port for landlocked Niger to the north. What intrigues and battles went into the construction of this place! Every inch of space carved out from another power's influence, still influenced by foreign powers.

The most compelling aspect of the town is the ocean-at-the-end-of-the-street. The visitor strolls absentmindedly down a shady, peaceful block when suddenly, without warning, the world dazzles open to infinity. Surrounded by the familiar and mundane, modest houses and leafy trees, you are shocked by the limitless expanse of ocean and the limpid brilliance of the light.

LEISURE AND PLEASURE

In the morning
—Buy some beautiful stamps at the post office philatelic desk.
—Wander through the African residential areas.
In the evening
—Walk across the bridge spanning the lagoon, in the moon-light.
—Go anywhere you hear outdoor drumming, and join the festivities.

GETTING AROUND

Taxis ply the main streets all day and night, picking up several passengers along the route for a 10-cent charge. Station wagons travel regularly between Cotonou and Porto-Novo.

PLACES TO VISIT

Not far from Cotonou are places of great tourist attraction easily reached on one-day excursions. Besides Porto-Novo, the towns of Ganvié, Ouidah and Abomey are the most outstanding. Transportation is frequent and cheap. It is easiest to travel between towns by group taxi (station wagon). Each popular destination has its own departure station (*gare*); taxi drivers know which is which.

293

Porto-Novo

Porto-Novo, eighteen miles from Cotonou, is the official capital of Dahomey. A city of great dignity and charm, it is one of the few old African cities to be found on the coast; the other great capitals of Old Africa are well inland.

From the 1700s the Atlantic Coast of Dahomey was a center for the slave trade. The town of Porto-Novo grew from two old villages on the site, and became a slave post founded by Portuguese traders. At that time Dahomey was an agglomeration of small, mutually suspicious principalities, most of them tributaries to the powerful kingdom of Abomey in the north. In 1851 Dahomey signed a commercial treaty with France; then, in 1863, the king of Porto-Novo, hoping for a measure of sovereignty, turned from Dahomey to the French for protection. France and England struggled over the region, but France finally subjected the coastal areas and drove five hundred miles into the interior, establishing the present borders of Dahomey.

Porto-Novo's distinction comes from its particular history. For one hundred and thirty years, slaves taken in coastal wars by the fierce kings of Dahomey or transferred to Dahomey from Central Africa were shipped to the New World. Hundreds of thousands provided labor on the burgeoning sugar plantations of the West Indies and Brazil while the Dahomean kings grew wealthy in the trade. With the revenues of slavery they outfitted their courts in splendor and bought armaments to equip a large military organization.

Despite its destructiveness, slavery could not eliminate talent and skill once learned, and many slaves in Brazil were remarkably enterprising in the use of these talents and skills. Though they were in bondage, they managed to work at their trades, and by winning concessions from their owners, to earn and save money. The most vigorous and fortunate were able to accumulate enough to buy their freedom and passage back to West Africa.

By 1835 they began to return: for the next sixty years, thousands of liberated Africans returned to Dahomey and Nigeria. Importation of slaves into Brazil continued until the 1880s, so, ironically, ships bringing captives to South America returned to the

African Coast carrying many former slaves, now prosperous and free.

The returnees were dubbed "Brazilians," which they are still called today. They came back with new sophistication and new skills; they were fluent in a European language, familiar with international conditions and experienced in business. Most of them had been converted to Christianity or Islam and thus belonged to sociocultural systems broader and more cosmopolitan than traditional African structures. Through correspondence and religious brotherhood they obtained institutional cooperation, encouragement and support.

The term "Brazilian" referred to their common historical experience and ideological orientation, but ethnically they were a diverse group. That diversity was now abandoned as dysfunctional. Since Brazilians settling in Dahomey and Nigeria did not return to their original homes, they were not among their own people and thus had no commitment or loyalty to local beliefs and traditions. Instead they established themselves as a mercantile force, modern and aggressive. They worked as intermediaries between the Dahomey kings and the European trading companies in a capacity of interpreters and managers, forming a wealthy, privileged elite. They welcomed French cultural influence and helped set up mission schools. Later, when the French succeeded in conquering Dahomey, the Brazilians became civil servants in the colonial administraton and continued to act as negotiators between local Dahomeans and various European powers. Their numbers grew as they married and formed large families, and since being a Brazilian was a matter of life style and ideology, not ethnicity, many local people adopted the new culture and melted in with the group—a very advantageous thing to do. Their names are still prominent in West African affairs—de Sousa, Ribiero, Talon, Zoller, d'Almeida, Pinto, da Silva, da Cruz, d'Oliveira. This is just a sketch of the incredible story; its full details will be revealed in the dissertation of Michael Turner, based on his research in France, Portugal, Brazil and Dahomey.

A walk through the streets of Porto-Novo brings a closer view of it and its people. There is no hotel in Porto-Novo, and no restaurant, and it has no towering modern edifice to mark its modernity. Instead it is a modest, quiet town, largely without European influence, whose charm and wholesomeness are refreshing.

The main stop for the visitor is the **Ethnographic Museum,** straight ahead a few blocks on the main road from the bridge. It is of unusual interest because under the influence of a brilliant Dahomean intellectual, Stanislas Spero Adotevi, a large number of objects have been arranged and displayed artistically and educationally.

In the long gallery there is a remarkable collection of *Gelede* masks. You will never again have an opportunity to see *Gelede* in such a great quantity and of such high quality. There are dozens of examples covering the walls; each object is displayed to highlight its particular characteristics. Next to each mask is a label describing the piece and translating its symbolism.

The *Gelede* mask is carved of a solid piece of wood. It is always composed of two parts—a mask face and a superstructure. It is worn like a helmet over the head of the dancer, whose body is then completely covered with swaths of cloth. The face is round and full, of frozen, serene mien; most likely the cheeks bear the three slashes of Yoruba ethnic identity. The superstructure reveals the subject and purpose of the mask. Images of swords, snakes, airplanes, pineapples, sewing machines, machetes, bicycles, ostriches, deities, birds, priests and chiefs. All allude to a story or incident, all are balanced on the head of the mask, and are thus comprehended and controlled.

Gelede is a cult and fraternal association documented to be at least two hundred years old. On its most serious level, the members perform in honor of the glorious goddess of the sea, and to appease volatile old women, and thus gain protection. On other levels, the association offers scope for expression in music, dance, song and sculpture. The amusing and socially critical dramatic presentations serve to ridicule the haughty, reorient the prodigal, and banish the malignant. *Gelede* associations are very popular in Porto-Novo, even attracting young men of high-level Western education and Christian and Muslim religious affiliation. The associations continue to display the dynamic qualities which many analysts of traditional society refuse to see: *Gelede* is constantly evolving, meeting modern conditions while satisfying traditional spiritual, social and artistic needs and tastes.

The streets of Porto-Novo wind into blind alleys or circle back on themselves. They are narrow and bumpy—no conquering army will march through here. The twists and turns, vacant lots and dead ends force the visitor to proceed slowly, flexibly, ready for the unexpected. Many houses are in the two-story balconied Brazilian style; others offer blank walls to the street as all activity of the household proceeds in the courtyard. In one spot there is a plaza, at another the ruins of a chief's palace. There are several markets, some of which display unusually beautiful *adire* hand-dyed cloth. In another section, artisans are grouped by trade—dyers, blacksmiths, potters; you are welcome to watch as they work.

As evening approaches you must make your plans. If you didn't bring some snacks with you, you may want to buy some market food. Night life here is home life, not for strangers. It is time to take the station wagon back to Cotonou.

Ganvié

Eleven miles north of Cotonou is this Village on Stilts—a fishing village of 8,000 located in the middle of a lagoon. Ganvié has no solid land; its houses are lightweight structures made of bamboo and thatch, perching on poles sunk through the water, reached by ladder; the streets are waterways crowded with canoes. It is marvelous to glide along looking at the jumble of houses, the floating markets, and the vendors of fresh water. You may be invited into a home to see how surprisingly comfortable and fresh they can be. One of these houses on stilts is a bar offering light refreshments.

Transportation: Take a cab at the Sakabo taxi station for the 11-mile journey; a canoe to the village and along the waterways costs about $2.

Ouidah (pronounced *whee*-dah)

Hanging in one of the rooms in the **Ouidah Museum** are large tapestries bequeathed by one of its prominent citizens. One shows political and economic history—fifteen tableaux of captives and kings, boats and beheadings, conferences, strife and riches. On the opposite wall is another—a tapestry illustrating sixty traditional Dahomean proverbs, a reflection of intellectual and spiritual life. They tell of love and longing, honor and pride, character, responsibility, generosity, peace of mind—lofty thoughts and deep emotions. Together these two works of art portray and express the history and mystery of Ouidah, a placid town of sad history.

Other exhibits in the museum document the story of Ouidah from its beginnings as a small independent coastal state to its subjugation by Abomey in 1727. King Agadja made Ouidah a center for the slave trade, an ocean port where hundreds of thousands of captives were shipped to the New World over the next hundred and forty years.

Several circumstances made for the longevity, violence and profitability of slaving from Ouidah. For one, Dahomey enjoys a smooth terrain without sharp geographical divisions of coast, forest and savannah. Since the strip from coast to Sahara is relatively easy to travel, slave raiders roamed the countryside with impunity, taking captives in the weak, exposed villages. The more the Dahomey kings were pressured by Europeans to produce slaves, the more they raided; the more they raided, the more arms they were able to buy to defend their own state and to use against weaker neighbors.

Later, in the 1800s, there were civil wars and local disputes among the northern and Yoruba kingdoms; captives in these wars were sold into slavery for revenge and to pay for arms and supplies. These once strong states became exhausted and enfeebled, their people easy prey to Abomey's vulturous soldiers. Around this same time the demand for slaves greatly intensified in answer to a call for manpower on the newly established sugar plantations in Cuba, Brazil and Haiti. Slavers moved down the coast to the Dahomean area because victims from previous slaving centers were becoming scarce: states would not sell their own citizens, and resourceful villagers learned to hide or protect themselves. More obviously, the countryside had been stripped and was almost empty of human resources. The densely populated areas around Ouidah and Lagos were next in line to be exploited. Africans by the thousands were forced onto ships and sent across the Atlantic.

Pause. The great Western arts are painting, drawing, sculpture, architecture and literature—arts of pen, tool, equipment. The great African arts are music, dance, drama and oratory—arts of the body and of time, portable, recondite, transported in the intellect and the muscles. Thus, naked and in chains, Africans arrived in the Americas. The invisible treasure they brought with them was their religion and their arts, culture unharmed and intact, culture which was to sustain them, keep their minds clear through adversity and their spirits strong, help free them. Another miracle of empty hands.

Several great scholars in Europe and America have dedicated their careers to the study of Dahomey life and history and its impact across the Atlantic. The slaves who passed through Ouidah were to have a stupendous influence on the New World. They brought even more African artistry, movement and philosophy to the Western hemisphere. Their enormous numbers intermingled and amalgamated with Africans already present, swelling the black population of the Caribbean and South America to make the entire Western hemisphere partly black *forever*. They brought to it the restless, angry, creative, dynamic spirit of *Blackness*—"honey and pimentoes"—to the New World. Ouidah is a holy land, hallowed ground, a cradle of civilization, a funnel, a space machine. The Creator had a master plan.

Visit to Ouidah: Ouidah is 25 miles west of Cotonou, easily reached by group taxi (which leaves from the Total gas station). The museum, Dutch fort, English fort, and Temple of the Sacred Python are all of great interest. Return via the scenic route along Lake Aheme. A half-day trip.

Abomey

Abomey became Danhomé, Danhomé is today Dahomey; the history of this part of West Africa radiates from Abomey, seat of the rulers of Dahomey. Following the logic of West African geography and tradition, Abomey is an inland capital, another crossroads of commerce. Today the town of Abomey is a vast museum of relics and treasures recalling the glory of the pre-colonial kingdom. Walls and buildings, objects and landscape recall the days when Abomey was rich and respected, remarkably well organized, victorious in war, splendid in pomp. The historian J. Lombard describes Dahomey at the height of its power in the 1800s:

> The Dahomey monarch also ruled an elaborate court, itself organized like a little state. It consisted predominantly of women: relatives, wives, and servants. The palace was the nerve-centre of the kingdom; its very name—Homé or Danhomé—was given to the country as a whole. It covered an area of more than fifteen acres and was enclosed by twelve-foot-high walls. Successive kings built their own palaces beside that of their predecessor, whose huts, altars, and tombs they were obliged to maintain. In this fashion, each king made his contribution to "making Dahomey always greater," since the palace symbolized the kingdom, which should extend its frontiers during each reign.

Visit to Abomey: Abomey is 90 miles from Cotonou, $1.50 by group taxi. The town is fresh and green, pleasantly designed. The visitor may be adopted by an erudite young boy and shown the landmarks—the palace, museum, residential areas, craftsmen's quarters, market. First stop for the visitor is the **Abomey Museum,** an amazing storehouse of art and history. Room after room is crowded with sculpture, ironwork, kingly accessories, tapestries and armaments. In one courtyard there is a wide display of crafts for sale. Renowned for the variety and quality of its folk art, Abomey is one of the best places in all of West Africa to purchase handsome objects at moderate prices. The museum guide will tell the visitor about local ceremonies and rituals, most of them open to outsiders. There is a small hotel (**Motel d'Abomey,** $7 for a double room, $3 for a simple meal), once sparkling, now seedy; there is also a small inn.

SHOPPING

Tourist Office Shop

The Tourist Office in Cotonou has a representative selection of Dahomean crafts; you can see the various items and get a general idea of price. One of the most extraordinary buys in West Africa can be found here—sets of hand-carved chairs. They aren't chairs, really, they are more like *thrones*. Made from a solid block of wood, the sweep from one arm to the seat to the other arm is one continuous U-shaped line; the back is sculpted open work. As beautiful as they are, you appreciate them even more when you sit in the smoothly contoured seat; the chair gives a feeling of comfort and support, endowing you with a relaxed, regal bearing. The price of these treasures is slight, around $25 apiece; alas, packing and shipping cost a mint. I dream of making my choice, leaving my order, returning to the States, forgetting all about them, and then four months later, when I have given up hope, these magnificent chairs arrive, mine forever.

Curios

There are trader stalls near **Hotel de la Plage** and near the post office; nothing special if you've seen trader stalls before.

Dantokpa Market

This market is held every four days. It is a huge, dusty, sprawling affair that begins at daybreak and goes on into the night. The West African market is the world of womenfolk.

Most women are sellers: they have just a small business and trade by the day. They live at home, bring their goods to Dantokpa on market day, have small booths in town the rest of the time. They do fairly well, using their profits to maintain their families, and reinvest in goods. A few rich and powerful women are entrepreneurs, wholesalers who buy from import houses and distribute to individual traders. You see them at Dantokpa, round and resplendent in their prosperity, sitting in the shade of their stalls giving instructions and assigning errands to assistants. Between the entrepreneur and the seller is the trader.

These trade women, more enterprising than the seller who stays in the neighborhood, travel on a circuit following the market cycle. Typically, she arrives in each town with a station wagon of wares early in the morning, negotiates for a place, then sits and bargains all day. She must purchase her goods, keep them in good condition; sell them at a profit; deal with wholesale distributors and market-license officials; find a place to sleep in each town; arrange for the care of her small children; maintain herself, her assistant and her car while she travels, besides contribute to the upkeep of her marital home and family. She may be gone from home for several weeks at a time; she starts out with her capital invested in trade goods— say, handbags—sells them as she goes along and returns when they are sold. A woman on a wider circuit continues to restock as she travels, or she may deal in different items as she goes along if she has a favorable deal with a distributor. She may start out by selling handbags, reach the fifth town where there is a wholesaler of head scarves, buy them for trade, and continue on.

All the time she is trading and traveling, the market woman is studying and learning. It is soon clear to her that there are many forces she must understand if she is to conduct her business profitably and provide for the future of her family. She is known to be hungry for information, determined and long-suffering, shrewd but somehow not cynical.

In many instances, market women have financed West African independence movements, and their support is necessary to any modern government. They are at once the bedrock of family, community and distribution system, of political and cultural life.

HOTELS

First-Class Hotels

Hotel du Port (B.P. 884, Cotonou; tel. 42-43) $14 single, $18 double; $19 single bungalow, $23 double bungalow. Completely air-conditioned. Rooms are clean and spacious; service is courteous. The bungalows are a joy: they offer privacy, comfort and a beautiful view of the ocean. Author's choice. There is a fine sparkling pool, very popular with the international set. Entry is about $1.50, for hotel guests. Behind the pool is the beach itself—the undertow is dangerous, but if you are careful you can play at the shore.

Hotel de la Plage (B.P. 36, Cotonou; tel. 25-60) $15 double, $22 double suite. Luxury class. Completely air-conditioned.   Rooms tend to be small, and without personality. The main attractions here—the excellent restaurant and pleasant pool—can be enjoyed without your being in residence.

Hotel Croix au Sud (B.P. 280, Cotonou; tel. 29-54) $15 single, $18 double; $20 single suite, $23 double suite. International standing. Completely air-conditioned.   On the oceanside, a bit out of town, this is a firmly French hotel with that old colonial atmosphere, popular with visiting delegations.

Lower-Priced Hotels

In Cotonou these vary widely, so you must check carefully before you move in. Some of them are clean and charming; others are plain crummy—sagging beds, creaky fans, dirt. Even the worst places, however, do have a couple of adequate rooms.

Hotel l'Asie, near Imprimerie Sotou, formerly the Hotel de France (tel. 22-62).   Rooms with overhead fans: $8 single, $10 double; $11 and $13 air-conditioned.   Rooms with fans are author's choice because they have big fourposter beds swathed in mosquito netting, firm mattresses, a good reading light, and lots of ventilation.

Hotel le Provence, on the road to Porto-Novo   (B.P. 446, Cotonou; tel. 21-78)   A small family hotel popular with Peace Corps people and always filled. The best room here is a single for $6 that overlooks the lagoon. A double air-conditioned room is $15; for that price you can stay at the Hotel du Port.

Hotel Pam-Pam and **Hotel le Concorde** are both small air-conditioned hotels near the Vogue cinema. Pam-Pam charges $13 for a double, Concorde charges $16. Again, for those prices you can stay at one of the luxury hotels, unless you just like being in the thick of things rather than near the ocean-at-the-end-of-the-street.

Hotel Triano (opposite Brossette) is newly repaired and white-washed, quite pleasant. $8 for one, $10 for two in ventilated room; more for air conditioning.

Hotel St. Bernard and **Hotel Babo** both are known to taxi drivers, both have rooms for $5 a night, and both can be buggy and grimy, though there are a couple of nice rooms. Both have good snack bars and a regular clientele of townspeople and Peace Corps volunteers. **Hotel Florida** (also called Château Suisse) has the nerve to charge $8 and up for some bad rooms, but also has some good rooms. Once more, look first.

RESTAURANTS

Hotel Restaurants

Hotel de la Plage has an indoor air-conditioned restaurant during the day, then in the evening serves out-of-doors in a lovely garden setting. The food is superb; if you hit it right you may enjoy one of the best meals to be found in West Africa. The fish is excellent, but terribly expensive considering it was caught across the street. **Hotel du Port** makes good fish, great omelettes and a choice fresh pepper sauce, served in a garden. The snack bar makes hamburgers and cheeseburgers.

The best restaurant out at the airport—the **Relais de l'Aéro-port.** Each night they present four prix-fixe ($6) gourmet dinners and a wide selection of well-prepared specialties. (Reservations by telephone 20-05.) The **Trois Paillottes** restaurant on the Porto-Novo road has dinner and dancing in a country setting. First-rate African specialties and French food at moderate prices; great *méchoui* (spit-roasted lamb) every Saturday night—really festive.

The **Pam-Pam** in town is crowded with people eating steaks and chicken out-of-doors in a café surrounded by a potted hedge, bustling from the general hubbub from the Vogue cinema next door. **Chez Pepita,** another popular place, makes good paella and bouillabaisse. **Paris-Snack** in the central-market area is very cool in atmosphere; they dish up excellent seafood, or you can buy your own at the splendid fish market next door.

The **Riviera** is a nice place for a relaxed drink in the afternoon; at night they make pizza, lasagna, and other Italian specialties. Have Shrimp Provençal at **Le Capri,** an omelette at the **Triano,** and the day's menu at **Le Provence.** The Vietnamese restaurant is called **L'Asie** (formerly L'Oiseau Bleu) and it serves fine food in tiny portions.

Observation: La Pâtisserie The pastry shop named **Gerbe d'Or,** and called simply "La Pâtisserie," is a landmark in the center of town. It is styled exactly like one of its counterparts in France. As you come in, you find to the left a long counter selling all manner of sweet baked goods; on the other side of the shop there are a few tables where you can be served tea, juices, petits fours, slices of rich cake, and imported ice cream. It is especially nice for breakfast coffee and croissants.

There is a shop like this in many West African coastal towns. Francée Covington pointed out what there was "about them." La Pâtisserie is a particular kind of enclave: as the door clicks behind you, you enter a sphere of air-conditioned sweetness, sealed off from the Africa "out there." This is a world of childhood indulgence in chocolate frosting, whipped cream, ice cream and angel food. You can order piles of butter and jam, warm rolls and steamy cocoa, little fruit tarts, a dish of sherbet—all treats savored in a certain kind of *safety*. The cash register jingles; the greetings are in high-pitched singsong, *"Bonjour, m'sieur-dame"*; to a Frenchman, the locale is Paris and home. No more Dahomey and strangeness, heat and humidity, insecurity and alienation. Africa has vanished and you are insulated in familiar surroundings.

La Pâtisserie is there because you will need some coddling along the way. Stop in and enjoy yourself: it is deeply satisfying. Just remember what it's all about.

*   *   *

Street Food

To eat well at small cost, pick up your evening meals from the ladies at the night-shopping area near the **Gare de Ouidah,** at the

Total gas station (where taxis leave for Ouidah). On the same side as the station, one woman sells pepper chicken grilled over coals at 20–25 cents a quarter portion. She also prepares a variety of stews, freshly made at home, accompanied by rice—all served to a steady line of bachelors. The shop next door has cold sodas and beer, and stays open very late. Across the street is another lady also selling chicken and stews.

The wares on the Total side of the street seemed tastier, but both cooks have their admirers, and all the food is wholesome and well prepared. You join hundreds who come to eat every evening. In any case, though, by the time you read this, the women may have changed sides, or been replaced altogether, or maybe you'll find a derrick on the spot plunging for oil.

NIGHT CLUBS

Drinks are $1 at the **Lido, Apollo** and **Excelsior,** $2 at **King's** and **Charlie Oscar.** The **Canne à Sucre** and **Apollo** are African-style places, **Calabasse** and **Poster Club** are very European. The **Poster Club,** out near the beach, jumps on weekends and sometimes shows movies. All the clubs are air-conditioned.

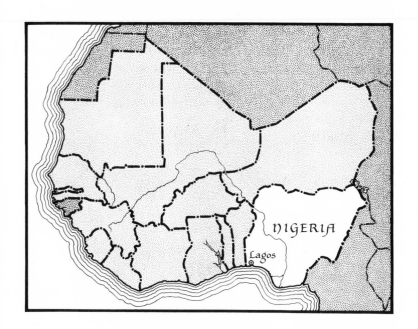

Nigeria
LAGOS

So far you've had suggestions on how to vacation in Dakar, stop over in Cotonou, beach-comb in Freetown, dance through the night in Accra, and purchase beautiful objects in Bamako. But now, when it comes to Lagos, there is no touristing around. This is no traveler's paradise; life in Lagos is rough and tough. No amount of money or sophistication can insulate you from the difficulties and trials of existence here. At best, you can learn a little about what to expect to roll with the punches and begin to appreciate Lagos' rambunctious appeal.

First some basic facts about the country itself, to set things in perspective. There are two countries of pivotal importance in black Africa: one is Zaïre (formerly the Belgian Congo/Congo Kinshasa), the other is Nigeria. Both have certain crucial blessings: a huge, well-watered land mass with mighty rivers and a coast on the Atlantic Ocean. Each has a variety of climates, soils and seasons to support a number of profitable products: cocoa, tea, peanuts, cotton, rice, rubber, food crops, fish and cattle. In natural resources above the ground, waiting to be harvested, they have timber and palm-oil kernels, as well as valuable skins and furs. Below the ground, both countries have oil, tin and iron; Nigeria is a producer of coal, Zaïre has copper, diamonds and cobalt. Underlying the natural wealth is a growing industrial infrastructure powered by fuel from the land and by electrical power from harnessed rivers.

Nigeria and Zaïre are the two countries the West thinks about most seriously; the neocolonialist powers do not kid about these two. Significantly, both countries have seen years of civil war and strife. (Some political scientists think that easy, largely bloodless transfers of power were effective in other states because they were of lesser importance to the economy of the West.) Western nations took sides in the assassinations, intrigues, bombings and bloodshed that have been part of the recent history of Nigeria and Zaïre. This is not surprising: recent struggles in Southeast Asia, the Middle East, the Caribbean, South America have shown Europe and the United States as deeply partisan, fighting in theaters for (high-school-textbook explanation) access to raw materials on favorable terms, a market for manufactured goods, and for political and cultural vassals. The stakes are high: power and riches untold.

The battle has been long and protracted and is far from over. For Africans, victory will mean control over their own land, politics, economics, culture and psychology. It will mean that decisions concerning the destiny of an African nation will be made *in* that country, *by* the country. At this point in time, this simply is not true. The price of raw materials and manufactured goods, the foreign policy, governmental structure, access to information and education—all of these have been formulated largely by foreign powers, to the impoverishment of Africa. As Kwame Nkrumah said: "Africa is rich but Africans are poor."

For three hundred years Western Europe has regarded Africa as some sort of appendage, a God-given limb supplying riches it lacked itself. Mother Africa in all her generosity has never been able to fully resist. First it was ivory and gold. Then it was slaves, black bodies by the millions, strong black backs to raise the sugar of the West Indies and the cotton of the American South, to construct and fuel the industrial machinery of the modernizing West. After manpower the West wanted vegetable oils for fuel and soap. The West wanted spices, chocolate for Europe's sweet tooth. Raw materials and produce for Europe's manufacturing plants were needed, then markets for finished products. A field of religious and cultural expansion, a safety valve for its misfit citizens.

Gold and diamonds for milady; tin, bauxite, rubber for cars; uranium and cobalt for bombs. Countless barrels of oil to turn the wheels of industrial life. Sculpture and bronzes for museums; new music, poetry and dance for entertainment and inspiration. A brain drain of scientists, professors and professionals to staff its institutions. All this Africa offered the West. Whenever Europeans (and Americans increasingly) have a need of something for their development and prosperity, they *find it in Africa.* Here is bounty and abundance, an inexhaustible storehouse, the bottomless well, the magic lantern, the chest of buried *treasure.*

Lagos is the federal capital of Nigeria. It is now the leading area in that country, the center of government and industrial development. By any measure, Lagos is certainly the most difficult city in West Africa. Nouakchott will eye you admiringly, Bamako will treat you with friendly respect, Accra will make you feel right at home, but Lagos! Lagos couldn't care less that you have arrived. Lagos has troubles of its own. First, the population jumped from 273,000 in 1952 to about 600,000 in 1962. In the following ten years it doubled, to 1.2 million in 1972, and continues to increase by about 12 percent a year.

Under the strain of rapid growth, the entire civil life of Lagos groans and sinks. Life is expensive, and harassing. The pace is hard. Not fast, but exasperatingly slow: two hours to get to work, and two hours back, unbelievable traffic snarls. Schools are on double sessions; hospitals are always crowded. The electricity falters, the water goes off, food prices go up, and another crack appears in the sidewalk.

There never have been any "good old days" in Lagos. The nucleus of the town began on Iddo Island, settled by fishermen and hunters from the mainland back in the 1500s. They spread to Lagos Island and were prospering by the time the Portuguese arrived looking for slaves. Lagos, with the placid waters of its lagoon and assured security in its detachment from the mainland, seemed a natural place for Europeans to set up a trading post. Starting in 1704, and for the next hundred and fifty-seven years, men were shipped out of Lagos for the New World, enriching local families and setting the structure for further development of the city. In 1861, when the trade was finally halted, Lagos received back hundreds of black people shipped from the Spanish and Portuguese plantations in the New World. These Africans returned to the home continent bringing proficiency in European languages, experience in modern crafts and commercial practices. This extraordinary group has played an enormous role in the new-style land, illustrating the never-broken links between Africans in the New World and the Old.

Lagos, the situation and the concept, are under great strain. The heart of the city is on three small islands in the Lagos lagoon; besides Iddo and Lagos islands, there is Ikoyi Island. The metropolitan region includes the adjoining mainland areas of Ebutte-Metta, Yaba, Surulere, Victoria Island, and parts of Mushin and Apapa. The fringes of Lagos, beyond the city limits and administration, continue to grow, spurred by the availability of cheap transport and housing.

It is sometimes hard to tell a rich man from a poor man in Lagos, because both are apt to live next door to each other in the same slum. There may be a two-story house with all facilities, and around it a swarm of temporary shelters, along with chickens, goats, dogs and cats. Families live crowded in one or two rooms; the unfortunate ones sleep out in the streets.

The sociologist Peter Marris has described the situation well:

> Only the chrome-tipped fin of a Pontiac, edged into the angle of
> a lane, may distinguish the home of a businessman with a profit of

several thousand pounds a year from that of his neighbor who earns perhaps £20 as a carpenter for the railways. A woman who shares two small rooms with her daughter and several grandchildren may be hauling loaves of bread for a few pounds a month; but equally she may be using her shabby parlour as an office from which she runs a valuable export business in handwoven cloth. Wealth is stored in boxes of clothes and jewelry, or invested in a son at Manchester University, a daughter learning nursing at a London hospital, or in the pious distinction in having made the pilgrimage to Mecca. Rich and poor live side by side, in the same crowded quarters. In one house, for instance, the head of one household made about six thousand a year and another seven pounds a month: a casual visitor would not have recognized which was which.

There are some of us, however, who can never get enough of Lagos. Recite to us the litany of its troubles and woes, and we will only say "Growing pains." Talk of overcrowding and the squalor, and we answer, "What do you expect after a civil war?" Mention all the inconveniences and we say, "Who cares?" All a small price to pay for the privilege of visiting Lagos.

The city is raucous and extrovert. It is congested, intense, full-blown, overripe; living there takes "a lot of nerve," and even more patience. Somehow or other, Lagos makes it through, survives, even prospers—all on the vigor and fortitude of its citizens. Their special characteristics seem, to the foreigner, part of the reason for the city's appeal.

First of all, there's their sense of humor, their appreciation of the wry and ironic. Lagosians repeat the latest stories of outrage and excess with great relish. The hurly-burly of life in the city and continued social dislocation throughout the country provide the background for hilarious anecdotes. People poke fun at themselves; they joke about their love of oratory and pageantry, their tendency to gripe and complain, the intractability of bureaucrats, the venality of politicians, the foibles of rich market women, the rudeness of telephone operators, the antics of cabdrivers, and the physical hazards of walking through Lagos streets.

Observation: Lagos Streets   How will you feel about Lagos streets? That all depends. Many first-time visitors are put off by the confusion, the reckless traffic, the ever-blaring horns, the stinking, unsanitary open drains, and the overpowering jumble of sights, smells, noises and sensations.

You cannot just amble aimlessly along—*you must look where you are going:* you might stumble into a ditch, trip over a crack or pitch forward into an open sewer. Then again, you might step on a toddler's barefoot toe, unbalance a mountain of eggs precariously placed on a little girl's head, or walk smack into a blind beggar. So watch out!

But what *are* you to do? In most places there are no sidewalks. You walk on the edge of the tarred road, people hot on your heels, deftly side-stepping other pedestrians walking toward you. On your left is a wide, open, fetid drain; to your right is a hurtling stream of buses, cars, lorries, bicycles, motorbikes and scooters. Movement is relentless, everyone presses on. But where do you scramble when a man-drawn delivery cart suddenly turns the corner into your path—you can't go forward or back; the ditch and the drivers both await their chance to *do you in.* It's a problem. Lagos keeps you alert and nimble, sharpens your ability to make split-second decisions and calls forth more humor and determination than you ever knew you possessed. Very good for getting you back in shape.

*   *   *

Lagos weather is terrible: the temperature stays in the upper eighties to low nineties and the humidity is high. In such a yeasty atmosphere, germs proliferate in abandon. If Lagos living is not a hazard to health despite the poor public sanitation, it is due to the personal cleanliness of Nigerians and their determination to bathe whether there is running water or not. The Lagosian who keeps his bit of personal space scrubbed clean enables the whole social body to exist in safety.

Men and women remain fresh under trying conditions, and their clothes are spotless. They are not only clean—hardly the issue—but more strikingly, there is love of beautiful clothing and personal adornment, care given to creating an attractive appearance, the obvious pleasure of a variety of styles and presences.

Observation: Lagos Dress   Traditional clothing styles in Africa and the Orient are usually simple and lovely. Each culture has developed classic designs that flatter the ethnic body type and meet the aesthetic demands of the community. Women generally are clothed from neck to toe (think of the sari and the kimono) in ample lengths of cloth that only hint at the outlines of the body as they sway with the wearer's movements. The basic style goes on year after year with only slight change; only the type and quality of the fabric vary to any extent. (This was also the idea of Mlle. Chanel, the great French *couturière*—a "uniform" of a perfect, flattering cut varied through material and accessories.)

There are three distinctive modes of West African dress—styles are set in Dakar, Accra and Lagos. Dakar women prefer billowing, flowing kaftans—yards and yards of cloth cascading from the shoulders to the floor. In Accra, clothes are worn close to the body: the bodice is fitted and the long skirt is wrapped tight. The ensemble outlines the figure conquettishly. Lagos prefers bulky, draped three- and four-piece ensembles that give a modest, matronly appearance.

Despite the Lagos heat, both men and women wear *layers* of clothing in very elaborate styles. At one time all the cloth was homespun, but now imported fabrics are the most popular. For everyday wear it is materials of lightweight wool(!), cotton worsted or percale, usually in prints, stripes or solids in shades of blue. For festive occasions the fabrics are sumptuous—velour and cut velvet, damask and brocade, lace and hand-dyed indigo, all extravagantly cut and richly embroidered. The men are usually more dashing and beautiful than the women.

*   *   *

Another element of the Lagos character that makes for high spirits is the enterprise shown by the average citizen. One survey pointed out that around 40 percent of the adults in Lagos are self-employed. That's easy to believe. There are only a limited number of jobs in government or industry, and large numbers of people are unemployed. The rest manage by engaging in some sort of trade or by providing some kind of service. The wealthy few are bankers and lawyers, owners of import-export firms and transport companies, building and road contractors, brokers for oil and timber, speculators in real estate. The more modest engage in trade; the poorest pick up small change doing odd jobs, such as car-sitting. All of them work at their own thing with ebullient self-confidence and boundless optimism.

A GBARIYE *of white cloth worn over voluminous cotton trousers*

A SAPARA, *a lightweight gown similar to an* AGBADA *but smaller and made from fabric other than handwoven cloth. It is embroidered at the neck. Sleeves extend beyond the arms to turn-back over the shoulders.*

A **LABARIKADA,** *a close fitting cap which together with* IKORI *is the older style of cap.*

An ONIDE *with hand embroidery*

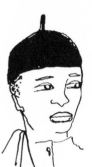

A Beret

A SEKOU-TOURE *cap of fur fabric*

An AGBADA *comprises three big gowns ranging from* GIRIKE *which is the largest, heaviest and most embroidered to* SULIYA, *the lightest.*

*Backview of
turban shows
intricate drapery*

GELE *draped in beautiful turban styles*

There are more than a dozen large markets spread around town; you find every imaginable product from greeting cards, hubcaps, flashlights and suitcases to snake jaws, lemonade, saddles, umbrellas, gold coins and typewriters, in addition to every kind of foodstuff. Along most of the main streets are rows of tables where women sit all day selling fruit and cupcakes, hard-boiled eggs, spices, hot-cooked meals, baby clothes and cigarettes. Dilapidated boutiques have records, wigs, handbags and bolts upon miles of dazzlingly smooth cloth. The entrance is a plank over the open drain; the displays spill out onto the street. Inches away from filth, immaculately clean fabrics flutter in pristine triumph.

Activity in Lagos never stops. The streets are filled during the days and into the nights. When the ramshackle stalls bolt shut near 8 P.M., the curb space is taken by someone new selling from a folding table lit by lantern. At midnight there are still crowds coming and going; private taxis, lorries and buses ply the main streets around the clock. In the wee hours there is still a steady stream of men and women who, as it is explained to the tourist coming home from dancing all night, are "going about their business."

The people who are late to bed are met by those early to rise. By 5 A.M. workers in the outlying districts are up, grooming themselves. By 5:45 they are waiting for the bus; by 6 A.M. the traffic crush is on, tens of thousands of people pushing, steadfastly cramming their way onto the islands of central Lagos, Lagos of the lagoons, cool of dreams.

Some Background for Understanding Nigeria

Twelve states make up the Federal Republic of Nigeria. The country's geography is unusually varied. It can be divided into four large natural regions. The first is the coastal strip, 35 to 50 miles wide. Sandy beaches give way to a wall of deep mangrove, and just on the other side of them are lagoons. These extend from the western border of the country to the great Niger delta, where they break up into a network of creeks and waterways that provide valuable means of communication in this part of the country. To east and west of the river there follows an area of tropical rain forest between 60 and 100 miles deep. In the center of the country, above the fork made by the Niger and Benue rivers, lie the mountains and plateaus of Jos and Bauchi. The savannahs to the north stretch from the plain of Sokoto to the great basin of Lake Chad.

Each of these regions has its own special mineral and agricultural cash products. On the sandy coast you find fishing and market gardening. The mangrove swamps provide lumber and skins; all kinds of fish and crustaceans are found in the rivers and creeks, and the delta forms excellent farm land for an extensive variety of food crops. Here too are found Nigeria's vast oil deposits. In the tropical rain forest, oil palm and valuable hardwood timber grow. In the west, cocoa is grown by thousands of farmers, along with a developing rubber crop. Tin, columbite and iron come from the central hills, while cotton, cattle, skins and peanuts form the wealth of the northern areas. Nigeria is self-sufficient in food, the basic crops being yams, corn, rice, beans, peas, bananas, sugar cane and citrus. Eighty percent of the working male population is engaged in agricultural production; "agriculture is the basis of the country's wealth and the root source of the implementation of all development plans," states the government.

Nigeria's exceptionally diversified agricultural sector, her growing industrial base and her mineral wealth (particularly petroleum) combine to give her the best prospects for sustained growth of any West African country. Farmers continue to improve their crops, work together in cooperatives and explore new marketing techniques. Prospecting has uncovered new sources of lead, zinc, iron and mineral oil. Industrialization is being intensified—Nigeria exports machinery, appliances, transport equipment and other manufactured goods to other countries in Africa and to England.

The other outstanding feature of Nigeria is her remarkable population. Sixty million men and women make Nigeria the most populous nation in the black world (the second largest is the nearly 23 million black population of the United States), and there is an incredible assemblage of varied ethnic groups, reflecting different traditional systems with complex historical interrelationships. The Yoruba, the Igbo and the Hausa make up 60 percent of the population. There are an estimated two hundred ethnic groups in addition (some names: Ibibio, Fulani, Nupe, Tiv, Kanuri, Efik, Ijaw, Beni, Birom, Urhobo, Edo, Itsekiri); each has its separate language, history and culture but is nonetheless closely interwoven with the life of its neighbors.

After you have been in Nigeria awhile, you will learn that the tribal label is supposed to inform you instantly about a man's attitudes about money, sex, work, family, government, politics, economics and artistic culture. When applying for a job, or for even a clinic appointment, or membership in a church, the Nigerian is asked to state his tribe.

Nigeria is hardly a "melting pot"; ethnic ties are strong, rivalry is often fierce and brutal. A Nigerian clearly is devoted to his family, and will identify with his group. He will often consider himself to be in sharp competition with members of *any other* group. (Only here you call it "tribe," because that is the word for the self-identification.) These ethnic squabbles are elaborate and intense. The tourist is advised to remain strictly, diplomatically neutral.

LEISURE AND PLEASURE

In the morning
—Go to the Federal Palace Hotel. Buy up a whole pile of local newspapers and magazines (there are over eighty daily newspapers published in Nigeria—fifty in English, thirty in vernacular languages), relax, and read for a couple of hours to get a feel for the country's concerns.

—Visit the Nigerian National Museum, particularly its fabulous display of Nigerian antiquities.

—Shop in the fabric and record stores all along Bridge Street.
In the afternoon
—Browse in Kingsway's Bookshop, looking at the African titles.

—Spend a few hours looking at hand-dyed materials and wax prints in the market.

In the early evening

—Take a cruise on the lagoon in a pleasure boat.

—Stroll the two-mile stretch along the marina.

—Walk on the sands of Victoria Beach, as the religious cults come for their rituals.

At night

—Dance in one of the small clubs where the music is cool and the steps intricate.

—Watch Nigerian television at least one night for the novelty.

Step by Step in Lagos

If Lagos is your first stop in Africa, expect to be temporarily traumatized by your experiences upon arrival. It is obvious to every reader by now that the author is extremely enthusiastic about West Africa, so when you are told that Nigeria is difficult and hard on the traveler, please *believe* me that Nigeria is difficult and hard on even the most poised, experienced and *serene* visitor. Be prepared to take many difficulties in stride.

Coming into Lagos is a great test of your equilibrium and strength of character. The following advice will help you prepare for the difficulties you will have to face initially so that your first encounters in Nigeria will not be discouraging.

1. Beginning back in the States, do your packing with the knowledge that you will be searched. Some items are limited, others strictly forbidden. You are allowed to bring in personal clothing, a typewriter, and one still camera and one movie camera. A pint of liquor, ten packs of cigarettes, or fifty cigars or one half pound of tobacco, and one half pint of cologne or perfume are the maximum amounts allowed. Arms and ammunition are *strictly prohibited.* You will be questioned about all medication and pills in your possession; only personal quantities of vitamins, anti-malaria pills and pharmaceuticals are allowed; all other drugs and narcotics are prohibited.

2. Nigerian friends in the United States will probably ask you to carry gifts to their relatives at home. They may ask you to take scarves, handbags, blouses, wigs, toys. *Be firm, say NO.* You have no room in your luggage to be carrying all that stuff, anyway.

3. Okay, you can't say no. Then be sure to ask your Nigerian friends to give you the value of the gift in cash, because you can expect to pay 100 percent duty on each item. It sounds cold and hard-nosed of you to ask for cash, but your Nigerian friends *know* the situation very well, better than you do. The customs inspectors will be firm, even if you were not, and that cute, chubby brown baby doll can cost you $15 in duty.

4. Undoubtedly your plane will arrive in Lagos a couple of hours late. If friends have come to meet you, chances are they have given up and gone home, and you are on your own.

5. An officer will ask for your passport and your landing pass. It goes without saying that your visa must be valid, and that all of your inoculations must be current. Keep an eye on your passport and get it back.

6. As the luggage comes off the plane, porters will pounce on it. Watch for your bags. Assuming you have two bags, each one will be grabbed by a different man; don't expect to carry them yourself.

7. The hardest part is customs. Even if you have been very careful, you can expect trouble. You must fill out a customs declaration and hand it to the examining officer. On your statement, "declare" that you have an old camera, a typewriter, or whatever, which is for your personal use. Anything new or meant as a gift will be taxed 100 percent of the value. The inspectors will search thoroughly, pulling everything apart. After the long journey, and in the hot and confused environment around you, you will feel your anger rising, augmented by your fatigue, hunger and general dismay. The nightgown you haven't worn yet, your new pair of shoes, a new shirt or your transistor radio, any or all of them may be considered liable for duty by the caprices of the customs inspector.

8. A currency declaration is required both on arrival and on departure. The import or export of Nigerian currency of any denomination is prohibited. Mark down the amount of money you have in travelers checks. Guard this declaration form well: you must present it at the bank when changing money and you must surrender the declaration upon leaving.

9. There is a cashier's cage in this same reception room where you can change a travelers check and obtain Nigerian money. Ask the clerk for small bills and be sure to get some coins so you can tip the porters.

10. Getting settled in a cab is the next hurdle. Probably the porters will already have chosen a car and put your bags in the trunk; there is little you can do about it.

11. Before you get in the cab you must negotiate the price. Do not ask about the meter—it doesn't count in this case. Prices for the ride from the airport to the major hotels in town are established by the federal government, but the drivers are rogues and will try to hassle you into paying an outrageous sum.

At this writing the charges are: 2 naira ($3) to the Mainland and Niger Palace hotels; 2 naira 50 ($3.75) to the Bristol and Regent hotels; 3 naira to the Federal Palace Hotel and Apapa; with 4 naira for the Ikoyi. Certainly prices keep going up, but use your judgment. In no case will it be more than 4 to 5 naira. No matter how you are hustled, stand firm. A driver will accept finally, and drive you for the legal fee. Remember again that the whole airport-taxi charade is a game played with everything against you, the traveler. The cabdrivers have been waiting a long time for a fare, so they are rested and strong, eager to make as much money off you as they can. You are exhausted, uninformed and naïve, and wishing for an air-conditioned chariot to whisk you away. (Courage—you are almost at your destination.)

12. Before you leave for Lagos you must arrange to have a room waiting for you. It is best to write weeks in advance and then send a telegram two days before to confirm your time of arrival. Even with these precautions your room may be given to someone else who has more pull than you do. Air Afrique will wire ahead for you.

13. Let's say you don't have a hotel reservation. Do not ask the cabdriver for advice. Do not ask to be taken from hotel to hotel until you find a room. Instead, tell the driver to take you to the Ikoyi Hotel on Ikoyi Isle; because it is the largest hotel, you have a better chance of finding a room there. When you get to the Ikoyi you may be lucky enough to find a cancellation. If not, from there

you can telephone around and find out if there are any rooms. There is bound to be one somewhere. As an alternative, pay five shillings for a cab to the airport hotel and stay overnight.

14. Once you are in your hotel room in town, check to see that it is set up with towels, linens, water, hangers. Relax, and just settle in. You have done the hardest part. You are in Lagos, Nigeria.

15. If it is daytime, go out for your first stroll; if it is night, need you be told to go to sleep for a refreshing rest?

GETTING AROUND

In Town

All forms of transportation in Lagos are a mess, and a particular menace for the inexperienced tourist. Going down the list—

Taxis

You'll probably depend on cabs. Good luck. They are hard to find, impossible a lot of the time. Even when you do spot one, you may not be standing at a place where they are allowed to stop and pick up passengers. The meters work sometimes, then again they don't, so fix the price before you get in. If you are going into the posher areas or into the government centers, you can expect to be fleeced. It helps to find out from friends or the hotel clerk the approximate fare to a particular place, and then be firm with the driver. (Try to have exact change, otherwise he may withhold the difference between what *you* say and what *he* says.) Since you were wished good luck you may indeed have it, otherwise expect to be frustrated and hassled.

Buses

Going by bus is very difficult. The routes are a mystery and the buses are always filled to bursting; lorries are out of the question. It would be nice if you met someone with a car (not that a car is much good for getting around during rush hours). Boats are best.

Out of Town

Nigeria has one of the best systems of transport of any country in Africa. Roads and railtracks, airways and waterways reach into the most remote areas of the country and serve almost every community.

Railroads

The Nigerian Railway has a main line from Lagos to Kano, in the north. It runs from the seacoast at Lagos through the forest country of southern Nigeria, into the hills beyond Ibadan and south of the Niger, across the plains and Bida, up the escarpment to the plateau country, to Kano and beyond. This is an extraordinary route. I once took a sleeper for several days along this route, traveling from the north to Lagos. I remember immense rock tables, and gigantic, somnolent turtles, and I recall a feeling of having "seen" Nigeria in all its variety.

Airlines

Internal air services link Lagos with other main towns; there are nearly a hundred interconnecting flights each week. Visitors are advised to make bookings far in advance because it is difficult to obtain seats on short notice. There are also three private charter airlines. Nigerian Airways in Lagos has all the information.

Intercity Bus Service

Greyhound (yes, Greyhound, but Nigerian-owned and -controlled) runs rapid bus services to all important cities. The office for tickets and information is at the Mainland Hotel.

SIGHTS TO SEE

Iga Indungaran, the *Oba*'s Palace At the center of a hive of social relations and reverence is the great *Oba* (king) of Lagos. Parts of the palace were built back in 1705 by the Portuguese. You are welcome to visit and see the works of art and the places of worship within the walls. When you arrive at a "reasonable hour" in the morning or afternoon, respectfully report to the *Oba*'s secretary and he will arrange for you to have a guided tour of the palace.

Walk from Independence Building
to the Supreme Court

The Independence Building is twenty-five stories high, the tallest in Lagos; it is located in the center of Lagos Island. Using it as a landmark, walk to the Town Council, then down the road to King's College and then to the Supreme Court Building, and back again.

Walk in the National Museum Vicinity

Nigerian National Museum, King George Park   Open daily 9 A.M.–7 P.M.   Admission free.

This museum continues to grow, increase its holdings and improve its displays. The archaeological researchers regularly come up with magnificent new additions to its holdings of antiquities. The museum has an especially fine collection of Benin court art and items from the ancient (2,000 years old) Nok culture. This is an absolute must on your list.

Senate Building, National Hall, House of Representatives and the **Ministries**   These buildings, seats of the Nigerian civil government, make for an interesting visit. Notice the style of the architecture and the layout of the grounds. The doors of the National Hall are carved with scenes of Nigerian life, aspirations and values—very inspiring. They are near the National Museum.

King George Park, Onikan   The National Museum is in this park, so when you complete your visit there, spend some time in the park. Its pretty grounds contain a huge swimming pool and a stadium, where soccer games are held regularly.

ART GALLERIES

There are several fine art galleries in Lagos that have shows of the work of contemporary Nigerian artists.

Gallery Labac   (34 Macarthy Road, near Ghana High Commission) is sponsored by the Nigerian Arts Council. Excellent displays of the creations of famous painters and sculptors draw visitors to this place. (*Note:* Gallery Labac is within walking distance of the National Museum.)

Bronze Gallery (39 Campbell Street, near Domo Hotel) is run by the renowned Nigerian artist Miss Aji Ekong.

Idubor Gallery of Fine Arts (29 Kakawa Street, in the Brazilian quarters) is named for its owner, Felix Idubor. You have seen and admired his work at the National Hall: he is the sculptor who carved the magnificent iroko doors.

SHOPPING

Lagos is West Africa's major metropolis and a great trade center. You can buy anything here you may need.

Books and Newspapers

English Sunday newspapers are available the same afternoon in Lagos; air-mail editions of U.S. and British papers and magazines come in a day or two after publication. So if you have been traveling for a while and want to depress yourself with the world news, buy lots of things to read at **Kingsway Stores.** They also have a fine bookshop, as does the **CMB Bookshop** on Yakubu Gowon Street.

Fabrics

Adire cloth is a length of cotton hand-dyed in wonderful patterns in colors of blue and green. These are for sale at Jankara Market on Lagos Island. The women traders sit in front of pyramids of cloth piled on tables, reaching twelve feet high. As you approach, one woman grabs you, pulling your arm, urging "Missus, come see her, I have everything you want." Another woman takes your other arm, and she too pulls, tugs and implores. You are surrounded and shoved; a dozen women swoop and shout at once. They clamber on the tables, pulling down lengths of cloth for your attention. The merest flicker of interest in your glance is noted and they uncannily yank out the particular piece of material that momentarily caught your attention.

It is all very disconcerting. A tiny ten-year-old pleads pitifully, "Please buy something from me." A dignified matriarch promises to protect you and send the others away if you will buy only from her. A younger woman casts admiring lecherous glances at you and says she has just the design to bring out your beauty. Another assures you that her prices are the cheapest. After a while the onslaught dies down as you walk through the aisles and when it is obvious that you are not buying, only looking. Now the tactic they use is scorn; they pretend not to notice as you pick your way along, daring not to linger too long in front of a piece.

Say you are interested in something, not interested enough to buy really, but interested enough to want to look closely and think about it. At last you find a woman who seems calm and pleasant. So you ask her to show you some things. You never once enter into bargaining, for to start discussing prices is to be engaged in actually buying. After a few minutes you thank her for her trouble. Mercurially, she flies into a fury, screaming and demanding a shilling payment for her wasted time. Give it to her and move on.

You have to be brave and able to resist all kind of blandishments to buy until you are ready. Your reward is the acquisition of works of art—hand-screened indigo batiks of gorgeous design and colors, treasures that are yours for a few dollars.

Curios

There are large stalls outside the **Ikoyi Hotel,** the **Federal Palace Hotel** and the **Mainland Hotel** selling a wide range of arts and crafts items. The traders have assembled good-quality items from all over Nigeria and displayed them in a very attractive manner. There are cushions and leather goods from the north; lovely glass beads and brass trays made by the senior craftsmen of Bida; blankets, reed zithers, handbags, carved ivory bracelets, good-quality drums, little cowrie boxes and carved calabashes.

You will have to bargain vociferously. Offer one third of any price the trader suggests on an item. He will ask you to "come up small"; you do, then ask him to "come down small." It's a friendly exchange and a friendly pastime.

AREAS OF INTEREST

Brazilian Quarters

Freetown, Monrovia—dotted along the West African coast are places where black men were returned from slavery in the New World. In the Brazilian quarters in Lagos, free men from Brazil were returned after the abolition of slavery.

Ikoyi Area

Ikoyi is really an island unto itself, in more ways than one. Formerly Ikoyi was the residential section where the English colonial administrators lived apart from the Africans.

Now the area is mixed racially, but still reserved for those of wealth and status. High Nigerian civil servants, prosperous businessmen, the residences for foreign commercial concerns, diplomatic missions—all this powerful group lives in the lovely homes in this area. The houses are large and rambling, in the colonial style. The gardens are lush with flowers and shrubs; the lawns perfect; the trees flower in brilliant blooms. Old, mellow, manicured, settled, yes, "settled," with that luxury look when whites come to stay.

The **Ikoyi Club** is one of the finest in Lagos, featuring—a bar, a ballroom, dining room, billiards, golf, tennis, squash, swimming, judo, film shows and a private library. Get yourself invited. There is a golf course and a polo club nearby. Ride along Queen's Drive. You might want to spend an afternoon in Ikoyi, ending up at the hotel for dinner.

Victoria Island

Connected to Lagos Island by a short bridge, Victoria Island is land reclaimed from the sea by a large hydraulic-engineering project. Now the island is a sort of wide-open-spaces, lungs for Lagos. Most of it is uninhabited sandy land and beach, dotted with scrub. When you are here you feel very relaxed and relieved, free from the hassle of the rest of Lagos.

The **Federal Palace Hotel,** in all its wilting splendor, is located

331

here. This is where visiting dignitaries stayed during the Independence celebrations in 1960, and it is here that prime ministers from the British Commonwealth met for their first African conference. When the hotel went up it was truly a proud acquisition for new Nigeria—a piece of luxury and "modernity" linking it to the larger world of progressive sovereign states, but now it is somewhat run-down.

Close by is the **Chapel of the Papal Delegate to West Africa.** This chapel has beautiful carved iroko wooden doors. The panels depict the image of the Risen Christ against a background of four Bible incidents that have special links to Africa. Other fine pieces of art are at the **Nigerian Institute for International Affairs;** the sculptured mural entitled "The Art of Understanding" and a bronze sculpture named "The Symbol of Knowledge" are both outstanding.

Victoria Beach (also known as **Bar Beach**) is certainly one of the most compelling places in Lagos. It is as cool and breezy as Lagos Island is hot and stuffy. Not surprisingly, many people drive out here every day when they can, to stroll, inhale and exhale. The beach itself is unusual. On the seaside, the surf pounds furiously and the undertow is very strong, so you may sun-bathe *but do not* go in the water. The beach is covered with the tents that shelter the various syncretic Christian church groups. The adherents come to the shore to pray and roll in the sands as part of their worship. Erosion causes an uneven terrain, with sudden clumps of vegetation and then a quick rivulet and pool. A very peculiar, engaging landscape, a lovers' lane at night.

Tarkwa Beach

This lovely spot is opposite Victoria Beach, and is a favorite place for the expatriate set. There is a ferry from the pier at the foot of Force Road on Lagos Island that makes regular trips to Tarkwa Beach. You can sun-bathe, do some swimming (depending on the undertow) and enjoy playing in the water. A nearby restaurant serves simple meals.

Apapa Area

Apapa is on the mainland. It is an industrial region and the site of Nigeria's principal seaport. You will find mills, factories, motor works, breweries, and all manner of light and heavy industry in this grim, gray area. Try to visit the Apapa Wharf, from which millions of tons of cargo are shipped annually.

Other Areas

In **Ebutte-Metta,** opposite the Mainland Hotel, you will find the **Botanical Gardens,** a lively spot for roaming and resting. The University of Lagos campus is in **Yaba:** it is still developing and is an interesting spot, with a bookstore. **Agege** is a quiet, out-of-the way spot whose main attractions are a bustling fruit market and a pretty resort hotel.

EXCURSIONS

Shagamu

Shagamu is a 49-mile drive from Lagos in the countryside. The town is famous for its "thorn" carvings, miniature models of everyday life in Nigeria carved in lightweight wood. On a small base, the artisan manages to reproduce a whole scene, at the market, the farm. There are limited numbers of chess sets available. Shagamu is also the home of the kola nut, the pink and brown fruit that is shipped from here world-wide as a stimulant and soft-drink base.

Abeokuta

This town, 64 miles from Lagos, has a population of 200,000. Abeokuta, meaning "Under the Stone," derives its name from the huge rock that gave shelter to its founders. The town is set amid a group of granite rocks of unusual shape and huge size. Abeokuta is famous for the skill of its weavers and dyers.

SPORTS ACTIVITIES

Horse Racing

Horse Racing is extremely popular in Lagos. As precious as land is on Lagos Island, the racecourse takes up a big chunk of it. Racing every Saturday and Sunday.

Yachting

Lagos has an extraordinary range of waters within its city limits, and the affluent enjoy sailing on all of it. The bight, lagoon, harbor, creeks and seas are all dotted with small, elegant craft. The **Lagos Yacht Club** has boating facilities on a choice tip of Lagos Island. The **Motor Boat Club** (Awolowo Road, Ikoyi) has a small boat landing, moorings and facilities for boat repair. Figure out a way to get invited; ask around. Membership is private and restricted, but if you are white-skinned you may be able to make the right contacts.

Other Sports

Well, the **Polo Club** has a polo field and stalls for the horses; the **Tennis Club** has twenty-four grass courts, and the **Aero Club** gives flying lessons and hires out aircraft. Again, the problem is getting access to the facilities.

National Stadium

Lagos boasts one of the world's most modern, well-equipped sports stadiums. It was triumphantly inaugurated in 1973 to welcome the second All-Africa Games (an Olympic-style festival of sports competitions). The stadium is a showplace of superlatives; every possible amenity and facility has been thought of, it seems. The most up-to-date timing and scoring equipment has been installed, along with advanced telecommunications and electronic devices. The main arena, with its spectator capacity of 50,000 is lavishly appointed with comfortable seats, restaurants, many snack bars and rest rooms. Designed for both track and soccer events, it is surrounded by a moat 15 feet wide and 15 feet deep "to prevent angry spectators from entering the arena to molest officials or competitors." In addition to the main stadium, the complex includes an indoor arena with seats for 5,000, an Olympic-sized swimming pool, courts for lawn tennis, volleyball, basketball, handball and squash, and fields for hockey and soccer, all regulation size, with stands for spectators.

HOTELS

The Lagos hotel situation can be trying and frustrating for the visitor. There is a scarcity of rooms, and most of them are high-priced; it is almost impossible to secure cheap accommodations. Compared to what you pay for similar facilities elsewhere, Lagos hotels have always been overpriced. Lately the faults have been compounded and enlarged. But remember that Nigeria is still rebuilding after a terrible war, and providing hotel facilities is not a priority. The few rooms available are in very heavy demand by businessmen and government personnel who crowd into the Nigerian capital on official duties, their bills picked up by their firms and governments. As for the small, neighborhood places, they may be crowded with local trades people, or in use as brothels.

Note: If you are traveling alone, you must insist on a single room, or on paying the single-room price. These hotels have few singles, and it will be hard for you to avoid paying the doubles price, even though you are alone. Sorry, no good hotel news about Lagos. Prices include breakfast.

More or Less First-Class Hotels

All the places listed below have air-conditioned rooms with private bath, radio and telephone in each room. They will have restaurants, and are spacious and well located. Rates include full "English" breakfast of cereal, eggs, bacon, juice and coffee. Please make note of the post-office-box numbers and cable addresses, and *write ahead for reservations.*

Hotels on Lagos Island

Bristol Hotel, Martins Street (P.O. Box 1088, Lagos; tel. 25901) $16 single, $27 double. In the commercial center of town, the Bristol is always fully booked, but you can try anyway. The air is heavy with important decisions, intrigues, casual sex and intricate financial dealings. Every foreign-service staff member, everyone working for an international firm or organization, every expatriate teacher—everyone comes to the Bristol. There is a good newsstand, a coffeehouse and a lounge.

Regent Hotel (P.O. Box 1088, Lagos. Cable: REGOTEL Lagos; tel. 26881) $16 single, $22 double. Author's suggestion for a fairly good choice of a bad situation. You go to the Bristol, they tell you they are completely booked, and they suggest you "go around the corner to the Regent," because "they may have something." The Regent tells you they are full too, but you should come back at 3 P.M. because someone may be checking out. The nice man tells everyone the same thing, and every day there is a first-come-first-served shifting of rooms in the middle of the day.

Ikoyi (pronounced ee-*coy*-yee) **Hotel,** Kingsway Road, Ikoyi (P.O. Box 895, Lagos. Cable: RESTOTEL Lagos; tel. 24075) $15 single, $23 and up double. Glossy, shiny, strictly European-American hotel set in a posh white residential area. The singles are tiny little "efficiency" boxes; the doubles are better. It has a swimming pool, and all sports (tennis, horseback riding, golf) are available nearby.

Federal Palace Hotel, Victoria Island (P.O. Box 1000, Lagos. Cable: PALACE Lagos; tel. 26691) $18 single, $30 double. This is the big blockbuster built for the independence celebrations and for the early days of visiting delegations. It has a lovely natural setting and a pleasant open-air terrace. Be sure your room has a view of the lagoon and the ocean. This place has seen better days, and the action has moved to the snappier, newer places, but the Federal Palace is still an old stand-by. When things are going well, its swimming pool is fresh, its tropical garden is in bloom, its shops are all functioning, and it offers a hairdresser and a library.

Hotels on the Mainland

Mainland Hotel, Denton Street, Ebutte-Metta (P.O. Box 2158, Lagos. Cable: MAINLAND Lagos; tel. 41101, 44033) $14 single, $25 double. Bright, clean, fresh, with nice gardens. Set up for parties and balls; well suited for conferences. When you telegraph to reconfirm your reservation, ask them to have their private bus meet your plane at the airport.

Excelsior Hotel, Ede Street, Apapa (P.M.B. 1167, Apapa-Lagos. Cable: EXCELSIOR Lagos; tel. 55904) $15 single, $23 double. Smaller than the other high-grade hotels, it really specializes as a restaurant and night club. Swimming pool.

Airport Hotel, Lagos Airport, Ikeja-Lagos (Cable: AIRPOTEL Lagos; tel. 33051) $16 single, $25 double. This is a nice, clean rambling place. The rooms are good and service adequate. The swimming pool is set into the pretty gardens and grounds. There is almost always a vacancy (but who wants to stay way out at the airport?)—so if it is late and you can't cope, consider cooling it here until tomorrow when you are rested.

Moderately Priced (by Lagos standards), Adequate Hotels

Lagos has a group of hotels that are not special, but are good enough. They are usually clean (check first), and fairly comfortable. The taxi drivers know where they are.

The **Maryland Guest House** in Ikeja-Lagos ($12 single, $15 double), the **Domo Hotel,** Lagos ($15 single, $22 double), and the **Niger Palace Hotel** on Thornburn Street in Yaba (tel. 44699; $11 single, $16 double) are small hotels that have air conditioning, private baths, and the other amenities. All three give good value for the price. Our thrifty traveler recommends **Angels Lodge** in Surulere ($6 single, $12 double) because it is clean and comfortable, and because good African food is available in the dining room. At the **Majestic Hotel,** in Surulere also ($7 single, $10 double), you may have to share a bath, but it has all the other comforts. **Victoria Hotel** in Ikeja ($9 single, $11 double) is a good buy. **Pension Smith** in Agege is a delightful place with guesthouses. The **Bobby Hotel** on Ikorodu Road and **Wayfarer's Hotel** are other names.

Student Accommodations

The **University of Lagos** offers a few rooms in its dormitories ($3–$4 per night) to students, and the use of its guesthouse ($7–$10) for teachers and professors. The **YMCA** and the **YWCA** always seem fully booked, but worth a try. (The YWCA serves good, reasonably priced meals.) Write your inquiries directly to Lagos; like the cabdrivers, the postmen know all the locations. **Boys' Hostel** (28 Hawley Street) and **Girls' Hostel** (30 Hawley Street) are quite plain and very cheap. Information about other student benefits is available by writing to NIGERLINK, P.O. Box 2069, Challenge, Ibadan, Nigeria.

RESTAURANTS

Restaurant dining in Lagos is, as you would expect, quite expensive. You can dine well in any of the first-class hotels, but you should try some of the eating places around town.

Cathay Restaurant, Yakubu Gowon Street   This place is first-class all the way. The atmosphere is cool and restful, the menu is extensive, the Chinese (Peking) cuisine is superb and the service is marvelously attentive. This must be one of the best Chinese restaurants anywhere in America-Europe-Africa; certainly you'd be hard put to find its match in the States. A well-heeled, well-dressed, international crowd keeps the place packed—businessmen at lunch, couples and visitors at night. Bring a big appetite, company (all dishes are made for two), and lots of money.

Antoine's Bar, Yakubu Gowon Street   This place is popular. It serves good food in pleasant surroundings. But the regulars come for the bar, which is famous for its wide range of drinks—three hundred—so you can have your choice at last. Lunch is crowded with Western businessmen.

Mogambo, Ikorodu Road in Ikeja   An attractive place, with gardens to look at and good food to eat. Also very popular.

Airport Hotel Grill, Ikeja   Recommended mostly because it is open twenty-four hours a day (unique in West Africa). It serves

T-bone steaks for you carnivores, and a wide variety of continental dishes.

Other Places Around Town   The **Maharani** restaurant on Martin Street, Lagos, serves excellent Indian specialties. The **Bagatelle** on Yakubu Gowon Street and the **Tam-Tam** on the marina do good things with steaks. The restaurant in the **Excelsior Hotel** has a fine reputation for Near Eastern and continental dishes; the **Tabriz** restaurant on Breadfruit Street is also recommended.

SNACK BARS

The place to look for snack bars is in the department stores. **Kingsway Stores** has the *Harbour Room,* a place where you can buy cafeteria meals and snacks at a modest price. It is open the same hours as the store. **Leventis Stores** on the marina serves snacks and coffee. **Banuso Stores** on Yakubu Gowon Street also serves snacks. The **Automatic Cafeteria** on Y.G. Street is popular. The *Koriki Bar* at the **Bristol** has sandwiches, beer, a jukebox and an international-intrigue atmosphere, as you'd expect (no telling *who* you'll run into there). The *Hungry Man* out at the **Airport Hotel** sells snacks, meals and drinks all around the clock.

Note: Feed yourself. Buy barbecued chicken from Kingsway, or stock up on some cans of salmon. Fruit, cheese, bread are all in good supply, not cheap, but certainly better than restaurant and hotel prices. Or, out on the street, find a lady selling oranges, another one selling kebabs, and another selling cakes; put them together and you have an adequate light meal.

NIGHT CLUBS

The night-club scene in Lagos is not to be believed: it is a kaleidoscope of colors and rhythms, graceful twists and smoldering turns. Some of the establishments are cabarets featuring a cast of Middle Eastern "interpretive" dancers and guitar groups playing continental favorites; others offer the rhumba, waltz and fox-trot. But in Lagos, night clubs are for hot dancing, and the dance is "Highlife" in all its variations. Highlife music and dance steps draw from pan-African sources—Afro-Latin, Afro-American, and traditional African court dancing; it makes a scintillating amalgam that is the blood medium of black communication and fellowship.

In the better places where the more affluent young people gather you find the most innovative, imaginative dancers, their feet flashing, torsos shimmying, their faces frozen in a mask of indifference. The steps change constantly: a country dance may be the latest craze, or a bit of Afro-soul. The movements may be warm and mellow or blunt and harsh. No matter what, each good dancer has his own particular style and the music lets him dance as he wishes to express his own rhythm and personality.

Here too are the best dance bands in West Africa. For musicians along the 7,000-mile coast from Dakar down to Kinshasa, Lagos is the Big Apple, a chance to make long money and gain fame in the clubs, or making records; a chance to match skills and frenzy with the most demanding, seasoned dancers. Where the clientele has less money to spend, the clubs are rudimentary—joints: a few metal chairs, a couple of light bulbs, beer, a dance floor and a loudspeaker. In these small places they do a form of Highlife called "juju dancing." Juju is rough and rude; it gets way down—more jerks and twists, more aggressive pelvis, looser hips.

In any category or class, Lagos dancing has a toughness about it, a bite, an energy, a funk, and at times a raw eroticism that is dizzying. Back in Accra there is an innocence and openness about going out, but here in Lagos there is a hard edge, a touch of vice, a sharpness that carries you along with its urgency and intensity. Night town, black light.

The night-club situation is in constant flux. A spot opens, flourishes for a while, and then passes away in a matter of months; other places go on for years. The names are wonderful—Enjoyment Palace, West End Colliseum, Black Rock, Hotel de Executive, Cool Cats Inn. The famous standby is the **Caban Bamboo,** where visiting men easily find dancing partners. The **Talk of the Town** in Apapa, the **Bagatelle** and the **Gondola** night clubs have long been favorites. The **Kakadu** has come back to vibrant life, while the **Afro-Spot** seems to have passed away. The cabdrivers know all the locations; hold the cab while one of you goes to investigate.

CASINOS

There are gambling rooms at the **Lagos Airport Hotel** and at the **Federal Palace Hotel.**

ART IN NIGERIA

Of all the countries in West Africa, Nigeria is the richest in sculptural traditions and in all the other plastic and performing arts. Nigerian art is more plentiful, more varied, more imaginative, more vigorous than any other in West Africa. One day Nigeria will be recognized as one of the great art-producing areas of the world, a concentrated space that has given birth through the centuries to the most extraordinary creativity and innovation.

Terra-cotta heads from Nok culture, the most ancient in West Africa, were uncovered accidentally in 1943 in tin mines near the Benue River. It is bitter certainty that for forty years before (since 1903, when the mines opened), workmen routinely and unknowingly crushed and buried hundreds of priceless historical objects, now lost forever. Radiocarbon testing dates Nok pieces from 500 B.C. to A.D. 200. Their refinement and artistic coherence indicate that they are examples of an already well-developed tradition.

This places the art of Nok concurrent with that of ancient Egypt before the flowering of Greek culture. It appears that art cultures in Nigeria have continued in a steady progression: Nok, Igbo-Ukwu, Ife, Benin, down to the present day. To put it another way, the art of Nigeria represents a *documented* artistic tradition 2,500 years long, *unbroken,* still fertile and strong.

Nigeria is a country where artistic and historical wonders continue to unfold. As in Italy or Mexico, wherever you put down a shovel you come up with a remarkable remain of an earlier civilization. And still, whenever you look over the wall into a contemporary courtyard, you find recently made objects of beauty and integrity, existing as a vital part of the social and spiritual life of today's Nigerian people.

The export of antiquities (which in Nigeria includes all ritual art objects even if made at the present time) is strictly controlled. There are severe penalties for attempting to export antiquities without a permit issued by the Antiquities Commission. Information about permits can be obtained at the museum in Lagos; you must leave plenty of time for the authorities to process your application.

Museums and Sites

Benin Museum   Benin City, Mid-Central State   The bronzes of Benin are the most widely known in the larger world because they are so well represented in great art museums. Though modest in size, this collection contains some of the earliest and finest pieces, most of them dug up accidentally during the development of modern Benin City, or excavated by the Department of Antiquities.

Esie Museum   Esie near Ilorin, Kwara State   The largest known group of stone figures in Africa was found near this Yoruba hamlet: one thousand human figures, half life size, many of high sculptural merit, all objects of myth and veneration. A new museum was built in 1966 to house these figures.

Ife Museum   Ife, Western State   The museum was built for the world-famous bronze and terra-cotta heads and stone sculptures of Ife, the ancient sacred city of the Yoruba. Visitors can see other objects of Yoruba history and culture and are recommended to visit some of the historic sites of Ife, among them the staff of Oranmiyan, an imposing 18-foot stone monolith, and the stone carvings in the Grove of Ore.

Institute of African Studies   Ibadan, Western State   This is an archaeological and ethnographic museum still building its collections, designed to enhance the artistic and historical studies at the university.

Carved monoliths Ikom, South-Eastern State There are a number of groves containing circles of stones carved in low relief to represent human beings. Their origin is not yet known, though they are still venerated by local people.

Jebba bronzes Jebba and Tada, Kwara State On the island of Jebba are some extraordinary bronze figures dating from the fifteenth century. Six of them are the largest cast bronzes ever found in Africa (including ancient Egypt). They have clear affinities with early Ife and Benin work.

Museum of the Institute of African Studies Jos, Benue-Plateau State Attached to the University of Ife, this fine little museum contains art and ritual objects of the major Yoruba cults and associations, terra cottas in the classical Ife style, and a collection of baskets from all over the world. Planned as an academic study museum in archaeology and ethnology, this is a delightful place to visit.

Jos Museum Jos, Benue-Plateau State The archaeological museum at Jos stands in a 60-acre park of extraordinary natural beauty. It shelters terra cottas from the ancient Nok culture, and other objects of great antiquity and beauty. Excellent pottery on display, and a good research library.

Makama's House Kano City, Kano State Located at the corner of Emirs Square, this is one of the oldest houses in Kano. It has been declared a monument and converted to a museum of antiquities, arts and crafts typical of the Hausa and Fulani people of the Kano area.

Oron Museum near Calabar, South-Eastern State This museum features a wonderful collection of hardwood figures depicting the ancestors of the Oron clan of the Ibibio people. These objects are among the oldest and finest of West African wood carvings.

343

Museum of the Institute of African Studies Oshogbo, Western State Embroidered cloth, leather appliqué, brasswork, carved doors and verandah posts, drums and shrine furniture, beadwork— this is a beautiful small collection donated to the institute by the renowned expert on Nigerian art, Ulli Beier.

Owo Museum Owo, Western State Another museum dedicated to a display of the splendid culture of the Yoruba people, Owo Museum specializes in examples of contemporary arts and crafts.

TOURING THE COUNTRY

Nigeria is one of the most fascinating countries in the world. Its economics, anthropology, sociology, history, law and arts are distinctive and original, and thus inviting to scholars and observers. Since independence in 1960, more than four hundred books about Nigeria have appeared, and articles without number. The processes of industrialization, urbanization, agricultural improvement and political change have been studied; banking, markets, taxation, unions, manpower planning, all have received continuing attention. There are biographies of Nigerians great and small, past and present, and historical studies of social and financial development. Similarly, Nigerian fiction, poetry, sculpture, religions, music, dance, popular literature and crafts are well documented.

The one book you will not find is a thorough guide and introduction to the land and the peoples of Nigeria. By its size and diversity and international importance, Nigeria certainly merits a detailed guidebook all its own—a guide that looks at its towns, its industries, the centers of its artistic creativity and its educational institutions. Furthermore, it should have a calendar and descriptions of the fairs, festivals and masquerades celebrated with costumes, drumming and dancing that spin the year around. My suggestion, your task.

Any extra time that you can spend in Nigeria is lavishly rewarded. Almost every place you turn you find a town whose history, culture and development are interesting. Each region is renowned for special crafts, and each ethnic group has its own artistic expression. (*Note:* At present, the *Nigeria Yearbook,* a paperback selling around Lagos for less than a dollar, has the only complete, up-to-date listing of Nigeria's towns and cities.)

IBADAN

On the 90-mile road journey north from Lagos to Ibadan, the bus weaves through the dense green of the rain forest, gradually climbing to the largest indigenous African city, city of one and a quarter million people, city of the Yoruba, city of hills.

Ibadan, capital of the Western State, is completely and thoroughly an African city, shaped by a remarkable history, steeped in legend. Twice the city has been razed to the ground: the first time by the wrath of the gods, the second time by internecine wars which the protagonists fought to the finish, destroying the town in the process. The Ibadan you see is the third one to grow on this site.

The city was founded around 1820 by Yoruba soldiers who began camping there. Gradually it developed along traditional patterns—small, low family houses and family compounds grouped in quarters. The city is still overwhelmingly Yoruba, but it is unique in the diversity of its population, which contains almost all the ethnic groups in the country, some of which form enclaves here and there in the city.

Ibadan is dominated by a range of seven hills, which runs through the center north to south. The local term for them is Oke, and the wards take their names from them, so there is Oke Bola, Oke Ado, Oke Foko, Oke Offa and Oke Aremo. As it happens, most indigenous Ibadan people live east of the range, while later immigrants from all over Nigeria are to be found west of the range.

The city is located on a border zone between dense forest and sloping grasslands. Most of the people who live in Ibadan are farmers; every morning they go out to their plots and return in the evening. Others live seasonally in an adobe cottage in the country and then keep a house in town. Tens of thousands of them are engaged in cultivating cocoa and rubber; others grow a wide variety of food crops. Ibadan is a major collection center for all rural produce in the area, and roads radiate from it in all directions to other big population groupings in the Western State, and to all the states beyond. It is served by rail and air services, linking it to the main cities in the country.

With its large, diverse population and its strategic location, Ibadan is an important trade center. There are huge wholesale exchanges for all manner of manufactured and handcrafted goods. There is a big business in imported china and enamelware, and in all kinds of cloth and pottery.

Internationally, Ibadan's reputation rests on the excellence of its university and teaching hospital. Its faculties have a world-wide reputation; its graduates have been extraordinarily creative in the arts and medicine.

Things to See and Do

University of Ibadan   One of the most outstanding institutions of higher learning in Africa, this university is a great place to visit. The campus covers an area of three and a half square miles and forms a very satisfactory universe. A student guide will show you around. At the School of Art and at the Institute of African Studies, there are collections of objects and artifacts of interest. The library is first-rate and you should try to see the architecture of the Protestant chapel and the carved doors of the Catholic chapel. Shop at the bookstore and stroll around. On the grounds there is a zoo with a small but good collection of Nigerian animals, and there is also a botanical garden displaying 868 species of plants (but who counts?). You may also tour the Univeristy Teaching Hospital if you wish.

Bower Tower   Looking rather like a minaret, this tower, named in honor of a former British administrator, stands on the highest hill in Ibadan. The tower offers a splendid view of the city day and night: from its top you can follow the spill of clustered brown-roof houses as far as the eye can see.

Mapo Hall   Standing on a hill in the middle of the original part of Ibadan, Mapo Hall houses the offices of the Ibadan District

Council, and is also the site of many local celebrations and festivities. There is a market nearby, Iba Market, which is held every evening. Very often, especially on weekends, troupes, drumming and dancing, will come from one of the streets and make their way to the grounds around Mapo Hall.

Parliament Buildings   By arrangement, you can visit the House of Assembly and House of Chiefs, currently being used as the High Court and Special Commissions. Within the Parliament Buildings are paintings of traditional Nigerian life, and doors and wooden ornaments carved by Nigerian artists.

Botanical and Zoological Garden   Spreading over 130 acres adjoining an artificial lake is an area where you can see the flora, fauna and fish of Nigeria on display. Official guides will take you through.

Mbari Club   This club is an art gallery showing contemporary African art. Originally founded in 1961, Mbari has been at the forefront of cultural developments in Nigeria. At various times it has published young writers, produced plays, and served as a forum and meeting place for lively artistic exchange.

Sports

Horse Racing   Horse racing was established in Ibadan in 1902, and the racecourse has been in use since 1906. Some beautiful horses, excellent riders.

Swimming   There are four pools open to the public, at **Green Springs Hotel, Lafia Hotel, Premier Hotel** and **Koko Dome.**

Shopping

Along **Lebanon Road** there are dozens of shops dealing in textiles. In the streets near **Mapo Hall** you can find the shops of small traders and craftsmen. Ask to visit the compounds of the weavers, dyers, carvers, smiths and potters.

Every ninth day, very early in the morning, thousands of people from all over Nigeria and West Africa flock to **Oje Market.**

Here is displayed woven and dyed cloth of incredible beauty and variety. If you are in town on such a day you must be sure to be there.

Places to Stay and Eat

Premier Hotel (P.O. Box 1206, Ibadan. Cable: PREMOTEL, Ibadan; tel. 23041) $14 single, $20 double. This is a deluxe hotel, meeting international standards. It has a restaurant, coffee shop, cocktail lounge, night club, casino, swimming pool and conference rooms. The hotel is entirely air-conditioned, and all the rooms have private bathrooms and telephones. The hotel sits atop a hill in the center of town; from its windows you get a haunting view of Ibadan.

Government Catering Resthouse (Cable: RESTOTEL Ibadan; tel. 24537) $6 single, $8 double. A bargain, if you can possibly find a vacancy. Old-fashioned, large, clean rooms, cheerful service and good African meals.

Green Springs Hotel $9 single, $15 double This is a nice, clean hotel with air-conditioned rooms, with bath or shower; there is a swimming pool and an adequate restaurant.

Lafia Hotel (P.M.B. 5353, Ibadan. Cable: LAFITEL, Ibadan; tel. 22851) $7 single, $14 double. Air-conditioned rooms, all with private bath, telephone and radio. Gardens, a swimming pool, restaurant and night club.

University of Ibadan Pleasant dormitory accommodations for students at $3-4 a night; the rooms in Queen Elizabeth Hall are especially recommended. The guesthouse for visiting educators costs $10 a night and is always in great demand.

Excursions from Ibadan

Thirty-three miles from Ibadan is **Oyo,** traditional military headquarters of the Yorubas and site of the ruins of the Yoruba kingdom, which once stretched to neighboring Dahomey. In Oyo, artisans make intricate calabash carvings; while you wait, a craftsman will engrave any saying you wish on the bowl. At nearby **Iseyin** the local craft is cloth weaving.

The 53-mile trip to **Ife** is a pilgrimage. This is the spiritual center for the Yoruba people and one of the oldest towns in Nigeria. Among the historical sights is the Staff of Oranmiyan, an imposing eighteen-foot monolith, and the holy Grave of Ore. The museum displays ancient bronze, terra-cotta and stone sculptures, some dating back to the thirteenth century. You may get permission to see **Oba's Palace** and perhaps see some of the three hundred shrines in the compound. On the way back, make a visit to the **University of Ife.**

Observation: Little Events   Africa is never obvious; its joys are not spread out before you; the traveler needs help to get the most out of his trip. This book has been an introduction to the Africa that awaits you.

It has been about looking—at African faces, African fashions, African scenery. About listening—to music, languages, surf, birds. About visiting—museums, towns, villages, waterfalls. About tasting— new dishes, like palm-butter stew, and bathing in new waters, like the Gulf of Guinea. About meeting people, and *really* seeing them in all their style and presence. It is written in a tone of appreciation and love because Africa has given me, as it has many others, so much inspiration and happiness.

*   *   *

It is late evening in one of Accra's downtown neighborhoods. As the night deepens, the streetlights come on, making their havens against the gloom. Into the brightness moves the eleven-year-old scholar, carrying along his small table. He sets it down under a lamppost, brings out his texts, pens and notebooks, then settles down for long hours of study and homework.

*   *   *

The solemn woman with the sculptured face has a small shop in Dakar where she does intricate embroidery on bodices of splendid gowns. As she gestures with her hands you see that her palms are dyed with henna in a burst of circles, diamonds and stars.

*   *   *

The baby in a Lagos market is lying chubby and contented on a stack of tie-dye cloth that her mother sells. As you approach you see the elaborate gold earrings and the boudoir-dresser-doll flounces of her little dress. Then you notice that her little eyebrows have been penciled in a thin black line, and the shiny eyes are circles in dark rings of kohl.

* * *

Follow-Up

MAKING YOUR TRIP LAST

Your trip to Africa is to influence and enrich your future, not to remain as some nugget in the past. Your travel is an integral part of your education if you are a young person; if you are older it is a way of expansion, refreshment and renewal. To put it another way—now that you have traveled, your life should be *better* because you have *more choices* and you *know more*.

Your three-week study tour in Ghana, your vacation in Togo, your explorations in Mauritania and your visit to Sierra Leone—all of it will pass in a swirl of song, color and movement. The time is swift and you are pushing to see each new sight, appreciate each new face, confront each new viewpoint. Try to *experience* as much as you can; absorb impressions and ideas. Listen to everybody's story. Keep your eyes wide open, and most of the time your mouth shut. Collect pamphlets and postcards, buy books, read everything you get your hands on. Turn around 360 degrees and see how things interrelate.

It will all begin to make sense to you *once you return home*. Don't even try to prove any theories while you are there; rather, strive to be as open as you can be to what is unique, noble, beautiful and enlightening. When you are back home you can begin to sort out sensations and thoughts, and get a sense of what you have really learned.

There are ways of weaving the benefits of your trip into the fabric of your daily life so that it will be a continuous spring of goodness.

1. **Correspond with African friends.** Write to thank the people who showed you hospitality while you were abroad. You can send a long letter or a short note, but let it reflect the warmth and appreciation you feel toward them. Keep up the correspondence with picture postcards and greeting cards when you are rushed, but

regularly take the time to write an air-letter telling what you are thinking and doing. Yes, Americans "hate to write letters," but do try.

2. **Eat African food.** Once in a while treat yourself and your family to a meal of African food, or prepare an African-style main dish.

3. **Wear African clothes.** With the right coloring and the right frame of mind, you might adopt African clothes for daily wear, or you might want a dress-up African outfit for occasions. Why not have some dresses or shirts made of African cloth, or acquire African beads or jewelry. Ashanti Bazaar (872 Lexington Avenue, New York City 10021) sells splendid things to replenish your wardrobe.

4. **Enjoy African entertainment.** *Go to see African dance and theater groups* on tour. In one season in New York, the national troupes of Guinea, Sierra Leone and Senegal came to play, followed the next year by a Uganda chorus and the troupe from Mali. On several of the college campuses the African students form musical groups also. *Go to see African films.* They can be rented or occasionally they play in an art theater, a film festival or on television.

5. **Continue to learn about Africa.** *Take courses on African affairs* at a local university or college. *Read African publications. Africa Report* published in New York City, *Africa Magazine* published in Paris, and *West Africa,* published in London, will all help you keep abreast of current affairs.

Documenting Your Trip:
In Case Your Pictures Don't Come Out

You document a trip as a way of keeping it in your memory and making it available to you as part of your experience. There are a couple of ways of making your trip last that don't depend on the use of hardware.

1. **Music Music Music.** Only music has the power literally to shape time in our imaginations. During your stop in Africa you will become attracted to a particular popular song—learn what it says and be able to hum the melody, pick up the accompanying dance

steps; then buy the record and bring it home with you. (*Note:* This has to be something you have heard and liked there; it *does not work* if you go to the record store and buy an album of, say, "Folksongs of Senegal.") Over time nothing but the music will have the power *to transport* your consciousness back to your African experience. Only when listening to "that particular song" will you actually recapture the whole feeling tone of your trip, see the faces, reconstruct the scene, remember the free way you felt and moved. Golden oldies. Oldies but goodies.

2. **Keep a diary.** This is a dead art, but an art nonetheless. Your writing can be as spare or as elaborate as you wish. The basic equipment is an ordinary date book, or buy (or receive as a gift) one of those books called "My Trip." A plain notebook will do as well. Record at least the bare bones of what happens, but also try to get down some of your impressions—of a wonderful sight, a delightful person, a new thought or new way of looking at things.

MY AFRICA HOUSE

Someday, somewhere, someone is going to make an Africa House. It will be a difficult task and will require lots of planning and probably lots of capital; more important will be imagination and fortitude. For the time being, Africa House exists only in my head. You are welcome to the idea.

In my Africa House there will be an African restaurant. So far as I know there is no black-African restaurant anywhere in the States. (There are a few Moroccan and Algerian.) This restaurant will serve real African food, on two plans, like the Cantonese and Peking sides of a Chinese menu. There will be the roasts, baked and barbecued meats that are so popular in West Africa: brochettes of lamb, broiled grilled chicken strong with onions or marinated and basted in lemony pepper sauce, small fish, dry-fried. Then national dishes of each country—the fish-and-rice of Senegal, groundnut stew of Guinea, palm soup of Ghana, Joloff rice of Sierra Leone. The delicious stews rich with palm oil or peanut oil, sauces made not of flour but of vegetables, served with rice, *kenkey, fufu.* Food will be as fresh as possible (there you will eat seafood

355

the same day it is caught) and will be served in as un-hokey an atmosphere as possible.

In my Africa House there is a woman's hairdresser. You come with your hair washed, or we wash it for you and make a traditional hairdo for you. The styles in Senegal and the Congo are so incredible—twists of braids, near the ear or on the crown of the head. A crown of flowers, an airy chignon, a motif of swirls. You will be able to make an appointment, come in, and in an hour emerge with a flattering, exciting design.

African fashions, for Africans know how to flatter and embellish the body and the skin. The clothes will be cut for men and women. Full-cut suits of pants, shirt and *bubu* top, in textured colored wools or cottons, shaped in sweep and majesty. Easygoing tops printed in waxprints or tie-dyes. For the women, a whole range of dresses and tops. Long dresses, in one-piece shifts, embroidered at the wrist and neckline. Simple day cottons and evening clothes of hand-dyed dull satin, cut and wrapped. Smaller editions for the children. Then all the accessories. Sandals, head ties, slippers, handcrafted leather pouches and bags.

Then, there should be a boutique selling African fabrics and jewelry. Most of it should be the handwork actually made in Africa. Less expensive should be the wax prints made in Holland or Japan from African designs. There should be the jewelry of Senegal, the Mauritanian bracelets made from silver from Mecca, earrings, bargain necklaces of seeds and beads.

One room of the Africa House will contain African home furnishings. Stools from Ghana, handwoven hammocks from Senegal, lamps, furniture woven of straw. The kitchen utensils, spices and the rest that you need for African touches: curtains and drapes and wall hangings of African cloth. Rugs woven of traditional designs. Leather hassocks.

That's all the bread-and-butter part. To move now to the Salon. There should be a gallery for the display of works of African art and design. Authentic objects are often extremely expensive, but in any case, they should be there. More so, there should be exhibits by contemporary African artists. This should be a gallery, museum, salon, bookshop. A good collection of all the contemporary literature written by Africans, works of art, records for sale at

356

as reasonable prices as possible. A place for receptions and for showing African films.

That's my Africa House, my building. Could there be a circuit—a restaurant here, a bookshop there, and hairdresser someplace else? Yes, but wouldn't you think that even one of them would work? Or that the profit from the restaurant and the hairdresser could help pay for the gallery and bookshop? It would be lovely.

ABC's of Coping

Air Conditioning

Air conditioning is increasingly popular in West African hotels, probably because it gives the Western tourist that old desired "enclave" feeling—an oasis of cool modernity carved out of hot, humid Africa, protection from all that "dark continent" outside. Hotels on the seaside in a cool place like Dakar are busy installing air conditioning—presumably for that one month of the year when the temperature rises. In places where it is hot, out go the cheap, efficient, quiet, adjustable overhead fans, and in come the expensive, temperamental, droning air conditioners.

Instead of using enlightened architectural design so that air currents are made to cool the air naturally, the trend is to build closed boxes and then refrigerate them. The problem is that air-conditioning machines require very sophisticated support systems and use an enormous amount of electricity. The drain on the dynamos is so great that even New York suffers electrical shortages and dim-outs during the summer months when air conditioners are in full use. If they knock out New York's spectacular electrical supply and generating capacity, imagine the effect on the fragile systems you find in West African capitals.

Airlines

The first choice for airline travel to Africa is **Air Afrique.** For variety and quality of its services, it cannot be beat. Air Afrique flies direct from New York to Dakar, and to literally every country in West Africa. The airline arranges a variety of low-cost, imaginatively planned tours and is always on top of the latest news about travel in Africa. The Air Afrique office is a landmark in every West Africa coast city and it frequently acts as agent for a number of foreign airlines.

Air Afrique has all the usual amenities of an airline, plus so many extras. They still give you all the party favors (slippers, puzzles, sleep masks) and souvenirs because they care about the comforts of all travelers, but more important, they want to create a favorable impression and make a good name for African-run enterprises.

Art and Artifacts: Serious Collecting

It is still possible this very year to begin a beautiful and valuable collection of African art that will form the basis of a small museum's holdings, or a fine personal collection that you can some day bequeath to the black college of your choice.

To do it well, prepare by reading seriously all about African art and by obtaining advice from astute art historians and dealers. Art prices are greatly inflated these days but you avoid the excesses by buying in Africa. So you should settle down in a West African coastal city for a year or two and let it be known that you are in the market for first-rate objects. You will, of course, need a pile of cash. Not *that* much—a few thousand dollars will give you a start.

All good collectors have some particular interests—say, in pieces made of iron, or dance masks or jewelry. It helps to have a discerning eye as well as some knowledge of what is available and how much it costs. Then you wait. You can expect a slow, steady parade of traders and dealers bringing pieces to your door. As you grow more selective and more definite in what you want, you become a very desirable and sought-after customer.

How do dealers get hold of authentic works of art formerly used in traditional contexts? In various ways. As pieces become old and termite-eaten, newer pieces are carved for use in the ceremonies; the old ones are just thrown in a pile somewhere. The trader can then buy them for a song, or often as not, he pays some local hustler to haul away the discarded pieces. There are times when chiefs sell pieces to get money for village entertainments or improvements. Sometimes a runaway will steal a few spectacular pieces to sell in the city.

(I know of one instance when the elders of an oppressed ethnic minority in a West African nation dug up their long-hidden works and gave them to one of their young men. A brilliant student, he was instructed to sell the scarce, valuable pieces to pay for his education abroad so that he could return and with his expertise come to the aid of his people.)

Generally speaking, the trader or dealer is the hot-goods man. Be assured that he is well aware of the price this art fetches in America and Europe; he knows you are getting a bargain. Because of the illicit nature of most of the trade, several countries have rules controlling the export of art objects, hoping to prevent master-pieces, part of the national heritage, from leaving. It takes time to have pieces inspected and certified; the national museums of the various countries take care of this. Naturally, some fine collections are gathered by members of the diplomatic corps because their baggage, under protection of international law, is usually not inspected.

Arts and Artifacts, Souvenirs and Gifts

Most of us have just a limited time for travel and not much money to spend on objects, but we still want to obtain things that are beautiful, and of fine quality and taste, things that help you recall your memories of Africa.

So, let me explain in a general way how the art thing works. At one end of the continuum are the pieces you see in museum collections and in art books—they are the stars of the African art world. You cannot expect to find similar pieces easily; they are usually not available for sale to the quick traveler. You may be shown carvings that do closely resemble the pictures—you know then that you are looking at fakes and forgeries, made for a gullible, uninformed public. Objects of that type are mass-pro-duced of inferior materials, then probably buried in the ground so that the raw newness will be somewhat blunted and the piece has a look of age.

At the other end of the spectrum are the common items called "curios" or "airport art" in the trade. These are the spears and shields, drums and masks, busts and lamp bases, letter openers and statuettes with metal coils around the neck—all glossy and crass, made frankly for the tourist trade.

In between these two extremes there is a fabulous range of African art and crafts, genuine, lively, handsome, produced for a local African as well as an international audience, easily obtainable for a fair price. Please try not to get your heart set on buying a rare item of authentic, traditional art, for you will only be cheated and disappointed. Consider instead these items by contemporary craftsmen, made to the exacting standards of their own guilds. In the chapters on individual countries I have tried to indicate the items of special interest in those areas; now I offer you a general listing of the best buys.

Beads. Some old, some not so old, made of glass, wood, silver, coral, cowrie shells, metal, bone, ivory or semiprecious stones. Choose them for their beauty of color and shape. A large number that match can be strung into a necklace, more singular beads make earrings or pendants, others are just lovely to play with or to look at in a jar.

Blankets. These are handwoven of cotton, wool or camel's hair, usually with geometric patterns on a white background. They are good for bed throws, blankets or as wall-hangings. They also make handsome wearing apparel. One that is not too large makes an excellent poncho if you make a horizontal slit in the middle for your head to pass through. To make a ruana, take a blanket, hold it vertically, cut a slit up the middle from the edge to one half the length of the material, hem, and it is ready to wear.

Cloth. Three general categories: handwoven, hand-dyed or wax print. **Handwoven** cloth can be made to order, or you can take your pick of what is available. *Kente* cloth, country cloth, Kano cloth—they go by different names in different localities. The prices vary widely, based on quality of workmanship, beauty of the color and design, scarcity of materials, and reputation of the craftsman. **Hand-dyed** cloth is printed by "tie-and-dye," batik or silkscreen process, usually colored with natural, organic pigments. **Wax prints** are machine-produced cottons of bright colors and indigenous designs. The prestige classical wax prints come from Holland or England, the largest selection comes from Japan, and many African countries, notably Senegal, the Ivory Coast and Nigeria, have established their own cloth mills.

Note: Care of your hand-dyed cloth

The fine hand-crafted tie-dye and batik cloth is made by using vegetable dyes. These dyes are unstable, and they have to be "set" to prevent their fading. Nebby Crawford says you can do it in two ways. Make a solution of cold water and white vinegar and let the fabric soak in it; then hang it up to dry. Or there is a longer, more effective process: rinse the cloth in a solution of cold water and salt (half a box of Morton's or Diamond Crystal will do nicely) and hang it dripping to dry. Do this three times (five is even better), after which the colors are colorfast. If you don't have time for all this, have the garments dry-cleaned.

Grass weaving.   Baskets, shopping bags, trays, mats and sun hats—all woven of grass, cane or raffia in attractive shapes with elegant geometric design.

Jewelry.   Necklaces, bracelets, rings and pendants of silver or gold. Though gold and silver sell in West Africa at international prices, fine jewelry is still a great bargain; there is little markup for overhead, and designs and workmanship are of uniformly excellent quality.

Leather goods, small.   Wallets and billfolds made of leather or reptile skin. Leather-covered amulets and grigris. The most pleasing item in this group is the nomad's purse—a long, slim pouch, tasseled and painted, with a tricky slide opening, strung on a long thong, meant to be worn around the neck like a pendant.

Leather goods, large.   Handbags, satchels, briefcases, cushions made of red goatskin (known as morocco leather or glacé kid), sheepskin leather or reptile skins; the best pieces come from the northern nations and states. There is a stunning large leather shoulder bag that is a medley of fringes and tassels, geometric designs and strong earth colors. Items of snake, lizard, crocodile or alligator are a good value only if carefully tanned and crafted. Embroidered cushions are a great buy; they can be shipped flat, then stuffed back home. Large fans of leather and ostrich feathers are handsome.

Metalwork.   Trays, bowls, ceremonial swords, kettles, figurines, toys and boxes made of brass. Also gold weights—miniature brass castings of symbolic geometric, animal and human figures, used traditionally as balance weights for weighing gold.

Musical instruments.   Reed flutes, thumb pianos of wood and metal, ivory or bone horns, lutes are compact and pleasing. (Most of the drums you see are made for tourists and scarcely playable.) *Balafons* (African xylophones concocted of wood and gourds) are treasures.

Paintings.   Occasionally you may find a canvas of merit. However, you should avoid those murky "village" scenes that come complete with round thatched cottages and hanging vines, and also don't buy those stick-figure pictures painted on cardboard; they are mass-produced frauds often made by Europeans.

Phonograph records.   Of folkloric music or the latest in West African popular dance music.

Shirts, blouses, smocks and dashikis.   These ready-made clothing items usually feature simple lines, hand-dyed or handwoven materials, and are decorated with pretty embroidery.

Stamps.   I made two young girls very happy by sending them each envelopes covered with stamps from every country I visited. Every central post office has a philatelic section where a large variety of colorful stamps are on sale. Buy a large number of those in small denominations, and mail them back to the collectors you know.

Wood carvings.   Masks, statuettes, dance paraphernalia, all masterpieces—all copies.

Wooden goods.   The most interesting buy is a game board for playing *Oware,* a pursuit game requiring skill and concentration. The *Oware* board is a rectangular piece of wood with 12 or 14 cups scooped into it; some boards are beautifully carved and decorated. (Commercial versions of *Oware* are available in the States: *Kalah,* by Products of the Behavioral Sciences, *Oh-Wah-Ree,* by the 3M

Company, and *Pitfall*, by Creative Playthings.) It is easy to transport this game board and, say, a carved walking stick, but stools and other furniture are very bulky.

Automobiles

In every country in West Africa, the Mercedes-Benz is the prestige car, the symbol of the B-I-G man—the wealthy merchant, politician, prosperous trader, government official. Arrive anywhere in a Benz—at a market, a private home, a school or an office building—and you will be accorded interest and respect. The car marks you as a person deserving of attention and deference. Properly tropicalized, the Benz will take you anywhere in great style.

Very few people in West Africa own cars; those who do usually choose the Volkswagen, Datsun, Citroën or Mini-Morris— little cars that use small amounts of gasoline and are easy to service and maintain. Because roads are often bad, good mechanics hard to find, spare parts out of stock, and fuel expensive, these modest autos are considered economical and virtuous. You rarely see an American car, for several reasons. The size of even compact American cars seems out of scale in relation to the roads and the other cars in use; the automatic gear shift and body construction make them too fragile under African driving conditions; and they consume a lot of gasoline.

Rental cars are available in almost every West African country at prices comparable to those in the States. Gasoline ("petrol" in English, *essence* in French) is around 70 or 80 cents a gallon.

Barbershops

Africans are not hairy people and in their system of aesthetics a lot of hair is often considered repugnant, animal-like. You will seldom see hair on a bared chest, and there certainly is no African prototype of the white, hairy he-man. Almost all the men you meet are clean-shaven. Furthermore, they will have removed the hair from under their arms, from their chests and backs, and from the nose and ears. Many older Muslim men have their heads shaved bald as well.

Shaving shops are everywhere you look. The barber merely

sets up his table and instruments under a tree, and he is in business. The barbers who also style men's hair usually have more elaborate establishments. They may have a little wooden shelter, mirrors, chairs for waiting, and the rest. They are most famous for the paintings adorning their shops of current fashions in haircuts. The names of the latest "do's" change rapidly. "Pointy Ship's Captain," "On the Way Up," "Ladies' Love" and "Afro-Monsieur" were all the rage a while ago.

Bargaining

You have to bargain over the costs of most items you want to buy in Africa. Department stores and some hotel shops mark their goods, but in most other places you have to take time to discuss price. Everything for sale has a price, of course, it just isn't stated. A set price—how dull and coarse! On the other hand, an unmarked item leads to lively human exchange.

Think for a moment about the *symbolic* nature of bargaining. Its essence is dialogue between two witty adults. In discussion they arrive at a compromise; both of them agree and are satisfied. They had time to think about it, so each is convinced, neither feels cheated. The price is not arbitrary and impersonal; rather, it is a human creation arrived at by mutual agreement. Bargaining is beautiful.

Minimum prices for most items are generally fixed by guild exchanges, and they vary according to complex prevailing trading conditions. For example, closing a country's borders will make its products rise in value; during a spell of poor fish catches, the price of fish will go up. The government often controls prices on staple food items. Thus, small everyday purchases don't take too much time. Let's say you want some tomatoes. They are not marked 25 francs for three, but that *is* the price. The vender asks 30; you offer 20; you both settle quickly on the regular price of 25 francs! Bargaining for an expensive item, a piece of cloth for example, is more complicated. You see the piece you want over *there*, but ask the price of a comparable piece over *here*. When the trader informs you, act completely shocked. Then you ask the price of the item you really want; she tells you. You say there is nothing to discuss.

She says, name your price. You suggest one-third her amount. She says no, and begins to tell you her troubles. You ask her to "help" you, to "come down small." She does; you say, still too much. How much? she demands. You give another price, and so it goes, until you agree. When the vendor stops bargaining and won't discuss any more, you have arrived at a fair price.

On tourist items the going gets harder. You want a particular carving—walk around, look, price a few things. Act totally uninterested in the carving. Start bargaining at about one-sixth of the amount asked by the trader and be adamant about it. He will gradually come down; you go up eventually to half the price he asked. This can take time, nearly an hour if you want a good buy on a special item. You must charm, smile, cajole. He will plead, get angry, decide not to waste his time, then go on to tell you the virtues of the piece. The final test comes when you walk away and are not called back for more discussion; then you know you have indeed reached his price.

See also "Shopping Hints."

Bargaining Rules

1. There is little bargaining in everyday food items, only a few francs or pennies either way.
2. For larger items be at your leisure; successful bargaining takes time. Avoid shopping in airports.
3. For a suitcase, a piece of cloth, sandals, dress or shirt, offer about one third of the asked price. (In Dakar or Abidjan, one sixth). Settle at one half. These percentages should not be considered rigid.
4. Go to the government tourist office to learn approximate prices on craft or curio items.
5. Bargaining on curios can be as ridiculous as the trader is—say about one sixth to one tenth of the asking price. Settle at one third. Traders are much softer after the Saturday and Sunday races, and at the end of the month, when they are low on cash.
6. Remember that a tiny deposit will hold your choice, once you have agreed on a price.

7. Never, never bargain unless you fully intend to buy the item; it's not a game. If you have second thoughts or something is too expensive, say so; and if the trader asks for a few francs for kola nuts for his time, give it to him. But never bargain in bad faith.

Beaches

West African beaches can be beautiful and inviting, but too often they are dangerous for bathing because of the rough waves and the strong undertow. Always inquire to find out local conditions, and never go in the water alone. Recreation at the shore is not very popular with African adults, though children turn out in great numbers. And as a general rule, Africans do not go out to sun themselves.

The seaside is most interesting to visit in the early evening when the fishermen return in their boats, drag in their nets and are met by the waiting women and children. It makes for a colorful, lively scene.

Bidets

That low-slung basin standing by itself in your bathroom may be puzzling. No, it is not a urinal for first graders or midgets; neither is it for washing your feet or your underwear. The bidet (bee-*day*), as it is called, is there for your intimate ablutions. You fill it with (warm, soapy) water, sit astride it at the wider part facing the faucets, and then you wash all between your legs.

Sure, people pee into it, do their laundry in it, and use it in all kinds of imaginative ways. For reasons of hygiene you are as wary of a strange bidet as you are of a strange toilet. But if you are staying for a while, and have used it a couple of times for soaking clothes, it will be about as clean as a bathtub.

The bidet is popular in Europe, where not every household has a bathtub. Since personal hygiene is the essence of cleanliness, the bidet, either as a basin or a bathroom fixture, is a permanent part of the international scene.

For Black People Only

A friend of mine went to see a black movie that was filmed on location in Ethiopia. When I asked how Africa looked to her, she confessed that she was disappointed. It looked flat and dry, not verdant and vivid as she had imagined. Africa was not *African* enough for her!

Many of us respond the same way. We are horrified that African women sometimes wear wigs and annoyed that African men are courteous to whites. We are distressed to see situations in which a handful of foreigners wield great financial and political influence. We have to realize that only in the States is natural hair a highly emotional issue, that African men deal as they must in present-day realities, and that the white people one sees are representatives of extraordinarily wealthy and powerful international cartels and monopolies, and citizens of mighty foreign countries.

Coming to Africa is an education in itself. Now the day has finally arrived when a trip to Africa is considered a necessary part of a black person's experience if he is to appreciate his heritage and understand the potentialities and the problems of his people. Afro-Americans travel to Africa by the thousands every year; for every one person who makes the trip there are ten others wishing and longing. Students from Bronx Community College, a group of presidents of black colleges, grass-roots community leaders, entertainers, schoolteachers, people in trades and civil service, everybody wants to "go to Africa this summer."

It used to be said that as Afro-Americans became better educated and more prosperous they would turn away from their African origin. But the opposite has occurred—we see now a burgeoning of interest in Africa and the development of greater rapport and understanding among black peoples.

The process is not always easy, but Africans and Afro-Americans must make a concerted effort to communicate, especially because there have been so much misinformation and slander spread in an effort to divide the two groups. In the last fifteen years since African nations became independent, black Americans used to hear that they were not welcome in Africa and that Africans would treat them with arrogance and even contempt. *Africans* were told that black Americans were inferior and shiftless, and just itching to go to Africa and "take over." And every year there has been a major newspaper report (New York *Times, Wall Street*

Journal, etc.) on how Africans and Afro-Americans "can't get along together." These false stories did much mischief, but all the myths are dissolving now as black people have the opportunity to meet and get to know one another and see things firsthand.

There never was a time when Africans and Afro-Americans were not in direct communication. People of foresight and wisdom on both continents have kept alive the spirit of unity and Pan-Africanism. New World blacks have made many contributions to Africans back home. Many outstanding African leaders were trained in Afro-American schools, for instance. Part of Africa's growing prosperity is due to our contribution—it was a West Indian who brought the cocoa plant to Ghana, and it is George Washington Carver's discoveries and methodologies that enhance the value of Africa's agricultural produce. You who journey to Africa now are part of that unbroken cord.

It would take a whole other book to go into the dimensions and ramifications of this new Atlantic crossing and new return. Certainly the experience is a catalyst for positive change both for Africans and Afro-Americans. Earlier I wrote about the effect the movies have had on our perceptions of Africa. For many years black Americans have been embarrassed and shamed by the screen image of Africans. When blacks began to reassert a positive self-identity by embracing their African heritage, the only information at hand came from the movies. So a hundred "primitive dance" groups copied and proclaimed as authentic characterizations and movements that were completely fraudulent, made for Hollywood. Now we turn away from the phony shields and spears, and look instead for genuine African creativity and thought.

Be open to experience, and to the real Africa. Some feelings will be overwhelming. Like the first time you are in a country with a black president, and the first time you see pictures of black people on *money.*

To a young woman: a free sense of beauty and femininity denied her on the plantation, a sense of being respected and cherished by a society. To a young man: an understanding of social responsibility and policy making, a beginning understanding of what it means to build a nation. To men and women, young and

372

old: a heightened appreciation of their own capabilities and an awakening of awareness.

Something special—intangible but nonetheless deeply meaningful—is added to your life once you have made the trip. *Africa makes you think,* makes you want to *get it together.* The broader horizons and possibilities you experience are a force for liberation, productivity and prosperity. *As-Salam-Aleikum.*

Books on Africa

The best way to prepare for your trip to West Africa is by reading books about Africa written by Africans themselves. They give you an insight into the African personality and an introduction to the African perspective.

First and foremost, read *The African Child* by Camara Laye (Noonday Paperbacks). This is an idyll, a praise poem to the Africa past, lyrical and bittersweet. Two other classics are by Chinua Achebe, *Things Fall Apart* and *No Longer At Ease* (Fawcett Publications). Together they chronicle the men of several generations of the same family in their confrontation with foreign, destructive Western domination.

All of Wole Soyinka's works are outstanding; Soyinka is one of the greatest writers in the English language. Read his *Three Short Plays: The Swamp Dwellers, The Trials of Brother Jero, The Strong Breed,* or *Kongi's Harvest* (all Oxford University Press), or his book of poems *Idanre and Other Poems* (Hill and Wang).

Amma Ata Aidoo has a collection of short stories entitled *No Sweetness Here* (Doubleday), indispensable because of its look into the heart of African women.

For an understanding of the African world view, turn to the work of African philosophers. *The Mind of Africa* by W. E. Abraham (University of Chicago Press) is excellent, and *The Cultural Unity of Negro Africa* by C. A. Diop (Présence Africaine) is a masterpiece. Any title by John S. Mbiti is worthwhile. *Muntu: The New African Culture* by the German scholar Janheinz Jahn is a good, popular introduction to African thought. *African Mythology* by Geoffrey Parrinder (Paul Hamlyn) is well written and full of good pictures. We are fortunate in having a new book about

African mathematics: *Africa Counts: Number and Pattern in African Culture* by Claudia Zaslavsky (Prindle, Weber, and Schmidt, Boston) but we are still awaiting a work on traditional African writing systems.

African history from the beginning of man in Africa to the present is well introduced in two large, gorgeously illustrated volumes. *The Horizon History of Africa*, edited by Alvin Josephy, Jr. (American Heritage Publishing Co.), is written by outstanding scholars in the field, including John Hendrik Clarke, A. Adu Boahen, Philip Austin and Jan Vansina. Basil Davidson's *Africa: History of a Continent* (Macmillan) is a rich, full, easy-to-read account. A compact book by Jacques Maquet, *Africanity* (Oxford University Press), discusses the African historical experience with succinct clarity.

Almost all the books on African art contain good photographs of beautiful objects, but the texts are generally inadequate and misleading. A good overview of African art is presented by Frank Willett in *African Art* (Praeger World of Art Paperbacks). Even better is *African Art* by Michel Leiris and Jacqueline Delange (Thames and Hudson, London), lavishly illustrated with a fine, informative text.

To clear your mind of misconceptions about Africa, this book is of extreme benefit: *The Africa That Never Was* by Dorothy Hammond and Alta Jablow (Twayne Publishers). Follow it up by reading the scathing analysis of European hypocrisy in *Discourse on Colonialism* by Aimé Cesaire (Monthly Review Press).

Contemporary ideas shaping African affairs are discussed by African politicians and statesmen. All the many books by Kwame Nkrumah are masterly and prophetic. *Africa Must Unite, Class Struggle in Africa* and *Consciencism* (International Publishers) are three titles out of some twelve seminal works. Several African leaders have written interesting political autobiographies, among them Sékou Touré, Nnamdi Azikiwe and Obafemi Awolowo. *The African Nations and World Solidarity* by Mamadou Dia (Praeger) and *On African Socialism* by Léopold Sédar Senghor (Praeger) are two more political titles of merit.

374

Bugs

One of my earliest Tarzan/African images has to do with bugs, insects, and other Crawling Things. In this one movie the evil white man stumbles into a cave and finds himself irresistibly caught in gummy cables, flexible as thread, strong as steel. It is the web of the denizen of the cave—a huge, hairy spider, as big as a room, and man-eating. A nightmare. I have never forgotten it.

After listening to me complain in terror about the omnipresence of tarantulas, black widows, poisonous lizards, scorpions and rattlers in rural northern Mexico, an exasperated friend shouted, "And what about Africa? Don't those things bother you in Africa?" Well . . . in Africa the bugs are different. The voice of authority has informed me that there are no poisonous spiders in Africa. There just aren't any, that's all. And if you're spiderphobic, that's nice to know. Certainly there are no common insects as ugly as the tarantula and as dangerous as the black widow. Scorpions generally stay out of sight under rocks. Big water bugs (those overgrown roaches) sometimes scuttle about, and housewives fight ants and flies. No. What you've got to worry about are the *mosquitoes* (see "Malaria," below).

Occasionally there will be a storm of winged ants filling the air with white fluff, and I've seen a horrible horned flying thing, known as a rhinoceros beetle. But by and large, West Africa is so huge and the population so sparse that bugs which are not domesticated prefer keeping to themselves in the great out-of-doors. As afraid of insects as I am—if *I* don't worry in Africa, you certainly shouldn't either.

Cards

Have some visiting cards printed up with your name and address. One hundred will be plenty and shouldn't cost more than a few dollars. They are nice to have to give to people you want to keep in touch with—so much more lasting than a hastily scribbled torn piece of paper.

Bring along a deck of playing cards also; card games will help you pass some quiet, lonely hours.

Climate

Here's a subject that would seem to be clear-cut enough! Everyone knows that Africa is *hot!* Well, again, it's time to look at an old idea in a fresh perspective. All of West Africa is *warm all of the time* (with the exception of Dakar, where it is cool from September through June); the temperatures vary usually between 78 and 88 degrees. It is milder along the coast, warmer in the forest regions, hotter and dryer with a wider range of temperature changes (chilly nights) as you go north to the Sahel zone.

In West Africa skies are always bright, and yes, the air is clean. In fact, living in West Africa all year is a pleasure of warmth and sunshine. Only Lagos and Abidjan have the kind of hot and muggy climate all year that we suffer in our U.S. Eastern cities during the summer, when you think you are going to *melt.* In the twelve other cities you are comfortable in cotton clothing; and you can always find shade.

African weather varies not in temperature, but in rainfall. Our summer is their winter, and as in all winters the weather changes to its inconvenient worst. In the States it is slush, hail, snow and freezing temperatures that make going outside unpleasant, uncomfortable and sometimes hazardous. In Africa, it is the rain.

In some places—Conakry, Freetown, Banjul, Abidjan—the rain comes down in buckets for days at a time. But luckily for most travelers who have summer vacation during the months of July and August, *most of the countries of West Africa enjoy a "little dry season" during this time.* The countryside is lush and blooming, and the earth is a palette of green; the rivers are full, the flowering trees are ablaze. The air is clear and washed, and spirits are high.

You were told in school that high temperatures make for laziness and sloth. Yet, you wonder, once you see the Lagosians, sleepless, and constantly active though the temperature is in the 90's and the humidity over 65 percent. Doctors now tell us to swing with hot weather for two weeks; the body gradually "adjusts" to perform more efficient cooling, so you can be at ease at much higher temperatures. The typical West African diet of highly peppered foods and generally low-calorie meals seems well suited for keeping the body heat moderated.

Compaisons

Making comparisons between the facilities in the United States and those in West Africa (or any other place, for that matter) is in very poor taste. You didn't come all this way to Africa for *things*—you came for new experiences and new ideas.

Currency, see "Money"

Directions

Nobody goes by street names and numbers in West African cities. You have to be prepared to tell the taxi driver about a landmark that is near your destination—a cinema, fountain, market, hotel, traffic circle. Whole areas are named for a healing church, a particular school, the home of a wealthy man.

Documents

Sophisticated travelers keep their *papiers en ordre*. You need a **valid passport,** of course. In it will be stamped your **visas;** make sure they have not expired (see "Visas"). Next in importance is your **International Certificate of Vaccinations;** again, be sure all your shots are current (see "Inoculations"). Next in importance is your **plane ticket**. Keep these three items with you while you are traveling; do not pack them in your luggage.

If you are planning to drive, you will need an **International Driving License**; the AAA will advise you. If you are planning to get rooms in college dormitories or to benefit from other privileges accorded students, be sure to have student identification. Your college I.D. card will usually serve; however, an official **International Student Identity Card** is much better received. Write for further information to Student Travel Services, Council on International Educational Exchange, 777 United Nations Plaza, New York City, 10017.

There are two approaches to handling valuables: some people keep everything together in one place; others disperse important items. I was taught to keep everything in one place. My handbag has several zipper compartments in which I carry papers, documents, money (men use a folding document case). So I know when I have that one bag with me everything is cool, and I am ready. Now if, heaven forbid, I should ever misplace it, I would be in deep stew; the terror of such a possibility keeps me finely tuned to its whereabouts. But because loss or theft of a central cache is ruinous, some people prefer to tuck different things in different places. Follow your own inclinations, but again, *always* keep your passport, health card and ticket *with you.*

Drains in the Street

Open drains are among the hazards of African city life, accepted stoically by African citizens. Many African cities experience long stretches of torrential monsoon rains and the drains are necessary for carrying off the water. Open sewage drains can be smelly, unpleasant and a danger to health. The renowned physician and medical historian René Dubos, writing in *The Mirage of Health,* appreciates drains because you can at least *step over* the filth while "industrial civilization has brought in a new kind of dirt which pollutes the air and thereby lifts infection from the intestinal to the respiratory level."

Eating

Cuisine is one thing—plain eating is quite another. Here is a general operating principle for eating on your West African trip. It is vacation time, and you are being very outdoorsy and active. Eat accordingly: grilled meats and fish, omelettes, fruits (peeled) and vegetables (cooked, no salads).

The cost of eating in restaurants in West Africa is high, especially if you consider how moderate the market prices are. Try improvising your own meals part of the time, using cans of tuna or sardines, cheese, ready-prepared main dishes and fruit. Delicatessens and supermarkets sell barbequed chickens and, in French-speaking countries, a wide range of roasted and prepared meats that you buy in small quantities. Shish kebabs and stews are available in the evening, made fresh daily at home by women who sell at the curbside. West African market food—rice, meat stew, gravy, fish in sauce, pound cake—is always thoroughly cooked and generally wholesome but very highly spiced. Bread in English-speaking countries is gummy, but in French-speaking countries there are always bakeries that sell an excellent Parisian-type *pain*. Mangoes, pineapples, oranges, bananas—the fruits are great, cheap and plentiful.

In French-speaking areas all the restaurants will serve a complete three- to five-course lunch and dinner for a set bargain price. The list of the day is pre-eminently displayed outside the restaurant. To order, you just ask for *le menu*. If you want to make separate choices, ask to see *la carte,* and be prepared to spend a great deal more. (Dinner is served around 8 P.M.) Local beer sells for much less than the imported, and Algerian wine is often available. Every barman can mix a gin and tonic, but if you require any other cocktail, be prepared to explain the details, get close enough to mix it yourself or give up graciously. If you ask for a martini you will probably be served a glass of Martini-brand vermouth on the rocks. American soft drinks are available everywhere you turn, called "minerals" in English-speaking Africa, *minérales* in French. There is no fresh milk but you can buy sterilized milk in sealed bottles, evaporated and condensed milk in cans, powdered milk and yogurt. The yogurt in French-speaking countries is superb. If you must have something resembling a hamburger, try the snack bars at the major hotels.

The food served in most of the dormitories, hostels and resthouses, especially in English-speaking countries, is appalling. You can expect to be defeated by the caterers and there is practically nothing you can do about it. They will try to serve you canned English breakfast sausage, tiny pieces of breaded fish, canned salad(!), canned diced potatoes, pale gravies over boiled meats, indescribable stews, and yellow, custardy deserts. Rant and rave, if you wish. The cook and the waiter are only doing what they have been trained to do.

Note: Little Shopping

Near where you are staying there probably is a little hole-in-the-wall shop that offers a variety of small staples. The proprietor will be selling matches, spices, soap powder, tins of margarine, sardines, cooking oil, bottled water, envelopes, safety pins, cigarettes and toilet paper. If he has a refrigerator, he will stock cool water, sodas and beer, maybe yogurt. He stays open all hours and charges delicatessen prices. Women who sit at the side of the streets or the road will sell you an orange (these are deftly shaved with a razor and a plug cut out of the top; you then squeeze and suck the juice out of the hole), some peanuts, kola nuts or chewing gum.

Electricity

In all West African countries the electrical system is 220 volts A.C., so if you are planning to use electrical equipment (for a short trip, why?) you will need a converter and an international plug. The exception is Liberia, where voltage and sockets match those here in the United States. A few of the more luxurious up-to-date hotels have 110 volt sockets in the bathroom for the convenience of American shavers.

Grooming

The standards of personal grooming in tropical Africa are extremely high. Young people often shower twice a day, and clothing is generally sparkling clean. When you get to Ghana it goes over into mania—a constant bathing, shaving, powdering, perfuming, pomading. Your dear friend in Accra will wonder how you can *stand* yourself with only one bath a day, and he will be amazed that you consider it any trouble at all to step in and out of a tub.

Africans take enormous pains with their looks. Hair is lint-free because it is washed and combed frequently. Elaborate hairdos have developed as a result of patient harem hours spent braiding, threading, twisting and being braided, threaded and twisted in return. Teeth are strong because they are scrubbed with brushes or chewing sticks until they glisten. Bodies are sleek because young people exercise and older people work hard; everybody gets massages and generally people just don't eat that much.

Slop around in the beginning if you want to, but be assured that it won't be long before you too begin to fuss and worry about your appearance. You are out from under winter wraps, mingling with people; the intense sunlight leaves you no place to hide. It is hard to understand until you've been in Africa for a little while and then greet friends coming off the plane from Europe or the States. Grime seems to hover over them like a gray cloud and it takes them a few days to get themselves washed off and aired out.

Hair

If you are an Afro-American woman, you will be continually delighted by the African hairdos you see. At the moment the vogue in some countries (most notably Senegal) is for elaborate hair styles in braiding and corn-rowing. How do you get yours done? First, if you know any African woman at all, *anyone,* tell her how much you like African styles and ask her to do your hair. Every little girl learns how to groom hair, so your friend is probably an expert. Or else you can look in the newspaper for an ad from a hairdresser; go to her and ask her to do your hair the traditional way. She'll say no because she only does "American styles," but she'll suggest the name of someone who can help you. Third, suppose you see a really interesting style on someone. March right up to her, explain that you admire her look, and that you would like to get the same fashion. Most likely she will be very complimented and will steer you to her hairdresser.

Hotel Pricing

As every budget-minded traveler knows, the key factor in the pricing of European hotel rooms is the presence or lack of a private bathroom. In Africa this is not the case. Perhaps because of the heat or because of the general African insistence on personal cleanliness, almost every room in even the scruffiest hotel comes with a basin and a shower.

But what you must look out for is air conditioning. An air conditioner in a room quickly doubles its price. This means that you are better off in a fully air-conditioned hotel that you are paying a high price for than in an air-conditioned room in an otherwise old-fashioned hotel. For comfort you need air conditioning in Lagos, Abidjan, Niamey and Ouagadougou all year round, but in other cities you can often manage with a fan or without, depending on the season and your tolerance for high temperatures.

Note that the French taste in hotels is very different from the American. The French like to be out-of-doors in cafés or on outings, and they spend lavish sums on sumptuous meals. We demand comfortable rooms with good plumbing, but the French economize on the facilities of the room where they really spend very little time. Rustic "vacation villages" so enjoyed by them may have only cold water and feature community showers and toilets; however, every meal will be a banquet. The average French holiday hotel has only rudimentary furnishings—even a fine, expensive hotel room at the Hotel N'Gor in Dakar, for example, seems bare to an American.

Inoculations

You must have your inoculations and immunizations and you must think about them early because several types require spacing of two- or three-week intervals between injections.

A valid smallpox vaccination is required for re-entry to the United States, and is required for entry to almost every country in the world. Most African countries will require that you have a yellow-fever injection. Note that this shot can *only* be obtained from the United States Public Health Service, and it is valid if not less than ten days old, not more than ten years old. Your local phone book lists the number of the dispensing clinic. The voice of authority recommends shots for tetanus, typhoid, typhus and polio. For a while now, some African nations have been requiring that you be immunized against cholera.

Try the health service at your university or inquire at your health group or city health department for low-cost inoculations. If you are in New York City, the Life Extension Institute (11 East 44th Street) and the Executive Health Examiners (777 Third Avenue) will give up-to-date advice and administer shots at a modest cost. Unfortunately but understandably, most private physicians are not well informed about tropical conditions, so you will get better help at a larger clinic.

Laundry

You will, of course, carry lightweight washable underwear (cotton or cotton-Dacron combinations are the coolest and most comfortable). For washing a special garment, ask one of the men who takes care of your hotel room or dormitory if he knows someone who does washing and ironing. Beware of giving your clothes to the hotel for washing. The prices can be exorbitant; check carefully first. At some student places there are irons and ironing boards available. A small travel clothesline and inflatable hangers will come in handy.

The small grocers of West Africa sell pure-vegetable-oil soaps that lather in cold water, rinse away easily, and also are mild enough for personal bathing. They are cheap, named Persavon in French, Sunlight in English-speaking countries.

Living Well

Touring is superficial, insulated and misleading about a country and its people. Travel, on the other hand, is rigorous, demanding a flexible personality, a sense of adventure and a desire to learn and love. While traveling it is satisfying to *live well* for a while, and feel you are a part of the good things going on around you. You do this by participating in the cultural life of the city, by attending events comprehensible even to an outsider, events that are part of the finest in the human experience.

An African coastal city has the range of cultural events of a college town, geared for an international audience. Almost every capital city is the home of the national troupe of musicians and dancers, and usually of some theater groups. Every night there is something happening of interest where large groups of people gather; you can join them.

Try to see local dance companies and choirs perform; perhaps an orchestra or pop star is in town. Newspapers, the radio and posters around town give announcements. When you hear of something you might like, go to the theater, buy a ticket and attend, on your own or with a friend, just as you would at home. On Sunday afternoon, join the crowds at the stadium to watch a soccer game or track meet. Again you are with people, participating in a shared event, communicating in a universal language. Go to the racecourse if you like horses; go to the conference on botany held at the university—you'll be welcome and you'll learn something.

In film-crazy African capitals, there is usually a popular and controversial picture making the rounds that you should see. Why not try to see an American film you missed at home?—see it now, dubbed in French and punctuated by the reactions of an African audience. Keep a lookout for films made by African directors with an African cast. The few available are fascinating. Several African film makers—most notably Ousmane Sembene—have international reputations. A while back Johnson Traore's film about Senegalese life, *Digùe-bi,* hit Dakar like a storm. *Hamili,* the Ghanaian version of Hamlet, is unique and exciting.

A personal experience: Once in Accra, I read in the newspaper that a neighborhood theater was playing a film entitled *Night at the Apollo.* Hoping to see something about that New York cultural landmark, I went alone to this open-air movie house; there were six or seven other people seated around. Before me unrolled a movie filmed at the Apollo Theater in Harlem simulating their vaudeville show; there was act after act of outstanding black singers, dancers and musicians. Because the film was made twenty years ago, all the performers—today's stars—were young, beautiful and fresh-faced. Strangest of all, however—as the camera scanned the theater picking out faces in the audience, there in one of the front rows, enjoying the show, sat my stepmother, Vella! She looked so young and very pretty and personable. It was remarkable to be sitting in Africa watching her as she sat watching the show I too was watching twenty years later. A time warp. I was transported!

Lottery

Almost every African nation runs a national lottery and the advertisements for them are prominent everywhere. Tickets come in bewildering combinations and denominations and are available in the post office, in kiosks, from street tables and from wandering sellers.

There are several reasons why you should buy a chance. For one, the lotteries are honestly run and their receipts benefit education and health services. Two, because the pictures on the tickets are often strange and wonderful, an example posted on your memorabilia bulletin board back home will be an interesting souvenir.

The third reason is more difficult to explain. Buying a lottery ticket when you *know* you will not be there for the drawing. Well, it engages you in a bit of charming, hopeful, irrational involvement with that particular country. It is a sweet link, rather like a bit in an Italian movie I remember: the forlorn heroine, slavey of an itinerant performing muscle man, would plant tomato seeds in vacant lots, although she knew full well that the next day they'd be off to the next town. You will think back wistfully, "I wonder if I won that lottery."

Mail and Post-Office Services

You *must* send all of your letters and cards home via air mail, otherwise they will arrive months later, if at all. The cheerful clerks at the post office consider only air-mail items worthy of prompt respect and dispatch. You can also have a letter or parcel sent special delivery or certified mail. The post office handles telegrams and telephone calls, local and international.

There is one young woman I know who tells me that she hasn't the slightest interest in receiving any mail while she is traveling in Africa. If, however, you would like to get letters you have a couple of choices of addresses. You can have mail sent to you in care of the United States embassy; there is one in every country in Africa and its consular section will hold your letters. (Since it is one of the few directly helpful services you know you can get for your taxes, you may enjoy this little bit of assistance.) Now, you may have friends, especially Africans, who will not write to you at the embassy because they do not want their names to enter there in any way, and others who find the remotest association with the embassy to be suspect. So you may want to receive your mail in care of the central post office. Have letters addressed to you marked *Poste restante,* the city and country. Your letters (telegrams, packages, and the rest) will be held at the post office for your arrival. (In patient Freetown they keep letters for years; in most other places they weed through every once in a while and return letters more than six months old.) Note that there are no American Express offices in West Africa.

See also "Shipping and Mailing."

Malaria

Try not to let a mosquito near you; their bite causes malaria. They are everywhere in West Africa and you must protect yourself from them. Use a mosquito net at night—make sure that it has no holes and that mosquitoes didn't come in *with* you. Wear coverings on your legs and arms in the evenings, and use "6-12" or other repellent. But, please, for general health, *do not* use a DDT spray and then shut yourself up in the room—inhaling the gas is injurious to your health, particularly to your lungs. Burn mosquito coils at night (a pleasant kind of incense whose scent nonetheless repels mosquitoes) and be generally vigilant.

Many African people have developed a kind of resistance to malaria. And many old Africa hands fancy that they also are immune. Don't listen to them. Rather, take your malaria pills regularly as suggested or prescribed. Malaria is a crippler, a killer; take something to prevent it. If you do not use contraceptives, you become pregnant. If you do not use malaria prophylaxes, you get malaria. Pregnancy is curable; malaria isn't always.

Paludrine and Nivaquine are excellent anti-malaria medication but difficult to obtain in the States; Aralen is the commercial name for the pills you can buy here easily. For complete protection you should begin taking your pills a couple of weeks before you go to Africa, and you should continue for a month after your return.

Measurements

They are all different from American measurements. Where people speak English they also use the ounce and English-mile measurements. But ready-made clothes and shoe sizes are different. If the language is French, the measurement system is metric. You'll need to know that a *kilo* is 2.2 pounds (3 ounces more than 2 pounds), or roughly 2 pounds; a *demi-kilo* is around 1 pound. A *litre* is about the same as a quart, and in measuring fabrics, a *mètre* is roughly the equivalent of a yard.

There are simple formulae for making some distance conversions. To change miles to *kilomètres,* divide the number by 6 and multiply by 10; so 60 miles becomes 100 kilomètres. To change kilometers to miles, divide by 10 and multiply by 6, so 120 kilometers becomes 72 miles. You will probably forget; I always do. Do try to remember that a mile is "much more" (almost double) than a kilometer (key: mile begins with the letter *M*, *M* is for more); so don't panic in Cotonou when the speedometer hovers around 90; that is only 54 miles an hour.

For Men Only

Most men traveling to West Africa want to know about their chances of meeting local women for casual sex. I think Nature intended the subject to be veiled in doubt and intrigue, and besides I'm not the best person for you to ask. All I can do is pass on some of the basic information that I've been told by male friends. When you arrive on the scene, check to find out the latest.

Girls from Europe and America you know about already. The opportunities for dates are manifold and varied; everyone meets everyone else easily. A woman doesn't feel afraid of assault in Africa, so she can relax and relate to men she meets with little worry.

Meeting African girls for flirtation isn't difficult either. Every African town has at least one night spot or dance hall where girls go hoping to be picked up by men. Available girls are easily recognized sitting together at tables; an invitation to dance or share drinks is usually enough to get things going. These young women are not hard, raucous hustlers; rather, they like the bright lights and seek male companionship. They will accompany a man home, expecting to spend the night and expecting a gift of money. The exchange is generally low-key. If you two agree, she will meet you regularly in a friendly manner; in fact, she may move in. Men are pleased because most girls try to be fun and seem almost as interested in having a good time as they are in making money.

In all the French-speaking countries, the downtown pastry shops and cafés are afternoon pickup places; the girls you find there are looking for excitement. A guy buys a soda for someone who looks likely and makes a date for later in the evening. In Dakar the pastry shops along Avenue Lamine Guèye, in Bamako the shop opposite the cathedral, in Cotonou the one on the central square—all are places where girls go because they want to meet men. Men report being approached more directly: a tap on the hotel-room door may bring an offer of female company for the night, or you may be stopped by girls standing near the entrance to your hotel. Generally speaking, the only girls you will be able to meet are the ones who want to go with men for money. Naturally, the transient foreigner rarely comes in contact with girls and women from better families.

Public morality varies greatly from city to city. Dakar seems the most libertine, while in Abidjan prostitution is a tough, organized business. Niamey, Conakry and Banjul are probably the most strait-laced. (*Caution*: In Ghana and Nigeria, schoolgirls are off-limits to males, most especially to visiting foreigners, horrors. These girls are known by their short-cropped, boyish hairdos. Fooling around with them can bring serious repercussions, i.e., a charge of statutory rape.)

Moment, Living for the

When you are traveling, it is so easy to get into a thing worrying about whether or not a certain something is "worth it," or whether or not "it can be shipped back to the United States." In a local market, 50 francs (around 20 cents) will buy you, for example, a beautiful, fragile, artistic hand-molded earthenware bowl, so fragile there is no question of shipping it back. Buy it. Put it in your room. Fill it with your beads, or sea shells, or soap, or fruit, or some of the stuff in your pockets. In a couple of days or a week when you move on, leave it behind. Your host will enjoy it, or the hotel cleaner will be pleased to take it home, and you, you will have been living nicely *for the moment*.

Money

The Gambia currency is the dalasi, while Liberia uses the U.S. dollar. Sierra Leone's money is the leone, Ghana's the new cedi, and Nigeria's the naira. Mauritanian currency is the ugiya, while Mali and Guinea issue their own national francs. All other countries discussed use the West African franc, abbreviated as CFA (pronounced say-*faa*). Relative values change often; a large bank can tell you the latest figures.

Avoid the necessity of changing money in airports, train stations or hotels; the banks give the best rates. Chase Manhattan, Bank of America, First National City and the other large commercial banks all have correspondent banks in West African cities.

Be sure to take enough money with you; if you run out and have to cable back to the States for help, the expense is high and the money may be slow in reaching you. Carry your money in travelers checks of small denomination. Also take along some cash in one-dollar and five-dollar bills; it will come in handy for last-minute purchases, airport tax, for drinks on the plane, and such. And while you are thinking about it now, tuck away $10 somewhere so that you will have cab fare when you arrive back in the States.

Packing

Clothes   In the movie *Around the World in Eighty Days* the English protagonist, Phileas Fogg, is preparing for his whirlwind journey. His valet goes to the enormous closet to try to select a suitable wardrobe for that fussy dresser. Fogg, in a grand gesture, reaches past him and takes down a large valise. In it he puts only two shirts; then he fills the rest of the space with pound notes. The lesson is clear—a suitcase crammed with dollar bills is really all you need to be prepared on every occasion. Such a lightweight, compact way to travel!

You don't need to be told again to travel light; airlines restrict the amount you can carry without paying extra. Besides, you need suitcase space for bringing things back. Bring only clothes of cotton; they are comfortable in the heat; leave synthetics at home. It is good to have a couple of changes of underwear and some practical shoes. Please, leave your trusty dungarees and T-shirts behind—what was so practical and fashionable in Philadelphia will seem shabby and smelly in Accra.

Bear in mind that the average African loves to dress well for occasions and is most likely to have numerous resplendent outfits. You will be much more at ease if you have brought along some clothes in which you feel particularly attractive. In Europe nobody

389

notices if you wear the same old drip-dries every day; but in Africa they do—everyone is very clothes-conscious.

Don't bring clothes to West Africa—buy them there! You will enjoy shopping shortly after you arrive (you won't be able to resist!). Men will feel relaxed in a *dashiki* shirt locally made of dyed cotton; women will find an enormous selection of long and short shifts, comfortable and flattering. The colors are muted and the prints aswirl. The quality and design of clothing is superior. You will have fun making new selections, and you will look good in your new purchases.

Note: Women, European or African, *never* wear shorts or pants in West Africa; dresses are knee-length or long. Also, they rarely wear gloves, formal hats or stockings. Men—no jodhpurs, pith helmets, white duck shorts, or any of the rest of the outmoded colonial outfits; too corny.

Other Items

Personal necessities. If there is something that you *must* have—prescription eyeglasses or a special bottle of pills—bring along two if you can, if its loss would jeopardize your well-being.

Personal cleanser. Vitabath is the name of a luxury all-over cleanser for men and women. Used as a face wash, a shampoo, a foam bath or shower, it always makes you feel fresh and exhilarated. For traveling efficiency, Vitabath comes in an unbreakable plastic bottle. Another, cheaper all-purpose cleanser in a plastic bottle is Dr. Bronner's Peppermint Oil Liquid Soap, available in health-food stores.

Health aids. "6-12" insect repellent, water-purification tablets, anti-malaria pills, birth-control preparations, paregoric or bismuth subcarbonate for intestinal upsets.

Pocketknife. Treat yourself to a Swiss army knife with all attachments; it comes in amazingly handy—the more gadgets the better. Bring a can opener, with bottle opener and can punch, and a corkscrew.

Portable radio. Small-sized only (FM and shortwave don't work and are bulky to carry) so you can hear all the African dance and folkloric music, and so that on Sundays you can listen to the programs of record requests and dedications.

Flashlight. Standard equipment; buy the rectangular kind that you can prop up, especially good for reading in bed.

Travel alarm clock. A really sturdy one (those cute folding "travel clocks" are notoriously unreliable). Westclox has a model named Travalarm that is highly recommended because it is so dependable.

French-English phrase book. It won't help you understand the answers, but you will be able to ask some good questions.

Kit. In a toilet kit or some kind of tough drawstring bag, stuff these odds and ends you will surely need: paper clips; rubber bands; Band-Aids; aspirin; Scotch tape; a roll of plastic Baggies (very helpful); a roll of soft toilet tissue.

NO GUNS. If you are planning to hunt, rent arms from your guides. Border officials and customs inspectors are positively phobic about guns. The weapons will be confiscated and you will be arrested.

Photos

There are dozens of mail-order companies in the States that will make up a batch of 25 wallet-size pictures for $1. While traveling you may need them for various visas and permits. Also, African young people are very fond of exchanging photos, so it would be nice for you to have some with you.

Photography

Both Agfa and Kodak put out booklets of excellent advice on photography in the tropics. Film is available in West Africa but the prices are higher than in the States. Dynachrome film by 3M is recommended because it better captures vivid African colors. Mailing film back for processing is risky; it is safer to hold on to them until you return. If you have some unused rolls of film left over, your African acquaintances will appreciate them as token gifts.

In some places in Africa you may have to get a permit to take photographs. If possible, try to bring along the receipts for your camera equipment; having them handy can save you some hassles. Do not try to photograph military installations or large industrial

391

complexes; they are out of bounds. Remember that many people are naturally camera-shy, while others object to being photographed for personal or religious reasons. Be sure to request permission to take someone's picture. It is rude and tyrannical to go around snapping people who look "interesting" to you—respect their humanity.

Pillows

No pillow is as good as the one on your bed at home, that's true. But the pillows in West Africa are just terrible. If you've been in England you remember how huge, hard and heavy they are. Those imported from France are rigid bolsters, as wide as the bed, implacable enemies of comfort and sleep. Air Afrique was nice enough to give me one of their little plane pillows; I could not have survived without it. Before I got that, I would fold up a *lappa* and put it under my head. You may want to bring along a small inflatable pillow.

Reptiles

Many people have irrational fears of reptiles (as I do of bugs) so they are terrified at the thought of Africa with its lizards and snakes. Maybe some facts and experiences will help you.

The lizards in West Africa are harmless, and afraid of humans. Small, transparent, benign lizards (geckos) live in many buildings, their nests in an unobtrusive corner. They are clean, feed on insects and are a positive addition to a household. Much larger and more menacing in appearance are the veranda lizards, black and scaly, with a long orange tail. They like to hop along cement walks and run along porches (the University of Ghana has many). Their antics are amusing and they too keep out of your way.

Now, about snakes. Over the past ten years in West Africa, I have participated in a rural work camp, gone hiking, tramped over forest trails, taken paths through the underbrush, wandered on isolated islands, walked along country roads, picnicked under waterfalls—and I swear to you that I have never, *never* encountered a snake on my path. I have been lucky, *touche le bois.*

Before writing this, I asked the advice of more than twenty

acquaintances who had lived and worked in West Africa over a period of several years. The same story—no personal encounters. Dead snakes on the road, yes, but *no one* has seen a live one up close. Your experiences living in town and traveling with friends will probably be the same.

West African snakes vary from the gentle garden snake to the extremely poisonous Gaboon viper, with a range of pythons, mambas and cobras in between. The appearance of a snake or its attack on a human being is a cause of frenzied community alarm, like our response to a rabid dog. Once the land is cleared, farms planted, and village or town living established, snakes are *not supposed* to come near or harm people. When they do, it is such a serious occurrence that Africans turn to priests and diviners for an explanation of the cause.

Shipping and Mailing

There are many reasons why you should try to avoid sending anything back to the States by a shipping company. The expense is very high and the journey is slow. Your package will arrive at a dockside warehouse in New York or New Jersey, no farther, and you will have to pay storage charges and spend days prying it out of the iron clamp of port officials. If you have an agent forward it for you, expect his service charges to be steep.

It is much better to send parcels to yourself by ordinary parcel post, *colis postaux* in French-speaking countries. U.S. mail will accept packages weighing up to 20 kilos, or 44 pounds, with no restrictions on dimensions. It is better to send several small packages rather than one large one. Overweight of books and woven blankets and leather bags and such will pack easily into one of the $4 cardboard suitcases you buy in the markets, and the package will be delivered right to your home in Seattle or Nashville.

Packages must be passed by customs officials before they can be sent. The parcel post office may be located in a separate building, so inquire first at the central post office for information. Go to the parcel office early with your package open for inspection; most places have a customs officer on hand to pass on your parcel.

(Note that in Dakar the customs inspection office is down at the harbor, a ways from the *colis postaux*.) Bring with you the wrapping paper, tape and cord (available in stationery stores) you will need to make the package secure. Another convenience of cheap suitcases is that they open and close with a snap for inspection, then lock for safe shipping. They come in a wide variety of sizes and are remarkably sturdy.

Always try to send your parcels from coastal cities; it is cheaper, faster and more reliable. It may take as little as four weeks for your parcel to arrive, or as long as three months.

As you probably know, you are allowed to bring $100 worth of merchandise acquired abroad into the United States duty-free. You can bring in goods over that amount if you wish; customs charges on most simple items are quite reasonable. If you have sent any parcels to yourself, you must note them on your customs declaration. There should be no duty on African artifacts and crafts entering the United States.

You may want to send gifts back direct to your friends. If the value is under $10 the recipient is not required to pay customs tax, and your gift is not counted as part of your $100 duty-free allowance. But if you send the package by air mail it could cost $10 or more in postage; if you send it by sea mail it will arrive long after you do. Write in large clear letters on the package:

GIFT—VALUE UNDER $10

Be sure to allow for the time to be spent shipping your extra things. Also it is wise to budget for postage and shipping charges; these are expenses that creep in and wreck all your careful figuring.

Shoes

Expect them to be ruined in a few weeks; and it is almost impossible to have shoes repaired in West Africa. High heels are doomed after a couple of wearings. Wooden sandals, tennis shoes and leather sandals are the most durable. (Clogs are dangerously clumsy.) For dress-up it is loafers for men, evening sandals for women. If you are planning a long-term move to West Africa or if you intend to stay for several months, ship yourself lots of good cheap shoes; they are abundant in the States but hard to come by abroad. Buy a dozen pair at an A.S. Beck sale and you'll be set. For women, the $3 Woolworth's granny shoe is a good buy. Men should carry their own shoe brush and polish.

Shopping Hints

If you are interested in buying a particular thing and do not have enough money, remember that a small amount of change will hold it for you. A "deposit" of 40 cents will hold a $40 item for a couple of days. The amount in advance indicates your sincere desire to buy and will engage the merchant in a bond of honor.

You can win a buddy for life by remembering to tip a trader a small bit for "kola money." If, after some hard bargaining, you are pleased with your purchase, it is nice to add on 25 or 50 francs (10–20 cents to you) saying that it is for kola, the bitter nut that the market men chew as a stimulant. His eyes will light up, you will be warmly thanked and receive extravagant admiration for your gracious gesture.

Sometimes you may be asked for a tip if you have taken a long time looking around and then decided not to buy. Have you ever "felt bad" because you overworked a Chicago saleslady and then slunk out of the store without purchasing anything? Well, savvy market women know how guilty you can feel; an aggressive trader may ask you to even the score by giving her a small bit of change—say, 10 new pence. No big deal; you're not being swindled.

Siesta

All over West Africa, work stops around noon and does not resume until two or three in the afternoon. Everyone heads home for lunch and a nap. It's a great idea. You'll find that you can't get anything done during these couple of hours anyway, so go back to home base and relax. Sleep a bit; or you may use this quiet time of the day to do a bit of reading and writing cards and letters. Later you take a shower and go back on the streets.

Special Savings for Students and Thrifty Travelers

Often the level of travel adventure and charming encounters diminishes as the level of living comfort increases. The affluent tourist is liable to be encased in such chilly, air-conditioned, antiseptic luxury that every country in the world looks exactly the same; he might just as well have never left home. The amount of money you spend is often a function of several factors—how much you have, how courageous you are, and whom you want to meet.

There are some general rules that will help you keep your living expenses to a minimum. Idell Weydemeyer is the expert on cheap travel in Africa; she taught the author these special tricks. Her general rule is—always check in with the local Peace Corps office. The volunteers manage expertly on limited budgets and know where the young crowds congregate. They will give you solid information on how to live in style on a minimum of expenditure; go to see them as soon as you can. If there is no Peace Corps around, ask taxi drivers, missionaries, garage men: they are usually willing to give you sound advice and insiders' information and tips.

Places to Stay

1. Peace Corps volunteers located in urban and rural areas are willing to lodge young Americans for a couple of days. The charge is small, about $1 for the night and $1 for the evening meal. Remember that Peace Corps volunteers are constantly on the move and staying with one another, so all extra rooms may be filled.

2. The best prospect for students is at the student dormitories on university campuses. The universities in Senegal, Sierra Leone, Ghana and Nigeria are especially cordial. They keep rooms open while their regular students are on vacation, at a cost of about $3 a night. You can write ahead, or upon arrival go to see the hall bursar and inquire. In French-oriented countries you will be helped by the *surveillant-général.* It will be easier if you can show your International Student Identity Card.

3. Many Protestant missions give you a bunk bed for about $1 a night, with simple meals in the same price range. You must look clean and respectable, however, or you may be turned away! Ask at the embassy or the Peace Corps office for the locations. There

are no official Youth Hostels in West Africa, but you may find hostels attached to "Y's" and missions.

4. If, traveling in the interior, you find no room at the local rest house, ask to see an elder of the village if it is a traditional setting or the local national government official, and explain your needs. An aristocratic Malian friend, Mama Ali N'Diaye, suggests that when you come to a strange place you inquire about a horse. Anyone who keeps a horse is a man of means who has extra food and space, and is thus in a position to accommodate you comfortably, sigh.

Places to Eat

1. The PCV, Protestant mission, hostel, secondary school, university, local government official or traditional villager that shelters you will naturally be your first source of low-cost meals. Also try the local "Y."

2. Buy bread and sardines and make a sandwich. Go to the market for a luxurious, low-priced (after bargaining) feast on those tropical fruits that cost so much back in the States.

3. Get to know the location of the *bonnes femmes* who prepare cheap home-cooked meals for working people and bachelors. At lunchtime or suppertime in the market you can get a bowl of rice, gravy, with small slivers of meat (the prices go up as the morsels of meat increase in size and number) or fish in a rich tomato-and-onion sauce—a serving is about 25 cents. Make your choice by the look and smell of the food, and general appearance of table and cook.

Getting Around

1. Ordinary West Africans travel fast, far, frequently and cheaply—all you do is tag along and travel their way. Find out prices and schedules for overland travel at the government bus depot and at the taxi and lorry park. As examples of prices: the 170-mile-by-bus trip from Accra to Kumasi is five hours long and costs less than $2; lorries are slower, leave more frequently and cost about the same; a seat in a station wagon holding nine passengers is around $2.50.

2. You may have luck hitchhiking. The easy part is that there

usually is only one major road to a particular place, and most drivers are going a long distance. The hard part is that private cars don't often stop. White travelers have a better chance than black ones because most whites have cars and usually only pick up other whites. Hitchhiking rules: know your destination and try to arrive before sundown; travel with one companion; be prepared to be good company for the person who picks you up. (*Note:* Please signal for cars with the palms out, the wave that Americans use for hailing a cab. *Never* make the thumb-up hitchhiker's sign; in West Africa that is an extremely rude gesture.)

Taxi Cabs and Drivers

Cabdrivers the world over are colorful characters with an interesting outlook on the world. Maybe it is in the nature of the job. Drivers are often stubborn, cantankerous men who are not able to work under direct supervision. They get around the city, overhear lots of conversations and generally get to know what's going on everywhere. And they always have cash in their pockets.

African cabdrivers are an equally independent, money-hustling lot; and if you let them, when you arrive, they'll rob you blind and drive you to anger and tears. If I had ever found a way of protecting myself from the avaricious crew stationed at hotels and airports, I would tell you, but I haven't, even though I have known the prices in advance. Once you come in at an airport, and your bags are being grabbed and taxi drivers are shouting at you, there is hardly any way to obtain a fair deal. If you comparison-shop and bargain for too long, you'll find all the taxis occupied and driving away. One time, knowing that there was a public bus that went from the door of the air terminal direct to my hotel in town, I waited for the bus. It was a long wait! However, the bus driver found it in his heart to fleece me anyway, figuring (rightly) that by that time I had no other means of transportation.

Even when the tariffs are government-controlled they are not posted, so it is difficult to find out what you will be charged. An airlines representative can tell you an approximate price. (In socialist Mali the rates are established.)

Bob Loomis has a great idea on how the harassed traveler can win the airport game. He suggests that you take a cab to your hotel, then let the desk clerk pay the driver—let the two of *them* argue it out; you'll be getting a much better deal.

Taxi service in town is generally satisfactory and the rates are low. In many cities, the taxis use meters; if there is no meter, they charge a flat rate which should be negotiated in advance.

Telephones

Telephone service can be very good or very bad in Africa. If you are living in a first-class hotel and you want to call an airline, no problem. Or if you are in an embassy and you want to call the university, your chances are excellent. But the moment your phone needs are personal—not official—you are in difficulty. First of all, hardly anyone has a telephone in his home unless he is a very prominent person in diplomatic or governmental circles. Then, as in Europe, no one casually uses the phone for visiting and conversing (if you want to talk with somebody, you go to his house to see him in person); the phone is a tool to be used for making arrangements and rendezvous.

The only public phones are located in the post office. To make an international phone call, go to the post office or to the international cable office (preferably a day in advance) and make a reservation for your call. You will be told when your call can be put through. In general the overseas connections are good; of course, this service is expensive.

Time

Local time in West Africa is five hours ahead of Eastern standard time, so when it is 12 noon in New York it is 5 P.M. from Senegal down through Dahomey. The exception is Nigeria, in the next time zone, 6 hours ahead of New York. When doing your calculations, be sure to make adjustments for daylight-saving time and for time-zone differences within the United States. If you are confused, pick up your telephone receiver and ask the International Information operator for the precise time in any location in the world.

The Tip and the Dash

My personal philosophy: when traveling, I try to tip generously and often. I like the idea that for a small sum I can become someone's pampered guest. I always follow the West African custom of giving a "dash"—a dash is like a tip, but it is given *before* the service is performed, in *anticipation* of the job being done promptly in a cheerful manner.

The American-European custom of leaving a tip that reflects your evaluation of the service—good service, big tip—seems vain to me now. How much better is the West African notion of giving money at the beginning of the job as a way of ensuring special treatment. Think of the dash (or *cadeau* in French-speaking countries) as a bit of encouragement, as an inducement, a bit of sweetening.

For example, when you first move into your room at the hotel, ring for the steward. Dash him immediately. Then ask him for extra hangers, or a bottle of water, anything you'd like. You can be sure he will be looking forward to helping you. In a similar manner, give a small coin to the waiter when he takes your dinner order and a small tip later, and a deposit to the seamstress when she starts to make your dress.

If you prefer to tip only, the 15 percent rule applies everywhere. When a service charge is added to your bill, European style, only a token amount is called for. There is little to be saved or gained by cheap tipping. If you are really interested in saving money, Learn How to Bargain.

The salary of the African worker is tiny and his expenses backbreaking; any extra cash is an enormous help with his family budget. No nonsense, please, about "spoiling" someone or upsetting the local economy. People who in the United States enjoy credit, expense accounts and Christmas bonuses somehow imagine that an unexpected windfall will "ruin" an African. That's bigoted thinking, mindless repetition of exploitative colonial practices.

Titles

There was once, in Accra, a sweet young thing who was introduced to a dazzlingly self-confident young man, with the words, "and meet the High Commissioner to London." She smiled with only moderate interest because she didn't know what a high commissioner *was*. He found her insouciance to be very refreshing. They fell in love and had an affair, but he wouldn't divorce his wife. In this particular instance, ignorance lent that young woman a certain naïve charm, a dumbness that some men often find delightful. But this author wants to make you knowledgeable and on top of the situation. There are social facts of life which you must understand if you are to be poised during your travels.

Here are some government titles you should be familiar with. A *high commissioner* has about the same rank as an ambassador. Commissioners are exchanged between countries that have especially close relations, such as members of the British Commonwealth, or between Senegal and The Gambia. An *ambassador* is an ambassador. Remember that the most prestigious foreign appointment is to the former colonial-metropolitan country; as in the United States the ceremonial appointment is to England, so it is in English-speaking African countries, while Paris is the center for formerly French territories.

A *chargé d'affaires,* or *chief of mission,* is a diplomat temporarily in charge of the mission in the absence of the ambassador. When you need information at any embassy, ask for the *consular officer.* A *minister* in a foreign national government is the same as a *secretary* in the United States Cabinet. Ambassadors, high commissioners and Cabinet ministers are properly addressed as "Your Excellency" or "Excellency."

Whether you find it appealing or not, West African governments are notoriously stuffy. People of government rank demand deference and respect for their person and their post. A casual man-to-man attitude, a warm brother-to-brother handshake do not work well with officialdom. West African functionaries are formal in manner and respond much better if you are the same.

In addition to the hierarchy among the political elite, the visitor should be sensitive to the high standing held by West Africa's traditional ethnic leaders. They too expect to be accorded the deference due their office. The honorable titles they hold are Nana, Na, Naba, Malam, Roi, Sheik, Emir, Chief, Oba, Oni, Alake. They "sit" on thrones, stools or skins.

The traditional ruler is often a man of royal lineage and of spiritual as well as temporal power and influence. Such a ruler may be chief of a ten-family village, or king of ten million people; he may have been appointed yesterday because of an outstanding public service, or he may be a descendant of a dynasty that has ruled for hundreds of years. He may be very casual in behavior outside of his official duties, or always stand on ceremony. He may have a dignified but simple manner, or he may have an imperious air reflecting his innate sense of natural superiority. In any case you will communicate with him best if you are mindful of his status, all a part of your developing new awareness and understanding.

Toilets

In the Anglo-Saxon world the Canadians are famed for their whiskey, the British for their textiles, and the Americans for their plumbing. You probably have lived your entire life with a flush toilet benefiting from cascades of water. With such a background you can expect to be occasionally dismayed by both public and private facilities in West Africa.

The toilets in all hotels at every price level in every country are, almost without exception, of standard model, clean and functioning. If you are in the cities visiting with the affluent, the facilities are also adequate. If you need to use the toilet, don't ask for the "bathroom"; in Africa the toilet and the bathing room are separate. The "john" is in a small telephone-booth type of room. Its English name, "water-closet," was taken over by the French, so you will see "W.C." (pronounced vay-*say* in French) used to indicate the toilet.

Once you move away from this circle of luxury, you may be confronted with challenges. There is the French-style toilet hole in the floor, two paw-prints on the sides where you are supposed to put your feet. The cabin is dark and slippery and there is no place to put your bag, so be careful. Many people in town as well as in the country use outhouses and commodes; there is a night-soil man who comes around to empty the buckets. Always carry Kleenex with you, and be quick about it.

U.S. Official Representation

It will help you to have a general, layman's view of our official foreign representation. In most West African countries there is an office of the United States Information Agency (USIA) called the American Cultural Center. It is usually on a downtown main street, and it often has a window featuring items of current events that show U.S. life in a favorable light: displays of American accomplishments, instances of cooperation between the host country and the United States, news about prominent black Americans because they greatly interest Africans. The Center has a library and also presents cultural programs. You may find current newspapers there and use the references.

The Peace Corps also has an office in almost every country, usually tucked away in a very simple, informal setup. Several countries are served by offices of the United States Agency for International Development (USAID). There may also be a military mission.

In West Africa, the U.S. embassy and its personnel are a force in every aspect of the political, social, economic and cultural life of the countries you are visiting. The U.S. embassy will matter a great deal more to you here than it does in developed countries, so be prepared to make use of its services.

The embassy is responsible for diplomatic relations with the country you are visiting. Without fail, the American embassy is well located and well housed. The U.S. ambassador is there as representative of "the most powerful nation in the world." Also, he is often the richest man in town: the repayment of U.S. foreign loans in national, nonconvertible currency means that the embassy has enormous discretionary funds in local banks.

Don't be surprised or crushed when most Africans assume you are in some way "connected" with the embassy, and thus cushioned from routine difficulties and financial embarrassment. If you are struggling along, it can be infuriating when people casually believe that the United States embassy is caring for you. In many African countries it is difficult for a citizen to obtain a full-fledged passport (most people have travel certificates enabling them to move about in West African nations only), and persons who have them are indeed privileged and do enjoy the concern of their foreign representatives (as well as a certain amount of control).

In the absence of American Express offices, you may want to have your letters delivered care of the embassy. There is always a courteous and efficient English-speaking receptionist, hired locally, who takes care of these things. The embassy takes a long break at lunch and is closed Saturdays and Sundays—an inconvenience; however, the Marine on round-the-clock duty may understand your plight and hand you your correspondence after office hours.

In case of difficulty, the person to contact is the U.S. consul at the embassy. You have difficulties if you lose your passport or it expires or you need extra pages for your visas. You have difficulties if you are arrested, asked to leave the country or want to get married right then. You have difficulties if you are in a place when there is a war or a coup d'état, or when economic problems arise affecting U.S. citizens. When conditions are unstable, it is wise to register with the embassy when you arrive and let them know when you are planning to leave. Learn from them about any travel or photography restrictions in the country, and about the general climate for Americans. If you need emergency cash, *the embassy will not give you any,* but the consul will wire home for you (at your expense) and try to get help from your family, friends or bank.

Visas

Visas are issued at the West African embassies in Washington, D.C., and at their United Nations missions in New York City. You are required to present your passport, Certificate of Vaccinations, a *round-trip ticket* (your travel agent can give you a certifying letter if your ticket isn't quite ready yet), a couple of passport pictures, and a fee (from $2 to $16); also, you will be asked to fill out an application blank. In the case of travel to Liberia, you will need a certificate of good conduct, obtainable at your local central police headquarters. It is always best to ask for a tourist visa of short duration. Anything more complicated will usually require consultation with the home Foreign Office, and that could take many weeks.

Obtaining visas is a tedious process; try never to have to get them for yourself. If you travel with a group, visas automatically become the headache of the leaders and organizer. If you are arranging your own trip, there are two avoidance techniques available. First, buy your ticket from a big, reputable travel agency knowledgeable about Africa (friends have had good luck with Hallmark Holidays in New York City, and Henderson Travel Service in Atlanta) and ask them to obtain the visas for you. They are well informed on the latest requirements and have people to do the legwork. Second, because obtaining visas is so time-consuming and inconvenient, there are special visa-procurement agencies that will do the job for you; Travel Agenda, 119 West 57th Street, New York City, has been recommended.

Some people who live in New York or in Washington, D.C., may find it educational to get their own visas. If you have the time and patience, you may enjoy a visit to an embassy or mission, and the chance to learn more about that particular country and perhaps to chat with some of the diplomatic personnel.

Whenever you complain about the difficulty of obtaining a visa, expect a chilly reply from the person taking your application. You will probably be told how incredibly complicated the procedures are for a foreigner to gain entry to the United States, and how arbitrary and mean some of the consular officers can be.

Walking

West Africans travel far and fast and light on all manner of boats, lorries, camels, horses, trains, planes, canoes, donkeys, taxis. They walk only by necessity and as little as possible: African cities sprawl out, distances are long, and it gets hot. Europeans almost never walk; it just *isn't done.* As a tourist, you will only make enlightening discoveries if you cover a section by foot, but it takes fortitude. Courage!

Water

In West African cities the tap water is treated with chemicals, fairly blah-tasting, and generally safe. In the better hotels the water has been filtered. There may be a risk in smaller places. Most experienced travelers use tap water everywhere for brushing their teeth and washing up, but for drinking they ask for bottled water; Evian and Schweppes are almost always available. If you are traveling to country areas, take along a bottle of water-purification tablets and use them whenever you are not sure of the source of the water.

Suppose, however, that you are living in a city in a dormitory or with an African family, or that you certainly have better things to do with your coins than spend them on water. Here's what you can do. When you first arrive, ask for fruit drinks, suck on oranges, and use ice in your sodas. Sip a few swallows of water, drink tea, and eat the sauces and stews served in the house. Your system will gradually be adjusting to the change of bacteria, and after four or five days you will be able to use the local water freely without any upset.

Every country on the coast (except The Gambia) has a brewery where it turns out foaming barrels of Dutch- or Danish-style beer. Local beer is cheap, and if it is well iced it is light and refreshing. Try Coca-Cola and Pepsi if you enjoy soft drinks, and also taste the various bottled light lemonades that are sold everywhere.

For Women Especially

West African women are people of unusual independence and verve. They are producers, not consumers; partners, not low-paid ornaments. Generally speaking, there are occupations shared by men and women (farming, for example), activities from which women are excluded (fishing), and others which they dominate— the crafts of pottery and long-loom weaving are examples. The visitor is most aware of women in business. In most West African countries, women dominate the retail-distribution trade. These "market women" as traders and entrepreneurs—many of them prominent and wealthy, all of them with cash to expend on their own concerns—are accorded admiration and respect.

Most West African women belong to strong protective families who look out for their interests. They join a variety of voluntary religious, social and business associations in which they share their time and resources with other women, and are helped and supported by them in turn. A woman who earns an independent income (no matter how modest) with strong family and social ties, is a power in her West African community, the backbone of its prosperity, and as such has a deep sense of security and personal worth.

Unlike many places where women fritter away the hours at home, African women are *out*—conducting business, visiting their families, meeting with their friends. To an outsider they seem passionately interested in making money, presenting a beautiful appearance, increasing the influence of their families, and rearing fine offspring. The successful ones manage home, husband, children, business and social life with confidence and ease. They are capable and hard-working while at the same time softly feminine and generous—a heady combination.

All of this is to say that you, a woman visitor to West Africa, will be accorded both the respect due a woman and the hospitality due a guest. It is all right for you to travel around alone or with a friend, and exercising prudence, you are free to go wherever you like. Women walking in the streets are not prey to insults or assault in any manner. You can generally make friends whenever and wherever you like. Invitations are always for public, sociable events where people come together for enjoyment. At a night club you may dance with anyone who asks you, as you choose; your escort won't mind.

You can relax in West Africa and enjoy a whirl of attention and good will. African men find something attractive about *every* woman, regardless of age, color, features or proportions; they overlook your faults and find something about you that is appealing (ever been loved because you have nice penmanship?). Things rarely get "faught" and there are seldom misunderstandings. If you are getting involved with an African, to be on the safe side assume he is married or betrothed; African men usually have a "personal" life outside of a "family" life, and besides, eligible bachelors are scarce on either side of the Atlantic.

For the sake of decorum, don't wear mini-skirts, and don't wear pants, long or short. Customs inspectors seem to find it hilarious to investigate the contents of Tampax boxes; it's an old joke by now, but they persist in brandishing them like cigars.

Tampax, by the way, and other sanitary supplies are for sale in all African cities. Don't be unduly alarmed if you miss a period while traveling; it is a very common experience, apparently a response to the excitement and abrupt change in activity.

FOR FURTHER INFORMATION

New facilities and programs for travel in West Africa develop, while others fade away. This is a listing of established agencies and organizations that offer information to the traveler.

Summer Study, Travel and Work Programs

Educators to Africa Associates
African-American Institute
833 United Nations Plaza
New York, N.Y. 10017

American Forum for International
Study
503 the Arcade
Cleveland, Ohio 44114

Association Internationale des
Étudiants en Sciences
Économiques et Commerciales
(AIESEC-U.S.)
Suite 1110
52 Vanderbilt Avenue
New York, N.Y. 10017

Program of Study Abroad
City University of New York
Graduate Center
33 West 42nd Street
New York, N.Y. 10036

The Experiment in International
Living
Kipling Road
Brattleboro, Vt. 05301

Division of Study Abroad
Programs
Institute of International
Education
809 United Nations Plaza
New York, N.Y. 10017

Director of Recruitment and
Selection
Operation Crossroads Africa
150 Fifth Avenue
New York, N.Y. 10011

For Further Information

Semester and Academic Year Programs

American Study in Africa
  Program
African-American Institute
833 United Nations Plaza
New York, N.Y. 10017

Inquiries Secretary
Schools for International
  Training
Brattleboro, Vt. 05301

West African Representatives

Dahomey

Dahomey Mission to the United
  Nations
4 East 73rd Street
New York, N.Y. 10021

Embassy of Dahomey
2737 Cathedral Avenue, N.W.
Washington, D.C. 20008

Ghana

Ghana Information Service
150 East 58th Street
New York, N.Y. 10022

Embassy of Ghana
2460 16th Street, N.W.
Washington, D.C. 20009

Guinea

Embassy of Guinea
2112 Leroy Place, N.W.
Washington. D.C. 20008

Ivory Coast

Ivory Coast Visa Office
521 Fifth Avenue
New York, N.Y. 10017

Ivory Coast Consulate
Suite 1402
9000 Sunset Boulevard
Los Angeles, Calif. 90069

Embassy of the Ivory Coast
2424 Massachusetts Avenue, N.W.
Washington, D.C. 20008

Liberia

Liberian Consulate General
1120 Avenue of the Americas
New York, N.Y. 10036

Embassy of Liberia
5201 16th Street, N.W.
Washington, D.C. 20011

For Further Information

Mali

Mali Mission to the United
Nations
111 East 69th Street
New York, N.Y. 10021

Embassy of Mali
2130 R Street, N.W.
Washington, D.C. 20008

Senegal

Mission of Senegal to the United
Nations
51 East 42nd Street
New York, N.Y. 10017

Embassy of Senegal
2112 Wyoming Avenue, N.W.
Washington, D.C. 20008

Mauritania

Mauritania Consulate General
and Embassy
8 West 40th Street
New York, N.Y. 10018

Sierra Leone

Consulate General of Sierra Leone
919 Third Avenue
New York, N.Y. 10022

Embassy of Sierra Leone
1701 19th Street, N.W.
Washington, D.C. 20019

Niger

Niger Mission to the United
Nations
866 United Nations Plaza
New York, N.Y. 10017

Embassy of Niger
2204 R Street, N.W.
Washington, D.C. 20008

Togo

Togo Mission to the United
Nations
800 Second Avenue
New York, N.Y. 10017

Embassy of Togo
2208 Massachusetts Avenue, N.W.
Washington, D.C. 20008

Nigeria

Nigerian Consulate
575 Lexington Avenue
New York, N.Y. 10022

Embassy of Nigeria
1333 16th Street, N.W.
Washington, D.C. 20036

Upper Volta

Upper Volta Mission to the
United Nations
866 Second Avenue
New York, N.Y. 10017

Embassy of Upper Volta
5500 16th Street, N.W.
Washington, D.C. 20011

Index

415

Index

Fourah Bay College (Freetown), 145, 148-49; rooms available at, 154

Freetown (Sierra Leone), 141-55; architectural design of, 145; beaches, 149-51; elite families, 143; getting around in, 147; hotels, 153-54; inhabitants of, 143-44; leisure and pleasure, 146-47; night clubs, 154-55; restaurants, 154; shopping, 151-53; sights to see, 148-49
See also Sierra Leone

French Sudan, *see* Mali

French-English phrase book, 391

fufu, 20; developing a taste for, 234-35

Fulani people, 322

Fyfe, Christopher, 143

Ga people, 240

Gambia, The, 121-28; currency system, 388; peanut industry, 39; tourist industry, 123-24, 132
See also Banjul

Gambia River, 125-27; boat trips, 126, 127

garra cloth, 151

Garvey, Marcus, 160

gasoline, cost of (per gallon), 367

Gelede, 296-97

Ghana, 94, 98, 144, 233-70; background for understanding, 238-40; currency system, 388; embassy in U.S., 410; excursions, 249-54, 264-70; geographic location of, 240; getting around in, 241-44; hotels, 256-59, 267-68, 270; independence, 239; intercity travel, 241-42; meeting girls in, 388; Middle Ages, 98-99, 238-39; northern and upper regions, 269-70; personal cleanliness in, 237; "personality" and image, 237-38; population, 239; regional division of, 240; styles of dress, 237; touring the country, 264-70
See also Accra; Kumasi

gifts, mailing back (duty free), 394

girls, meeting (for men only), 387-88

gold, 55-56, 165, 185, 206, 265, 289, 311; sale of (by gram weight), 56; "special bargain," 56-57
See also jewelry

Gold Coast, *see* Ghana

goldsmiths, 54, 55-56, 112

golf, 331

Gorée, Island of (Dakar), 34, 78-83; historical background of, 78; hotels, 78; museums, 80-81; restaurants, 78; sights and things to do, 80-83; slave trading house, 81-83

Gorer, Geoffrey, 38-39, 63

grand bubu, 86

grass weaving, 365
Greene, Graham, 154
Griaule, Marcel, 119
grooming, personal, 380-81
group taxi, 293
Guèye, Mor, 56
Guinea, 131-39; anti-tourism attitude of, 132-35; currency system, 388; embassy in U.S., 410; travel permits, 135; visa, 132
See also Conakry
guns, renting from guide, 391

hairdos, 381
Hallmark Holidays (travel agency), 405
Hamdullahi, caliphate of, 98
Hamili (film), 384
Hammond, Dorothy, 374
handbags, 111, 206, 249
hand-dyed cloth, *see* cloth, tie-dye
Harris, William Wade, 177-78
Harrisme (religious sect), 177-78
Hausa (ethnic group), 200, 201, 321
Hausa language, 240
health, 22-24
health aids, 390
Heart of the Matter, The (Greene), 154
Henderson Travel Service, 405
Highlife (dance), 263, 340
hitchhiking, 397-98; with palms out, 398

Horizon History of Africa, The (Josephy), 374
horse racing, 63, 109, 208, 256, 334, 347
Hotel de l'Amitié (Bamako), 114-15
Hotel de France (Conakry), 137-39
Hotel Ivoire (Abidjan), 175, 179, 182, 188; gift shops, 187
hotels: air conditioning, 361, 381; drinking water, 405-6; pricing, 381-82; restaurants in, 69-70, 91, 115, 191, 226-27, 260-61, 304-5; shopping stalls, 211, 224; student accommodations, 258-59, 338, 348, 396; thrifty places to stay, 396-97
See also under names of cities and countries
hunting, 122-23; guns, 391

Ibadan (Nigeria), 34, 345-50; excursions from, 348-50; hills surrounding, 345; places to stay and eat, 348; shopping, 347-48; sports, 347; things to see and do, 346-47
Ibibio people, 322
ice skating (Abidjan), 179
Idanre and Other Poems (Soyinka), 373
Idubor, Felix, 329
Ife culture (Nigeria), 342, 348
Igbo people, 321

About the Author

SYLVIA ARDYN BOONE has made seven trips to Africa and has lived there for extended periods of time, visiting most of northern, western, central and eastern Africa. Fluent in French, she has traveled in a variety of roles—work-camper, student, teacher, lecturer, researcher, translator, writer, radio announcer, escort-interpreter, guide and journalist.

At present, Miss Boone is a Fellow of the Yale University Graduate School, where she is a candidate for the Doctorate in the History of Art, specializing in the Arts of Africa.